Gender and Justice

The Johns Hopkins University Studies in Historical and Political Science
128th Series (2010)

1. Eliza Earle Ferguson, *Gender and Justice: Violence, Intimacy, and Community in Fin-de-Siècle Paris*

Gender and Justice

Violence, Intimacy, and Community in Fin-de-Siècle Paris

Eliza Earle Ferguson

The Johns Hopkins University Press
Baltimore

© 2010 The Johns Hopkins University Press
All rights reserved. Published 2010
Printed in the United States of America on acid-free paper
9 8 7 6 5 4 3 2 1

The Johns Hopkins University Press
2715 North Charles Street
Baltimore, Maryland 21218-4363
www.press.jhu.edu

Library of Congress Cataloging-in-Publication Data
Ferguson, Eliza Earle, 1970–
   Gender and justice : violence, intimacy, and community in fin-de siècle Paris / Eliza Earle Ferguson.
     p. cm.
   Includes bibliographical references and index.
   ISBN-13: 978-0-8018-9428-2 (hbk. : alk. paper)
   ISBN-10: 0-8018-9428-X (hbk. : alk. paper)
   1. Crimes of passion—France—Paris—History—19th century. 2. Marital violence—France—Paris—History—19th century. 3. Women—Crimes against—France—Paris—History—19th century. 4. Working class—France—Paris—Social conditions—19th century. 5. Murder—France—Paris—History—19th century. I. Title.
   HV6053.F47 2010
   364.152'3094436109034—dc22   2009018177

A catalog record for this book is available from the British Library.

Special discounts are available for bulk purchases of this book. For more information, please contact Special Sales at 410-516-6936 or specialsales@press.jhu.edu.

The Johns Hopkins University Press uses environmentally friendly book materials, including recycled text paper that is composed of at least 30 percent post-consumer waste, whenever possible. All of our book papers are acid-free, and our jackets and covers are printed on paper with recycled content.

*To women everywhere
who have suffered
intimate violence*

Contents

	Acknowledgments	ix
	Introduction: Problematizing Crimes of Passion	1
1	*La Vie Intime*	18
2	Material and Symbolic Household Management	56
3	Networks of Knowledge	93
4	Reciprocity and Retribution	128
5	Local Knowledge and State Power	156
6	Reading and Writing Stories of Intimate Violence	186
	Conclusion: "Men Who Kill and Women Who Vote"	209
	Notes	219
	Bibliography	247
	Index	261

Acknowledgments

In preparing the research and writing of this book, I received financial support from a Foreign Language and Area Studies Fellowship (U.S. Department of Education), a Chinard Fellowship (Institut Français de Washington), the Frederik B. M. Hollyday Instructorship in History (Duke University), and an Ernestine Friedl Fellowship (Duke Program in Women's Studies). In the spring of 2008, a semester's release from teaching at the University of New Mexico finally enabled me to revise the manuscript for publication. An earlier version of chapter five appeared in the *Journal of Social History*. Elements of this project have also appeared in the *Journal of Family History* and the *Journal of Women's History*.

I am very grateful to executive editor Henry Y. K. Tom, assistant editor Suzanne Flinchbaugh, and the anonymous reader for the Johns Hopkins University Press for helping this work come to fruition at last. I also wish to thank fellow Salem Academy alumna Julia Ridley Smith for her expert copyediting.

Between Duke and UNM, it was my privilege to serve on the faculties of Wake Forest University, the College of William and Mary, Reed College, and Juniata College. Along that journey, I accumulated more intellectual debts than I can ever hope to repay. William Reddy, my dissertation advisor, has offered ceaseless support and encouragement throughout these many years and many drafts. My work has benefited enormously from his insightful readings and challenging questions. Claudia Koonz, Donald Reid, and Malachi Hacohen have also been my teachers since even before this project began; their confidence in my work sustained me even through the darkest nights of the job search. Thanks are due to Laura Edwards and Irene Silverblatt for their support as dissertation committee members and to Kristen Neuschel for her support as a master's thesis committee member and beyond. I owe special gratitude to Jean Fox O'Barr, whose leadership of the Women's Studies Program at Duke created a truly interdisciplinary intellectual community where this project first took root. I would also like to thank Rachel Fuchs, Nina Kushner, Ronald Schechter, and the habitués of the UNM new faculty happy hour for much encouragement and moral support at crucial points in this project. My uncle, Tim Earle, has given me decades of impeccable advice. Maria and Ronald Bobroff, Cassandra Briggs, and Heather Deal have enriched my life immeasurably through their wonderful gifts of friendship.

Finally, I would like to thank my parents, James and Eleanor Ferguson, for inspiring me with their love of France and their unswerving support.

Gender and Justice

INTRODUCTION

Problematizing Crimes of Passion

"Today I regret what happened, but anger did not allow me to be master of myself," testified Joseph Maxant, two days after shooting his wife Margot. "She had caused me too many troubles."[1] Maxant was accused of murder, but in fin-de-siècle France, his act would have been understood as a "crime of passion." Exactly what constituted a crime of passion was and is open to debate, and it has never been a legally defined act in France. At the most basic level, the "crime of passion" was an act of violence between a man and a woman. Although any murder or attempted murder might involve passions of rage, hate, or jealousy, the "crime of passion" was more specifically understood to be a crime between a couple, whether married or not, and therefore to involve love.[2]

A crime of passion is thus by definition a love story gone awry—love betrayed, love unrequited, love lost—and lurid tales of such unhappy love affairs proliferated in the popular press of the nineteenth century. Resulting acts of violence were likely to go unpunished. Though it is not possible to quantify crimes of passion precisely,[3] it is certain that the overall acquittal rate for all cases tried in the assize court during the Third Republic was around 28 percent.[4] Rates of acquittal for crimes against persons—precisely the categories that would include crimes of passion—were significantly higher than those for crimes against property.[5] In my own study of cases of intimate violence in the fin de siècle, I found that 28 percent of male defendants and 64 percent of women were found not guilty, while men outnumbered women three to one as defendants in such cases.

Contemporary criminologists, jurists, and politicians were greatly alarmed by the high rate of acquittal in such cases. Criminologists understood crimes of passion to be caused by a sudden loss of rational control; the individual was overcome by a wave of emotion or madness when he or she committed an act of violence. They worried that more people would be inspired to commit similar crimes by reading about them in the popular daily papers. Politicians understood this kind of violence to be symptomatic of the dangers of modern urban life and the decay of the family. Yet, from a legal standpoint, since the defendant almost always admitted the deed, acquittals in crimes of passion defied the letter and the spirit of the law. Maxant's case seems to fit the definition of the crime of passion perfectly. He claimed to be carried away by extreme emotion at the moment that he shot his unfaithful wife, and he was acquitted. However, a closer look at the testimony in this exemplary case indicates that far more was at stake than the judicial validation of a love story gone wrong.

On the day that Margot Maxant was shot by her husband, she spent part of the afternoon chatting with her friend Joséphine Guillot, who lived in the same apartment building at number 6 bis, rue des Récollets, a street that runs between the Gare de l'Est and the Hôpital St. Louis in the tenth arrondissement. "She told me that she didn't know what was wrong with her husband, that she believed he was crazy, because he was making false accusations and that she had to leave their room to put an end to it," Joséphine testified to the investigating magistrate. That evening Margot returned to the Guillots' place, having been locked out of her apartment, and sat with them while they ate their supper. At one point Margot's husband Joseph appeared, demanding, "Is my cow here?" and Margot followed him out the door. "Barely a few seconds went by when we heard the explosion of a firearm," Joséphine explained, "and we immediately thought that something bad had happened. At the same moment, la femme Maxant arrived, dragging herself along, and fell in front of our door, never again to rise. She was dead." Joséphine further testified that she heard Joseph call for the police from his window, heard him try to make his wife stand up, and saw him holding his gun immediately after the attack.

Joséphine Guillot was nearly an actual eyewitness to Margot's murder, but the investigating magistrate did not ask her for any further details of the crime itself. Instead, he questioned her about Margot's conduct prior to the crime. "I cannot say if la femme Maxant conducted herself badly," she replied, "I have never seen her in suspicious company. I happen to know that the two spouses did not get along and that Maxant never had a good word for his wife. Already a week ago he almost killed her by hitting her with a chair, and the bruises and injuries to her head that he gave her that day could be seen by everyone." (Rather than rendering them into the more familiar *Madame* or *Mrs.* I have chosen to leave the titles *la femme* and *la dame* untranslated, in order to preserve the more nuanced meaning of the French. Jurists and witnesses alike used these terms to designate a married woman from the popular classes. *Madame* was used for middle- and upper-class married women and almost never for working women.)

Based on Joséphine Guillot's testimony, it would appear that Margot Maxant had been a long-suffering victim of her husband's abuse. Although the other nine witnesses in the case all agreed that the Maxants had an unhappy marriage marked by numerous violent fights, they disagreed with Joséphine about the cause of those conflicts. In the words of one of the building's concierges, "The misconduct of la femme Maxant was notorious; the accused, on the other hand, was esteemed by everyone." Neighbors volunteered specific details illustrating her bad behavior. One man whose window was directly across the courtyard from the Maxants' could easily see into their room. Joseph, he said, "was a man who was entirely calm and of a peaceful nature, always staying at home, sober, and never going out with anyone. As for his wife, she gave herself over to drink. I saw her drunk many times. She yelled very loudly and picked fights with everyone. Sometimes, as I happened involuntarily to look through my window, I saw strangers at her place, in her husband's absence. Each time this occurred, I closed my window so as not to be suspected of indiscretion." Another neighbor, Pauline Crovisier, could not escape knowledge of the Maxants' household so easily. "My bed is placed right next to the bed of the Maxant couple," she testified. "Only a thin partition separates the two lodgings, and you can hear distinctly on one side all that is said or done on the other." Ill with tuberculosis and arthritis, she apparently spent a great deal of time in bed and had ample opportunity to overhear her neighbors' activities. "From the very first days, I noticed that la femme Maxant conducted herself badly, that she profited from her husband's absence to receive men at her place. Old and young men came. I saw them come to her place many times, and I heard what happened on the bed and what they said to each other. Once she asked a young man for a one-hundred franc note, telling him that she needed it to go to her native region." Apparently, the money was exchanged for sex.

The neighborhood business owners also confirmed that she spent time in suspicious company. Victorine Brevet, who ran a restaurant (*crémerie*) in the same building where they lived, asserted that la femme Maxant often came to her shop with men whom she kissed and called by the familiar second-person pronoun, *tu*. She became a more frequent customer once liqueurs started being sold there. "Sometimes with a young man of the age of nineteen, sometimes with a butcher," Brevet continued. "It happened that I would see her bring these men by way of the porte cochère of the house, without doubt to lead them to her place." The wine seller next door also asserted that Margot behaved in a familiar manner with a group of masons at his establishment and once provoked a fight with her husband by throwing a glass of wine in his face and calling him a pig.

Yet these neighbors were not idle observers of la femme Maxant's behavior. On the day of the crime, Victorine Brevet told Margot that her husband was watching her, and, consequently, her butcher friend, believing that she really might be under spousal surveillance, decided not to go up to her apartment with her after all. Pauline Crovisier claimed that she advised Joseph, "Think of your children and leave her instead of causing a scandal." On 14 August, Pauline said that she was so frightened by the sounds of a fight at the Maxants' place that she fled to another neighbor's room, where she fainted. As a result of this noisy fight, Alexandre Guichon, a concierge, told the Maxants that they would have to move out. Arriving just after the fight, he told Joseph

> that the neighbor woman had had an attack of nerves and that he had to stop the racket at his place. At the same time, he pointed to his wife and called her a cow and a whore. He told me that she carried on with men for the pleasure of having a drink. He showed me the debris of a terrine on the floor that he said she had thrown at his face. Both of them had bloody faces. Maxant had scratches, and his wife had a cut on her forehead and scratches on her face. The wife, when I arrived, made a step toward me as if she had hoped that I would take her defense. But when, after her husband's accusations, she heard me respond that, unhappily, we all knew, she moved away with an air of ill humor. After this moment, la femme Maxant became a true fury; she insulted everyone, la dame Crovisier, myself, my wife. She had insults in her mouth without addressing them to anyone. She incited her three-year-old little girl against the other children in the house.

It seems that Margot had alienated all of her potential allies in the building, except for her friend Joséphine Guillot. Everyone knew about the violence in her household, but at the same time, almost everyone had judged that she was the cause of her troubles, not her husband.

Joseph himself claimed that his attack was precipitated by the information (provided by Pauline Crovisier) that Margot had received a pair of new booties from a shoemaker, supposedly in exchange for sexual favors. "When one has endured as I have endured," he declared to the investigating magistrate, "I no longer knew what I was doing." According to the autopsy report, Margot was shot in the lung and the heart. It is perhaps not surprising that Joseph fired so accurately; he was a patrol officer by profession, and he used his service revolver in the crime. Furthermore, he took an active role in shaping his defense.[6] He turned himself in immediately after the crime and then wrote several letters to the investigating magistrate, requesting to be moved to a double cell and suggesting witnesses who could testify to his wife's misconduct. One of these, a chef named Alexandre Mallet, was indeed summoned to testify. Mallet described himself as "one of Maxant's closest friends," who had known him for six or seven years. He testified that three months earlier, Margot had sat on his lap and lifted her skirts, revealing "all her nudity," but that he had rebuffed her advances. Most of what Alexandre had to say actually concerned his own wife, whom Margot was supposed to instruct in glove making but whom she allegedly corrupted into prostitution instead. Alexandre's mother, who lived in Châteaudun (Eure et Loire) also weighed in on this point. Though it is not clear if she volunteered to give a deposition or was summoned to do so, she blamed Margot for turning her daughter-in-law away from her wifely duties and said she had learned of the murder in a letter from her son.

For all the discussion of his wife's misconduct, nobody ever doubted that Maxant was the one who shot her, and indeed Maxant readily admitted having done it. According to French law, any defendant who, like Maxant, had intentionally killed another person was subject to a specific range of punishment: execution or forced labor. Although the law provided for an "excuse" under certain circumstances that would reduce the penalty, it did not permit any manifestly guilty person to escape punishment entirely.[7] Nevertheless, an assize court jury acquitted Maxant of murder on 6 December 1884. Something other than a strict application of the law was operating during his trial, but what was it? After reading their testimony, it would be impossible to maintain any notion that Maxant and his neighbors were the passive objects on which the state-sponsored system of justice imposed its power. Making sense of trials like Maxant's requires analyzing a complex set of interrelated practices and processes. That analysis must turn inward, toward the couple, their expectations for and beliefs about each other, and the history of their relationship. Equally, such an analysis must turn outward, to investigate how the couple interacted with their local urban community and, in turn, how the members of this community interacted with the state-sponsored judicial process. Such is the trajectory for this project.

The Nature of the Evidence

Judicial archives, Arlette Farge has cautioned, "only exist because some practice of power has caused them to be born."[8] The people whose lives are briefly recorded in the archives have entered the historical record only because they have come into conflict with the official apparatus of justice. Unless proven innocent, their encounter with the law could define defendants as deviants or criminals, people who have overstepped the bounds of acceptable behavior. Yet, following Farge, this study suggests that judicial archives can offer more to historians than a record of fluctuating definitions of crime and deviance, or the effects of official discourses of social control. Testimony by defendants, victims, and witnesses in judicial settings often did not answer the purposes of the magistrates, whether in the eighteenth-century police archives studied by Farge or in the fin-de-siècle dossiers of the assize court of the Seine. To be sure, court documents are produced under very specific circumstances and for purposes quite other than the gratification of researchers a century or more in the future. This is true of virtually any historical text, however, and it is always of critical importance to know in detail precisely what the circumstances of the text's production were in a given time and place.

It is actually an advantage of judicial archives that the institutional practices governing their production can be known with great accuracy, although few recent historians who have studied the archives of the assize court have given adequate attention to the circumstances of the trial dossiers' creation. Doing so helps elucidate the interactions between the ordinary people involved in the trial and the elite members of the judiciary. That these two social groups had limited areas of commonality concerning standards for the comportment of men and women shaped the content of court testimony in important ways.

Specifically, in cases of intimate violence, witnesses were called upon to articulate what normally went without saying in their daily household interactions, precisely because their interrogators were from a different social world than their own. Most of the defendants and witnesses were among the working people of Paris, employed in a range of professions from day laborers to seamstresses to grocers, but all shared a financially precarious existence. Their auditors did not take for granted many of the same things that they did, as moments of disagreement between judges and witnesses about such key issues as honor and fidelity demonstrate. The rhetorical occasion of court testimony, therefore, put into play the disjunctures between the two groups. For a man to testify in court about how his neighbor's poor housekeeping skills incurred her husband's wrath was certainly not the same thing as chatting about it in a bar or writing about it in a letter to relatives back home on the farm. If the relationship between interrogator and witness was in some ways antagonistic, though, it was precisely that conflict that clarified the position of each. Thus, court testimony preserved in the judicial archives makes plain the conflicting assumptions and expectations, and the dynamics of power, between these two groups. But trials were also occasions where witnesses spoke in relatively unfettered ways about the minutiae of daily life in their communities, and this candor is what makes these records such a rich source for understanding the intimate lives of ordinary working people.

While it is true that the acts of violence that brought defendants to the assize court were extreme—people were shot, stabbed, disfigured or maimed by acid—the disputes out of which these acts arose were common. Indeed, the act of violence itself was only a small part of what occupied the depositions and interrogations. Defendants almost always admitted that they had committed the act of which they were accused. What was at issue in court testimony was not the fact of the violence but its legitimacy. Therefore the bulk of the testimony concerned the circumstances of the conflict and who was involved in it: the relative social positions of the attacker and victim, what their relationship had been like prior to the attack, and what the witnesses thought about their reputations. Most cases involved testimony from ten or more neighbors, friends, and family members, some from the native region (*pays*) where the antagonists were born—the testimony examined in this study altogether records more than two thousand men and women talking about each other's daily lives. These trial documents, therefore, do not present a strictly two-way battle between accused and accusers, or even a little more broadly, between lower-class testifiers and higher-class judicial officials. Rather, in any given case there were many voices arguing for different interpretations of the crime.

This study encompasses 264 dossiers from the Cour d'assises de la Seine, from 1871 to the end of the nineteenth century, concerning violent crimes between domestic partners.[9] I use the term "domestic partners" to refer to couples who maintained a household together, whether they were married or unmarried. Most of the people involved in these trials were among the working poor, and a significant proportion of the working poor in fin-de-siècle Paris lived *en concubinage*, delaying or avoiding marriage. The violent acts that they committed against each other came under the purview of the court as cases of assault, murder and attempted murder, homicide and attempted homicide, and poisoning.[10]

Trial dossiers contain all legal documents related to the investigation and trial of the case, including lists of witnesses and jurors, a list of material evidence seized, and reports from expert witnesses, along with various administrative documents concerning procedure. Often, police interrogations, letters written by or for people involved in the case, photographs, clippings, and other scraps of lives long past are tucked in. Of most interest to this study are the *acte d'accusation*, the indictment summarizing the case for the prosecution written by the investigating magistrate, and transcripts of depositions by witnesses and interrogations of the accused. Following the conventions of the court documents, I use the term "witness" (*témoin*) to refer to anyone who testified in the case besides the defendant—but most witnesses were not actual eyewitnesses of the crime. Also included in the dossier is the *procès-verbal* of the trial, which, given the title, might be expected to be a verbatim account of the proceedings but in fact simply records the legal procedures that were followed in court (noting that the session was convened, the jury sworn in, and so on). The only source of direct transcriptions of what took place in court is preserved in the popular press. For forty-three cases, I have compared testimony given to the police, testimony given to the investigating magistrate, and testimony given in court and reported in the *Gazette des Tribunaux* and popular dailies like *Le Petit Parisien* and *Le Petit Journal*. Based on this sample, it is safe to say that the depositions of witnesses and defendants varied little as they repeated their stories to the police, to the investigating magistrate, and in court, so I consider newspaper accounts to be reliable.

Finally, the sources for this project extend beyond the various documents produced around assize court trials; they include a comprehensive range of pub-

Fin-de-Siècle Assize Court Cases

Total number of cases: 264
  Male defendants: 200 (76%)
  Female defendants: 64 (24%)

Total number of acquittals: 96 (36% of total defendants)
  Males acquitted: 55 (28% of male defendants)
  Females acquitted: 41 (64% of female defendants)

Accusations of premeditated violence
  Defendants accused of *assassinat*: 66 (55 men, 11 women)
    Acquitted: 16 (11 men, 5 women)
    Convicted on a lesser charge: 24 (20 men, 4 women)
  Defendants accused of *tentative d'assassinat*: 91 (70 men, 21 women)
    Acquitted: 35 (20 men, 15 women)
    Convicted on a lesser charge: 27 (25 men, 2 women)

Reduced charges and sentences (all cases)
  Convicted with extenuating circumstances: 64
  Convicted on reduced charges: 80

Source: Approximately 500 dossiers concerning (nonsexual) violent crimes against persons survive for the Cour d'assises de la Seine from 1871 to the end of the century. These are cases of *assassinat* and *tentative d'assassinat* (premeditated murder and its attempt); *meurtre* and *tentative de meurtre* (unpremeditated murder and its attempt); *empoisonnement* (poisoning); and *coups et blessures* (aggravated assault).
  I consulted 442 of these dossiers in order to determine which cases concerned violent conflicts between couples who were married or living together. Thus I identified and transcribed 172 dossiers that were relevant to this study. These court dossiers are supplemented by accounts of 92 similar cases published in the *Gazette des Tribunaux* during the same time period, for a total of 264 cases.

lications by contemporary criminologists, sociologists, jurists, and politicians concerning crimes of passion. These publications help illuminate the attitudes and assumptions of social elites and provide contrast with the views expressed by lower-class witnesses. Even if those elites did not have the power to control what ordinary people said in court, they did have the power to shape social policy in ways that had a real impact on how intimate violence was understood as a social problem in this era.

Method

Historians of the early modern and modern eras have tended to handle materials from judicial archives quite differently. For the early modern era, historians have long relied on various kinds of judicial archives to create rich analyses of subordinate social groups that have left few other traces of their lives in historical records.[11] By contrast, recent work by historians of the modern era has been more concerned with using judicial archives to investigate the effects of official discourses produced by magistrates, medical professionals, and other members of the elite, rather than illuminating the social and cultural world of the ordinary people who were caught up in the judicial process. This preoccupation is part of the legacy of Michel Foucault and thus perhaps is best illustrated by his own presentation of the case of Pierre Rivière. In reproducing the documents from Rivière's judicial dossier, Foucault leaves the author of the crime virtually unexamined, except as an illustration of the dissonance between juridico-medical discourses on crime and madness, and the peasant culture of which Rivière was a member.[12] Foucault and his collaborators invite the reader to join them in their stunned astonishment before the "monster" and his outpouring of words—in effect, reenacting the incomprehension of Rivière's early nineteenth-century judges. Indeed, Rivière and his words must remain opaque without an in-depth analysis of the social and cultural world that informed his actions and ideas. As Carlo Ginzburg has observed, "We are dazzled by an absolute extraneousness that, in reality, results from the refusal to analyze and interpret."[13] Like Ginzburg's sixteenth-century miller Menocchio, it is certain that Rivière was neither without nor outside of culture, in spite of his manifestly deviant acts.

The Foucauldian preoccupation with dominant discourses has deeply influenced recent work on crimes of passion in fin-de-siècle France. The existing historiographical literature about crimes of passion has focused on the discourses produced by these contemporary elites, especially in law and medicine. In seeking to explain why authors of crimes of passion were let off, one historian has argued that defendants were acquitted because of the growing influence of criminologists and psychologists on the legal process: that is, defendants would be exonerated if a doctor judged them to be insane.[14] Other historians have argued that defendants would be acquitted only if they could enact the crime as a kind of melodramatic narrative and thus make their story conform to the expectations of the bourgeoisie.[15]

While this kind of work provides important insights into the intersections of medical, legal, and literary discourses in the construction of crime, I contend that acquittals in crimes of passion were due to an entirely different set of factors. Drawing on a much larger sample than previous historians in this field, I have found that the intervention of medical professionals was actually quite rare, occurring in less than 10 percent of all the cases in this study.[16] In those few cases where they did provide an official evaluation of the mental health and criminal responsibility of the accused, no correlation exists between their judgments and the verdicts of the court. Also, it is not at all clear that a defendant who said something like Maxant's statement, "Anger did not allow me to be master of myself," was invoking the latest psychological theories about temporary insanity. The medicalization of crime, therefore, did not have a significant impact on the outcome of the trials. It could be more fruitful to investigate the social world that legitimated Maxant's anger and the violence it generated.

Furthermore, one can well admit the availability of the melodramatic narrative of the crime of passion, whether in the popular daily press or publications destined for bourgeois professionals, but the simple availability of a cultural script does not assure its enactment. It is not satisfactory to suppose that anyone would stab a lover or hit a spouse with no more motivation than some abstract norm of proper behavior extracted from a serial romance in a newspaper. Instead, it is necessary to know much more about how ordinary people read and thought about the kinds of discursive sources on which historians of crime have relied. If it is possible that the social and cultural lives of these violent offenders involved something more complex than the reflection and reproduction of norms, rules, or discursive models, then a different methodological approach is necessary to address the roots of intimate violence.

To account for the steps between the availability of a certain narrative or cultural script and the choice of one individual to wield a knife or a gun requires a deeper understanding of the social context in which that individual acted. As the anthropologist Sherry Ortner has noted, without a meaningful understanding of the degree to which a given discourse can impose itself on people, it is impossible to fully assess its power or significance. Any claims about the possibility for the people on trial to resist or appropriate a dominant discourse must include an analysis of the range of factors conditioning their choice and its possible effects.[17] The challenge here is to uncover a complex social and cultural world through an analysis of violent conflict, triangulating among the different accounts articulated during the trial. This is, fundamentally, an ethnographic endeavor. It is also informed by the perennial concern of feminist scholars to recover women's experiences in the past and to explore the connections between the lives of individuals and larger systems of social organization.

My approach has been inspired by practice theory, particularly as it has been elaborated by Pierre Bourdieu. Practice theory casts individual actors as savvy strategizers who improvise within a given context. Yet that context—the social institutions and symbolic order—is understood to be created, maintained, and modified through social practice. Thus individuals' choices and actions can have an effect on larger structures of social organization. This approach does not dismiss the importance of "discourse" but conceives of discourse as one of many kinds of meaningful action. After all, a left to the jaw or a knife in the belly during a domestic dispute is not reducible to an effect of language, although they certainly take part in systems of meaning. The task here is to understand the discursive artifacts of the trial as being deeply embedded in a social world and willfully produced by the people who articulated them. As Ortner explains, "The challenge is to picture indissoluble formations of structurally embedded agency and intention-filled structures, to recognize the ways in which the subject is part of larger social and cultural webs, and in which social and cultural 'systems' are predicated upon human desires and projects."[18]

One of the great advantages of practice theory for historians of culture and society is that it renders the minutiae of everyday life relevant to the analysis of large-scale phenomena. For example in Bourdieu's well-known work *Distinction*, he demonstrates how individuals' preferences in music, film, interior decoration, and food—among many other things—only apparently depend on their personal, deeply felt senses of aesthetic value. Rather, he identifies certain Kantian criteria of aesthetic value to be an artifact of the dominant class, arguing that such standards have become camouflaged as an innate sense of judgment. Thus the manner in which someone performs apparently mundane and trivial activities becomes symptomatic and partly constitutive of his place on the class scale.[19]

According to Bourdieu, the relationship between the individual actor and the social world he inhabits is mutually constructive. The habitus, in his terms, is what mediates between the two. It is a modus operandi that generates ways of understanding the world and ways of acting in it. The habitus is not a rigid, external set of rules to be followed, but a flexible set of perceptions and dispositions, built from and responsive to the individual's experience and education. It follows that people with similar life experiences, such as the wage-earning laborers of fin-de-siècle Paris, share a common habitus, enabling them to make common sense of their social world. In Bourdieu's theory, social actors are like players in a game: the habitus is their "feel for the game," their savvy about when to make the right move, which may or may not be the result of conscious strategizing. Each player chooses his moves in consonance with his interests, that is, toward the goal of maximizing his advantage, in the form of economic, social, or symbolic capital. The game continues precisely because each player has a stake in its continuation, hoping to secure his position relative to the other players.

For the working people of fin-de-siècle Paris, economic capital—money and property—were difficult to obtain. In this milieu, intangible forms of capital were therefore at least equally important. The symbolic capital of a good reputation could be like armor in a risky situation, elevating a person above suspicion when a crime has been committed or magnifying the gravity of an offense made against him. Social capital, one's useful connections with other people, could also be protective, perhaps providing a reservoir of friends to offer positive accounts of one's character or neighbors to give shelter from a violent attack. As they gave their depositions, the accused, the victim, and the witnesses all mobilized these resources. If they were players in a game, they were gambling that their interpretations of events, backed by the power of whatever capital they could muster, would win out and "fix" the meaning of past events, with the ultimate result that certain actions would be judged to be criminal or legitimate.

When it comes to real human beings who assault and murder each other, the term *games* may seem inappropriate, and Bourdieu's assumption that everyone is motivated to maximize their advantages over everyone else may seem overly rationalistic and competitive. Actual social interactions are more complex than the schematics of any theory. As Ortner points out, "there is never only one game" at stake in social interactions.[20] To illustrate this point, let us consider the hypothetical case of a husband who beats his wife when he returns from work to find that she has not prepared his dinner. This household conflict takes place on many levels. First of all, there is the immediate contest between the husband and wife, who apparently disagree on the level of domestic service that she is to provide him. Second, there is the question of how this conflict relates to community standards of proper behavior for men and women, as well as the acceptable uses of violence. If the husband or wife appeals to their neighbors for help, they put into play the gendered standards of proper behavior for men and women, and their relative positions—within the community and within the household—become salient. Next, if the matter ends up in court as an assault case, judges and jurists join the fray. Perhaps the case will figure in stories in the popular press or in the analyses of some professional studying crime and society. All these fields—the household, the local community, the state justice system, the representation of the act in the media and professional discourses—are arenas where the legitimacy of the violent act is contested. The husband, the wife, their allies, jurists, journalists, and perhaps even criminologists, psychologists, and sociologists, offer their interpretations of the event. Which one will stick depends on the relative status of the antagonists within a given field, with the ultimate result that certain acts of violence may be judged to be legitimate or not in the eyes of the community and of the court. In Bourdieu's words, the discursive strategies of various agents "depend on the balance of symbolic forces between the fields and on the specific resources that membership in these fields grants to the various participants."[21] Thus the discourses produced around cases of crimes of passion are deeply implicated in the complex, overlapping systems of cultural meaning and social interaction in which they were produced.

This kind of analysis is of particular interest for studying the working people of fin-de-siècle Paris precisely because they constituted a population in flux. The city's population grew rapidly in the last decades of the nineteenth century, primarily with migrants from the French countryside.[22] Many of these migrants left behind longstanding peasant traditions of household organization that depended on a gendered division of agricultural labor, where the tasks specific to men and women (as well as children and elders) were all necessary for the household's survival. Although patterns varied significantly in different regions, choosing a spouse was at least as much about creating a viable farm as it was about creating a harmonious personal union, and the partners' extended families were usually involved in the choice.[23] In the city, by contrast, the same considerations did not apply. The survival of the household as an economic unit depended on the wage labor of its members, not their joint work on a farm, and it was entirely possible for single people to support themselves on their earnings alone—though it was considerably more difficult for women, who usually earned much less than men. Far from their families of origin, city dwellers did not necessarily heed the advice of parents and relatives in their choice of a partner. They could follow their preferences in joining a partner to establish a household together, and they could also do so in leaving one that was unsatisfactory. They were, in short, more mobile. It does not follow, however, that they could do whatever they pleased. Indeed, a significant part of what cases of intimate violence reveal is an ongoing struggle to define the mutual obligations that men and women owed each other in urban households. Although it is possible to glean normative standards from witnesses' testimony, it is also clear that many individuals were testing the boundaries of what was acceptable, and violence marked the places where they crossed the lines.

Intimate Violence and Gender

In 1998, Michèle Perrot wrote that a "complicit silence" surrounded battered women, "especially in the popular milieus" of the nineteenth century.[24] Integrating intimate violence into the social and cultural history of the working people of Paris is an important step in the historiography of violence, in recovering not only the traces of its existence but also its place in social organization. Following Max Weber, historians have long agreed that the transition to modernity entailed a monopolization of violence by an increasingly centralized state.[25] Private feuds that had previously been settled by brawls, duels, and battles were to be carried out by other means in the judicial arena, and the murderous impulses of individuals were channeled into the service of the state and its wars. In Norbert Elias's formulation: "The monopolization of physical violence, the concentration of arms and armed men under one authority, makes the use of violence more or less calculable, and forces unarmed men in the pacified social spaces to restrain their own violence through foresight or reflection; in other words it imposes on people a greater or lesser degree of social control."[26] Elias's celebrated exploration of the "civilizing process" reveals his assumption that, prior to the state's monopolization of violence, it had already been monopolized by men. They are the ones who required new kinds of self-control in this new order; it is men's violence against other men that concerns Elias most. Men's violence against women within the family, much less women's violence of any kind, is omitted from this narrative. The exclusion of intimate violence from a major work centered on the history of practices of violence stems from deceptively solid conceptual boundaries between public and private that have persisted too long in social and cultural historiography.[27]

Work much more recent than Elias's perpetuates this distortion, for historians of the family have also avoided in-depth analyses of intimate violence, operating from the assumption that families are essentially harmonious private units, whose members share an untroubled solidarity.[28] The exceptions are generally among recent works that stem from an ethnographic methodology, such as Frédéric Chauvaud's study of "village passions" in central France.[29] While he finds that in rural France, "masculine brutality was presented as self-evident" by one battered wife, somehow this banal rural violence has disappeared by the time he describes urban families later in the century.[30] Although he suggests that family violence declined over the nineteenth century, his analysis depends more on evidence about public, group actions, rather than intra-household conflicts.

Historians who study marital breakdown nonetheless have found ample evidence of violence against wives from the early modern through the modern eras.[31] It has proved difficult, however, to integrate such evidence into compelling accounts of family life. The venerable Eugen Weber's discussion of intimate violence is extremely limited. In his analysis, family life among the poor was characterized by "an unpredictable succession of cuffs and cuddles, kicks and kisses." Consequently, he argues, "People become suspicious, easily feel slighted, and are easily roused to aggression. The better-off have options, hence something to discuss. The poor regard talking as useless, which it usually is."[32] According to Weber, what was interesting about the ubiquitous violence of the working class is how and why it was curbed through the moderating influence of the bourgeoisie. He writes, "What deserves explanation is not the rigor of the times or their violence, but the attempts made to temper both" through education and literature. "School and mimicry of the upper classes slowly taught that restraint and self-control could proceed from something other than fear: good manners and social virtues."[33] It is unclear what evidence Weber has for this alleged trickling down of peaceful bourgeois habits. Between his lists of peasant proverbs condoning wife beating on the one hand, and his reliance on novels and reform literature on the other, it seems likely that he reproduced the bias of contemporary upper-class observers. His conclusion that the violent lower classes were colonized by the peaceful practices of the upper classes is consistent with his larger narrative about the making of barbaric peasants into civilized Frenchmen, but this kind of analysis tends to assume that the lower class was in a sort of stasis, incapable of change without influence from above.[34]

Intimate violence is crucial to the history of gender and gendered power relations in the household. It is a key practice in testing and enforcing the bounds of acceptable behavior for men and women, a tool largely but not exclusively used by men. A regulating practice that is itself regulated by local communities and state systems of justice, intimate violence is deeply implicated in the history of shifting constructions of masculinity and femininity. This analysis of practices of intimate violence in fin-de-siècle Paris lays bare the connections between the ongoing household conflicts of ordinary men and women and larger systems of social organization. Episodes of violence recorded in judicial dossiers reveal that the bases of domestic partnerships—the conditions under which a man and a woman would join together or break apart—were constantly negotiated and tested. Such conflicts activated closely knit networks of friends and neighbors, who were intensely involved in monitoring and resolving them. Acts of severe violence brought these community methods of control into contact (if not conflict) with state-sponsored systems of control, like the police and the judiciary. They also came under the analytical eye of the educated elite—criminologists, psychologists, sociologists, and jurists—who articulated competing interpretations of the causes and consequences of intimate violence. A historical analysis of intimate violence thus facilitates insight into social organization and cultural expectations of men and women from the most intimate to the broadest levels.

For Joseph and Margot Maxant, ongoing conflicts about sexual fidelity were ultimately resolved with a gunshot. With his wife's death, Joseph also put an end to her infidelity and his own shameful position as a cuckold. He had endured too much unhappiness, he testified, and he was carried away by anger when he shot Margot. Reinforced by a chorus of neighbors who confirmed his wife's misconduct, Joseph's account was validated by his acquittal. His neighbors as well as the jurors ultimately agreed that his wife deserved her fate at his hands—in short, that his use of violence as a retributive tool of justice was legitimate. Hundreds of other defendants in the fin-de-siècle assize court sought to establish that they too had legitimately taken justice into their own hands in seeking vengeance against their partners. The social, cultural, and legal conditions under which this could be possible constitute the focus of this book.

CHAPTER I

La Vie Intime

The following exchange occurred on 1 December 1886 between an investigating magistrate named Prinet and an umbrella maker named Angélina Merle, age twenty-one.

> QUESTION: Le sieur Henri Béziade began to court you during the year 1884, he promised you marriage. On the faith of this promise you had the weakness to surrender to his desires. You went many times to his room at rue Danville 2 and had intimate relations with him.
>
> ANSWER: Yes, monsieur.
>
> QUESTION: After having possessed you, he showed himself to be less eager to keep his promise of marriage. He made evasive replies to the questions you addressed him on this subject. Irritated with him, you threatened him... saying that if he did not keep his word he would be sorry?
>
> ANSWER: Yes, monsieur; even before I gave in to him, I had declared as much, from the moment I set foot in his room. If he seemed to say "no" to marriage, I would be capable of killing him. The first time I went to his place, as I was resisting him, he told me that if I did not give in, he would write an anonymous letter to my parents, which is why I had relations with him. [...]

QUESTION: Béziade was wrong, without doubt, to make promises of marriage to you and then to try to escape them. But you, if you hoped to become his legitimate wife and the respected mother of his children, you should have begun by maintaining respect for yourself and not giving yourself up to him. We must tell you that he did not obtain your favors by surprise nor following a momentary clouding of the senses, but you went to his room, his bachelor apartment, more or less for that. In a word, you went looking for what happened to you.

ANSWER: No, monsieur, he had invited me to go to his place, assuring me that he wouldn't ask anything of me. I didn't give in to him until after several visits. [...] I did it with premeditation because he kept telling me no. If he had said "yes," I wouldn't have done it. [...] I am no more coquettish and easy than other young girls.[1]

Angélina Merle later would be acquitted of assaulting her former lover with sulfuric acid, but her vivid personal account reveals something of her motives and expectations in beginning a sexual relationship with a man she hoped to marry. The judge implied that she could have had sex without blame had it been against her will, had she been taken unawares and overwhelmed by her emotions, but Merle asserted that she had made a conscious choice. Even in the face of the magistrate's disapproval, she insisted that her choice to have sex was a step in a regular courtship. She certainly knew that her decision to go to Béziade's room was fraught with risk—after all, she threatened him about the dire consequences of breaking his promise even before they had sex—but she did not express regret either for sleeping with him or for attacking him. Indeed, her mother's first action when Merle revealed her relationship with Béziade was to confront him and try to make him keep his promise of marriage. It was only when this effort failed that Merle decided to seek violent revenge. Although the judge scolded Merle for having sex, neither she nor her mother believed that this choice was a barrier to contracting a satisfactory match. It seems that choosing to have sex based on a promise of marriage was a gamble in which there would only be a loser if one person broke his end of the bargain.

Henri Béziade was apparently the only one of her many suitors Angélina chose to have sex with. The trial dossier contains letters from four young men (and their families) who were courting her between 1881 and 1884. The Merle family made and sold umbrellas on the avenue d'Orléans and was prosperous enough to offer a dowry of ten thousand francs for Angélina, the oldest of three children. They had long known the family of Henri Béziade, whose father was a locksmith on the nearby rue Sophie Germain. Although her family was actively involved in seeking a suitable partner for her, Merle made her own choice among her suitors.

Was Angélina Merle a rebel against prevailing norms of courtship and sexual propriety? Was she a pioneer of freedom and individual choice in the pursuit of pleasure? Or was she a typical young woman of her milieu, no more of a coquette than other girls, who only happened to enter the historical record because she bet on the wrong man to fulfill her desires? Her story speaks to important issues in the history of sexuality and the history of the family, as well as the historical ethnography of the working people of Paris. Read together with the hundreds of other dossiers from so-called crimes of passion in the fin de siècle, Merle's story illustrates the conflicting expectations, desires, and disappointments that played into the creation—and rupture—of intimate relationships.

Much traditional family history, informed by demographic sources, does not problematize sexuality, while more recent work on sexuality tends to focus on behaviors defined as deviant that fell under the purview of medical and judicial control, rather than on normative heterosexual practices.[2] The occasional historical work that purports to address the issue directly can fall prey to class-based (if not also sexist) distortions. Historian Guy Richard describes the sexual life of the popular classes at the end of the nineteenth century thus: "In the workers' milieu, it was simpler [than among the bourgeoisie], you screwed the girls in empty lots or on piles of rubble; you took a wife or a concubine, you gave her children, and when the girls were grown, you screwed them in their turn. Let us not forget that it was in the industrial regions of the Nord that in the year 1979 the rate of incest was the highest, facilitated by the workers' row houses and lodgings."[3] What is striking about this passage is not only the exclusively male perspective but the gross stereotype of workers' sexuality as brutal, deviant, and ahistorically unchanging. Richard's statement can serve here to demonstrate the pitfalls for historians of reproducing the biases of past eras, since he was drawing on information from bourgeois observers (such as Zola) who were shocked at the apparent disorder of workers' sexual relationships.

Other social historians have provided a wealth of demographic information about such important topics as the ages at which people married in cities and the countryside and how many children they had. Sifting through endless registers of births, marriages, and deaths, they have compiled monuments of statistical analysis. On the broadest level, scholars agree that throughout the nineteenth century, rates of mortality and fertility fell, age at first marriage fell, and migration to urban centers intensified.[4] A few local studies have examined the dynamics of these trends in specific contexts. For example, Elinor Accampo's painstaking study using the method of family reconstitution reveals the impact of industrial transformation of the town of Saint-Chamond on family formation among workers.[5] Accampo argues that pressure from industrial work organization was the primary cause of the decline in family size in Saint-Chamond. Such local studies provide important insights into the effects of large-scale demographic trends, but by the very nature of the sources they employ, they cannot describe in depth the experience of individuals. Marriage registers do not record personal motivations, after all, and they exclude the numerous couples who lived together without marrying and so escaped official record-keeping.

Detailed accounts of the lives of working people are hard to find. In her study of fin-de-siècle working women in the Nord, Patricia Hilden based her analysis of *la vie intime* largely on information from government-sponsored studies of working-class life, local leftist newspapers, and cultural material such as popular songs.[6] These sources enabled her to describe the general material conditions under which women gave birth, raised their children, and made ends meet, but they do not permit much insight into individual women's struggles and choices. This problem plagues virtually any historical work that aims to describe the intimate lives of the laboring poor. Sources that provide anything like a firsthand account are difficult to come by and are far outnumbered, if not overshadowed, by contemporary and historical works dealing with the lives of the upper classes. For instance, Laure Adler's *Secrets d'alcôve* poses the question, "How are couples born, how do they live, and how do they break apart?"[7] Drawing on a rich variety of medical, religious, and literary sources, Adler argues that the bourgeoisie and upper classes invented the notion of the couple in the nineteenth century, promoting the attainment of romantic love and sexual satisfaction within marriage. This model, she claims, only spread to the lower ranks of society after the first World War, and indeed, the glimpses of lower-class couples that appear in her account—gleaned mainly from prescriptive literature produced by educated elites—depict nothing but hardship and betrayal. In this narrative, the sexual and affective comportment of the lower classes were modernized through the example of the upper classes, yet the sentiments, desires, and deeds of the lower classes prior to this colonization remain almost entirely unexplored.

Michel Foucault's *History of Sexuality* also follows this top-down narrative. The key to the consolidation of the bourgeoisie as a class, and its power as a politically and economically dominant group, he argued, was the creation and control of its sexuality, beginning in the mid-eighteenth century. "For their part," Foucault wrote, "the working classes managed for a long time to escape the deployment of 'sexuality.'" Having successfully resisted the controls of the Catholic Church in an earlier era, he claimed, in the nineteenth century the lower classes nonetheless fell subject to bourgeois efforts to "moralize" them, remaking them in the bourgeois image, "with the development of the juridical and medical control of perversions, for the sake of a general protection of society and the race." He continued, "It can be said that this was the moment when the deployment of 'sexuality,' elaborated in its more complex and intense forms, by and for the privileged classes, spread through the entire social body."[8] If Foucault was correct that the end of the nineteenth century saw the greatest influence of bourgeois norms and controls over the sexuality of working-class people, then one might expect to find stricter controls on such practices as sex before marriage, women's sexual satisfaction, and nonreproductive sexual practices in general during this era.

Historian Anne-Marie Sohn, however, has argued that exactly the opposite was the case. Drawing on seven thousand judicial dossiers concerning private life in various ways (including many from the Cour d'assises de la Seine), she has found that as the nineteenth century drew to a close, ordinary people became less rather than more inhibited in their sexual practices. Vocabulary referring to the body and to sexual acts became more precise, and practices such as nudity, kissing on the mouth, and premarital sex gradually became more widespread. As the number of arranged marriages declined, Sohn argued, the value placed on finding sexual and emotional satisfaction with one's spouse increased, especially for women. "No desire without love, no love without pleasure, said these frustrated wives," in Sohn's interpretation. She concludes, "It is above all incontestable that an ethical rupture took place under the Third Republic which opened the way to sexual freedom," contrary to official "Victorian" discourses. Sohn found that the fundamental cause of this shift was the increasing use of birth control and abortion, which enabled women to risk more extramarital sex. And it was urban working women, "with neither status nor patrimony to protect" who first took the risk. "They showed the way to wealthier women who would imitate them one or two generations later."[9] According to Sohn, then, the eroticization of the couple moved from the bottom of the social hierarchy up, rather than from the top down, and resulted in a diversification of sexual practices, not their repression. Her interpretation coincides with that of Edward Shorter, who argued earlier that a rise in illegitimate births in the nineteenth century betokened a rise in extramarital sexual activity and the pursuit of pleasure among the lower classes, a trend that would move up the social ranks.[10]

Stories like Angélina Merle's suggest that the process of change in the sexual and affective lives of ordinary people was much messier than either of these linear narratives suggests.[11] The last three decades of the nineteenth century appear to be an era of transition, during which the working people of Paris hotly contested different notions of propriety as they struggled to balance emotional satisfaction and material security. The trial dossiers of the *cour d'assises* often document how conflicting expectations in intimate relationships led to violence. Given that a large portion of the Parisian population was comprised of immigrants to the city, it is perhaps not surprising that no single standard of sexual propriety had been established by the end of the nineteenth century. As Martine Segalen has abundantly demonstrated, conventions regarding sex before marriage and the choice of a partner varied considerably by region in the rural areas from which these new Parisians came.[12] Among fin-de-siècle workers, some men and women considered only pleasure in choosing a partner while others' choice of a spouse depended more on family and business ties. For most couples, however, finding and keeping a suitable partner depended on carefully balancing personal interests of love and desire on the one hand, and financial or familial considerations on the other. A deficit on either side could lead to a rupture, as could a miscalculation of a potential partner's capacities in either area.

Furthermore, the diversity of views articulated by lower-class witnesses stands in sharp contrast to the predictable bourgeois views of the jurists, who thought that sex before marriage was always wrong, that women were not supposed to seek sexual pleasure, and that genuine, passionate love among disreputable people was impossible. Yet assize court cases do not provide evidence that bourgeois jurists successfully imposed their standards regarding love and sex on the lower-class people involved in court cases. On the contrary, people like Angélina Merle defended their own standards even where jurists pointedly expressed their disapproval. Individuals sought satisfactory partnerships on their own terms—testing, stretching, or enforcing the limits of legitimate intimate relationships. Practice theory posits that individuals pursue their interests in social and cultural contexts that constrain and enable them in certain ways but are themselves responsive to individuals' actions. In fin-de-siècle Paris, some participants in assize court trials expressed normative standards for intimate relationships, while others implicitly or explicitly challenged those standards in their pursuit of a partner. All were improvising within the context of a burgeoning city, where the material conditions of life and social ties with neighbors and family members inflected the possibilities for intimate relationships.

The Formation of the Couple

Marriage was not necessarily the goal of a partnership between a man and a woman among the working people of Paris. Since the Revolution, legal marriage in France had required a civil ceremony in the town hall that rendered an additional, religious ceremony legally superfluous. While Catholic leaders decried the nineteenth-century decline in marriages, the notoriously irreligious Parisians did not find the sanction of the Church compelling. At the same time, the civil ceremony required the proper papers—birth certificates, parental permission for those underage—which could prove difficult to obtain. The expense of the celebratory meal (*la noce*) that followed the ceremony presented a financial obstacle. Whether they avoided marriage because of these difficulties or perhaps rejected it on principle, many couples in this milieu lived together for years and even had children without being married. It is impossible to determine the precise extent of this practice, though Rachel Fuchs has suggested that such couples comprised about one-third of domestic partnerships.[13] About half of the couples in this study lived together without being married. Officially, this was termed living *en concubinage*, or *maritalement*. Lenard Berlanstein reports that a period of concubinage appears to have preceded half of the marriages of humble white-collar employees.[14] Neighbors and acquaintances might accord a cohabiting couple the titles used for married people, or the couple might purposefully adopt the names themselves. Marie Gadel was called "Madame Paul" after her lover, with whom she lived for many years.[15] Marguerite Clément used Friart, the name of her longtime lover, even after their relationship had ended.[16] Similarly, men referred to wives or concubines they lived with as "ma femme." "I lived with the widow Dhuyck for four years; I called her my wife," declared Dominique Millim.[17]

This elision of names and titles reinforced a fundamental similarity among the relationships they described. Whether married or not, the mutual obligations of a man and a woman living as domestic partners were the same: both were expected to work and contribute financially to the household; the woman was expected to take care of provisioning, cooking, cleaning, and childcare, as well as remaining sexually faithful to her partner; men were not obliged so strictly to be faithful, as we shall see. For an established couple, then, the difference between concubinage and marriage was not so great, and indeed one was often a step to the other.

Living *en concubinage* could be a trial period before contracting a marriage, testing not only personal compatibility but also the financial viability of a more permanent union. The two criteria were often in conflict. Marie Rochat had taken great care in determining her husband's compatibility, though she later shot him when he abandoned her for a mistress. "Before marrying, I lived with him as husband and wife [*maritalement*] for thirteen or fourteen months. He proved himself to be very decent. That's what convinced me to accept his proposal of marriage."[18] Louis Badran did not pass the same test. Having unsuccessfully courted the elder of two sisters, who rejected him for his laziness, he ran off with the younger one, Blanche Gallier, a seamstress for the department store Printemps. "Blanche was the one who preferred to wait [to get married]," he claimed. "She wanted us to save some money for the expenses of the *noce*. Blanche had a certain situation at her store, and she did not want to get married in a poor fashion."[19] She was concerned with marking her social position with the public display of a suitably copious celebration. But after several months of working long hours and literally starving to support her lover, Blanche changed her mind. Badran was convicted of attempted murder for stabbing her when she threatened to leave him, though he offered to atone for his crime with a promise to marry and support her.

In a comparable situation, Sophronie Martinage agreed to live with Jean-Baptiste Verhoost until his parents would permit their marriage.[20] When he proved unwilling to give her enough of his pay to support the household, however, Martinage broke off their deal and left him. Philippine Thomas lived with Pierre Beulle for about five years and had a child with him, but she resisted his proposals of marriage: "Beulle only worked very irregularly and sought only to live at my expense... When I understood that there was nothing to hope for from such a man, I broke with him definitively."[21] Women like these did not seek partnership at any price. They were willing to test the waters and invest a certain amount of time in evaluating their partners, only then committing to a partner who fulfilled their expectations.

A handful of women (and no men) went so far as to express their intention never to marry, indicating that for them, an independent life was not only feasible but desirable. One woman wanted to stay single apparently for moral reasons. A widow, Victoire Langot said she did not want to remarry so that she could "consecrate herself entirely to her children."[22] Other women who asserted their desire for independence cited less pious motives. "The accused... did not think of becoming his wife because marriage did not suit her flighty and changeable nature," reported the investigating magistrate about Edmée Chervey.[23] A widow named Estelle Pluchet enraged her former lover when she told him, "I am perfectly free in and of myself [*libre de ma personne*]. I am allowed to do what I want."[24] Marie Traber also resisted marriage proposals from her lover, Guiseppe Deffendi, who shot her when she left him. She explained, "Since he was very helpful to me at a time when I was in difficulty, I did not want to leave him suddenly, and that's why I stayed with him for a while. This man is extremely violent. He made a scene every time I talked about leaving, threatening to kill me if I carried out this plan. I did not, however, hide my intention from him; since no legitimate tie bound me to this individual, I was free in and of myself [*libre de ma personne*], and I meant to make use of my liberty and my independence as I saw fit."[25] The phrase that both Traber and Pluchet used, *libre de ma personne*, has a legalistic connotation referring to one's personal rights as a juridical subject. While the civil code accorded husbands numerous rights over their wives, such as determining where they should live, Marie Traber's explanation of her behavior is remarkable for identifying her legal rights (or rather, her lover's lack of a legal claim on her) with her own personal, emotional inclinations. A friend of hers testified that Traber had met Deffendi as soon as she arrived in Paris from the countryside. He had helped her financially at that time, and she had continued to stay with him whenever she was between jobs as a chambermaid, although Traber would also claim that she took those jobs as a domestic servant precisely to get away from him. Traber judged that Deffendi's economic assistance had been repaid by her time with him and thought that no further obligation should ensue from their liaison.

Such fierce claims of independence were rare, however. In contrast to these women who did not seek permanent relationships, many more appeared in court claiming that their lovers had promised marriage and then abandoned them. In such cases, it can be difficult to distinguish between couples who were going through a trial period of cohabitation to determine their compatibility for marriage and couples where one partner was exploiting the other for sexual services or economic support. The stakes could be very high, as in the case of Marie Féral and her erstwhile intended Jules Courtois, where each person had a different understanding of the nature of their relationship. Courtois was openly cynical when he told the investigating magistrate: "I promised marriage to her as one does to all young girls. Since she was a novice, this is how I was able to get something; otherwise, she wouldn't have given in, since I had enough difficulties to overcome her resistance."[26] She had been a domestic servant in the same building where he was a chef in a restaurant, and she only agreed to have sex with him two days after she lost her job. Perhaps economic necessity added fuel to her romantic inclinations. At any rate, they moved in together, and she wrote her family for permission to marry, while Courtois secretly made plans to marry a cousin with whom he had had a child five years earlier. It was only when Féral became pregnant herself that she discovered her lover's duplicity and shot him.

Whether or not a woman could parlay a pregnancy into marriage was a question of grave economic and emotional importance. To be sure, even married men might fail to support their legitimate children, but a woman with an illegitimate child had no hope of making a legal claim for support against the father, since paternity suits were illegal until 1912.[27] However, in the assize court, seduced and abandoned women who had been promised marriage were almost invariably acquitted for seeking violent revenge. Four years after the birth of their child, Marie Croissant finally realized her lover was never going to keep his promise of marrying her; she shot him and was acquitted.[28] Much of the investigation centered on who knew he had promised marriage and when: in a sense, the legitimacy of Croissant's vengeance depended on the validity of his promise of marriage.

Even as Croissant sought retaliation for false promises of marriage, other women suffered no permanent damage to their reputations after choosing to have sex *without* the expectation of marriage. Among the working people of Paris, a consensus did not exist about whether or not it was proper for a couple to have sex before marriage, and witnesses expressed contradictory views on this point. While Jean-Baptiste Dubien, for example, said he wanted to marry Joséphine Jacques specifically because she was known to be a virgin,[29] Marie Boizot chided her nephew for worrying that his wife had had sex before marrying him: "All young girls have lovers before getting married," she said.[30] But if the propriety of sex before marriage was open to debate among the ordinary people who testified in court, there was no ambiguity for the investigating magistrates or the judges of the assize court. For professional jurists, sex before marriage could only be excused by a woman's naïveté; it was never acceptable as a calculated risk on the way to a permanent alliance.

The choice to have sex or not would seem to indicate a personal decision based at least in part on the pursuit of the individual's own desires. In many cases, however, individual desires contended with the interests of parents and other family members. Family involvement seems typical of marriages among families already well established in Paris or families with a small amount of capital to distribute, and of marriages undertaken in the couple's native region. For instance, in the Nièvre, Amable Bartholémy negotiated marrying his daughter Alexandrine to François Clément through the mediation of the suitor's aunt. Although Bartholémy only met the young man a month before the wedding, he had known his father and believed his family to be respectable. The couple were married in the country and then returned to Paris to live.[31]

As in Angélina Merle's case, however, parental involvement did not necessarily betoken parental control of the match. In Paris, Victorine Guerval's mother arranged a match for her with Adolphe Goury and then authorized him to walk her daughter home from work every evening.[32] Meanwhile, Guerval, known to be a serious young woman who supported her family through her work making chains for a jeweler, made dates with her suitor in private rooms of a restaurant—a typical location for sexual trysts. Thus her family's surveillance went only so far, and she secretly thwarted her mother's efforts to maintain a chaste courtship. Esther Clerc was more circumspect with her suitor, Jean-Pierre Gendarme, to whom she was introduced by female friends in her neighborhood. She spent time with him over six months, having a relationship that she described as that "of [a] future husband and wife, consequently very honest."[33] She specified, "During our relationship, Gendarme took me to the theater sometimes in the company of my parents, and I dined with him once. He didn't give me any gifts besides a scarf and a knit shawl." In fact, she broke up with him in mid-December so that he would not give her a New Year's gift, which would signify a level of commitment that she did not want. "Since affection for him did not come," she explained, "I was afraid of making a bad match, and I broke with him definitively." Her emotional preference, within the bounds of a courtship monitored by her parents, was the deciding factor.

Parents had several resources to facilitate or hinder a marriage. In addition to keeping important legal documents like birth certificates, which were necessary for identification at the time of the wedding, parents were legally required to give their permission to children under the age of twenty-one, either in person at the town hall or through a notarized declaration. Choosing the latter method could indicate a parent's disapproval of a prospective spouse. The widow Augustine Bertal declared that her son had married against her will, explaining why she had only given permission by *acte notarié*.³⁴ Even though her son and future daughter-in-law lived together for six months before marrying, she had refused to meet the woman. Similarly, Georges Langlois explained his father's reluctance: "My father was opposed to my marriage, because he thought I was too young and because my future wife had no fortune. He gave me consent before a notary and did not attend the marriage," though he did pay for the *noce*.³⁵ Although couples who did not obtain parental consent could certainly still live together, a few took the denial more seriously. Eugène Henry obtained his father's permission to marry Augustine Vasseur, a prostitute with twelve thousand francs in savings.³⁶ Her mother, however, delayed giving her consent, even after receiving a letter from Henry's hometown mayor attesting to his good conduct. In response to her apparent opposition to their union, the couple attempted a murder-suicide. Recovering from her gunshot wounds, Vasseur declared that having now reached the legal age of majority, she would marry the man regardless of her mother's wishes.

Perhaps Vasseur's mother had reason to be suspicious about the suitor's motives. After all, it appears that the most persuasive argument Henry used to obtain his father's permission was that Vasseur's savings would allow him to establish his own business. By law, whatever property a wife brought to a marriage came under her husband's control. Women who negotiated formal marriage contracts had more legal protection. They could stipulate a separation of property (called *séparation des biens*, defined in article 1536 of the Civil Code), allowing them to keep their own property and even to run a business independently. Such a contract could also require a husband to manage his wife's property responsibly. Of course, women with few economic resources were unlikely to create such a document, and in practice, it was not a solid protection of their interests. With little or no legal recourse, women were extremely vulnerable to financial exploitation by the men they married—or who promised to marry them. For example, by the time she met Jules Cattiaux, Hélène Guillet was in her late forties and had amassed the remarkable sum of ten thousand francs by working as a chambermaid on a steamship and then running a small bar. Cattiaux promised to marry her, they moved to Paris together, and he proceeded to dissipate her entire savings before running off with another woman. "Cattiaux betrayed me," Guillet complained bitterly. "He promised me marriage, he ruined me—that's what pushed me over the edge."³⁷ Her only regret was that she had targeted his new mistress with sulfuric acid, not him. Modeste Guillot, who met his wife during a business transaction, twice drove her grocery business bankrupt through his drinking and laziness, in spite of her family's frequent interventions.[38]

The case of Ernest Teste demonstrates how tangled business and emotional interests could become. On 28 February 1889, Teste married Blanche Lecoeur, who was the head of a prosperous little business in feathers and hat trimmings.[39] Before he shot her in September of 1890, the business had already gone bankrupt two times. Witnesses at the hearing for the first bankruptcy blamed it on the "disastrous influence" of the husband, and by the time of the crime in 1890, Blanche Teste declared to anyone who would listen that she had been better off on her own and that she would soon divorce her lazy, incompetent husband so that her business would once again prosper. Nonetheless, at the beginning of their marriage, their association had seemed to be a mutually beneficial proposition.

Ernest Teste was a broker of feathered accessories (*courtier en plumes*) and had known of his future wife's work in the same business for a dozen years. Initially, he was her employee, and then, by all accounts, she was the one who suggested marriage to him—a gesture that some witnesses found unusual. Teste's oldest sister, Emilie Belot, considered the proposition advantageous to her brother, if not ideal. "Ernest told us about his plans to go into business. At that time he was living with a woman [*un faux ménage*], and since he said that the person whom he wanted to marry was in the same business as he, we saw certain advantages in the union. Instead of remaining a middleman, he could work for his own account, since the person was established in business. Certainly, there was an illegitimate child [by another man], but since we wanted to see his state of concubinage end, we pointed out to him that sometimes one has to set aside one's pride. Besides, he told us that the lady did not displease him." Teste's other sister was surprised by the marriage, but her brother told her "that this woman was intelligent and she had taste, and that between the two of them they could probably set up a good business." Apparently, the lure of becoming the *patron* outweighed the stigma of legitimizing a child not his own—a girl who was four years old at the time of the marriage.

Although several people, including her husband, claimed that she married him primarily to legitimize her daughter and atone for her faults, this suggestion made Madame Teste furious in more than one argument. She seems to have been more forthright about her business interests in marrying him; Teste claimed that she needed a man in her business to give her more authority over her workers. Nonetheless, she maintained a certain superiority: not only did she control the purse strings ("I had no salary," Teste admitted, "but when I needed something my wife gave it to me.") but also she remained the titular head of the business, thanks to the *séparation des biens* stipulated by their marriage contract. Although Teste claimed that they lived with their property in common, she was the only one held legally responsible and sent to jail when the business failed. Madame Teste was also quite strict about her husband's business practices. According to their maid, "It didn't take anything for an argument to break out. If monsieur wrote a bill badly, or if he made a mistake in recording something, Madame got angry." Toward the end of the investigation, Teste would claim that he never touched the cash box or the account books, but testimony like this from the couple's employees indicated otherwise.

Their business interests may have been an important factor in bringing them together, but it does not necessarily follow that Ernest and Blanche had no affection for each other. The concierge attested to their frequent quarrels but also said that they were inseparable and never left the house without each other. They shared the same bed every night until the night before the crime—except on the occasions when Blanche was driven from the house after a fight, when, her husband would later claim, contrary to all other testimony, that she slept with a lover. By all accounts (except Ernest's, who claimed that his wife had no feelings for the child) they were both devastated by the death of their baby while in the care of her nurse in the spring of 1890.

Nonetheless, whatever common ground they shared had eroded completely by the summer of 1890, which was marked by noisy arguments, mutual insults, and violence. Madame Teste found refuge with the concierge when her husband beat her and often sought the help of the police captain of the Gaillon quarter where they lived. After an episode where Teste threatened to stab his wife, the *commissaire* called Teste into his office and extracted from him a promise that he would not create such a scene again, while the captain's secretary suggested that Madame Teste seek a legal separation.[40] She eventually followed this advice and went to see a lawyer about it the day before her husband shot her. This action seems to have sparked Ernest's attack. He reported that, right before he shot her, as she reclined on the bed after lunch, she said, "I will be alone in the future to carry on my business. I'm going to get a divorce—get him out of here! In twenty-four hours I will make him leave."

The timing of the crime made Teste appear less like a long-suffering husband who finally cracked under the strain of a difficult life with a nagging, domineering wife, and more like a frustrated opportunist who was about to lose his meal ticket, at least in the eyes of the investigating magistrate. He made his interpretation clear in his final interrogation of Teste in December of 1890: "Many times there was the question between you two of separation, or, at least, your wife talked about it. But this idea was repugnant to you because you only married out of commercial interest, to become the boss, and you would not have consented to a divorce without your share of the business." Teste replied that he was the titular head of their third and final attempt at business together, although the testimony of all five employees interviewed reinforces the fact that Madame Teste remained in charge. Nonetheless, when Ernest was questioned on this point during his trial, he confirmed that he would never have agreed to split the business. "I did not speak of sharing," he testified. "I was the master."[41] His insistence on his dominance, even in the face of so much evidence to the contrary, indicates a desperate struggle for control, where business and emotional interests inseparably twisted together. His wife no longer shared his bed and intended to take away "his" share of the business, too. On a sexual level, he had been rejected; his own child had died, while he had legitimated the daughter of another man. In business, he was blamed for failure and insulted for his incompetence in front of other people.

Was the jury sympathetic to his plight as a disempowered man? They found him not guilty of murder but guilty of attempted murder with extenuating circumstances, and the judges sentenced him to six years of prison and ten years of banishment from Paris. It is impossible to know, however, if the jurors believed Teste's version of the story, or if this was one of the very rare cases where medical testimony made a difference in the verdict. Noting that none of the bullets had actually penetrated the victim's skull, Dr. Jules Socquet concluded in his autopsy report that the victim's heart disease had "fatally diminished" her resistance to the wounds, and he was unable to confirm that the wounds had been the direct cause of death. The final interpretation of the trial's results must therefore remain uncertain, but this case illustrates the many factors that could bring a couple together—business or monetary interests, legitimation of a sexual relationship or a child, love or desire, and family influences.

Sexual Partnership

As the story of the Teste couple suggests, marriage was a partnership, but not of equals. Men and women owed each other reciprocal but dissimilar obligations: as stated in Article 213 of the Civil Code, a wife owed her husband obedience, while he owed her protection. In practice, too, a key element of a man's legitimate authority in the household was the ability to master his wife, a notion that was strategically invoked by men and women alike when a relationship went wrong. For, just as the head of a corporation could be held liable for an employee's fraud, a husband could be blamed for failing to control his spouse. Her errors ultimately could be ascribed to his faulty governance, and nowhere more so than in issues of sexual conduct, for sexual services and fidelity were at the core of the reciprocal obligations between domestic partners.

This reasoning informed Alexandrine Duc's attempt to lay the blame for her infidelity on her husband's neglect.[42] She was a middle-class woman (with a dowry of twenty-five thousand francs plus five thousand francs more in trousseau and jewels) who married a doctor twenty-eight years her senior, and she carried on affairs with three men before her husband found out and shot her. Although her experience is not typical of the vast majority of women who passed through the assize court, she articulated certain standards of the marital relationship against which her lower-class sisters were measured by judges and juries in court. She describes the difficulties of her marriage as follows: "I married Monsieur Duc in the month of February, 1860. I was young. I wasn't even eighteen, and I needed my husband to take care of me much more than he did. Although he was married, he continued his bachelor habits and left me to spend all my evenings at home alone. He hardly ever went out with me." She took care of their children for twelve years, "but my heart, you understand, did not have the satisfactions that my husband should give me, and little by little the affection and devotion I had for him went away." As she tells it, if she was unfaithful, it was because her husband was not sufficiently concerned with her; since he left her to her own devices, she could hardly be blamed for seeking a lover. Her need for love (and, implicitly, for sexual satisfaction) was a given. Her explanation sought to turn to her own advantage her inferior status as a weak woman in need of guidance. Her arguments were unsuccessful, though, and her husband was quickly acquitted for shooting her in the neck (a wound from which she recovered). The *Gazette des Tribunaux* reported that the trial ended with the husband's total vindication. "An enormous crowd waited for him and gave him a kind of ovation while his friends threw themselves in his arms and congratulated him on the happy outcome of the trial."[43]

Other cases, however, illustrate that a husband could effectively be held responsible for his wife's infidelities. The investigating magistrate and a witness reprimanded Simon Richelet for allowing a male friend to board with him and his wife in their one-room apartment. "You corrupted her by the examples you gave her; in a way, you threw her into Benotte's arms," scolded the investigating magistrate.[44] Another man, Georges Koenig, allowed his unfaithful wife to go to public balls on Sundays. When a friend reproached him, Koenig had shrugged it off, saying, "My wife works a lot during the week and it doesn't matter in the least if she has fun on Sundays, and besides, I trust her fully."[45] A policeman advised Koenig "to supervise his wife in order to avoid a scandal" and not to take her to low-class dances, which would be "imprudent." The wife's mother explained that her daughter needed not permissiveness but husbandly direction: "This child has a frivolous character, but she isn't mean; in leading her with gentleness one could have made anything of her one wanted to." Ideally, the balance of power in the couple required the man to be on top. If he failed to control her, she might fail to be sexually faithful to him.

Yet this equation depends on the implicit assumption that women, as well as men, desired sex. It was extremely rare for either men or women to express directly in a judicial context their enthusiasm for sex. When the investigating magistrate asked him why he and his mistress had rented a hotel room (where they stayed in bed all day and ultimately staged an attempted murder-suicide) instead of going home, Jean Ancelin explained that they simply could not wait: "After having lunch, wanting to have relations together and being far from our respective lodgings, we took a room in the rue Geoffroy Marie, next to the place where we had coffee."[46] Hillairain de Saint-Priest claimed that he and his lover were enthralled by "an entirely sensual passion" that precipitated intimate relations three days after they first met.[47] Paul Lelong first made the acquaintance of his lover Rose Méhu only two days before they slept together for the first time; two weeks later, she moved in with him.[48] But this kind of eagerness for sex was rarely admitted in judicial dossiers.

It was undoubtedly more problematic for women than for men to articulate their desires in the context of criminal investigations. Although many women engaged in sexual activity outside marriage, the professional jurists who interrogated them advocated the stricter norms of the upper classes, which eschewed sex outside of marriage for any honorable woman. Whatever their feelings may have really been, women who testified in the assize court did not portray themselves as actively pursuing sexual pleasure. Rather, they "surrendered" to the man's demands or gave in to irresistible emotions. Marie Bière, for instance, "admitted that she gave in to the compulsions of a violent passion."[49] By the same token, it is sometimes difficult to determine where a woman's rhetoric ended and real resistance began. Marguerite Herbellot admitted that she had had sex with her husband before marrying him: "He profited from finding me alone one day to have sexual relations with me; I was living with my mother."[50] They were married shortly before the birth of their first child. Was it truly against her will to have sex, or was it convenient to absolve herself of responsibility for something that was, in many cases, an acceptable step in a couple's relationship? The court documents cannot resolve the dilemma in this case.

A single woman named Jeanne Cabrol also absolved herself of responsibility when she admitted that she had had sex years earlier with a cousin whom she now rejected as a suitor: "I was fourteen, I was very inexperienced, and I couldn't defend myself against Paul."[51] Besides, she continued, she could not stand the sight of him and they quarreled all the time. Perhaps Paul believed that consent once given could not be revoked. Certainly, Edmé Lechevallier would have agreed, since he resorted to blackmail in order to force his lover Louise Méro to continue to sleep with him. She said that he had promised to marry her, and they had had sex in hotel rooms and carriages, but when she wanted to break off their relationship, he dragged her into his room and threatened to tell her employers that she had a lover—which probably would have caused her to lose her job as a domestic servant.[52] Méro describes the scene as follows: "Once we arrived in front of his door, I didn't want to go up. I even told him that I intended to break up with him because he promised me marriage but kept putting it off. He took me in his arms and dragged me into the corridor and the staircase. In the room, I resisted him. I didn't want to undo my dress. I pushed him away and threw my umbrella to the ground. He threatened me, saying that he would go to my masters and make a scene, that he would force me to be fired. I consented to have relations with him again." A few weeks later, after going to bed together, he shot her (and himself) when she got up to leave.

More decisive evidence that many men and women purposefully sought sexual pleasure with their partners lies in the complaints that one partner was not fulfilling the other's expectations, either not having sex in a proper way or not having sex at all. "You didn't even look at me; you scorned me. When you have a husband, it's not to spend five minutes with him," complained Eulalie Jean to her husband, after she shot at him. "You took me like a prostitute."[53] Apparently, a quick sex act was not what she felt she was entitled to as his wife. Her comment implies that she wanted him to take the time to show her some affection. She had a definite idea of what she wanted from a sexual encounter with her husband, and he failed to provide it.

Although it was not articulated in these terms, it is clear that men and women expected their domestic partners to fulfill their sexual needs. For married people, the *devoir conjugal* was indeed a legal duty, but unmarried couples seemed to have felt it was just as serious an obligation. Refusal to have sex could be a symptom of profound problems in the relationship and was often described along with other injustices a partner felt he or she had suffered. François Lerondeau complained that his wife neglected the housework, failed to feed him enough, and made him sleep in a barn. At her trial for poisoning him, five of the couple's friends reported that she complained he did not fulfill his sexual duty towards her. Lerondeau said to one of his friends, "She complains that I'm not gallant towards her, but how could you be to a woman who always causes you such misery? It repulses you!"[54] One of his friends summed it up: "The reason for their discord came from the wife always wanting the husband to fulfill the conjugal duty. He used to say, 'If she were nice to me, maybe I could rediscover the energy to satisfy her.'" But when the wife was confronted with these statements, she denied ever speaking of it. "I have too much modesty to say such things. I would barely dare to share such a confidence with a close female friend [*une intime amie*]." It hardly seems likely that her husband would have started such an unflattering rumor about himself, but, although she may have shared it with others before, Mélanie Lerondeau was unwilling to describe her problem to the investigating magistrate, who was far from being an *intime amie*. Significantly, this is the only case where a woman claimed she was wronged because her partner refused to have sex with her. This case adds evidence that men and women had very different attitudes about their entitlement to sexual satisfaction with their domestic partner.

Unlike women, some men were quick to respond with violence when they felt their sexual needs were not met, regardless of other factors in the relationship. Perhaps certain men were more willing to discuss their sexual disappointments with judicial interrogators, or perhaps men resorted to violence more readily than women no matter what their motive. It is likely, however, that they felt a stronger sense of entitlement that women should serve their sexual needs. The judicial archives provide numerous stories of women who were beaten or killed for refusing to have sex, or to perform certain sex acts, with men. Louis-François Forestier spelled out his reasoning quite explicitly during his trial for killing his mistress. "Around one in the morning, I wanted to have relations with her; she did not consent. I said to her: 'Don't worry, I won't torment you. It's all the same to me.' Then, when I got up, I thought about her refusal and all the misery she made me endure. All this passed through my head. I said to myself, She's wasted 700 francs of mine, she who has caused me so much trouble. When I want to go with her, she replies: 'Ah! That's for tomorrow.'"[55] Since he supported her financially, he thought her refusal was unjustified, and he attempted to enforce an implicit bargain where sexual access was guaranteed by financial security.

Yet the obligation worked in both directions, and a woman's refusal to have sex could be considered punishment for a man's failure to make a sufficient financial contribution to the household. Sophronie Martinage refused to have sex with her lover or share a bed with him after he lost his job.[56] Blanche Gallier explicitly linked her refusal to have sex with Louis Badran to his failure to work properly.[57] In her first deposition to the investigating magistrate, made as she convalesced after the crime, Gallier described what caused Badran to attack her. "He approached to kiss me; I understood that he wanted to put me on the bed and have relations with me. I pushed him away very lightly with my finger, saying, 'Wait until I've finished my work.' Then he began again: 'You don't want to screw with me anymore.' I believe I replied, 'No, because you are a lazy bum.'" At this point he began to stab her with a sharp tool, but she did not get up to defend herself right away, choosing to wait until her sewing machine had stopped so she would not spoil her work. The investigating judge made much of this circumstance when he interrogated Badran, although Badran omitted it entirely when he summed up the confrontation himself, focusing only on her rejection. Speaking to Gallier in the presence of the investigating magistrate, he said, "When you came in, I wanted to have sex with you [*avoir affaire à toi*]. You didn't want to, so I was overcome with anger. An instant later you said you would leave me. I took out the three-square file and I struck." He connected the motivation for his attack to her refusal, while she explained her refusal of sex in terms of his failure to work. To her what was at issue was a question of exchange; to him it appeared to be a question of satisfying his desire.

Women also refused to have sex for reasons of physical health, whether they were recovering from childbirth or trying to avoid disease. A woman hired by Lolote Nodin to help her after the birth of a child reported that Julien Nodin tried to have sex with his wife three days after the birth. "Naturally, she didn't go along with it," the woman said, but Julien dragged Lolote out of bed by her hair and kicked her for her refusal.[58] Julie Marie refused to sleep with her husband after she discovered he had contracted a venereal disease. Her husband complained in a letter to a friend: "Like I told you the other day when I want to kiss her she pushes me away as if I were a viper so my nerves are frayed and there are moments when if I didn't hold back I would do something stupid."[59] Ultimately, he shot at her when she left him. Léonie Besson also cited venereal disease when she confided to her mother the reasons why she would not sleep with her husband. "She told me many times that her husband had passions against nature; that he had an illness, and that, to avoid it, she sometimes slept wearing underpants [*un pantalon fermé*]. My daughter told me many times that her husband brutalized her during the night because she rejected him."[60] While these women claimed to have refused sex in order to protect their health, their partners clearly did not respect this explanation.

These women were attacked when they refused to have sex with their domestic partners; many others were at risk of attack for real or suspected infidelity. Indeed, more than thirty cases contained accusations of infidelity against at least one of the partners, with accusations against women outnumbering those against men by almost two to one. Questioned about whether or not he had bragged he would have vengeance against his unfaithful wife, Jean Legrand replied, "I might have said that. What man would not have said as much?"[61] He was acquitted for killing his wife by throwing her out the window. Many other men, through their actions, would seem to have agreed with Legrand. Emile Michaud confessed that when he saw his former mistress go to a hotel with her new lover, he decided to kill her.[62] Jean-Baptiste Verhoost, whose fiancée intended to leave him because he could not provide for the household, stabbed her through with an épée. Explaining his motive, he exclaimed, "Sophronie is so pretty! Because she rejected me, I didn't want her to belong to someone else! I love her today as madly as the day I wanted to kill her!"[63] When Emile Robert returned from an extended trip to La Plata to find his wife had been having an affair with one of his friends, he shot her on the spot when he encountered the two of them by chance on the street.[64] Eudoxe De Verneuil took action immediately when he was informed of his wife's infidelity. He saw her take her lover's arm at the Cirque d'hiver and stabbed the lover dead and cut his wife's arm before bystanders could stop him.[65] Both Robert and De Verneuil would be acquitted.

Granted, any of these men could have chosen a different reaction to their partners' infidelity or abandonment— leaving their partners or taking lovers themselves, for example—but they chose to inflict physical harm on the bodies that had betrayed them. Surely not all men responded to their partner's infidelity with the kind of potentially lethal violence that could bring them to the assize court, but some male attackers obviously considered sexual jealousy a legitimate reason for violence. Whether or not jurors would condone these men's actions depended on a variety of factors in the case—not just the attacker's explanation. For these men, however, maintaining exclusive sexual access to one woman was very important to their status; it demonstrated perhaps more than any other factor his control of her and his position as the dominant member of the couple. It is true that if a woman left a man, he lost more than just sexual access to her, since women were responsible for most chores, in addition to contributing financially to the household. Men hardly ever articulated these losses, however, focusing instead, as we have seen, on their outrage at a woman's sexual infidelity.

Counter to the male focus on sexual access, women were quick to link sexual jealousy to other things that were being taken away when men abandoned them. Very few women said they sought vengeance against unfaithful lovers or husbands for the sole reason that they had been unfaithful. Dire financial need almost always played a key role. "Pay. This is for you!" Rose Méhu cried, as she threw acid on her lover. She was pregnant, and he had just abandoned her, leaving all her belongings in the possession of the landlady as collateral for unpaid rent.[66] When Marie Pourcher shot at her husband's mistress, she did not say a word about wanting to keep him exclusively for herself or about loving him madly. Instead, she accused the mistress of "eating my children's bread" and bragging about the gifts her husband had given her, which would be the financial ruin of the family.[67] Similarly, in a letter to her brother, Adèle Pautard explained her motives for attacking her husband's mistress: "I can no longer hide my position. After eight years of marriage, my husband is abandoning me to follow a piece of trash aged eighteen whom he is going to make a mother... I am going to find myself alone in Paris without any resources. Rent to pay on 8 April or my poor furniture [will be] sold. I avenged myself on the woman yesterday. I slapped her next to him in a big restaurant on rue St. Honoré."[68] When her husband still failed to end his adulterous relationship, Adèle threw acid on his mistress's face. She burned her horribly but was acquitted. Marie Gy was acquitted for a similar crime. She had followed her husband from Nancy to Paris, where he had fled with his mistress, and had thrown acid on his mistress's face.[69] Targeting the mistress suggested that she still wanted her husband back, healthy enough to work and support the household. For women like Marie Gy, an unfaithful partner caused not only jealousy but financial ruin.

While infidelity could lead to such serious ruptures, it was not always a simple matter to determine whether or not a partner had strayed. The presence of venereal disease was a far less accurate indicator of infidelity than contemporaries believed. "If I left [my wife] it's because she had venereal disease, and I wasn't the one who gave it to her," declared Georges Masset.[70] A disease seemed to be proof that a partner had had sex with another person. Considering that common venereal diseases like syphilis go through active and dormant phases, and can be transmitted even when physical symptoms are not visible, however, it was often baffling for contemporaries to determine who had infected whom. The Marie couple accused each other mutually of infection; he claimed she gave him "illness twice and vermin once." She asserted that she would not sleep with him for fear of catching a disease from *him*.[71] Georges Koenig was reluctant to tell his interrogators about his venereal disease, but, he insisted, "the illness came from my wife and not from me, because I have always had good conduct. Six months ago, I caught the same disease from her, and I'm sure she still suffers from it."[72] In fact, he had sent her to a convent for eight months for medical care, and it is possible that the disease went into remission and then appeared again.

A wide range of behavior—indeed any gesture of familiarity between a man and a woman who did not have an acknowledged, legitimate relationship—was also open to interpretation as evidence of infidelity, and women were far more vulnerable in this area than men. A neighbor once saw Julie Marie walking arm in arm with a man who was not her husband, and her five-and-a-half-year-old daughter testified that her mother once had coffee with a man who kissed her.[73] These actions were enough to fuel her husband's suspicions of infidelity, even though they had previously agreed to live apart. He must have assumed that it was all too easy a step to go from walking down the street together, or kissing over a cup of coffee, to having sex. François Clément heard that his wife had sewn a button onto another man's pants, and that was enough for him to suspect that they had a sexual relationship.[74] In another case, the husband and wife of the Catherine family accused each other of infidelity, and rumors flew in the neighborhood that both were guilty. The husband claimed to have seen conclusive proof with his own eyes: "I had seen, one day at home, Lepage pass his foot under my wife's skirts. I intended to kill them both."[75]

The slightest misstep could bring a storm of suspicion and retribution, at least for women. Neighbors might suspect women of promiscuous behavior if they dressed coquettishly or went to public balls and cafés. One concierge cast suspicions on her murdered tenant's conduct by describing habits that could only be those of a loose woman. "I never saw men come to her place, but some men used to make signs to her from outside, and she would go out with them. A pork butcher especially had the habit of whistling; she would go out with him right away."[76] The implication was that a woman a man could whistle for would have sex with him. The concierge's understated observation highlights the fragility of a woman's reputation. Although by the same act she may have been asserting her claim to freedom of movement, a woman's careless behavior could easily bring about violent retaliation from her lover or husband. A more lenient man might have been undisturbed by his partner socializing with other men, and suspicious behavior witnessed by neighbors might not have been interpreted in a detrimental way until after other problems arose between the couple. Violence certainly was not the only possible consequence of infidelity. The fact remains, however, that no man in these cases was attacked by a woman on the mere suspicion of infidelity, whereas many women were. Clearly, the costs were much higher for women who tested the bounds of sexual propriety than for men who did the same. Some men were willing to use violence to reinforce their control of a woman's sexuality, while women only used violence against unfaithful partners when other important issues were also at stake.

Illicit Pairings

Infidelity was not the only illicit sexual behavior that was the focus of testimony in court. Details about a person's sexual behavior sometimes emerged as part of the effort to vilify a partner's character, and certain practices were marked as deviant in judicial testimony, either by witnesses' judgments or the harsh verdicts of the court and its magistrates. As if it were not enough that her neighbors and brother supported her accusations of long-term physical abuse by her husband, Ernestine Perney claimed, "My husband asked me to commit the most ignoble and obscene acts that one can imagine."[77] She specified during the investigation: "He wanted to introduce his virile member into my mouth. He wanted to commit acts of sodomy on me, and I assure you that one time he did commit one in spite of my resistance. Finally, he liked to have sexual relations with me when he had just beaten and martyrized me, and the time he made me all bloody and blackened my eyes, he had relations with me two times in the state that I was in." The only reaction of the investigating magistrate recorded in the dossier was to continue with another question about whether or not she drank. Ernestine Perney may well have provided him with more information than he wanted; her explicit description is without parallel in all the other cases. During her testimony in court, she reduced the detail of these events considerably. "He required things of me... Oh! He will not deny it. He knows well what I mean, monsieur, he knows it."[78] With her husband, sex appeared to have been just another means to wound, control, and humiliate her. In their relationship, violence was sexualized, and sex was integrated into other acts of violence.

In the case of Louis-Marie Lestevan, the very commission of his crime hinged on his demand for "acts against nature," an ambiguous phrase that was usually taken to mean anal intercourse. When Mathilde Forty, a prostitute, refused to satisfy his request, he beat her, stabbed her, and threw her out the window.[79] Amazingly, she survived. In a truly macabre case that took place in the Parisian suburb of St. Ouen, Pierre Schumacher strangled his mistress Rachel Duflot in bed with a belt and then had intercourse with the cadaver—the whole episode witnessed by an upstairs neighbor through a hole in the ceiling.[80] To defend himself, Schumacher asserted that he was jealous because Duflot had had sex with six men consecutively, that is, "*passée à la série.*" Although several witnesses had heard the rumor, the men who allegedly participated in this act fled town during the criminal investigation of the case, so the allegation remained unsubstantiated. Schumacher was condemned to forced labor for life, while Lestevan was sentenced to death. Whereas other men could have argued successfully that they were entitled to sexual access to their partners or to retaliation for a partner's infidelity, the deviant nature of these men's sexual practices earned them the harshest penalties for their crimes.

However grisly these crimes between men and women may have been, the practice that elicited the most intense response during investigations and trials was male homosexual contact. Rumors and vague accusations caused a flurry of curiosity among witnesses, and a focus on alleged homosexual acts could obscure all the other facts in a case. In the trial of Georges Langlois, whose life story was filled with ample evidence of fraud, theft, blackmail, and infidelity to his wife, the investigating magistrate chose to interrogate him about an incident that had occurred more than a decade before he was brought to trial for murdering his wife. Langlois had spent the night in the bed of an army officer known to be a pederast, from whom he allegedly took twenty francs in the morning.[81] Langlois's own father explained that the affair had been hushed up by another officer, who repaid the stolen money. The implication, of course, was that Langlois had been paid to have sex with the man—damning evidence against his character, even though the incident took place long before he married. Langlois was convicted and sentenced to forced labor for life.

Similarly, when François Lathouwers was tried for stabbing two of his fellow domestic servants in 1870, he was interrogated at length about an 1867 incident in Belgium when he had been accused of soliciting sex with a man in a park. The presiding magistrate also insinuated that Lathouwers took liberties with the paralyzed man who employed him. Lathouwers denied everything, saying, "When you are accused of one thing, people throw stone after stone after stone until you are completely buried. But as long as I stayed [in that man's employment], nobody ever reproached me for it."[82] The judge replied, "Oh! Surely, if it had been known, you would not have been kept." While Lathouwers expressed his frustration at having a label he could not leave behind, the judge confirmed that it would be used against him without a doubt. Lathouwers submitted to a medical examination, and the doctor concluded, "We observe no certain indication of habits of sodomy." None of this had anything to do with the question of whether or not he had committed murder, but it had everything to do with how deserving he would be of punishment. Lathouwers was sentenced to death.

It is conceivable that Ernest Teste also received a harsher sentence because of his rumored sexual involvement with men. Given that his wife had heart problems that reduced her resistance to injury, was well known as an irritable nag, and was threatening to divorce him and end their business, too, Teste might have been acquitted altogether. Yet he was convicted and sent to jail, if only for six years. Asked about Ernest Teste's reputation, one patrol officer only commented that "I have happened to hear, jokingly: 'he's an old *chass... d'aff...*,' and he had, one would add, habits against nature; but I repeat, I don't know what this gossip is worth."[83] One of Teste's employees echoed these rumors, saying that Madame Teste claimed her husband was partial to men (*il était porté pour les hommes*). These observations were offered amid more general descriptions of Teste's business dealings and his relationship with his wife. It is worth noting once again that even if these rumors were true, they dealt with his behavior before his marriage; nonetheless, the witnesses considered them relevant in assessing Teste's guilt.[84]

Two other cases in this study involved men who were apparently homosexual lovers. A murdered man named Flet was found half-naked, lying on his back on his bed, with his feet on the floor. The investigating magistrate deduced that he must have been killed instantaneously, "in the course of the accomplishment of an act against nature, by the individual who lent himself to his desires."[85] His murderer, Louis Perrette, had a particularly bad reputation, according to the official indictment. "Suspected of giving himself over to pederasty in the prison of Moulins, the accused continued his hideous trade in Paris. The investigation has revealed that, like Flet, he often frequented the places where pederasts habitually meet. The notebook seized from him shows that he accepted many rendez-vous with men; and finally one day he exchanged his hat with one of his pals, because, he told him, his was too well-known on the Champs-Elysées." Traces of a community of homosexual men emerge here—or, at least, traces of a network of men who had established places and procedures to find one another to have sex.[86] If Flet and Perrette shared anything more than a single physical encounter, the historical record is silent. To the investigating magistrate and the police, the evidence of their sexual relationship alone was culpable enough.

The other murder case involving homosexuality was of a man decapitated by the friend (*copain*) with whom he shared a one-room apartment. The official indictment specifies, "For nearly a month they had shared the same room and the same bed. They had accepted a community of existence from which their tastes, their habits, would have driven them... Were there habits against nature between this man of thirty years and this adolescent, who was called 'la gosse?'"[87] The answer was "no," according to the conclusion of medical exams and testimony by friends of the two men. However, Vaubourg, the attacker, had tried to commit a "coupling against nature" (*rapprochement contre nature*) with a prostitute, had asked another prostitute to find him "a young little man," and had narrowly escaped conviction for the rape and murder of a girl years before. He was convicted of murder but not of an offense against morals. Neither investigation focused on the topics usual to domestic conflicts between heterosexuals—the couple's relationship, work record, or contributions to maintaining a household, for instance. Even the motive for the crime remained unexplored. Rather, in both cases, the investigating judge was most interested in discovering the extent of the victims' and attackers' known homosexual activity, to the exclusion of all other considerations. Their deviant sexual practices disqualified them from any consideration as respectable men.

Accusations of lesbianism seemed not to have such serious consequences. They appeared in only two cases in this study and never spurred an investigation into the details of the allegations. One jealous husband, having chased his wife from their apartment, sent a package to the friend's house where she had found refuge, addressed to "Ernestine, ex-dame Grodet, chez sa concubine la fille Guebel."[88] But only the friend who received the package seemed offended, and the incident caused no further comment in the investigation. The other case involved a woman who was a theatrical performer, and, indeed, the identification of female actresses and singers with lesbianism was well established by the end of the nineteenth century.[89] According to one witness interviewed by a police commissioner, Marie Daouze, *artiste lyrique*, was "known to be a lesbian."[90] But this observation was not repeated, and she was acquitted of killing her lover Hippolyte Richard. Whatever the sexual practices of these women may have been, they were both in long-term relationships with men, which may have reduced the apparent threat of a lesbian relationship to the patriarchal social order and, hence, its importance in cases about household power struggles.

Women who were prostitutes posed a more paradoxical challenge to the social order. They represented both the antithesis of respectable relationships between men and women and their logical extension. As professional sex workers, they were outside the bounds of propriety, but as individuals, they were integrated into the fabric of local communities, with lovers, husbands, and friends of their own. Prostitution operated on many levels in fin-de-siècle Paris, from the *filles soumises* who were registered with the police and subject to medical examinations, to the unregistered women who made a living as sex workers, to mistresses who were more or less supported financially by male lovers.[91] Whether or not she had accepted gifts of money was a critical question for any woman who had a lover. While a scarf or an occasional meal could be innocent gifts, receiving cash put a woman beyond the pale of respectability.

Perhaps the greatest perversion of the normal social order was when a man forced his wife or lover to sell her body for sex. He was supposed to provide financial support for the household, and she was supposed to remain sexually faithful to him, and yet he turned her sexual services to his own financial gain. Ernestine Perney accused her husband of trying to make her prostitute herself. In the investigation, she said he wanted her to work for a certain Gantier and that she was as nice as the other women who worked for him, "which made me suppose what I would be occupied with at his place."[92] During the trial, she developed this theme further: "He wanted to make me leave my little business [as a *marchande ambulante*]. He told me I still had four or five good years to spend, that I was still fresh, and that it wasn't in business that I would earn the most and that I could please people."[93] Eugénie Schlesser was unable to resist being prostituted by her lover, Joseph Oudot. "I would have liked to work," she explained, "but he forced me to walk the street. He told me that, if I didn't bring him the money, he would hit me."[94] The presiding judge asked how much money Oudot required each day, and she answered, "Ten francs, fifteen francs... when I only brought back five francs, he used to beat me." He never left her a penny for herself. The courtroom audience likely would have known how many men she would have had to have sex with to earn that much money. One historian's estimate puts the average charge for a prostitute during this era at two francs, and several women in similar cases cited this as their fee.[95]

Prostitutes who supported their lovers financially were vulnerable to violent reprisals when they sought to end the relationship and, thus, the material benefits that went with it. Charlotte Gérard appears to have supported a lover the way a man would support a mistress; she earned enough money as a prostitute to hire her own domestic servant and to keep Honoré Leroux dressed in the latest fashion.[96] According to their neighbors, he never had a job. Other situations where a prostitute supported a lover appeared far more sinister. Henriette Damotte seems to have been a victim of an emotional attachment that degenerated into an exploitative relationship. She met Eugène Dogmatschoff while working as a domestic servant, two years prior to being registered as a prostitute. She rented and furnished an apartment for him, and paid for all his meals at a wineshop, while maintaining a separate apartment of her own. When she finally tired of his constant demands for money and tried to cut back her support, he stalked and stabbed her. The official indictment characterized the crime as "the act, long and coldly premeditated, of a pimp who avenged himself, in killing her, on a mistress resolved to break her chain and no longer give him money."[97] Louise Jorand's lover also stabbed her when she tried to leave him and cut off his source of money. "Me, I went out in the evenings to exercise my profession of *fille*, and him, he beat me when I came back bringing a sum of money that was, according to him, too small."[98]

The investigating magistrates consistently found it difficult to believe that women who sold their bodies for sex could also be subject to the usual rules of love affairs, most notably, the sexual fidelity supposed to characterize intimate relationships. A prostitute belonged to everyone for the asking, they believed; she could neither demand nor inspire fidelity. The actions of some prostitutes, however, proved that they themselves believed otherwise. Margeurite Zick, registered as a *fille publique* on 25 December 1870, met her lover Charles Roché when she accosted him on the street. Later, she saw him at the Bal de la rue St.

Martin, and, "finding myself a little aroused," he said, "I consented to follow her."[99] They saw each other once or twice a week at first, then much more frequently, but he refused to move in with her. According to some of Zick's friends who were also prostitutes, she was trying to escape a former lover who used to beat her. A need for protection thus may have heightened her professed passion for her new lover. In any case, while she did time in St. Lazare, the women's prison in Paris, Roché sent her money, food, and letters. The day she got out, she saw him having lunch "very intimately" with another prostitute, Cécile Brunette, and he told her he was ending their relationship. She boldly threatened to "lard" him if he left her. Three days later she tried to stab him in retribution for his faithlessness. During her trial the presiding judge made it clear that she could have no permanent claim on a man's affections. "By what right were you jealous of this man, you who give yourself up to the most ignoble prostitution? How could you have had rights over him?"[100] She replied, "But if I exercised that profession, it wasn't without his knowing it. He knew perfectly well what I did; he certainly consented to it and had a [financial] interest in it."

Whether they exploited them financially or not, men did claim to love women who were prostitutes just as ardently, exclusively, and jealously as they would love an honest woman, much to the consternation of the professional jurists to whom they told their stories. Jean Bernicat met la fille Desesquelles at the Cirque Fernando and became her lover the next day. They lived together for two years, but he returned from a stint in prison to find that she was living with another man and stabbed her to death. At his trial, the presiding judge scolded him for abandoning his legitimate wife to live with such a woman. Bernicat explained that he was already separated from his wife before he met la fille Desesquelles, and, furthermore, "Passion carried me away. I couldn't do without that woman."[101] The judge replied scornfully, "An honest man doesn't surrender to such compulsions, and it is difficult to believe that you had compulsions of that nature for a *fille publique*."

A similar case involved Marie Iltis, who was not a registered prostitute but was characterized in the indictment as a woman "of easy morals."[102] Although she listed her profession as milliner, she supplemented her meager income with money from her lovers. Emile Perrin was one of them, but his work earning one hundred francs per month as a clerk for an oyster seller did not provide much for Iltis. She left him and took up with a man who, in her words, "helped me and still gives me everything I need." Perrin shot Iltis and himself, wounding them both only slightly, when he happened to meet Iltis and her new lover at the

Folies Bergères. Even though he had an affair with another woman after Iltis left him, Perrin claimed he was consumed with passion for her. The investigating magistrate was skeptical, saying, "It is very difficult to admit that you conceived such a violent passion for this girl, who belonged to everyone." How could he claim any exclusive right to her affections, when she could "belong" to anyone who paid her? To the investigating magistrate, a prostitute was unworthy of such love. Perrin was acquitted, perhaps due in part to the minimal amount of physical harm he inflicted, and perhaps also because Iltis stated she did not want to pursue the case.

Perrin had a certain amount of education—enough to give him refined handwriting and a propensity for expressing himself at length in writing. He submitted for his defense a long essay titled, "My Life, from 10 December 1881 to 8 November 1882," completed in prison on 21 November. It was not the story of his life but of Marie Iltis's, from her fall into prostitution to her salvation by Perrin. According to Perrin, he took on the role of Pygmalion, molding his lover into the ideal, modest, hard-working woman.

> I promised to pardon her, to forget her past, if she remained faithful to her repentance... Until the month of May, I could only praise her good conduct. She had become unrecognizable: clean, tidy. Simplicity, modesty—she had all the qualities of the best housewife, being very orderly. Following my desire, she had changed her hairstyle, her clothing, her manners, her words; she watched herself in everything. Nobody questioned her past. I gave her lessons. She applied herself to copy pages of writing in a book, and, all proud of her progress, she showed them to me on my return. I had come to love her without noticing it, not as a mistress but as my student, as the woman who must be the purpose of my existence... [She took work as a seamstress and a maid when the oyster season ended.]... That's when I believed my work was complete, and I promised to reward her for it. I believed I was sure of her, and her work was a sure guarantee of her fidelity. She must have loved me sincerely to do what she did, after having been what she was! One day when we were speaking of the future, I asked her if she were happy. She threw herself on my neck, crying and thanking me for what I had done for her... I made her kneel with me. Hand in hand, we both prayed. We asked God to unite us until we could do so at the foot of his altars. We swore to belong to each other, and death to the one who would betray his vow![103]

But then, he concludes, Iltis couldn't find any more work, and her sister Adèle led her back into corruption.

If Perrin aspired to reform his mistress, Iltis took a more pragmatic view of their relationship. In his version of the story, her reward was to be marriage with him, but her own description of their life together indicates that she would hardly have been tempted by such an offer. Perrin only gives the briefest mention of the economic difficulty that Iltis said was her main concern. "Our position was becoming more and more difficult. Sometimes I didn't even have anything to eat. My sister... told me I was a fool to stay with a man who wasn't in a position to keep me alive."

Perhaps Perrin's strategy was to cloak his relationship with Iltis in romantic terms, to make it appear that it was not his failure as a provider, but her own weakness and the influence of her sister, that made her leave him. He presents himself as an arbiter of proper behavior, an authority on dress and comportment, a patient and generous teacher. Iltis is transformed into someone unrecognizable, allowing him to dictate the smallest details of her appearance and behavior. She is not only tractable but grateful for Perrin's control—not at all the kind of woman who would ridicule him publicly, as she did when she saw him at the Folies Bergères, where he shot her and himself without seriously wounding either. It is impossible to know if Perrin really did give her lessons in penmanship, or if she really was grateful for his attentions, but it remains significant that Perrin chose to tell his story of legitimate love for a prostitute in terms of her redemption through his control. In his view, the way back to respectability was to belong to one man, affirming the normative standards of sexual fidelity.

Love

Whether or not Marie Iltis or other prostitutes in these cases were worthy of love was a serious question, for love was supposedly at the core of every domestic partnership, at least according to the sentimental novels and *feuilletons* of the day. Violent conflicts between domestic partners were widely characterized as crimes of passion: carried away by the irresistible force of their emotions, spouses and lovers did physical harm to the people they claimed to love the most. Yet, deferring a discussion of love to the end of this chapter on *la vie intime* serves to emphasize that many different factors were involved in establishing and maintaining a couple's relationship. Surprisingly, love was not the fallback justification for acts that could be characterized as crimes of passion. Indeed, less than a quarter of the cases in this study contain any kind of explicit reference to "love" or "passion." Nobody in the assize court claimed they killed for love alone. Witnesses and investigators closely scrutinized declarations of love, for not everyone was worthy of it, and not everyone was able to show love properly. Love was open to debate; it had to be proved authentic.

As the preceding analysis of prostitution suggests, the sign of a person's worthiness for love seems usually to have rested on the question of exclusive sexual access to his or her partner: love was suspect outside the bounds of a normative partnership. Charles Joulain lamented his attachment to his lover, who belonged to another man. "I loved her too much, and I couldn't resolve to leave her. I knew my love was criminal, since it directed itself toward a married woman; I knew the husband could burst in from one moment to the next, but all these considerations disappeared before the desire to always remain the lover of la femme Paisant."[104] Joulain despaired that his lover was not his to keep. Félix Pellentz claimed he stabbed his former mistress Louise Cajon because he loved her, but the presiding magistrate expressed serious doubt that this could be true. "Come on!" he cajoled. "You could not love a girl to this extent, whom you had only known intimately once, whom you went such a long time without seeing, who lived with another man and was seven months pregnant, at that moment, by her [other] lover?"[105] Pellentz only replied, "I couldn't stop myself from loving her." He continued, "I no longer knew what I was saying and what I was doing. I loved her too much. I didn't want her to stay with that man. I couldn't keep my head anymore." He portrayed himself as helpless in the throes of a passion that the presiding judge considered dubious.

If not everyone was a worthy object of love, not everyone was capable of love, either. Jean-Baptiste Bernou protested that he killed his mistress because he loved her, not because she was no longer willing to aid him financially. But none of the witnesses believed him. Bernou's friend from his student days described the two of them as follows: "[His] was a cold, spineless, indifferent nature, which seemed incapable of any violent passion... Bernou seemed to have remained the insouciant young man I had known, without resources... I don't believe he was capable either of loving this person or of being jealous of her... [She] did not seem to me at all to be a woman able to inspire a great passion."[106] Other witnesses noted that she was quite fat and past her prime. A widow, now in her second marriage in her early forties, she was altogether unbelievable as a romantic heroine. Similarly, a friend of Louis Léra was surprised at the dramatic turn his friend's romance had taken. In an odd elision of the emotions necessary for marriage and murder, he explained, "He wasn't a man partial to women [*porté pour les femmes*]. I am very surprised that he was so taken with la fille Ballot to the point of wanting to marry her and to the point of wanting to kill her."[107] Passion, it seems, was rightly the domain of the young and beautiful.

A man named Hillairin de Saint-Priest was also involved in an unlikely affair, in which an avowed passion weighed against an unspoken desire for free food and lodging. For five months he lived with a woman twice his age, and the investigating magistrate refused to believe that the motive for his attachment was love. "This woman is forty-nine years old and you are only twenty-four. It is difficult to believe that she inspired a very lively passion in you. But she ran a *hôtel meublé* at Vincennes, and you could hope to find with her what you lacked, which is to say food and shelter. Speak sincerely: Isn't that the only explanation for this singular liaison?"[108] Hillairin replied, "The truth is on the contrary that I felt for this woman a love of which she was not worthy, and that is the true reason for our relationship. If I had simply wanted to live at the expense of a woman, I would have started by choosing a woman who had money, while she had none. In addition, I would not have worried about her conduct, while I went so far as to follow her to find out if she had other lovers. You see very well that it was passion alone that guided me, a completely sensual passion, since this woman knew how to work a lot of action on my senses... I remember having asked her one day how she accepted me so easily, and she answered me that I had exercised on her an attraction that she didn't understand herself." Only a genuine lover would worry about his partner's fidelity, he argued, and their unusual pairing was explainable by the mysterious magnetism of passion. His erstwhile lover, however, did not share these illusions for long. She affirmed, "What he loved about me is not my person, it's my cooking." His material interests rendered suspect his protestations of love.

Among so many examples of dubious passion, it was important to determine the sure signs of genuine love. Public displays of affection could offer such proof. The Boudets' concierge believed that they were a loving couple because she often saw the husband kiss the wife when she left their building: "Boudet always appeared to me to love his wife; I saw him many times accompany his wife as far as the exterior door and kiss her."[109] This behavior between a married couple was unusual enough for the concierge to take it as a sign of special affection. In another case, Madame Tarisse found herself in the position of having to prove that a male employee of hers who tried to kill her was not her lover, as he claimed. She relied on conventions of gift giving between lovers to prove her point.[110] He had argued that their exchange of gifts was evidence of a romantic relationship, but she insisted that his gifts were unwanted. "As for the scarf you gave me on my saint's day," she said to him during his interrogation, "remember what happened? I didn't want to remain your debtor, and on New Year's Day I gave you one back, saying that I could buy myself what I needed and it didn't suit me to receive presents from the employees." The accused then said she'd given him a ring, which he had thrown away. "That's what condemns you," she retorted. "When you love a woman, you keep like a relic what she gives you, you scoundrel. You want to tarnish the reputation of an honest woman to absolve yourself, but you won't succeed. People know you, but you'll have what you deserve." As a lover, he was not credible, she argued, since he did not observe the proper social rituals. The court seemed to agree with her; he was convicted of attempted murder and condemned to forced labor as well as to pay damages.

True love, at least according to some attackers, could also be proved by a willingness to resort to extreme action in its name. When Nicolas Becker moved out of Célestine Béal's apartment and went to live in his sister-in-law's building, Célestine bragged to her concierge that she was going to go stab her supposed rival. The concierge expressed doubt that she would actually do such a thing, and Célestine replied, "One can see very well that you don't know what jealousy and love are!"[111] Constance Dreyfuss took a more elaborate approach to test her partner's love, leading him into a deception that almost cost them their lives. "The origin of this unhappy affair must be sought in a childish notion whose consequences I couldn't foresee," she explained during the investigation for an attempted murder-suicide.

> I had a deep love for Ancelin, and at the same time I was prey to a violent jealousy that was only too justified. Often, to test Ancelin's affection, I suggested dying together to him, not wanting him to say yes except to know how much of a sacrifice he would make for me. With the same purpose I often told him that I had tuberculosis, which is actually false, and that I was condemned by the doctors. I wanted to know if I would make a big impression on him like this; I believe he loved me a lot because what I tried always succeeded. It is true he didn't really want to carry out the double suicide I talked to him about, reasoning that nothing hindered the relations we had together. But when I spoke to him about my lung disease, he rolled on the ground and melted into tears.[112]

Just before he shot her, she had told him she was leaving him to live with another man, because, "having to die soon from my lungs, I wanted to give myself all pleasures possible." So she tested his love and piqued his jealousy. Although she got the answer she wanted, it came at the cost of a bullet in her jaw (and one in his arm), for which he was acquitted.

If love could be proved by a willingness to resort to extreme behavior, it could also be invoked as the only possible explanation for acts that were illogical by any other standard. A few women who stayed with their neglectful or abusive partners claimed they stayed out of love, although other powerful psychological and material forces likely were at work in such situations. "I must love him to stay with him since he gave me forty centimes for our food every day. He said that was enough for us," wrote Marie Sanglé to the investigating magistrate.[113] Her husband took all the money she earned and barely gave her enough to subsist on—why else would she stay with such a poor provider if not for love? Confronted with the corpse of her husband, whom she had killed after years of abuse, Marie Rault uncovered his face, held it in her hands, and kissed it repeatedly. "I was very unhappy," she said to the investigating magistrate who was with her, "but, that doesn't matter, I loved him. When he had a good moment I was, my God, so happy. He had a good heart, but when he was angry, he no longer knew anyone, and when he had been drinking, it was even much worse... My poor old man, I won't see him again!"[114] In a later interrogation, she said, "In spite of everything, I regret what I did, since, in spite of everything, I loved my husband."

On the other hand, when attackers claimed that they loved their victims, they believed their love entitled them to jealousy, anger, and violent reprisals if the object of their affections did not reciprocate. Alphonse Catelier, who had been particularly controlling and abusive, lamented over his lover's dead body, "It's because I loved you too much, my poor wife, that I did this to you."[115] Henri Schmittgall admitted he stabbed Lucie Olivier with a butcher knife, but only because she had left him. "I loved this woman profoundly; I was desperate from her abandonment."[116] Yet this claim that love was a license to kill was met with skepticism or disbelief by surviving victims, as well as members of the court. "What makes me angry with you," said Louis Badran to his mistress Blanche Gallier, whom he had stabbed when she tried to leave him, "is that I still love you. Would I have struck you like that if I hadn't loved you?" She replied dryly, "If you loved me, you had a singular way of proving it."[117] Henri Jean had a similar reaction when his wife explained her motive in attacking him. Although their marriage had been far from idyllic, Eulalie Jean said she tried to kill her husband because she loved him. "I still love you as much as I used to love you. I wanted your death because I loved you," she said to her husband during the investigation.[118] "That's a strange way," her husband replied. She insisted that he knew she loved him, since she had allowed him to have sex with her just prior to the attack, however unsatisfactory the act might have been. She blamed him for the crime. "It's really his fault if all this happened. He shouldn't have pushed me away. He should have spoken to me nicely, not scorned me and treated me like a stranger." If only he had loved her in return, she would not have attacked him.

Sometimes statements of love during court testimony seemed entirely irrelevant and insincere.[119] Investigators and jurors were certainly not convinced by Augustin Froquières's declarations of love for Jeanne Douët, the woman he murdered. The investigating magistrate confronted him with her cadaver at the morgue—probably not such a dramatic gesture for a man who worked as a porter for an undertaker. There, he asked the accused why he committed the crime. Froquières answered, "Because I loved her. If I hadn't loved her, I would not have killed her. I asked her if she wanted to come with me, and since she answered no, I struck her."[120] Jeanne had lived with him briefly but then chose to return to live with her child's father, who could support them. The official indictment clearly stated that Froquières's defense based on passion would not be successful. The investigating magistrate wrote that the defendant "claims he acted under the compulsion of the passion that dominated him, the love that he felt for la fille Douët having misled his reason... After an exchange of words communicating... the most ardent sentiments, he was taken by vertigo and struck out unconsciously, no longer master of himself. This Romanesque story imagined as a system of defense does not bear one minute of examination... The true motive of the crime is therefore vengeance. Froquières only struck under the empire of the most vulgar spite, not wanting the woman who left him to belong to another." Such a statement on the part of the investigating magistrate indicates a certain savvy about Froquières's narrative strategy. Froquières was trying to fit his motives and actions into the classic story of a crime of passion, but the magistrate called Froquières's bluff and accused him of telling tales in bad faith.

Love was neither a necessary nor sufficient cause for violence between domestic partners, although much has been made of its importance in "crimes of passion." But love was only one element that could inspire people to join together, form a domestic partnership, and then perhaps split apart. The choice of a partner depended on not only affection and desire but also economic interests, family intervention, and sexual propriety. As a motive for violent crime, the preservation of the household as an emotionally fulfilling entity seems to have been secondary to the more pragmatic goal of preserving the household as a materially viable partnership. The eroticization of the couple had not eclipsed other considerations: love did not conquer all.

CHAPTER 2

Material and Symbolic Household Management

The word most frequently used by witnesses in the *cour d'assises* to designate the domestic unit was not "family" (*la famille*) but "household" (*le ménage*).[1] Though the term *le ménage* usually refers to the people who comprise the domestic group, it can also denote household goods—furniture, linens, utensils—that they own and use. At once a set of people and a set of material goods, the household fulfills symbolic and material functions. The household is a nexus of exchange for socially useful relationships among people and for the conversion of economic capital (wages) into the material goods necessary for survival. Economic capital also translates into symbolic capital, the markers of status that define the household's relative position in the community. As Pierre Bourdieu has observed, women are central to this transmutation of one kind of capital into another.[2] In an intensely patriarchal, rural society like that of the Khabyles that Bourdieu studied in the 1960s, women themselves were the medium through which symbolic capital was exchanged. Women appeared as passive signifiers, mere carriers of meaning that were actively traded and defended by men.[3]

Women's role in the urban, wage-based economy of fin-de-siècle Paris was inflected by quite a different context. Not only were they wage earners themselves, they also were responsible for mediating the intersection of the economic and symbolic domains through their management of household resources. They were the ones who decided on purchases major and minor, from furniture to daily provisions. As caretakers of household goods and clothing, they managed the image that members of their household presented to the world. Women's management of economic *and* symbolic capital thus was essential to the proper functioning of the household. By contrast, men's primary role in the household economy was contributing cash from their wages.

More broadly, the household's survival depended on maintaining a careful balance between the contributions and interests of its members. The household was essentially a unit adapted for survival in an unpredictable world: the mutual obligations and multiple skills of the partners ideally created a safety net in times of crisis. It was when one of the partners failed (or seemed to fail) to fulfill his or her end of the implicit household bargain that discord arose, and the wronged partner sought retribution or left in search of a more worthy partner. When discord led to violence and then to a trial in the assize court, aggrieved partners' claims delineated the boundaries of normative household obligations.

The distribution of resources and services reflected and constructed the gendered distribution of power in the household. For a man, his superior earning power ordinarily worked to reinforce his social status. In this milieu, a man's status derived primarily from his reputation as a good worker and provider. Ideally, a worker would earn enough to support his household properly and have money left over to fund his own pursuits in bars and cafés, key sites of male sociability. But a man could become unemployed or disabled, or could simply be too lazy to make a living, opening the possibility that his female partner could become economically superior. In fin-de-siècle Paris, women could earn enough to survive without male support, and men could purchase the services (such as laundry and prepared meals) that they had traditionally received from women. Economic necessity did not bind men and women together permanently, and the precarious balance of their mutual obligations was frequently put to the test.

Thanks to earlier social historians who applied tools of statistical analysis to the study of populations in the past, we now know the essential outlines of material living conditions for the working people of fin-de-siècle Paris. These historians, largely preoccupied with the social and political development of the French working class, have made it possible to situate the experiences recounted in trial dossiers relative to the generally prevailing levels of wages and standard of living. The task now is to analyze the social relationships that were interrelated with these material conditions at the level of the household, to explore how earning and spending wages translated into strategies of household management. Household management was not simply a matter of cobbling together enough resources to ensure physical survival—although that in itself was often no mean feat. It also meant choosing how to spend money on goods like furniture, food, and clothing, which were at once physical necessities and signs of status. With limited financial resources, choosing how money would be spent was a zero-sum game and, therefore, a frequent source of conflict between domestic partners. While men usually earned more money than their female partners, it was typically the women who spent it. This system rested on a gendered division of labor, but it was not a clear-cut division between men as producers and women as consumers. While men's primary responsibility towards the household was contributing sufficient cash from their wages, women were also expected to work for wages, and a failure by either partner to contribute financially was cause for serious complaint. These mutual, if incongruous, obligations were the cornerstone of the domestic economy. They were the basis on which men and women's worth was judged, together with the considerations of sexuality discussed in the previous chapter.

Historian Lenard Berlanstein has usefully defined "working people" as "Parisians who owned no property and depended on their earnings from one pay day to the next," a group that he estimates at about seventy percent of the city's population.[4] Property is understood to be real estate and other productive capital, not just household goods. The term "working people" is preferable here to "working class" because the political consciousness of the working class is beyond the scope of this study. Political matters appeared to be largely irrelevant to the domestic disputes that brought couples to court. References to politics rarely appear in court documents, and people virtually never identified themselves as members of a politically coherent group of workers.[5] "Working people" is an admittedly broad category, and for the purposes of this study it designates a range of people from the most destitute (for instance, a laundress living alone) to the relatively comfortable artisan or small shopkeeper. On a financial level, all these people experienced a basic insecurity that made obtaining the necessities of life a daily imperative. Even a small shopkeeper could sink into poverty in a matter of a month or two, if ill health, bad luck, or bad decisions interfered with his business. Perhaps even more importantly, on a sociocultural level, the thousands of depositions in this study do not reveal significant variations in ideas about work, love, sex—all the areas in which men's and women's status and behavior was evaluated. Among working people, ideas about social behavior were generally coherent and, in the context of assize court trials, stand in sharp contrast to their higher-class interrogators. It is reasonable, therefore, to speak of the working people of Paris as a group with common experiences and a shared outlook and expectations about their social and cultural world.

Obtaining Material Resources

People who lived off their wages alone were financially insecure, and it was all too easy to slip from the ranks of the self-sufficient to the desperately poor. The seasonal nature of many professions, not to mention financial crises caused by sickness, accidents, or childbirth, could all tip the balance. To be sure, a margin of security existed in the accumulation of household goods that could be pawned for cash, perhaps some carefully hoarded savings, and of course the networks of family, friends, and neighbors that could be called on for assistance in times of trouble. Yet when sociologists Octave Du Mesnil and Charles Mangenot performed a study of the Parisian working poor in the late 1890s, they determined that only 65 percent of male-headed households and 30 percent of female-headed households met a minimum standard for self-sufficiency. They had estimated that every person required a minimum of one franc per day to survive "without want and without assistance."[6] These statistics help illustrate the precarious nature of working people's lives at the end of the nineteenth century. According to Berlanstein, the overall trends were toward deflating prices and slightly higher wages. Women's average wages rose from 43 percent of men's wages at midcentury to 51 percent at the end of the century, a real but not dramatic improvement.[7] The ups and downs of individual working people's fortunes thus occurred in a larger economic context that was largely stable in this era.

Perhaps the most distinctive characteristic that most sharply distinguished working people from other urban sociocultural groups was their assumption that women as well as men would work for wages. Wage labor decisively divided a woman of the people from the middle class. Historian Anne Martin-Fugier has defined bourgeois status by the fact that *la bourgeoise* did not engage in productive labor.[8] Bonnie Smith has explained in detail how middle-class women withdrew from active roles in their family businesses in the earlier part of the century and moved into domestic roles of homemaking and charity work.[9] As the nineteenth century progressed, the leisured ladies of the upper classes cultivated their roles as consumers rather than producers of value. The lower classes, however, made a virtue of necessity, and productive work remained central to women's roles as household partners. Women's work went beyond a matter of simple economic need; their skills, integrity, and even morals were evaluated in light of the work they performed. Among the women who appeared in assize court cases, the vast majority worked for wages, but it was always assumed that men should provide the larger portion of money to the household purse.[10]

Citing 1896 government statistics, Christophe Charle notes that highly skilled male workers in Paris earned between seven and eight francs a day on average during the 1880s, while less skilled male workers earned around five francs per day.[11] Working women rarely earned more than two francs a day, and in feminine professions, it was often difficult to earn one franc per day. Although wages were not recorded in all of the trial dossiers, the working people represented in the *cour d'assises* were economically average. Male defendants included, for example, a man who hung wallpaper for forty to fifty francs a week, a jeweler who earned two hundred francs a month, a furniture maker who earned seven francs a day, and an excavator who earned four and a half francs daily.[12] Among women, one earned three or four francs a week sewing pants, another was paid one franc a day for trimming hats, a milk carrier earned thirty-five francs a month, and a fish seller earned one franc a day.[13] One woman explained that she could earn thirty francs a week posing as a painter's model, instead of three or four francs doing laundry, or one and a half francs as a maid for the boardinghouse where she lived.[14]

Even in cases where men and women performed the same work, women were paid significantly less. For instance, Mathilde Bourdeaux and her domestic partner of seven years, Alexandre Larue, were both hired to run a laundry in 1881. They received free lodging, plus two thousand francs for Larue and only twelve hundred for Bourdeaux annually, though it was her good reputation and skills that got them the job in the first place.[15] Such inequality can be interpreted as a remnant of rural hiring patterns, where the male head of household was paid for the labor of the whole family group, or as an indication of women's supposedly inferior skills, or as an avatar of patriarchy designed to ensure women's dependence on men. Nonetheless, it is certain that wherever a woman earned significantly more money than her male partner, this inversion of the usual order was attributed to some gross failure on the man's part. Of course, some women ran their own businesses, even employing men, and made a good living. In spite of their generally low wages, women could and did support themselves and a child or partner through their work alone. They likely enjoyed no more than a minimal standard of living, but the possibility of surviving on their own was an important factor in their decisions to stay in or leave bad relationships.

If every domestic partnership was inherently an economic one, it was nonetheless rare for a couple to prioritize finances above all other considerations. Five couples in this study said they married—or hoped to marry—for the express purpose of going into business together. Once the partnership was established, however, both partners did not always pull equal weight. Zélie Cachet married Modeste Guillot after making his acquaintance during negotiations for the purchase of a grocery store (*fonds d'épicerie*), for which she was an intermediary. "I kept the cashbox," she testified. "I had learned commerce in three businesses in Paris successively and I had a certain experience." In fact, she had come to Paris at age eighteen to learn the trade from her uncle. She went on to describe their business: "We had six employees. My husband was supposed to supervise them and make them work, but he was not a hard worker himself and a few months after my marriage, I could see that he had another fault, that of drinking." Within two years, the store went bankrupt, so the wife opened a new one, with her mother's funding, and talked about getting a legal separation. In response, her husband resolved to kill the whole family but only succeeded in strangling their young daughter in her sleep.[16] Désirée Solhart was already in the business of selling butter and eggs at the Halles Centrales when she married her husband. "I was established [in business] nine years ago," she explained to the investigating magistrate, "and we would have prospered if he had followed my example, but he did not want to work."[17] Frustrated with his laziness and an incident of infidelity, she finally decided to leave him. He attacked her the day she was removing her belongings from their apartment.

A joint business could become the stakes in domestic disputes that had their roots in other causes. When Marie Ecoiffier argued with her husband, she would shut their wineshop and lie down in bed—not only damaging the business but also keeping her husband locked out of the house.[18] For her, abandoning her work was a means of protesting her husband's mistreatment. Philiberte Brossier had another dilemma. She wrote to the court to plead for the release of her husband, who was held in jail for ten months before his trial for shooting her. Expressing certainty that her husband had already learned a lesson from his time behind bars, she argued, "My business...is interested in his return."[19] The two ran a restaurant together, and la femme Brossier preferred the risk of future injury to herself to the risk of damage to the business.

In these particular cases, discord in other areas led to financial trouble, but it was also true that financial trouble could lead to domestic discord. A few couples separated apparently because of financial difficulties alone. Louis Benoit had no doubts about why his lover left him: "Our relations only ceased because I was not equal to satisfying her expenses."[20] In another case, Alphonsine Ancel ran a brasserie on the rue du Temple and was raising a young child when she took Louis Martinière as her lover. Martinière, however, quit working and went into debt, prompting Ancel to return to her child's father for support. "The coolness which Mademoiselle Ancel showed me for several days, the comparisons that she made between my inactivity and the fruitful activity of Monsieur Monnery made me suspect a *rapprochement*, which did in fact take place," the spurned lover remarked. She had told him "that she had renewed relations with Monnery because he would procure resources for her that I was incapable of giving her."[21] These cases demonstrate the difficulties that could result from one partner's financial dependence on the other, and they show that intimate connections were formed and broken according to financial need, with affection playing an apparently secondary role.

All the same, financial problems could be an opportunity for mutual assistance between men and women, rather than just a source of conflict, and some people intervened to secure or improve their partners' employment. One person's friendly relationship with an employer could be translated into a job for his or her partner—whether or not the partner would have obtained or kept the position on his or her own merit. Alfred Grodet asked his employer to hire his wife to do some piecework, but she performed poorly and was later fired.[22] François Badault requested that a friend hire his mistress to work as a bread carrier, and she worked for thirty-five *sous* a day, plus two *livres* of bread, until she left Badault.[23] It is unclear whether she lost her job because she left her lover or quit because her new lover was supporting her.

Women also influenced men's work, either through their contacts or through eliciting sympathy for their plight. Sophie Martinage's father helped her erstwhile fiancé get a job at a factory, which could have assured their financial security, had he been a hard worker.[24] Gustave Bazin, a wine seller, hired and rehired François Clément because his wife was a valued servant. "I employed Clément as a cook on two different occasions for around thirty-five days," he stated. "I fired him the first time because he was very violent and inclined to drink. Then, on the pressing solicitations of his wife whom I employ as a laundress, I was pleased to take him into my service again... He brutalized his wife, who was however very sweet and who put up with the poor treatment from her husband almost without complaining."[25] Jeanne Guerrier was also protected by an employer's goodwill. She and her husband were employed as concierges, but his performance was not satisfactory due to his excessive drinking. Nonetheless, for his wife's sake, the woman who owned the building did not fire him: "I kept him because of his wife, who always seemed to me to be very honest and very correct."[26]

How far would an employer go to retain one valued worker where two partners were employed? The case of Mathilde Bourdeaux illustrates an unusual sympathy between employer and employee and reveals the friction that could arise between a couple who worked with unequal success at the same job. Bourdeaux and her lover of seven years, Alexandre Larue, were hired to run a laundry by Marie Fragonard, who had known Bordeaux for a long time. About a month later, Bourdeaux declared that she would leave unless her employer fired Larue. "On 31 August, she arrived at my place around ten in the evening, all in tears," testified her employer. "She told me that Larue was drunk and had mistreated her more than usual. Her face was marbled from blows; she had a split lip that was bleeding; she had one hand all swollen from a blow with a boot. She told me that she did not want to be mistreated anymore, that she no longer wanted to live with Larue, and that she would go away if Larue stayed at the laundry. I had received many complaints about Larue. He was vulgar and insolent with the clients. I had reproached him, but he did not listen. I decided to fire him in order to keep Mathilde."[27] Larue demanded a month's pay as indemnity before refusing altogether to leave the premises of the business. He purchased a gun on 1 September and shot Bourdeaux to death two days later. His final interrogation by the investigating magistrate illustrates his reaction to his mistress's success in employment, and his own failure:

> QUESTION: How, after living with her more than seven years, did you come to have this excess of hate? To conceive of such a crime?
> ANSWER: It's because of her change in conduct. I'm talking about her character since we came to the laundry. Until then she had been very sweet. Since, she became quarrelsome. She wanted to put her nose into everything. She spoke badly to me. If I gave an order to a *garçon* or if I spoke to a [woman] client, she

would contradict me. Finally, since our quarrel on Wednesday, she had slept somewhere else, and she did not want to tell me where she had slept.

QUESTION: But after the quarrel on Wednesday evening, she told Madame Fragonard that she no longer wanted to live with you, that she would leave the laundry if you stayed there. You were fired. Isn't it rather because of this that you committed the crime?

ANSWER: There's also that. I was unhappy that they kept her and fired me. I was also ashamed to become a steward [*commissaire*] again after having been the administrator of a laundry. And so I wanted her to leave with me.[28]

Larue simply could not stand to lose his job, its status, and his mistress all at once, and he identified her as the author of his misfortune, which in a sense she was. She had become more assertive once they started work at the laundry, publicly chastising and contradicting him, blatantly challenging his authority. Indeed, their fight on 31 August began with her scolding him for speaking rudely to a child. Then, because of his abuse of her and her superior performance at work, he lost his job. When he was arrested, he said to the police, "I want to be the master. I don't want anyone to dominate me." Fragonard and Bourdeaux may have hoped to be rid of him forever, but instead he took vengeance for the damage to his status as a man and a worker. The court was unsympathetic; he was convicted of murder and condemned to fifteen years' forced labor.

This case reveals a relationship between employer and employee based on personal sympathy as well as business interests, but employers were not always so sympathetic to the plight of women in abusive relationships. In fact, testimony from a boss sometimes came into opposition with testimony from neighborhood witnesses. All her neighbors praised Esther Bonjour as a hard worker, although she drank fairly often, while her lover Deschutter was known to be violent and often failed to bring home his pay. Deschutter's boss, however, only knew about their relationship from the occasions when Bonjour came looking for him at work. "Deschutter was a good worker," he testified. "He lived with la fille Esther. Many times she came and caused scenes with him, calling him a slacker and a pimp [*fainéant et maquereau*]. So Deschutter got angry, and it is very rare that I have seen him hit his mistress. She had to provoke him first."[29] Charles Dabon's boss also had a higher opinion of him than his neighbors did. According to a police report, Dabon's boss believed him to be a good worker who got along well with others and said he had never appeared violent or quarrelsome. His neighbors, though, countered that he often got drunk and beat his mistress.[30]

Joseph Alazard, a shoemaker, received such praise from his employer and coworkers that evidence of his violent behavior at home seems to have been disregarded by the jury. Alazard, age sixty-two, stabbed his wife in the neck after she mocked him for wetting his pants. His allegation that she had been unfaithful to him seemed ludicrous to the court, since she was fifty-one years old herself. Alazard's employer, Monsieur Blot, testified during his trial: "I have known and employed Alazard in my workshop for more than thirty years. I have always known him as an honest man, and during thirty years we have never had the least reproach to make against him... I cannot believe, knowing him like I know him, that the accusation [of murder] is founded." Three male coworkers agreed. Two neighbor women asserted, however, that the couple fought frequently. Célestine Schuylen said, "I have often heard la femme Alazard complain and cry out. Many times she even has made me see the traces of blows that she said her husband gave her." Anne Gaultier added, "Madame Alazard was a good woman. She told me about her husband's scenes of jealousy. She even showed me a knife, telling me that he had threatened her with it... The accused mutilated his wife all night long. One used to hear cries and moans and abominable things."[31] Alazard's behavior seemed grievous enough to the neighbors, but the jury may have thought that his good work record eclipsed his misconduct in the household because they acquitted him.

The picture that emerges here is of a male workplace unified against the claims of wives and their neighbors. Here men's testimony trumped women's testimony. Yet while such gendered antagonism operated clearly in these cases, it would be an exaggeration to draw a clear-cut distinction between the workplace as masculine and the domicile as feminine. After all, these women worked for wages as well as men, and men were often perfectly willing to testify about their neighbors' doings in their homes. Nonetheless, men's status as workers was primary; the economic realm was the most significant one where a man could prove his worth.

It was a particular sign of virtue for working men to hand over all their pay to their partners.[32] Sometimes this one masculine virtue was a man's entire line of self-defense in a domestic conflict. Edmonde-Auguste Duhault asserted that his wife could have no complaints about their life together. "From time to time we had words because of the children, but that's all. I used to give her everything I earned for the household."[33] After his wife threw acid on him and his lover, Marius Cholat argued that, on balance, he had treated his wife well. "I do not deny that I have given my wife reasons to be jealous," he said, admitting his infidelity, "but I have always been good to her. I have never used violence toward her. I have never let her lack for anything."[34] In short, he argued, since he didn't beat her and always gave her enough money, any other lapses on his part were excusable.

Confronted for the first time with the accusation of attempted murder for beating his mistress of twenty-two years, Henri Durban defended himself by describing his performance as a provider. "I worked every time I found something to do and I brought my salary to la fille Eizenkreimer. The last week we spent together I gave her sixty-two francs in two installments."[35] Likewise, Lucien Derreux, who hoped his wife would return to him, claimed that he had fulfilled his obligations toward her in a satisfactory way. "I admit having beaten my wife a few times, when I was drunk, but I always worked to provide for the needs of the household."[36] His wife contradicted his claim, noting that, "since I am no longer there to feed him, he sings in courtyards to live." In her view, it was she who supported him, and he was unable to support himself alone.

If a woman did receive adequate money from her partner, it was then her responsibility to use it carefully for the needs of the household. Poor household management was one of many failures that François Lerondeau attributed to his wife. According to his cousin, he consistently gave his wife everything he earned. "He always brought his wife faithfully all the money he received, keeping nothing for himself." This reliability made his wife's neglect of his meals and clothing seem inexcusable.[37] The wife then would not give any of the money back so that he could go out with his friends, forcing her husband to borrow money from the masons he employed.

Complaints like Lerondeau's about women's poor management were far outnumbered by complaints about men's failure to provide adequately for their households. This incongruity can easily be attributed to the basic scarcity of cash among poor working people, as well as men's superior economic power. After all, if a man did not like how his partner managed the money, he could simply withhold his pay from her. Conversely, his partner could only rely on his goodwill and sense of proper behavior to share enough money to meet the household's needs. Nicolas Jacob and his wife fought constantly because of his lack of support; their conflicts ended only when he threw her out a window and killed her. He denied any responsibility for their disputes, saying, "She constantly made scenes when I came home, under the pretext that I did not bring back enough money."[38] Marie Probst said the only reason she left Denis Roulland was his lack of financial support. "We ended up living on rather bad terms because he contributed very little to the cost of our common household, and when I demanded money from him, he was furious."[39] Jean-Baptiste François's wife had an eminently practical solution to her husband's lack of support, which unfortunately also aroused his jealousy—she took a lover. "As long as he would not change, as long as he would not work," she told him, "I would not leave Tallet, because I could not support myself alone."[40] Tallet affirmed that he gave her money and food, noting that she seemed to lack for everything. In turn, la femme François added her lover's gifts of money to the common purse for household expenses. "During the month of April," she explained, "I might have received twenty to thirty francs from my lover; I put this sum in the household purse, and my husband, who knew about it, nevertheless lived on it."[41] She added that her husband could not have been unaware of the fact that she ate all her meals with Tallet instead of at home. By using money supplied by her lover and allowing her to eat with him, her husband not only condoned her illicit relationship but profited from it, while abdicating his own responsibility to provide for her. In a milieu that prized women's sexual fidelity and men's ability to work, the François couple failed to meet key standards of propriety.

Madeline Bock was perhaps not as resourceful as la femme François. Her husband worked intermittently and then drank most of his pay, so she had to try to support them with the paltry wages she earned doing embroidery. Her patience finally failed, and she stabbed him one day when he refused to give her money. "On Sunday morning, we had a quarrel," she declared in court. "Nothing remained for me from my weekly wages after paying all the expenses of the household. I asked him for twenty *sous* from his week's wages, which he had just received at eleven o'clock. He refused."[42] The next day, she waited for him after work on the sidewalk. "I no longer had a *sou*, no more bread, no more provisions... I told him that he should have come sooner, since he had quit work at five o'clock and he was leaving me without bread." He insulted her and hit her, and then she stabbed him. Since she was known to have had several lovers and was suspected of being a prostitute, her presentation of herself as a long-suffering victim was apparently not convincing to the jury, who convicted her of murder. Had Madeleine Bock been a more sympathetic character in the courtroom, her crime might have been attributed more to her husband's failure as a man than to hers as a woman.

What was worse than a man failing to provide for a woman was his allowing her to support him financially, abandoning the primary criteria for his masculine worth and thus inverting the roles of support and dependence. Several men attacked the women who had left them and thereby deprived them of financial support. Esther Bonjour was reputed to be a hard worker, unlike her lover, Jean Deschutter, with whom she lived for several years. Their landlady knew they did not get along because of financial problems. "Often there were disputes between them. They always arose because Deschutter did not bring back enough money, and la fille Esther complained of working for two. She was always the one who paid [the rent]."[43] The landlady's husband was even more specific about their fights. "These disputes always came from Deschutter earning small salaries. Many times I heard his mistress say to him, 'How are you only bringing fifteen or eighteen francs! How can you run a household with that! If I didn't work like a horse myself, we wouldn't even be able to pay our rent!' Deschutter didn't answer anything, but from the woman's cries I knew that blows were being exchanged." Though Deschutter normally earned four or five francs a day as a furniture maker, in the days preceding their final conflict, he was getting only one franc a day on advance, since there was no work for him. Bonjour earned four francs a day making mattresses. It was during this period of hard times that la fille Bonjour finally decided to leave Deschutter, renting another room for herself after a brutal fight. A few weeks later, he stabbed her to death. The landlord attributed his motive to the loss of her financial support. "If Deschutter struck la fille Bonjour, it was rather because she refused to go back to him and therefore he no longer knew how to meet his needs." Deschutter himself denied this accusation. With a trace of pride, he insisted, "I did not need her to live, I am a worker, and everywhere I've worked, I've found enough to maintain myself."[44] Although this was manifestly untrue—he could not even pay his room rent after his mistress moved out—he clung to his identity as a self-sufficient working man. Perhaps with his mistress's departure, he lost the means to prop up that deception along with her financial support.

Charles Duchène, a cook, also lost his means of survival when his wife left him. Married for ten years, his wife Eugénie said that he had only been a good worker for the first five. "During these last five years," she remarked, "my husband has only worked in a continuous manner for nine months, and the rest of the time he has only done... He did not contribute to the expenses of the household and that was the cause of frequent arguments between us. I naturally reproached his laziness, and that set off his violent rages."[45] While la femme Duchène's profession was listed on court documents as seamstress, a form for a bill imprinted "Madame Duchène, robes et confections" appears in the dossier, suggesting that she had her own business. Although it is impossible to say how large her business was, she was surely above the ranks of the seamstresses who eked out a living doing piecework, and she was well able to survive on her own. When she left her husband and he demanded her return, she replied "that she would not return to him until he set himself to working seriously." Perhaps she meant to leave the door open for a possible reconciliation, but his response was to shoot her. Both la fille Bonjour and la femme Duchène left their partners after extended periods in which their men failed to work hard and earn enough money. The women decided that their partners had failed definitively in their financial obligations, and they refused to be the sole supporters of their households.

A brief period of financial difficulty could be tolerated, though, for the great advantage of a partnership between two working people was the security of having two separate sources of income. Each partner could shoulder an extra burden to pull the household through a crisis if the other lost his or her job, fell ill, or had a baby. This kind of arrangement most often came to light in the *cour d'assises*, however, when one partner failed to reciprocate with the proper assistance. Rose Méhu finally threw acid on her lover, Paul Lelong, after he abandoned her, pregnant and with the rent due. She believed that he owed her support not only because he was the father of her baby but also because she had helped him through hard times. "I was pushed to the limit by my lover's conduct toward me," she claimed. "When he was without work for two months, I was the one who fed him. Later, I was without work myself, and he never wanted to give me anything... When I asked him for money for my needs, he said that he had none for me. He'll never give me a centime."[46] Victorine Lelong also supported a man through hard times, only to be abandoned during her pregnancy. "I worked night and day at the military equipment factory, and he never lacked for anything, although he did not work himself," she testified.[47] When she gave birth to their child, he did not give her any assistance, though he still lived with her. He only grudgingly gave her food and a little money until the child died barely two years later, after many illnesses for both mother and child.

In a comparable situation, Catherine De Moor worked steadily as a shirtmaker while her husband drifted in and out of employment. Repeatedly, whenever she was on the point of giving birth and would thus be unable to work for a few weeks, he would take his pay and abandon her, only returning when she was again able to work and support him. "He wanted to be fed by her for doing nothing, and he made her work like a slave," asserted Phillippine Grillon, a longtime friend.[48] Such behavior earned universal condemnation from their neighbors and the following accusation from the investigating magistrate: "You were attached to your wife, not at all because you loved her, but because, being laborious, economical, and a good housekeeper, she represented productive capital to you." Where marriage was meant to be a partnership based on a reciprocal exchange of services, De Moor was accused of reducing it to nothing more than the economic exploitation of his wife, without even a pretense of affection. He was convicted of murder.

Parenting

Although some assize court cases hinged on fathers' abandonment of mothers and children, parenting was rarely a focus of court testimony. In numerous cases, witnesses never mention children, and the fact that a couple had any children is only recorded in the official "Tableau des Renseignements," a listing of information on the accused or in police reports. Statistically, the family size of households considered in this study was similar to those of Parisian working people in general during this time period—very small. Although most of the women involved in these cases were still young enough to bear more children, more than 90 percent of them had two children or fewer, while those couples with larger families often included children from more than one union, especially if the couple was unmarried. It appears that couples either purposefully limited their family size or they did not practice effective contraception at all, and, of course, child mortality was also a factor. The case of Marguerite Eizeinkreimer (age thirty-nine) and her partner illustrates just how complex a family could become, at least from an administrative point of view. "I had been living with Durban for twenty-two years, when I left him;" she testified, "I had eleven children with him. Five are still living, of whom he has recognized only two—Henri Durban, age twenty-one, and Félix Durban, age nine. The other three were registered with the État Civil under my name because I gave birth to them at the [charity] hospital."[49] Her family was unusually large; very few other women in this study reported having had as many pregnancies as she.

Fathers had clearly defined financial and emotional responsibilities toward their children.[50] When a new baby arrived, it was the father's responsibility to provide pay for medical care for the birth, as well as to provide compensation for the time when the mother would be unable to work or to pay the cost of sending the child to a nursemaid. Even though Jules Courtois chose to leave his pregnant mistress in order to marry another woman (with whom he had also had a child), he signed papers promising to give her forty francs a month for seven months to cover her food and rent, an amount that would have been barely adequate. He also promised to legally recognize the child. Such gestures did not placate the wrath of his lover Marie Féral, who was infuriated by his refusal to marry her. Féral would be acquitted for shooting him, although some witnesses believed her lover had behaved with perfect decency.[51] In a comparable case, the investigating magistrate reprimanded Victorine Lelong for attacking her lover, Langlois. He had abandoned her during her second pregnancy but had sent small sums of money until the baby died. "According to the witnesses collected, Langlois conducted himself toward you and conducted himself toward his children in the most appropriate manner," the judge remarked. "Each week after your separation, and the whole time that the children lived, he helped you from his purse in the measure of his means." But Victorine Lelong protested, "He never gave me more than eight francs a week, and that was what he earned in a day. He could have done more, and one will never know the misery that I have endured because of him." In her view, the assistance he gave her was both hard won and inadequate, and the final insult came when the child died and Langlois refused to pay for the burial.[52]

As proof of paternal affection, a certain amount of physical affection was expected along with financial support. Indeed, paternal love and money were often mixed together in the stories witnesses told. Kissing a child was a key sign of affection. Langlois, for instance, had never once kissed his child, a further proof in the eyes of the child's mother that he was an utterly inadequate father. For Marie Gy, the decay of her husband's paternal affection for their three children was among the costs of his affair. "Oh, that woman, that woman, she has ruined my household. My husband no longer spoke except through her, no longer looked at his children. He jumped over them. He stepped over them without even kissing them. He no longer took them by the hand." As Marie Gy told it, her husband was so preoccupied with his mistress that he ignored his children, leading her to fear for their abandonment. Indeed, he ran off to Paris with his mistress after receiving his pay, leaving his family nearly destitute.[53] In a similar case, the police reported that Ernest Cotard only rarely visited his wife in order to kiss their child and did not provide financial support for them. His wife, Marie Cotard, invited him to her apartment one day to discuss placing their four-year-old daughter in the care of a convent. The father's ready agreement to give up the child spurred her to attack him. "I asked him what he would give me for our child, and he answered me with a negative gesture," she recounted. She elaborated in a later interrogation, "I hoped that in calling my husband to the house and speaking to him about his child, that he would return to better feelings and that he would not consent to her abandonment. When I asked him to place her with the sisters, and I saw that he consented, I understood that everything was over between us. I grabbed the vitriol that was in the kitchen, and I threw it at his face." To Marie Cotard, her husband's lack of overt affection for his daughter reflected a real indifference to the child's welfare.[54]

While fathers expressed affection for their children through financial support and the occasional kiss, mothers had far greater responsibility for the proper care of the children. Yet, in court, where the establishment of a good character was so critical, women were rarely praised or condemned for their performance as mothers. Only extreme cases of virtue or neglect seem to have elicited detailed comment. Children and motherhood played only an accessory role in establishing a woman's goodness in the context of these assize court trials; her work record and sexual fidelity were far more frequently a focus of evaluation. Those women who did receive special notice as excellent mothers epitomized the virtues of devotion and self-sacrifice. Victorine Lelong, a cook, was an exemplary mother in the eyes of her concierge, the widow Blet, who testified:

> I must say that one can be a good mother, but that one cannot be a better mother than she was. She would almost die of hunger to be able to give [her son] something to eat or to buy him medicine, because the poor little one was often sick. She went as far as to beg for him. She had successively pawned everything she had of her own linens to be able to care for him. She had only the child's little bed in her room. As for her, she did not lie down; she stayed there without resting and without eating, always near the little one, working as much as she could to give him care. I assure you, messieurs, that this tore my heart. I have never seen a better mother.[55]

If the supreme maternal virtue was self-sacrifice, however, it was impossible for a working woman to devote herself full time to the care of her children without risking starvation. Given their limited economic circumstances, mothers like Lelong were all but doomed to failure if they sought to fulfill this ideal. Perhaps frustration with her impossible situation was what drove her to throw acid on and stab her estranged lover (the child's father)—she punished him for not fulfilling his duties towards his family.

Indeed, paid labor and motherhood were always at odds. Without doubt, this was one reason why so many people paid for their children to live with someone else during their youngest years, when they required the most intensive care. It was extremely common for working people—really, anyone who could afford it—to send their children to wet nurses to be raised for the first few years of their lives, and then to schools, or simply into other families to board while they grew up. According to Rachel Fuchs, about one-third of all Parisian children were sent to wet nurses throughout the nineteenth century. The practice of wet nursing provided a source of income for some women, with wages comparable to those of domestic servants or seamstresses, usually about twenty to forty francs per month.[56] Certainly, the employment of wet nurses contributed to the infant mortality rate, since women who hired themselves out as wet nurses were generally poor and lacked the resources to provide a sufficient diet for themselves. But the great advantage of sending a child away was that it freed the mother to work. Juliette Legrand, for instance, paid for her son to board with a grocer a few doors down from where she lived with her husband.[57] Taking advantage of a more recent innovation in childcare, Marie Neu took her child to the *crèche* every day.[58]

Occasionally, children's paid caretakers were called upon to testify about the parents' qualities. Such depositions usually focused on the material conditions of the child's maintenance, not the emotional attachment that parents demonstrated for their children. Perhaps the former stood for the latter. Although Jean-Marie Marie had written to his father-in-law complaining that he had to force his wife to stay home and care for their sick daughter, the woman who ran the daughter's school wrote a letter to the court, saying that she had nothing but praise for the mother and that the girl was "very properly maintained."[59] After the Testes were married, and the husband legally recognized his wife's daughter Marcelle, she was sent to a boarding school in Vincennes, where her mother visited her weekly. The *institutrice* testified that they regularly paid the costs of her education and that "Madame Teste was an excellent mother. I was struck by it, as was everyone at our house. Little Marcelle adored her and always rejoiced to see her mother. She had the greatest desire to see her little girl well brought up." Although the teacher was not impressed with Madame Teste's personality ("she had a very weak character, and I believe was very scatterbrained"), she noted approvingly that Madame Teste did not take the slightest offense when she suggested that the child should stay at the school during vacation, since the mother might have difficulty supervising her at home.[60] In this instructor's opinion, an important part of being a good mother was knowing when to put your child into someone else's more competent hands.

Historians have long argued that intensive parenting, especially by mothers, is a defining feature of the development of the modern family.[61] Yet economic need clearly played a role in the kind of parenting that was possible for working people in fin-de-siècle Paris. For a woman to tend her own children full time would have required a level of income and financial security beyond the reach of most couples, much less a single woman. Witnesses attested that mothers and fathers could fulfill their parental obligations admirably without the kind of constant personal care that was becoming the norm elsewhere. Although parenting was a peripheral issue in most of the cases in this study, it is notable that conflicts about proper parenting always fell along gendered lines, with mothers seeking the emotional and financial support they believed fathers owed them.

The Distribution of Household Resources

While both partners contributed their wages to the household, women typically managed the household budget. Charged with acquiring food and other provisions to furnish the household, they were normally the chief consumers in the household economy. Their savvy bargaining could stretch limited funds, and their careful saving could create security against hard times or facilitate major purchases. Yet conflicts almost inevitably arose between the needs of the household and the woman, on the one hand, and the desires of the man who earned much of the money, on the other hand. When men and women fought about the distribution of household resources, they often drew their battle lines along the distinction between necessity and pleasure, the communal domestic interior and the selfish amusements exterior to it.

Paris at the end of the nineteenth century offered unprecedented opportunities for public sociability and for the consumption of household goods.[62] The contrasts between interior and exterior are sharp in many depositions. "This is a man who does not work, regularly at least, and when by chance he does work, he goes to spend his money at the races and the café instead of bringing it to his household," commented Marianne Naour in a case involving her brother-in-law.[63] He put his desire for entertainment above providing for his family. "It doesn't matter if I work," complained Marie Gadel, who was a greengrocer, "this unlucky man wastes everything I can earn in partying [*faisant la noce*] from time to time. If this continues, I will be obliged to sell my store. If he wasn't such a good purchasing agent, I wouldn't be able to keep him."[64] Her lover's wastefulness nearly outweighed his value to her business. Clearly his priorities focused on sociability and pleasure, while she was focused on making a living. By all accounts, Désirée Solhart's husband spent money as fast as she could earn it in their butter and egg business. "When he was drunk, which often happened to him, he picked quarrels with me, and above all when I refused him money to satisfy his tastes," she declared.[65] He in turn claimed that she had driven him to drink by stealing his rightful share of the profits.

Like these couples, the Fétats fought when the woman refused to give the man money to go drinking. A women the wife employed as an embroiderer described their usual pattern. "I have always seen scenes between the husband and wife. She reproached him for his spending at the cabaret; he went into a rage over everything and nothing... Fétat constantly required money that he spent drinking, and if the poor woman attempted a refusal, he threatened her with death."[66] Another employee confirmed that just such a scene took place before the husband shot at his wife, inadvertently wounding their son. Cécile Genet also tried to keep her partner from drinking up their money, with similarly dire consequences. "Yesterday evening, following a discussion that I had with my lover Berquet, to whom I refused to give money, he kicked me out of his place," she told the investigating magistrate. "If I was refusing him money like that it was [because] I knew that he would use it to go get drunk, as often happens to him... I've known Berquet one year. He ate up not only his money but also mine either in drinking or with other women."[67] He attacked her when she returned to his room to retrieve her belongings for a permanent move.

In the few households where men reportedly managed the household finances, this unusual arrangement appears to have been part of a particularly controlling and abusive situation. Charles Aubriot, for instance, was a brutal man who was known to beat his children with a whip and who beat his wife to death in their presence. "It was papa who held the purse strings," testified his fifteen-and-a-half-year-old son, "to assure that if my mother got drunk, he would get drunk with her."[68] In another case, Marie Sanglé made twenty-five to thirty-three francs a week as an upholsterer. Her excessively controlling husband came to get her at work every Saturday, so that she was compelled to give him all her pay, and he did not give her back enough money to live on. By the time of the crime, she had lost at least two jobs and was planning to become a wet nurse after the birth of her next child. She went to trial for throwing acid on her husband's friend, Auguste Delinon. In a letter to the investigating magistrate, she explained that she had targeted this man because he encouraged her husband to squander their resources. " Delinon and my husband are never apart.

He incites him by saying 'you are young.' 'To have a wife and children every year, that's nothing,' he used to say to him. So these monsieurs went to balls and brasseries all over Paris, while I was about to die of hunger as well as my poor little children. He slept away from home very often. When I asked him where he had been, he answered that he had slept at the police station. A word was enough for him to do me in."[69] She went on to describe her financial strategies for feeding and clothing herself and her children: begging money from her mother and his, pawning household items and clothing, and, ultimately, selling her sewing machine. When all her resources had been depleted, she attacked the man whose bad influence she believed had turned her husband away from his household obligations.

Clearly, la femme Sanglé and her husband had very different priorities for the use of their wages. The discrepancy between his priorities and hers highlights the gendered division of labor in the household. While he amused himself with his friend, she was left with the impossible task of provisioning the household and feeding herself and her children. Although many working people bought ready-made meals from wineshops or street vendors, the purchase and preparation of food was by and large women's work. Numerous studies have determined that food consumption varied considerably among the ranks of working people, depending on an individual's status in the household as well as on economic factors.[70] Men, for example, often enjoyed larger portions of meat and wine. People might eat well during seasons of employment and quite poorly during the low season, but food was always the largest category in any working person's budget. A contemporary survey of budgets from the last decades of the nineteenth century indicates that food expenditures required 46 to 77 percent of the household budget, on the average about four times as much as housing.[71] Working people's diet was generally characterized by a heavy reliance on carbohydrates for energy, especially in the form of bread, with small portions of meat, fat, vegetables, and dairy products, although Parisians' diets became more varied and substantial during the second half of the century.[72] The purchase of wine and spirits all too frequently drained financial resources away from affording more nutritious food.[73]

Food that was sufficient in quantity and nourishment was a goal rather than an everyday certainty in this milieu. The frequency of metaphors referring to food attests to the centrality of this concern in everyday life. Quite often, money that had been wasted in high living was said to have been "eaten" or "drunk." Alfred Massacry testified that his sister's husband had squandered her savings:

"All this money was drunk and eaten by him."[74] Also, the verb *nourrir* signified not only to feed or nourish but also to support in a more general way. When Virginie Jouault wrote to the Procureur de la République asking for a legal separation from her husband, she complained bitterly that she was "obliged on pain of being beaten to feed [*nourrir*] my husband, whose laziness equals his intemperance for drink."[75] A former landlady reported that François Boullevaut was content to live supported by his lover. "He was perfectly willing for this woman to feed him [*il aurait bien voulu que cette femme le nourrise*]."[76] The investigating magistrate scolded Louis Badran for the same shortcoming: "It was your mistress who fed you [*qui vous nourrissait*] and paid the rent," he declared, also describing the mistress as "a poor, exhausted girl...who...had used up her strength and her health feeding your laziness."[77] Blanche Gallier confirmed this description of her lover, saying, "Badran found me to be good for exploitation; he found me to be good for working to feed him." Badran was doubly culpable—for failing to provide for his partner financially and for obliging her to support him.

Implicit in any discussion of food was an understanding about the distribution of resources in the household. Although women were responsible for preparing meals, men were supposed to provide money to purchase the food. Indeed, the preparation and consumption of food were defining activities of the household, encapsulating the economic, affective, and even sexual exchanges on which it was based. In a few instances, men and women offered their partners the continuation of their food-related services even after ending their association as partners living together. At least two women continued to provide meals for their estranged partners, perhaps in an effort to pacify them. Zélie Guillot continued to send her maid with soup, bread, wine, coffee, and meat to her estranged husband and his sister. He was not earning enough to support himself, while her grocery business thrived. The supplies she sent were not enough to assuage his anger.[78] Charles Dabon admitted that his mistress had discussed leaving him prior to the evening of his attack, and he knew that she had already rented a room for herself. "She wanted to go live there and talked about coming back each day, nevertheless, to prepare my meals for me, but I let her know that from the day she left me, I would not want her to come back to the house anymore."[79] Although she may have reasoned that he was most attached to her as a cook, he declared he wanted all of her services or none.

The obligation to provide meals for their partners could lead women to the extreme of depriving themselves of nourishment. In some cases, a woman's self-deprivation was part of her efforts to pressure her partner for further concessions. Blanche Gallier, for example, believed that her hard work and sacrifices would persuade her lover to shape up and marry her, although she was soon disillusioned. She told him, "People used to ask me why I was getting thin, why I was pale... I didn't say that I was always hungry, being obliged to feed you, while you stayed in bed."[80] Likewise, Victorine Lelong had worked to support her lover when he lost his job, although he had already left her once before. "I was two months pregnant," she wrote in a letter to the *juge d'instruction*, "but he was so delicate and in such bad health that I used to give him my portion of meat along with his. I even used to give him the small amount of wine that... [a charitable former employer] brought me."[81] Unfortunately, he was unwilling to reciprocate. After he abandoned her, and she became unable to work because of an infection in her hands, Lelong persuaded her former lover to subsidize her meals at the local wineshop in exchange for doing his laundry every week. "Pushed by need and having no other support but him, since he was the father of my child, I then asked him to allow me to take my meals with him chez Monsieur Bruno. He agreed to it, but gave me two *sous* of bread, two *sous* of wine, the bouillon and the beef," a very minimal allowance. Perhaps by extending the exchange of materials and services between the two of them, Lelong hoped to preserve some semblance of the domestic partnership they once shared, but, after the death of their child, even this grudging support from him ceased.

More often than not, if a woman was deprived of food it was part of a larger pattern of mistreatment. La femme Lecoeur, who had employed Clémence Derreux for twelve years, expressed her concern about her friend's bad marriage. "I soon saw that her husband—who is a drunkard, a lazy bum—mistreated her and spent in orgies everything she could earn. Nonetheless, she was not discouraged and often used to deprive herself of food while her husband spent all of his earnings at the cabaret."[82] His financial irresponsibility led to her to the brink of starvation. Eugène Lacoste testified that his concierge of fifteen years, Georges Guerrier, used to beat and deprive his wife. "He used to take her money and keep her from eating," he said, "or at least that was the general opinion." Another neighbor, Lucie Gilbert, testified that she often fed the woman when her husband left her without resources.[83] Marie Sanglé sent the *juge d'instruction* a long letter describing her unhappy marriage, including her husband's financial control of what she ate. "Every day I used to bring my food in my basket [to work]," she wrote, "a little soup in a tin and for [a] drink a little herb tea. It [was] to such a point that all the women workers had pity on me. [They] helped me a lot, just like Madame Maurice, who was the forewoman."[84] Her husband spent all his money going out with his friends and beat her when she asked for more money.

Exposing a man's failure to provide sufficiently for his household was a powerful claim against him, for his failure to uphold his end of the domestic exchange was acceptable grounds for ending a partnership. Several women articulated explicitly the reciprocal nature of their obligations and their partners' by focusing on the purchase and preparation of food. According to her mother, Marie Neu had protested her lover's failure to provide his part of the household finances by ceasing to cook for him. She had told her mother, "He does not want to work, and I do not want to work to feed him. When he works and gives me money, I will feed him."[85] So Marie Neu started eating with her mother, who seemed to believe that this strategy led Gaspard Keiffer to leave her daughter (though only briefly). Conversely, Antoine Charrier decided to cease giving his wife money to run the household because she never served him enough food. His neighbor Omer Guilment informed the investigating magistrate that Charrier had frequently complained that his wife Marie did not feed him properly. "In recent days, he no longer ate at home," he explained. "Charrier no longer brought her his pay and resolved not to contribute to her expenses, which obliged her to spend her personal resources to live."[86] In an incident prior to the crime, Charrier feared his wife had poisoned him with a cup of hot chocolate, although a doctor disagreed that his illness could have been caused by poison.

When Marie Charrier actually did attack her husband, she chose to use sulfuric acid, but that he feared poison attests to the exclusive power that women had over the preparation of food. Ann-Louise Shapiro has argued for a certain coalescence of "a set of widely recognized cultural references" identifying the female poisoner as a particular focus of fin-de-siècle anxieties.[87] Shapiro bolsters her claim with reference to medical and legal professionals. Whatever impact these professional discourses may have had on people's behavior, it is certain that struggles for power within a household played out in terms of the mutual service obligations that men and women owed one another, and the preparation and consumption of food was one site among many where the battles took place. As historian Laure Adler has noted, women were stereotypically associated with poisoning, not only because they were the ones most involved in food preparation but also because poisoning requires cunning rather than physical strength on the part of the attacker, a characteristic that was considered feminine.[88] Nonetheless, women outnumbered men only slightly as defendants in poisoning cases in nineteenth-century France, with a total of 1,041 women and 949 men, from 1825 to 1900.[89] Adler has documented a surge in the number of poisoning cases around midcentury,[90] but the last three decades saw a real decline in such cases, usually fewer than a dozen per year. The fin-de-siècle plague of poisoning was thus more apparent than real.

In the dossiers available for this study, wherever poisoning was alleged, there is evidence that disputes concerning the preparation of food had been ongoing for months—if not years—before the alleged poisoning took place. Thus, while Shapiro associates the story of Mélanie Lerondeau with the stereotype of a scheming, deceitful poisoner, testimony from more than forty witnesses in the dossier itself reveals the far more complex story of the husband and wife's relationship. Shifting the focus from elite discourses to popular practice, Lerondeau appears not as an illustration of the *empoisonneuse* of bourgeois fears and fantasy but as a woman engaged in a continuous struggle with her spouse. She was initially tried and convicted on 16 January 1878, in the Cour d'assises de Seine et Oise, for the poisoning death of her husband. The sentence was revoked in June of that same year in the Cour d'assises de la Seine, thanks to new medical evidence proving that François Lerondeau could not have died by poisoning with oxalic acid.[91]

Witnesses who knew the couple in the town of Chateaufort described a marriage characterized by years of open discord.[92] Although they mostly blamed the wife, they also reported that she was dissatisfied with her husband's reluctance to perform the "conjugal duty,"[93] his failure to pay for repairs to their house after the invasion of 1870, and his decision to place their daughter in a boarding school. She showed her displeasure in a number of ways. She made him sleep in the barn, she refused to mend his clothes, and she frequently did not cook meals for him. Jules Bigot declared that François Lerondeau had told him that "he was obliged sometimes to feed himself at the wineshop because she [his wife] refused to prepare food for him." Lerondeau's second cousin, Françoise Chrétien, testified, "Sometimes, while he was eating, she tore his plate from his hands." His cousin Clementine Larcher complained that the wife made the husband "suffer all kinds of privation. She refused to give him anything to eat and he was forced to go feed himself in the places where he had work." Emile Ernue agreed that Mélanie Lerondeau did not prepare food for her husband, and furthermore had neglected to feed his aging, blind mother properly.

"Good bouillon would have been necessary for this poor old woman, but her daughter-in-law refused it to her, nor [did she] prepare anything to eat for her. This poor mother fed herself with sausage and other foods that her son and other people brought her." Other witnesses echoed these allegations, and, in her interrogation, Mélanie herself confirmed that she did not cook or wash for her husband when they were fighting. She chose to protest what she perceived as his shortcomings toward her by refusing to perform her household duties towards him. Thus, Mélanie had frequently sought to punish her husband through the medium of food, and so, when François died of a stomach ailment, it was not at all surprising that she was suspected of poisoning.

Mélanie Lerondeau was far from the only woman to express her displeasure with her partner through her handling of food. Eulalie Jean had been unhappy with her brutal husband for years and resisted cooking for him. One of his workers, who had room and board at the couple's home, witnessed her subversions and the reactions it provoked. "They often quarreled... Rather often when we came back to the house, the supper was not prepared and we were obliged to do our cooking ourselves. So he reproached her for being lazy and spending part of the money she took from him on fripperies... It also happened that she would season [the food] in such a way that we were unable to eat it. It was so peppered and salted, and she seasoned it this way very intentionally, since she was careful to take her own portion that wasn't seasoned the same way before serving us. Seeing that we could not eat the food, she laughed whole-heartedly."[94] Eulalie Jean made a deliberate choice to subvert her responsibilities to provide food for the household and apparently took pleasure in the dismay it caused. According to another witness, she also took bread, wine, oil, and money to her father, while refusing to take food to her husband at his worksite—again reinterpreting the proper distribution of household resources.

Such protests did not occur without retribution, however. Victor Dubuisson listed Marie Buire's failure to have supper waiting for him when he returned from work as one of his reasons for leaving his mistress to marry another woman.[95] Presumably he planned to marry a woman who was more reliable in her services. In at least one case, an unprepared supper led directly to a fatal attack. Suzanna Devaguet overheard the beginnings of a fatal quarrel between her neighbors Charles Dabon and his mistress la fille Jamaux. "I heard him reproaching her. 'Here's the dinner not ready again,' he was saying to her. 'There is no fire; you have been drinking; you are disgusting... You're really not going to make dinner for me? I have walked for an hour and a half to come home and eat dinner with you quietly, and I find you drunk. I'm going to eat elsewhere.'"[96] At this, la fille Jamaux declared that if he couldn't wait to eat with her, then she was going to go live with her brother. Dabon stabbed her while she was gathering her belongings to leave.

Food could also be used to indicate status and favor, which was problematic if the man who received special food from a woman was not her husband. A business associate of a wine seller named Biver testified that he was certain of an illicit relationship between Biver and Marie Fournet, his cook. "La fille Fournet was very attentive to Biver. She reserved all the good pieces for him, and one saw that she loved him madly."[97] Jean Vigineix-Roche argued in a letter (most likely directed to the *juge d'instruction*) that his wife had a lover named Alphonse Châtel. He gave as evidence of their intimacy the fact that his wife "sent him food daily." He reasoned, "After all this familiarity between them, it is impossible that they limit themselves to looking at the whites of each other's eyes."[98] His wife's generosity with the food she prepared seemed easily translatable into generosity with her body.

These men were supposedly receiving culinary marks of favor that the women should only be giving their husbands, but the opportunity for such transgression was widened considerably when male pensioners or friends were invited to take meals regularly at a couple's table. Lacking a woman to cook for him, a single man could pay to eat with a family. He could hope for better food than at the local *marchand de vins*, and the couple could earn a little extra income. Alexis Leca testified that his sister lacked for nothing in her household, that "her table was rather that of a *bourgeoise* than that of an *ouvrière*," but it was the introduction of a stranger to that well-endowed table that eventually undermined its security. Simon Richelet had invited his friend Arthur Benotte to live and eat with him and his wife in their one-room apartment, and an adulterous relationship between his wife and friend ensued. Eventually, she left her husband, and Richelet shot her.[99] Similarly, Augustine Catherine and her husband Pierre were milk vendors who lived together harmoniously until they allowed two of their male employees to take meals with them. The husband soon suspected the wife of infidelity, she fired the two men, and her husband ended up shooting her when she left him.[100] Thus, while food was a daily necessity, it could also be used to create discord, mark protest, or indicate affection.

Clothing was also invested with meaning beyond its material necessity. Clothing functioned as a sign on whose surface could be read messages about disorder or sexual incontinence. On a physical level it could serve, quite literally, as armor against an attack. Whatever can be said of the confining and deforming effects of the corset, at least half a dozen women in this study were saved from serious injury, if not death, by the thick fabric and hardware of their corsets. In examining Blanche Gallier's twenty-four stab wounds, Dr. Jules Socquet also analyzed the clothes she was wearing at the time of the attack. Her black satin corset, edged with blue velvet, had numerous rips and bloodstains. "[W]e must say," Socquet asserted in his report, "that it is probable that this article of clothing preserved la fille Gallier from a certain number of blows... its whalebones serving as a cuirass."[101] When Marguerite Eizenkreimer was attacked by her partner of twenty-two years, who stabbed her with a mason's compass, she attributed her survival to her clothing. "At the moment when I was struck, I was wearing a corset with stays made of steel, and I suppose that it is because the metal point slid on these stays that I was not more seriously injured."[102]

Likewise, the relatively meager firepower of inexpensive handguns could also be stopped by a corset's hardware. Juliette Legrand only suffered a bruise (albeit fifteen centimeters in diameter) when she was shot by her husband; the bullet was stopped by an eyelet of her corset lacings.[103] Virginie Jouault was also saved by the whalebones in her corset when her husband shot her.[104] At the trial of Pierre Beulle, an arms expert testified that the bullet he fired at his lover went through a package wrapped in newspaper, a wool shawl, and several layers of clothing before lodging against the corset. Bullets from the gun "could have pierced clothing and an ordinary corset," he said, but the victim's was particularly thick. Phillipine Thomas agreed, "The ball was flattened against the busk of my corset, and I was not hurt."[105]

Of course, the physically protective properties of clothing were ordinarily not as important as their appearance. Clean, mended clothing indicated that a woman had sufficient, time, skills, and resources to devote to its maintenance. A tidy appearance thus signified a well-managed household, while wearing inappropriate clothing was a sign of disorder. Marie Charrier was known for her slovenly appearance, a symptom not only of her stinginess but also of the poor quality of care she gave her household and her husband. "This woman dressed herself in rags to economize, and loves money a lot," one female neighbor testified. Charrier's husband elaborated, "My wife is sordidly greedy. In the house, everyone would tell you. To economize she often went out without stockings and dressed in rags."[106] She apparently had the resources to dress better, so her choice to save money by sacrificing her appearance was widely condemned. In another case, Mélanie Lerondeau was so negligent in mending her husband's clothes that they had rents in them through which one could see his *parties*. She also failed to provide him with clean clothes and tore new garments that he purchased, apparently as part of her general refusal to assume her household duties.[107] Conversely, Catherine De Moor used gifts of clothing to reward her husband when he had a job. A female friend of hers noted, "As soon as he worked a little, it seems that she took courage again. She used to buy him clothes and would put a certain amount of *coquetterie* in [ensuring] that he had a good appearance."[108] It is notable that even where a man's clothing was concerned, it was always his female partner who was held responsible for maintaining his proper appearance.

Indeed, witnesses virtually never commented on men's appearances, except in connection to a woman's intervention, whereas women's appearances were subject to intense scrutiny, again reinforcing women's greater participation in maintaining the household's symbolic capital. What a woman wore could signify many things about her economic status, profession, and sexual availability. Thus the proprietor of the building where Charlotte Gérard lived identified her as a prostitute because of her dress: "I was not slow to notice by her outrageous toilette and her allures that this was a girl of light morals."[109] Flamboyant dress could indicate that a woman was promiscuous or, at the very least, that she was not a hard worker, for, dressed in finery, how could she labor at a job or perform housework? Eulalie Jean protested firmly against her mother-in-law's accusations that she was a "toiletteuse,"[110] and Octavie Levielle's husband scolded her for going out *en toilette* during the day, when she should have been working as a laundress and cooking his dinner.[111] Wearing the wrong kind of clothes could also create confusion about which social category a person belonged to. "Although she was a registered prostitute, she was very presentable. One would have taken her to be a worker," commented a female baker, who lived across the street from Henriette Damotte.[112] She appeared more respectable than she really was. The opposite was true for la femme Jacob, who was known to be a flashy dresser and to affect a particularly unusual hairstyle. In spite of her appearance, none of her neighbors could confirm anything negative about her conduct. "In effect la femme Jacob might have had a look that was a little singular, showy; however, I have never heard that she frequented public balls or that she was seen in the company of men she could give herself to," commented one neighbor.[113]

Using clothing in deliberate attempts to hide one's true identity seems to have been acceptable as long as the ruse was obvious and temporary. La femme

Jacob took her taste for unusual clothing to extremes one day when she dressed as a man. She went to her husband's employer and declared she was looking for her husband, who had been away from home for four days. "I dressed as a man to look for him more easily," she explained, and yet the employer apparently had no trouble at all recognizing her.[114] In other cases where people put on disguises, they too remained perfectly recognizable. Marie Pourcher also dressed in a disguise and went searching for information on her husband's activities, though again, the concierge she spoke with had no trouble recognizing her on subsequent visits.[115] Estelle Pluchet always wore a thick veil when she visited her lover at his apartment, despite the fact that the concierge—the only witness to her trysts—knew perfectly well who she was.[116] It seems that for these women, the gesture of being in disguise was more important than actual success in hiding their identity.

In other cases, the messages encoded in clothing and fabric seemed to provide unambiguous proof of misconduct. Since she had spotted Marie Rochat early one morning wearing the same dress she wore the night before, a *"robe pompadour,"* Blanche Varin concluded she must have slept away from home. "I did not doubt that she had spent the night with the monsieur who accompanied her to the Montagnes Russes," she asserted. Varin's accusation was suspect in itself, however, as she had already admitted to being the mistress of Rochat's husband. And Rochat read her own messages in fabric that inculpated Varin: "The bed, where I had put clean sheets, had stains proving that he [her husband] must have slept there with a woman."[117] Marie Gy also found "revealing stains" on her husband's shirt that confirmed her suspicions that he was carrying on an affair. His lover Malvina Wuillaume was known for her coquettish ways; her employer said she was "excessively *recherchée* in her toilette, and [spent] her wages even in advance to satisfy her tastes in fashion [*toilette*]."[118] In no case was a man accused of such sartorial excesses.

Inappropriate dress may have brought censure, but disputes over expensive household goods could bring deadly violence. The discrepancy between men's and women's priorities became even more acute when the financial stakes were higher, and it was a question of purchasing household property, especially furniture, not merely the daily expenses of survival. After four years of physical abuse and excessive control by her lover, an umbrella maker named Étiennette-Marie Monchanin finally threw acid on her lover's face and blinded him.[119] Previously he had beaten her so badly that she went to the hospital, and he sometimes locked her in their room without any food. According to her testimony, what finally spurred Monchanin into action was that he spent forty of the fifty francs she had been saving to purchase a wooden bed frame. "I wanted us to have a little home [*chez nous*], I had persuaded him not to live in furnished rooms anymore," she testified at her trial. For the vast majority of the couples who appeared in the *cour d'assises*, furniture was the most significant property they would ever own—significant not only in its price and size but also for its value as a sign of financial stability.[120] Purchasing a set of furniture on a worker's wages required years of careful saving or months of payments by installment. This achievement required good luck as well as discipline, for if a worker fell ill or lost his or her job, savings could rapidly disappear. The possession and maintenance of furniture and other household goods thus indicated not only a significant degree of financial security over time but more largely the proper function of *son intérieur* where each domestic partner contributed sufficiently to ensure the unit's survival. Furthermore, on a legal level, an apartment furnished by its inhabitants qualified as a private residence, whereas furnished rooms were open at any time to search by the police.

Women usually shouldered the burden of purchasing furniture for the household, like Monchanin, and when portable property appeared as a subject of dispute in cases at the *cour d'assises*, it was usually the women who were said to own the furniture. For instance, the police report on Louise Jamaux noted that most of the furniture in the household she shared with Charles Dabon belonged to her, although she earned only one franc per day selling fish.[121] But why would the partner with the more limited financial resources invest so heavily in the most expensive purchases a couple would ever make? Women's connection to household property may seem like a logical extension of their responsibility for managing household resources, as well as their primary role in performing household chores. Furnishing the household, however, added a further burden to women's already overextended wages. As we have seen, men were not always reliable in giving their partners enough money to purchase necessary supplies, much less expensive items like furniture. In addition, some men did not hesitate to sell or pawn items purchased by their partners in order to obtain money for their personal use. Based on strictly economic calculations, women's responsibility for furnishing the household made no sense. They could only achieve their goal with a reliable man's wages.

On a more abstract level, women's responsibility for furnishing and maintaining the household was a function of their role as the curators of the household's symbolic capital.[122] The working women of fin-de-siècle Paris were active, even aggressive, in their pursuit of symbolically important goods. The sacrifices they made to obtain them and the violence some were willing to deploy in their defense attest to the profound commitment that many women felt toward maintaining and increasing the household's symbolic capital.

This is not to say, however, that working women participated in the domestic ideals espoused by the upper classes at the end of the nineteenth century. Aside from the basic fact of owning furniture, working women rarely articulated any desires regarding the material trappings of their interior. Artists' rendering of crime scenes illustrate the few adornments of their rooms: candlesticks, a clock on the mantle, or a few illustrations cut from popular publications. Clearly, priority was not given to accumulating decorative knickknacks or achieving a harmonious unity of interior decoration, as it was in bourgeois and wealthy families.[123] Accumulation of items beyond the strictly necessary seems to have been directed toward stockpiling useful items—say, a dozen bed sheets, towels, or handkerchiefs. If working women were concerned with the furnishing and appearance of their interior, it was not due to an *embourgeoisement* of their taste but rather a domestic arrangement assigning the management of the household's symbolic capital to women.

Fortunate couples were able to begin cohabitation equipped with furniture given by their families, indicating families' concern for the new couple's status and comfort. Indeed, some couples waited to marry until the necessary household goods could be accumulated. "My mother and I, we already had the money to buy the furniture," stated Isodore Trouvé, expressing his great disappointment that his intended had broken their engagement to be married when their preparations had already progressed so far.[124] Mérantine Gallier, who worked for the department store Printemps, commented that she had intended to give her own set of furniture to her sister Blanche and her lover Badran when the two of them married and to buy new things for herself.[125] On a rather higher social level, Henri Laforest regretted that he could not give his sister a dowry after their father's death, but he did pay to furnish her household when she married. "With my own money," he declared, "I set up their household [*j'ai monté leur ménage*], 40 rue des Martyrs."[126] Eugénie Ballot's mother, whose profession was recorded as day laborer also furnished an apartment for her daughter, even though she had not yet had any marriage propositions.[127] Nonetheless, most couples whose conflicts over property helped bring them to court had to work to purchase furniture after they started living together. The Koenigs, for example, paid 401 francs for a set of furniture and paid it off in installments over ten months.[128] Earlier, the couple had argued when the husband retracted a promise to buy more furniture, because, he said, the wife wouldn't apologize to him for her loose behavior. The accumulation of furniture, like any other allocation of household resources, depended on factors other than the purely financial.

Indeed, the fact of having paid for furniture did not indisputably entail its ownership. When a couple broke up, the division of the household goods was frequently an occasion for conflict, with couples arguing for possession based on their sense of entitlement, whether they had purchased the items in question with their own money or not. That Zoé Barbier took a large portion of the furniture when she left her husband fueled his anger against her.[129] "My resentment was increased by the fact that in leaving she had taken all that I had," the husband explained during his interrogation for shooting her. She, on the other hand, claimed that every object she took was hers because she had purchased it with her own money. "I took away my clothing, and a few pieces of furniture that I had bought with my personal savings, such as a cabinet, a table, four chairs, a mirror, a clock, a mattress, and some linens." Since the wife worked as a cigar maker and the husband worked maintaining roads (as a *cantonnier*), it is unlikely they would have owned much else. In contrast, Jeanne Douët never claimed to have purchased the goods she took from her former lover Augustin Froquières when she left him, but she did feel entitled to them. He formally accused her of theft when she took a mattress, a coverlet, an eiderdown, three sheets, a coat, and several household utensils. "I did not consider the removal of these objects as a theft," she insisted during her interrogation, because Froquières had not kept his promise to support her and her child.[130]

Although Douët willingly returned the goods at the police's request, most former partners were not so compliant. Marie Buire, for instance, said that she stabbed her former lover in the Gare de l'Est because she suspected him of having packed some of her belongings in his trunk when he left her.[131] In a parallel situation, Georges Solhart declared that his wife's removal of some furniture angered him even more than her leaving him. "[Her leaving] was not what exasperated me," he confessed. "I was angry because she had stolen everything in the house." He beat her severely when he caught her in the process of moving goods that, in the skeptical words of the *juge d'instruction*, "right or wrong, she considered her personal property." Solhart believed he was not to blame for his violence against her. "All this happened by her fault. Why did she want to steal from me?" he protested.[132] In a twist on the usual storyline, Octavie Levielle appears to have plundered the household goods after her husband attacked her for her alleged infidelity. He shot her on 14 March and was tried on 4 June. Meanwhile, it seems that she took the furniture and went to live with another man sometime in April. Her husband demanded that she be investigated for adultery, and he protested her being given receipts from pawning her jewelry "because she stole my furniture."[133]

On a strictly legal level, Levielle and other husbands in similar circumstances were perfectly correct in their assertion that all the household goods were under their control, unless other arrangements were specified through a marriage contract or a formal settlement in legal separation or divorce. Nonetheless, these numerous disputes about the ownership of household property illustrate that the question of possession was not simply dependent on the conventions of law any more than the actual purchase of the goods. Rather, household goods were stakes in the complex struggles for power between domestic partners.

Occasionally, women tried to use furniture as a bribe to help rid themselves of partners from whom they feared reprisals. In these cases, however, the women also had been supporting their partners financially, so a gift of furniture would hardly have been an adequate substitute for ongoing support. Elisa Delpic claimed that she offered several times to divide the furniture evenly with her lover Louis Périchon when she left him, although she had purchased all of it. One day, he came home from work to find that Delpic had taken most of their household goods, moved into a new apartment, and dumped his belongings outside. Lacking the money and initiative to find a place of his own, Périchon slept in the rain, hoping his former mistress would have pity on him and take him back. He finally stabbed her after her repeated refusals to give him shelter.[134] In a more dramatic case, Henriette Damotte, a prostitute, had been obliged to lodge and feed her erstwhile lover and pimp, Eugène Dogmatschoff, and tried to break with him by furnishing a room for him alone. Her sister reported, "To try to deliver herself from him, she had given him the furniture which is currently in the room where he lives, rue Saint Julien le Pauvre number 12. This furniture did not have great value, but my sister hoped that Dogmatschoff being housed would go back to work. He continued to extort money from her, to threaten to kill her, and to hit her." Ultimately, he stabbed her when she stopped paying for his meals.[135]

Household goods represented a kind of security because they could be reconverted into cash during difficult times, through sale or pawning. Conflicts arose, however, when one member of the couple—invariably the man—appropriated this resource for his own personal use. When a man sold furniture and drank up the proceeds, not only did he squander a resource that could have been crucial to the couple's survival in a future financial emergency, he also attacked the woman's efforts to save for and purchase the goods. Ernestine Perney listed among his infractions her husband's plundering of their household. "You know already that he hit me continually, that he made me sell my whole household [*tout mon ménage*] to get drunk with the product of the sale," she affirmed in one of her pretrial depositions. Her husband, who had sold everything they owned before abandoning her, blamed it all on her. "If my wife had a valuable set of furniture and it is gone, it is because she sold it herself. I never touched a *sou* of her money," he protested. The furniture had been valued at 2,000 francs, quite a sum for a woman who sold cress from a basket and a man who was a porter at the Halles Centrales.[136] Virginie Jouault had the same complaint against her husband. "Every day, some objects from my household disappeared, which my husband sold, to drink. Recently, he sold my best mattress, worth 45 francs, for 5 francs, my cabinet for 20 *sous*," she lamented.[137] Likewise, Anne Breffeil confirmed that her husband had decimated their belongings. "It is not true, as you tell me he has claimed, that I had sold any of the furniture," she declared to the investigating magistrate. "It was he, on the contrary, who, on his return from the prison ship [where he had been sentenced for taking part in the Commune] sold the whole household in order to drink, and who, when he no longer had a *sou*, began to persecute me."[138]

Although all these stories are about household goods sold for drink, it is not necessary to conclude that these men were all alcoholics with serious drinking problems. At least, the historical record is not sufficiently detailed to make such a diagnosis in hindsight. What is certain, however, is that drinking could function as the opposite of working: rather than make money to support the household, a drinker squandered money for selfish satisfactions. Of course, he could only get away with it as long as his partner was able to support him, willingly or not, or until the reserve of furniture to sell was depleted. Before relegating these delinquent husbands' behavior to the realm of pathology, then, it must be considered that their decision to drink could have been a rejection of their responsibility in the household contract. Drinking was typically done in public, at a café or bar, surrounded by male friends, away from the domestic interior managed by a woman.[139] Socializing in a bar required money that could not be spent to fulfill a man's household obligations. In converting the household's symbolically important goods back into cash to pay for their drinks, men may have raised their status among their male peers in the cafés, but this activity was inherently contrary to the women's project of gaining status for the household through the accumulation and care of furnishings.

Even in a context where some women were able to earn enough money to live on, a woman's culturally determined investment in maintaining her appearance and her household could only be abandoned at great cost to her own status. In the best circumstances, a two-income household could provide more financial stability in hard times. When the system broke down, it did so along gendered fault lines. Men failed to work and contribute sufficient funds, while women failed to maintain the household properly. Men chose to spend money on their own pursuits, while women protested and cajoled to obtain it for the expenses that they felt were more important for the household. It is certain that only a fraction of the couples who argued about money ended up in the *cour d'assises*. Yet there is no reason to doubt that the kind of conflicts that escalated into serious violence in the cases represented here had the same bases as conflicts between couples who did not end up in court. After all, before resorting to violence, these men and women used many different strategies, such as cutting off financial support, choosing to spend money differently, or refusing to perform household chores like cooking and mending. These kinds of conflicts and strategies likely were widespread.

When financial resources are limited, the competition for cash is a zero-sum game. Conflicts over property had their roots in a larger gendered division of labor that oriented men toward seeking status in the exterior, public setting of the cafés, and women toward seeking status through the provisioning of the domestic interior. These conflicts were probably only exacerbated by the expanding consumer economy, as opportunities for outside entertainment competed with readily available goods for household decoration and maintenance. Bars, cafés, and dancehalls proliferated in fin-de-siècle Paris, while new methods of mass production and marketing made ever more clothing, decorative objects, and furniture available to the masses. Even as these new economic areas developed, though, old patterns of the gendered division of labor in the household were reinscribed.

Although women often controlled the purse strings, they usually did not control the superior portion of money flowing into the household budget. The price of abandoning the struggle to maintain appearances was high, resulting in a woman's being condemned as slatternly and lazy. Each woman thus had a personal stake in continuing to fulfill her prescribed roles. Women were therefore doubly burdened by a smaller income and a culturally conditioned greater desire for more expensive goods. Understanding how and why individual conflicts about the management of household resources took place thus illuminates the perpetuation of a larger system of gendered domination. In fin-de-siècle Paris, this was one way by which working women's economic dependence on men was ensured.

CHAPTER 3

Networks of Knowledge

The cases of violence tried in the *cour d'assises* reveal ruptures between domestic partners, but they also reveal networks of alliance and assistance among the friends, neighbors, and family members surrounding the couple, sometimes even extending through time and space into the rural regions of the couple's origins. Disputes between couples were common knowledge for their surrounding community, and many victims of violence purposefully spread awareness of their plight among friends and family to gain their support. Testimony in the trial dossiers illuminates the networks connecting people in urban communities, revealing who knew what about whom and how they assessed each other's behavior. While kinship, region of origin, or work-related ties were salient in certain cases, the connections that mattered most in virtually all *cour d'assises* cases were those created by daily interactions between couples and their neighbors, who made it their business to know the intimate details of each other's lives. Such knowledge may have been all but unavoidable in the crowded housing where the working poor were obliged to live, but they nonetheless recognized it as a resource, strategically garnering and deploying it for their own purposes.[1]

The knowledge that an individual's neighbors had about his character and behavior—the facts of his daily life—was of crucial importance, for it was the stuff from which his reputation was made. A good reputation was invaluable, making it easier to gather allies in a crisis or deflect suspicion when malicious gossip threatened. It was what entitled a person to his neighbors' assistance. A woman who fled her partner might need food, money, or shelter; her attacker would need allies to confirm the legitimacy of his deed. Both would draw on the people they knew to attest to the merits of their position. These useful connections with other people are what Pierre Bourdieu has termed social capital. Other people's memories were the bank where the individual's social capital was stored. It could be put into circulation as gossip and hearsay, and it could be "cashed in" when a domestic partnership was in crisis—and a violent attack certainly constituted a crisis.

Thus, intimate violence activated the complex social web of every urban quarter. These networks of knowledge, ultimately, were what defined local urban communities. David Garrioch has used a similar definition for urban communities in his work on eighteenth-century Paris, arguing that communities are constituted through the self-regulation of members' behavior.[2] In the same vein, Roger Gould has argued that neighborhood ties became more important in the middle of the nineteenth century, after the rebuilding of central Paris forced so many working people to live at a distance from their places of employment.[3] Parisian social life was especially dynamic in this era, as the city grew dramatically in the second half of the century, thanks to the influx of immigrants from other regions of France and abroad. According to contemporary social analysts, urban population growth was connected to the decay of traditional rural work and family organization, higher crime rates, and the fragmentation of society.[4] Although Joëlle Guillais has argued that antagonists in crimes of passion were characterized by "rootlessness" and "isolation,"[5] this study finds that crimes of intimate violence were more characteristic of settled migrants and Parisians. Far from being isolated, anomic individuals, participants in assize court trials were active members of close-knit urban communities.

Links to the *Pays*

The geographic origins of the couples who ended up in the *cour d'assises* reflect the ongoing trends of migration to the city. The majority of defendants were not native to Paris—only about thirty were born in the city. Besides a few representatives of foreign countries, notably Belgium and Prussia, the accused came from regions throughout France, with a certain concentration in the regions of the Massif Central and the German border areas. This regional distribution is entirely typical of patterns of migration to Paris at the end of the nineteenth century, which saw an important influx of people from these regions, especially after the loss of Alsace-Lorraine.[6] While it is not always possible to determine precisely how long a given couple had lived in Paris before an act of violence brought them to the assize court, hardly any had lived in the city for less than a year. Even if they were not native-born Parisians, it is apparent that they had lived there long enough to establish ties with their neighbors, if not find a new domestic partner. Furthermore, married couples who appeared in the *cour d'assises* on average had been together more than a decade, while unmarried partners had usually been together for about three years. All this evidence suggests that intimate violence was not a crime of vagrant loners, even if many of the people involved were migrants.

The basic fact of leaving the *pays* (one's native region in the countryside) to come to Paris did not necessarily make a migrant socially disconnected. Historian Leslie Page Moch has argued cogently that migrants to the burgeoning cities of fin-de-siècle France experienced their move as continuity rather than rupture.[7] Although the trial dossiers rarely address the question of an individual's motives in coming to Paris, or what their expectations were of city life, they do suggest that connections to an immigrant's region of origin remained significant for a portion of the people in this study. About thirty cases contain information from the hometown of the accused, a sufficient number to illustrate important continuing ties. In some cases, witnesses appeared who had known the accused in the countryside and as well as the city. Information from the *pays* could be either solicited directly by the police or investigating magistrate or presented spontaneously to the authorities by people who had heard about the case through the press or personal lines of communication.

Witnesses from the *pays*, as well as the jurists who sought their input, believed that the conduct of the accused and the victim even years before a crime took place was relevant in assessing the merits of the case. "What I need to know about," wrote the *juge d'instruction* Ragon to the public prosecutor in the Meuse, "is the time at which the accused left the *pays*—what his records were—the memory that he left—his character, his relationships, his habits, and the trace of any fact that would be of a kind to explain the crime of which he is accused."[8] The police captain of Le Creusot (Saône et Loire) responded to a similar request for information on Jean-Jacques Guignot in the following succinct terms: "deplorable record; integrity sometimes put in doubt; dissolute morals, which he flaunted even being married; faculties imbalanced, very intelligent, but without heart, low, servile, a liar, sometimes violent, always cowardly."[9] The mayor of Feuquières (Oise) sent a letter describing Jeanne Vasseur, who was a victim of an attempted murder-suicide. He wrote that she was a registered prostitute, who "comported herself in a truly regrettable manner according to different reports."[10] Her lover Eugène Henry was described by the commissaire de police of Beauvais (Oise) as having irreproachable behavior during the time when Henry courted his lover at the *maison de tolérance* in that city. The investigating magistrate also received three unsolicited letters from Henry's former employers, plus one letter from his former schoolteacher. The foundations of the accused's reputation were laid in the *pays* and remained relevant in Paris.

It was fairly rare for the officials writing reports from the *pays* to state exactly whom they consulted to construct their reports. In small towns, it seems likely that the officials could have known the objects of their investigation personally. Two gendarmes from Nogent-le-Roi (Eure-et-Loire) specified that they had consulted the "principal notables" of the town to discover Eugène Thauvin's background.[11] The Commissariat de Dieppe must have consulted the lower-class milieu of Edouard Genuyt de Beaulieu's mistress Melina Thévenot to discover the details of their affair and the gifts he gave her, since the author of the report noted that "the *grand monde* Monsieur de Beaulieu frequented was in large part ignorant of his life of debauchery." The *grand monde* would probably not have been impressed by the price of the bouquets he regularly brought his mistress—a detail that appears to have been supplied by two close female friends of Mélina Thévenot.[12]

Reports solicited from local notables were not the only source of information sent from the *pays*. For instance, the police commissioner in the town of Gap wrote the *juge d'instruction* Pauffin to say that the accused "left the worst memories at Gap," where he was known for squandering money. However, this letter was countered by an apparently spontaneous and unsolicited statement, signed by members of the *conseil général* (departmental council) and by the mayor and other government officials of St. Firman, asking the judges and jury for indulgence in light of Bernou's past good behavior. They wrote that they "certif[ied], to render homage to the truth, that the man named Bernou Jean-Baptiste, health officer... passed a large part of his life at St. Firman, where he rendered true services. He belongs to an honorable family that enjoys the greatest consideration and public esteem and that the misfortune of which he is a victim has plunged into despair. His easy character, his goodwill conquered for him the esteem of his compatriots."[13]

Being himself a member of the town's educated elite, the level of the local luminaries who wrote on Bernou's behalf was exceptional, but such a show of support was not unique. Jean-Baptiste Santin, an intermittent employee at an omnibus manufacturing company, was supported by a letter signed by sixty-eight residents of his hometown, St. Quentin, plus the mayor. "Le sieur Jean-Baptiste Santin has never ceased to enjoy general esteem," the letter declared, in a dignified tone. "They [the undersigned] think that it was following a conjunction of circumstances stronger than his will that this unlucky man, whose character was as gentle as anyone's, is called today to appear before the Cour d'assises de la Seine... They dare to hope that he will touch the heart of *messieurs* the jurors."[14] The mayor and residents of Guérigny (Nièvre) also wrote a letter when one of their own was on trial for murder in Paris, but this time they wrote in support of the victim, not the accused. Eighty-three people signed the following statement: "The undersigned have the honor of certifying that the Barthélemy family, residing in Guérigny for more than thirty years is very honorable and very sociable in the *pays*; and that la fille Annette Barthélemy married to François Clément comported herself well during the entire time of her stay in this town."[15] Since Clément claimed he murdered his wife because he suspected her of infidelity, her behavior was as much at issue as his at the trial.[16] Remarkably, in what may have been an imitation of letters like these sent from residents of the old *pays*, a group of seven men from a quarter of Paris where the accused Henri Schmittgall used to live sent a letter to the *Procureur de la République*, stating that Schmittgall "had never been the object of any blame, as much from the point of view of integrity as the point of view of morality."[17] Such letters indicate durable connections with places of origin, ties strong enough to withstand temporal and physical distance.

A few people actually traveled to Paris to attend a trial, apparently at their own expense. Individual witnesses who had known the accused in the *pays* presented themselves to testify in person. When François Bouin testified in the case of Adèle Pautard, he blamed her husband for the circumstances that drove her to crime, basing his judgment on a long association with the couple. "Pautard had poor conduct for a long time not only in Paris but also in Bry-Sur-Marne. He dissipated all that his wife brought him [when they married], which is to say around 3,500 francs. Since the month of January... he left her in misery. We took her in and fed her, and if we hadn't come to her aid, she certainly would have killed herself."[18] Apparently he was motivated to testify by a strong personal commitment to the victim's welfare. Not so for la femme Lacaille, who came to Paris from the Meuse to testify at the trial of Célestine Béal. "I am from Vaucouleurs, the *pays* of the accused," she stated. "In the country, she was called 'the madwoman' because she had a deranged brain. She has an aunt who has been in a madhouse for a long time." Indeed, Béal's disorderly behavior in the courtroom was that of a woman who was, if not mad, at least disdainful of ordinary social decorum.[19]

Yet the flow of information went both ways, and if the *pays* was a source of information for the investigation in Paris, what happened in Paris could also have consequences in the *pays*, especially if the family of the accused still lived in his or her hometown. When Georges Koenig wrote his brother Louis in Besançon a breezy letter about how they could tour the city and amuse themselves if Louis came to see his trial, his brother answered with the following invective: "Unhappy man! You thus did not think of your parents nor of your poor little sisters? You therefore do not fear the shame that has spread over the whole family. Everyone knows this frightful story here, and we no longer dare to lift our eyes in the street... Don't you see, poor mother is sick, father is in despair, and it's worse than a burial at our place... But upon your release from prison, do not return to Besançon for at least a year. It is necessary to allow this painful memory to pass in the mind of the population." In a gesture of support, however, he sent his brother ten francs for tobacco along with the letter.[20] Marie Traber had similar concerns when she confronted her lover after he attacked her. Insisting that she would not forgive him, she stated, "No, I do not pardon you, no. [Not] only did you want to kill me, and it is extraordinary that I did not succumb to my wounds, but you lost my position and my future by the scandal that has resulted from it. My father, who is in Alsace, knew of this affair and fell sick following this revelation."[21] She may have survived the attack, but she felt that she could not live it down. Agathe Georges was also worried about the effect that her plans to commit a murder-suicide might have had on her family in Frouard (Meurthe et Moselle). She wrote to her brother Pierre, sending him her linens and her favorite teacup, and explaining the crime she was about to commit. She admonished him, "May our grandfather not learn of it, since this blow could kill him, too... I recommend silence for our grandfather as for everyone in the *pays*."²² Much as they may have wished it, these people could not extricate themselves from the web of connections tying them to their regions of origin. The ties persisted, and how they comported themselves continued to matter to the people they had left behind.

Connections to the *pays* could also function as safety lines for people in difficult situations. Most often, returning to the *pays* was an escape route for women wishing to end an unsatisfactory or dangerous relationship. Marie Thiéron escaped from her lover Charles Balade twice and returned to Chatel-Chéry (Ardennes) to live with her parents, but he followed her there and frightened her into returning with him to Paris.²³ On the multiple occasions when she left her husband, Eulalie Jean sought refuge with her father in Blanc (Indre).²⁴ In an inversion of the usual storyline where women were the ones who escaped a bad partner by returning to the *pays*, Berthe Paisant only consented that her lover Charles Joulain be released from jail because he promised to return home to Gallius-la-Queue (Seine et Loire). His promised departure turned out to be only a ruse, however, and he stalked and attacked her in Paris after his release. Interestingly enough, the two lovers had known each other when they were younger and lived in the same region; they renewed their relationship after meeting by chance in the city.

All in all, even after an extended stay in Paris, the *pays* that immigrants left behind continued to offer support in difficult situations and to be a point of reference from which their reputations were assessed. Investigators looked to the past to shed light on the deeds of the accused, while those deeds also had an impact on the network of kin and acquaintances remaining in their hometowns. The lines of communication and assistance that existed among many immigrants and their regions of origin remained strong.

Family Ties

Family members were often important links in this network. They played active roles in over a quarter of the cases in this study, including in many situations where the family still resided in the *pays*. Parents, sisters, brothers, and cousins often had knowledge of a couple's relationship, intervened to help end conflicts, gave material aid to a household, and provided refuge for victims of violence. However, no witnesses explained this intervention by saying that it was obligatory to help a family member nor did people always side with the person to whom they were related. They did not habitually advise couples to stay together to preserve the family's integrity or reputation, and sometimes they even turned down pleas for help. Though it was usually true that relatives assisted each other, family relationships did not create binding obligations. Instead, assistance was contingent on the circumstances of the case.

Family members were among the first people women turned to when their partners became abusive, and families' knowledge of troubled relationships was often quite thorough. La femme Morand knew of her son-in-law's threats toward her daughter: "He never went to bed without a knife under his pillow. Often Virginie would say to me in the evening, 'Maybe it will be tonight.' "[25] Henriette Damotte had confided to her two sisters about her fear of her lover: "Many times my sister told me that Dogmatschoff threatened her with death because she didn't want to give him money anymore. Dogmatschoff would say to her, 'The day that you won't give me any more money, I'll kill you.' My sister said it to me again the very day she was killed."[26]

These people gained knowledge of their relatives' relationships from face-to-face contact in the city, whereas communication among family members living at a distance naturally required greater effort. Visits to the *pays*, letters, and word-of-mouth through acquaintances circulating between the *pays* and the city all facilitated communication, but the transmission of information was not necessarily transparent. In a *cour d'assises* case, it was apparently a standard procedure for the investigating magistrate to search out the parents of the accused and the victim, and very occasionally this research turned up a parental relationship that had gone sour. The judicial investigation could reveal details of a son or daughter's life of which the parents had remained ignorant—deceptions that appear to have been facilitated by the geographical distance between them. Sometimes one parent knew more than the other, as was the case with Marie Thiérion, whose mother knew she had a lover in Paris but whose father only knew that she was supposed to be working as a seamstress. (She was really a waitress in a café.)[27] Eugénie Ballot's mother also believed her daughter was working as a seamstress, but she was actually registered as a prostitute and living with a lover.[28] Ballot's mother said she visited her often, so the daughter must have purposefully kept her activities secret—after all, no mother would rejoice that her daughter had been registered with the morals police. Likewise, in an effort to keep the bad news of her arrest from reaching them in the *pays* (Meurthe et Moselle), Elisabeth Prévost told the *juge d'instruction* that she had never known her parents. It did not take him long to locate her father, however, who said he had not heard from his daughter in two years.[29]

Some women purposefully hid information about abusive relationships from their family even when they were in touch regularly. Marie Cantel knew why her sister would not tell her about her troubles with her husband: "Since her marriage, I often saw my sister, and I certainly noticed that she wasn't happy. She did not complain to me about her husband because she knew I had done everything to keep her from marrying Boudet."[30] Although her sister lied about her husband's violence, Marie Vinot was suspicious of her bruises. "I saw her once with a bruise on her face. She told me that it was in play that Catelier had done it to her, pushing her on the bed. Another time, she had a bruise on her leg; she told me that she had fallen from a tramway, but I always suspected that she had been beaten by Catelier, whom she never complained about."[31] Other witnesses described the sister as an unusually passive person, who had "an extreme gentleness of character, she was a true child without will." Her personality, together with the fear of reprisal from her lover, seems to have accounted for her silence. Amable Bartholémy, who lived in Guérigny (Nièvre), was distressed to learn about the violence of his daughter's marriage: "My daughter never complained to me about her husband; I only knew after her death, from the concierge of the house where she lived in Paris, and by the neighbors, that she was very unhappy. These same neighbors used to tell her, 'So tell your father that your husband makes you suffer.' She told them, 'I beg you, don't say anything to my father, since if my husband knew about it, he would make me even more unhappy.'"[32] She was frightened of his reprisals if she made her plight more widely known—her father knew his father and had helped arrange the marriage. Perhaps she believed that revealing the dismal state of her marriage would disrupt a long-standing connection between the families.

While these cases illustrate disjunctures in the relationship between parents and their adult children, it was more common for parents and other family members who appeared in *cour d'assises* trials to be knowledgeable, active participants in domestic conflicts. Whereas families in about a dozen cases either knew nothing of a bad relationship or refused to help, around fifty families did know about and respond to troubled relationships. Their response could be ambiguous, though. On the one hand, frequent and illegitimate violence or neglect was not acceptable, but on the other hand, the family might not be willing or able to help the disadvantaged partner put a decisive end to a bad relationship. A family member's decision about when and how to intervene depended on the individual circumstances of the couple and their own preconceived notions of what was acceptable in a domestic partnership. There were no hard and fast rules about a family member's duty to a relative in trouble. Célestine Fontaine's behavior demonstrated this ambiguity. Although she deplored the way her son-in-law, Ignace Trudersheim, treated her daughter, she always sent her daughter back to him. As her son explained it, "My sister was barely married when she had to suffer brutalities from Trudersheim. He deprived her of food and let her go without everything. Most of the time she came to eat at the house. It happened several times that he kicked her out; my mother always exhorted her to return to the conjugal abode."[33] In fact, Trudersheim physically attacked his mother-in-law for trying to force him to allow her daughter to return to their apartment. At this moment, one of his wife's brothers shot him—an extreme form of assistance, to be sure—but the brother was acquitted of murder.

It was actually quite rare for family members to function as intermediaries to help a couple stay together. There is only one case where a witness articulated the idea that a couple should stay together, come what may. The wife's cousin, Jules Magnus Timmerman, took credit for persuading her not to leave the violent man to whom she had been married for almost twenty years. He testified to the investigating magistrate:

> La femme Kemps had often confided to me about the violence that she suffered on her husband's part. Once when she lived at Passy, she had told me that one day when he was drunk, he had pursued her with a knife in his hand and that she was only able to escape him thanks to the intervention of the neighbors. This woman was unhappy to the point that she told me about her plans to leave her husband. I was the one who dissuaded her from it by telling her that the mission of the married woman was to remain at her duty, that should the need arise, pushed to the limit, she could find a refuge with us but that it was not necessary to have recourse to this means, except in the last extremity. I used to see Kemps very often, and I often reproached him for his conduct. He admitted his wrongs.[34]

A clear explanation for this view of a wife's "duty" is not readily apparent from the evidence in the trial dossier. Although the cousin was sixty-one years old, and the wife was in her fifties, there were many other cases involving people of similarly senior ages who did not share such views. On a socioeconomic level, they seem to have been firmly within the ranks of average working people.[35] Such strong views on the indissolubility of marriage were atypical of their milieu.

Even in cases where children were involved, witnesses asserted that unhappy unions could be dissolved. While François Lerondeau said he would not leave his wife because of their little girl and the consequences a separation might have for the family reputation, others in his family disagreed with his choice. "To any argument that everyone made in his interests," explained his cousin, "he responded, 'And the little one?' I tried to show him that it would not be a dishonor for his family nor for the child if he separated without a trial from a wife as mean as his, but he feared that this separation would harm his daughter's future. He always refused it."[36] On the other hand, Eulalie Jean's father wrote to her urging a separation from her husband. "Think of your little one," he wrote. "I do not counsel you at all to live with him."[37] Likewise, Joseph Maxant's neighbor advised him to leave his unfaithful wife. "Think of your children and leave her rather than making a scandal," she said. But he replied "that he could not leave her, that nobody knew her like he did, that nobody knew what she was capable of."[38] Here, the choice seems to have been between the potential violence of the husband, if he stayed and confronted his wife's misconduct, and the potential violence of the wife, if he angered her by leaving. Neither outcome appeared propitious for the children. Thus, considering the divergent views on the subject, the presence of children was a factor weighed seriously in deciding whether or not to preserve a domestic partnership. The results of the choice, however, were debatable.

It was not even certain whose side a family member would take in a dispute. The assistance of parents and relatives was contingent on their own determination of whose behavior was most worthy of defense in a domestic dispute. This meant that they did not always take the side of their own kin, nor of the victim of the crime. It was her mother-in-law, for example, who wrote a letter to Eugénie Duchène advising her to get a divorce.[39] Catherine Fenet was also ready to believe her son was the guilty party in a bad relationship. She immediately suspected him of murder when she found her daughter-in-law's corpse, and she contacted the police. "He drinks and is very violent," she stated. "I forbade him my door a long time ago. I did not attend his marriage. On the contrary, I esteemed the deceased woman. My first husband had warned her, before her marriage, that she would be unhappy with his son; but she did not take this advice into account. She used to come to see me from time to time. She told me her troubles, saying that her husband did not give her money and got drunk. On many occasions, I gave her gifts of money and linens."[40] In the case of Jean-Marie Marie, a husband was able to make his in-laws believe the worst of their daughter. He wrote several letters to his wife's father in the *pays* (Seine et Oise) and succeeded in convincing him that his daughter was an unfaithful wife and an irresponsible mother. The wife, Julie Marie, consequently did not find a warm welcome when she sought refuge with her parents. Her father confirmed that he believed her husband's story, blaming her for neglecting their daughter and transmitting a venereal disease to her husband. "In sum," the father testified, "my daughter behaved badly; on the contrary, I have a good opinion of my son-in-law."[41] Jean-Louis Demaison claimed he was displeased with the behavior of his son-in-law and his daughter, who could not seem to extricate herself from an extramarital affair:

> Although I had the right to be unhappy with my son-in-law, who had forgotten what he owed his wife and child, I expressed to my daughter no less the chagrin that her conduct caused me. She explained that, abandoned by her husband and without resources, she had been forced to use the skills she had in linens to make herself a laundress, and that having met Joulain, finding herself without support and without guide, she had the weakness to surrender to him. I have, since this time, received my daughter several times, and at each of her visits, I asked her if she had completely broken with Joulain. She always answered me that she was unable to do so; he came back to her with so much more determination that she had sent him away with the order never to appear at her house.[42]

The implication here was that, lacking her husband's direction, the wife was easy prey for a man who wanted to seduce her. The father's authority, apparently, was not strong enough to bring her back to the straight and narrow either, even though he registered his disapproval clearly.

This pattern—that parents and relations chose the side of whomever they perceived to be the offended party, whether male or female, blood relative or not—appears to have held true among the upper classes as well. In two cases involving upper-class families, the husbands' relatives condemned the men's behavior and praised their unfortunate wives. Alexandre Langlois expressed his discomfort at having to condemn his son's conduct, but he considered it his duty to tell the truth. He testified for the *juge d'instruction*:

> My situation in these horrible circumstances is very difficult and very painful. It is impossible for me to say anything bad about my son, and I can't say anything good about him. The dear departed was the most charming, the most honest, the most pure and adorable of women. I loved her with all my heart and as if she had been my daughter. This story is atrocious... It is my duty as an honest man to say here that my poor daughter-in-law was not at all a spendthrift and that she was on the contrary perfectly orderly. In the very moments when the pecuniary situation of

my son seemed to be the best, he barely gave his wife enough to clothe herself with. He made scenes with her over a dress, a hat. It is from my son's hands that the money flowed, God knows how..... [sic] Why would I hide it, since you already know it? It was in the bars with girls that Georges spent the money he measured out so rigorously to his wife.[43]

He went on to describe his son's mistresses and his great skill with firearms, suggesting that the son had aimed to kill his wife, but had only feigned an attempt at suicide. "Why would I tell you more about my son? But about my daughter-in-law, this poor child, for whom I weep with all my tears, I can speak and I will speak without hesitation. She had all the honest seductions of a woman. Loving and good, as pure as she was pretty, she would have been adored, if my son had ever been able to adore another person besides himself."

Emilie Genuyt de Beaulieu also won the unqualified approbation of her husband's family. A former opera singer who married a member of the aristocracy, she would be acquitted—and indeed, not even arrested—for shooting her unfaithful husband in the back. All the witnesses agreed, however, that she had acted in desperation, after suffering serious injustices. Edouard Genuyt de Beaulieu's great-uncle described the marriage as follows:

> A dozen years ago he married Mademoiselle Emélie [sic] Muller, his current wife, who was the daughter of a mechanic from Nancy and who had neither his rank, nor his condition, nor his fortune. His maternal family, who alone knew of his plans for marriage, was opposed to its celebration, but he ended up obtaining, I do not know by what means, the consent of his father, with whom I do not have frequent contact. After his marriage, he introduced his wife whom we recognized as being very well brought up, a very good musician, and whose excellent character we noticed; consequently, we had excellent relations with this young household.[44]

The couple got along well, he said, until the middle of the previous summer, when the wife started having nervous crises and the couple began to quarrel. "He attributed this bad humor of his wife to a nervous illness, but I think it was on the contrary the indignation of the wife manifesting itself since she was not unaware at this time of the relations her husband maintained with a demoiselle Mélina who lived in Dieppe."[45] A man who described himself as a "relative to the eighth degree of Monsieur de Beaulieu" also reproached Genuyt for his reckless spending and his plans to leave his wife for his mistress. He praised the wife, however, and took her in after she committed the crime. Perhaps these wealthy family members only differed from their working-class counterparts in the eloquence of their speech, but it is surprising to find families so willing to condemn their blood relations at a social level where family solidarity, for financial reasons at the least, would seem to be more highly valued. It is possible that they were trying to paint their erring scion as the black sheep of the family in order to make themselves look better for coming to the aid of his embattled wife. Still, revealing their own failures to restore harmony to the marriage, as well as the ungentlemanly behavior of the husband, was painful to them. They could have chosen instead to portray the wife as a hysteric or a fortune hunter had they wanted to try to exculpate the husband. Instead, these people judged the situation based on their knowledge of the couple's behavior, not on blind loyalty to their kin. Commitment to certain ideas about proper behavior for men and women could outweigh commitment to family ties.

More often though, in cases where family members were fully informed about the bad conditions of a relationship, notions of good behavior coincided with family ties, and family members acted decisively to assist their relatives. From advising a man or woman to leave, to facilitating his or her departure, to planning elaborate schemes for revenge, families could be instrumental in resolving disputes. When Joséphine Rispal confided to her mother that she had a presentiment of death at the hands of her lover, her mother simply advised her to find another place to live.[46] After telling the long story of her daughter's unhappy marriage, Eloïse Péronne testified that she advised her daughter and son-in-law to get a divorce, a suggestion the son-in-law met with hostility.[47] In a letter to his daughter Marie Biver, her father offered a detailed strategy for revenge against her unfaithful husband, as well as a way out of the relationship: "If he continues to make you unhappy try to take as much money as possible and make the largest debt possible with your suppliers and then you only have to come back to my place returning with your two children. There is still bread for you and your children and for him vitriol."[48] Adeline Iltis helped her sister find a job after convincing her to leave her lover, Emile Perrin, who was not violent until she left. "I knew about my sister's relations with Monsieur Perrin," she testified. "He was a very sweet, gentle man, and very hard working. Unfortunately, he only earned 100 francs per month; with that he could not support a woman. Consequently, I tried to make my sister understand reason. She finally listened to me and came to live with me for three months."[49] After much persuasion, the widow Denizet took her father's advice and left her lover. Her father explained, "She was unhappy with him, but she didn't dare leave him because he threatened to kill her. He used to say that if she left, he would buy a revolver for fourteen francs and he would do her in... He mistreated her sometimes; he sometimes slapped her. I saw my daughter come to my place with black eyes. I counseled her to leave him; she answered, 'But he'll kill me.'"[50] Unfortunately, about a week after she moved in with her father, her ex-lover did just that. Marie Neu's father also tried to keep his daughter away from a dangerous man: "I did everything I could to prevent Marie from seeing [Gaspard Kieffer] whom I considered to be a leader of the pack, a thief who never worked, but I couldn't keep her from going with him. I knew later that it was out of fear that she did not want to leave him."[51]

Although these fathers did not succeed in protecting their daughters, one of the primary forms of assistance family members could give was refuge from a dangerous partner, as they did in about twenty cases. Both the legitimate wife and later the mistress of Georges Masset escaped his mistreatment and returned to live with their parents.[52] Marie Sanglé stayed with her mother on three occasions when her husband kicked her and her child out of their apartment.[53] Jeanne Vigineix-Roche went with her two children to stay with her brother after her husband threatened to kill her.[54] When Zoé Barbier left her husband, she went to live with her adult daughter and son-in-law.[55]

In addition to shelter, in about one dozen cases family members also provided services and material goods to women in crisis. After her husband abandoned her for another woman, Adèle Pautard wrote desperate letters asking her mother and brother to help pay her rent, but she did not wait long enough for a response before taking revenge against her husband's lover with a glass of sulfuric acid. Another brother invited her to stay with him in Belgium following the crime.[56] Several women were given food in emergencies. Marie Sanglé once went to see her mother-in-law at midnight to get two francs to feed herself and her child when her husband did not return home with his pay.[57] Célestine Trudersheim's mother regularly fed her, as her husband did not give her enough money to buy food.[58]

Sometimes family members were instrumental in averting a fatal attack. Marguerite Eizenkreimer's two oldest sons saved her from a brutal beating by her lover of twenty-two years.[59] But it was not only men who intervened in violent situations. Eugénie Duchène often took refuge with her sister when her husband became violent, and she was at her sister's apartment when he shot at her. Her husband confirmed that she frequently left their apartment to escape him, revealing the network of people she relied upon for help: "My wife had the habit, when the least discussion arose, of leaving the conjugal abode and taking refuge either at [a neighbor's] place or with other friends, or also with her sister." The sister, Marianne Naour, had tried to protect her. "He never struck her in front of me because I always interposed myself between them, but, many times, he shoved her."[60] When he shot his wife, Marianne Naour knocked him down, and he pointed his gun at her before he ran away.

Neighborly Knowledge

If contact with family members was potentially optional, contact with neighbors was unavoidable, and neighbors performed much the same functions for each other in domestic disputes as family members did. Indeed, urban structures made physical isolation out of the question for working people. Crammed into crowded tenements, sharing common stairways, courtyards, faucets, and outhouses, neighbors could hardly avoid gaining intimate knowledge of each other's existence. Walls were often so thin that they functioned not as barriers between households but as permeable membranes allowing for the constant transmission of auditory information about the lives on the other side. Actions were visible through open windows and doors. Neighbors could become so accustomed to coming and going in each others' apartments that they dispensed with the minimal formality of knocking on a door. In short, the structures inhabited by the working poor, and the patterns of sociability facilitated by those structures, confounded the distinction between public and private space, and public and private lives.

Floor plans or artists' renderings of the apartments of the people involved in court cases occasionally appeared in trial dossiers. The purpose of these drawings was to illustrate the course of an attack or the placement of a body, but they also provide information about the size and contents of the dwellings. Many of the working poor lived in one-room apartments, perhaps with one window and just enough space for a bed, a table and chairs, a stove for cooking and heating, and a chest or trunk for storage. Nicer apartments would have two or three rooms and, of course, more furniture. Without the buffer afforded by the thick walls and closed doors of finer dwellings, the kind of separation between public and private so essential to a bourgeois way of life was impossible for the lower classes. It was all but inevitable that neighbors would hear or see evidence of interpersonal violence, enabling them to interpret what was happening and decide whether or not to intervene.

In court, witnesses took pains to describe the precision with which they could hear what happened in a neighboring apartment, doubtless to reinforce their credibility. Louis Delattre heard the prelude to a crime next door: "I hear what happens in the lodging next to mine when one speaks loudly there... A short time before, I heard [Millim] come home from work. He said to his wife, 'Serve us dinner.' From the way he spoke, I told myself, 'He is completely drunk.' There were a few words of quarrel, and then I heard chairs moving. Then, nothing more. I thought they were eating, but almost immediately the woman cried out like she had the habit of doing. He used to hit her daily." Then Millim came to confess to his neighbor he had just stabbed his wife with a table knife.[61] An attacker like Millim must have been aware that the sound of his actions would carry to neighboring apartments, but few tried to dissimulate.

Neighbors' knowledge of a couple's habits could be decisive in establishing the conditions of a crime, as the case of the Kemps couple illustrates. Elisabeth Ganet could describe the frequent beatings her neighbor la femme Kemps received, asserting, "I have said that my apartment was situated below that of the Kemps. The floor that separates us, made out of pine boards, is thin to the point that I can hear at my place the least noise produced at the Kemps'."[62] Another woman who lived below the Kemps, Evélina Guérin, also heard what went on in their apartment. "The Kemps couple lodged above us, on the fifth floor. The husband frequently brutalized his wife, and I was almost used to hearing the discussions that arose above me and the blows that ordinarily followed them." The Kemps' neighbors were furthermore well informed about the health of la femme Kemps, and two of them testified that they had often seen her vomit, due to her "retour de l'âge," which is to say menopause. After he murdered his wife, Kemps arranged the body neatly in bed, left the apartment for the day, and locked the door behind him. On his return, he tried to persuade his neighbors—and the police—that his wife had been ill that day and he had merely returned home to find her dead. The neat position of the body in bed and the testimony of the neighbors who had heard a fight the night before gave the lie to his story. In addition, the investigating magistrate found it impossible to believe that a man would leave his wife at home alone without notifying any of the neighbors that she was sick. In the official indictment he wrote, "This story was completely inadmissible. How can it be believed that knowing his wife was ill he would abandon her without warning the neighbors nor the concierge and would even shut her in the room, leaving her deprived of any help?" Even an outsider, the *juge d'instruction*, expected that a man would tap into the neighborly network of knowledge and assistance to help his wife if she were truly sick.

Witnesses emphasized knowledge of bodily functions—presumably the activities that should be most shielded from public view—for if they knew about intimate physical processes, then their knowledge of different aspects of a couple's relationship must also be credible. Two male neighbors of Alphonse Catelier and his mistress testified that he kept her locked in the apartment so strictly that "she was reduced to doing her business [*faire ses ordures*] in her room."[63] In another case, Madame Orset, the proprietor of the apartment building where she and the De Moor couple lived, explained that she could hear everything that went on in the De Moors' apartment above her: "Since the end of December, my bed is just below your wife's," she said to the accused husband. "I hear the tiniest movements. The house is made of cardboard; we can hear each other urinate from one room to the next."[64]

Jean-Jacques De Moor claimed that he killed his wife because she had a lover. He said that he himself had secretly returned from Belgium and had been living with her for weeks before the crime, and that the two of them had fought all night before he finally cut her throat. The neighbors disproved all of these claims and played a particularly important role in establishing the facts of the case. "Everything is so thin that, although we can't see each other, we really are in each other's rooms," testified the woman who lived directly above the De Moors. In actuality, Catherine De Moor had seen her husband for the first time in months on 5 April 1891, just five days before the crime. She told her sister and a neighbor about the effect it had on her. "My sister was extremely disturbed by seeing her husband on Sunday," her sister explained. "The same day she showed me her chemise, saying, 'Hey, look, I was so upset seeing him again that my period [*affaires*] came back early.'" Françoise Fischer, who lived in the room next door to the De Moors, also knew of this situation. She observed that on Monday, 6 April, Catherine stayed in bed all day because she had her menstrual period. "On Tuesday the seventh, she went to work; Wednesday morning, 8 April, she told me that she had seen her husband on Sunday, that this had turned her blood and made her *affaires* come too early." On Wednesday evening, Madame De Moor did not come to say good evening, "as was her habit," so Madame Fischer visited her the next day and learned that she had a sore throat.

The two women clearly had a close friendship, and the familiarity that Madame Fischer had with her friend's habits, as well as her household, was important to the case. "Many times, Madame De Moor borrowed household utensils from me," she stated. "I was on good terms with her. I used to go to her room, and I knew perfectly everything that she possessed. I saw the knife with which she was butchered, and I can affirm in the most positive and certain manner that this knife did not belong to the victim." The implicit argument here was that if the knife had not been used in the household, then De Moor had bought it himself for the express purpose of killing his wife with it, establishing premeditation, which he denied. The victim's sister Madame Vendenéede also confirmed that the knife was new. "I am sure, absolutely sure, that the knife that served to kill my sister did not belong to her. I knew her whole household perfectly well, all her utensils, and I say that the knife did not belong to her."

The picture of neighborly relations that emerges from a case like De Moor's is of a closely knit network, mostly of women, who were intimately aware of each other's daily lives. Similar relationships clearly existed in many other cases. Flore Vanier, for instance, had already visited her neighbor Anaïs Sauvan twice before 9:30 in the morning on the day when her estranged lover attacked her— once to give Sauvan a lemon she had asked Vanier to purchase and once to loan her a pot lid.[65] The neighbors of Marie Gy wanted to prove to investigators that she had not abandoned her children without resources in Nancy (surely a comparable urban setting) when she traveled to Paris in search of her unfaithful husband. Her neighbor Rose Riplinger could give a complete inventory of the household supplies: "She did not leave her children in destitution. They were supplied for several days with sugar and coffee, and she had left them at least 10 *livres* of bread, a kilo of *saindoux* [rendered pork fat], some potatoes, and about 1 franc 70, which the older boy gave to me to take care of the small needs of the household." Marie Gy's thirteen-year-old son wrote to her while she was detained in Paris to say that he and his four siblings were well cared for: "Madame Michel makes our food every day. She makes our beds. Madame Kantzler gives us many things and la dame Klein, too. Until now we have not been hungry; we have in our purse four francs and more bread. My boss has augmented our purse. We are taken care of; only we find the time very long without you."[66] The care of these children became a community effort during their mother's detention.

While neighbors' positive knowledge of each other's households was clearly very important, what neighbors did *not* hear or see could also be crucial. As in the De Moor case, where all the neighbors agreed that he must have attacked his wife in her sleep because they did not hear any struggle or argument, Jean-

Baptiste Santin was also implicated for attacking his wife unprovoked. Genève Torcheboeuf affirmed to the investigating magistrate that she heard nothing from the Santin apartment next door on the day of the crime.

> My lodging is only separated from the one the Santin couple occupy by an extremely thin partition. However, on that day, I didn't hear any kind of noise. Santin claims, you tell me, that his wife, following an argument between them, gave him a kick, that he then seized his hammer, that he struck his wife, and that she fell to the floor, and that later he placed her on the bed. I don't believe any of it. Things must not have happened that way; it's impossible. If there had been a discussion, quarrel, fight, fall of a body onto the floor, I would have heard all that. In my view, Santin must have killed his wife while she slept or rested on the bed, and from the first blow she received, she must have been killed, since I did not hear anything.[67]

Based on her own sensory experience, Torcheboeuf concluded with perfect confidence that the absence of evidence constituted evidence of absence of a struggle. Likewise, Jean François thought Louis Forestier must have killed his lover in her sleep: "I did not hear any noise, and it's very surprising, because one easily hears everything that happens."[68] And Eduoard Gardin, whose room was next door to Esther Bonjour's, was positive that her ex-lover had attacked her without a previous fight: "I am certain that no argument preceded this scene. I would have heard it because all the windows were open, and I declare that I was only awakened by the woman's cry of distress."[69]

In such closely knit urban neighborhoods, positive knowledge about one's neighbors' doings came not only from directly witnessing disputes and their aftermath but also from the rumors and reports in constant circulation throughout the community. Hearsay was treated as a legitimate source of information in and out of the courts, even if in retrospect damaging rumors could not be substantiated by anyone's direct experience. *L'opinion général* (general opinion) or *la rumeur publique* (common report) were powerful forces, circulating information about people's behavior as well as their neighbors' judgments of it. In the case of the Catherine couple, the wife's possible misconduct was clearly the subject of much debate among their neighbors. "One spoke, in the house, about the conduct of la femme Catherine. My husband had forbidden me to say hello to her. I heard tell that this woman had been seen going out with Lepage," testified one woman who lived on the same landing as the Catherines. An older man who used to take his meals with the Catherines made a number of speculative remarks about the source of their discord before concluding, "I have no personal view on the point... In the quarter, the opinions are divided."[70] In the case of la femme Gy, much discussion among her neighbors did not turn up anything to her discredit: "Since she was arrested, she has been talked about a lot, but I have never heard a single voice accuse her of conducting herself badly," affirmed a woman who lived next door.[71]

Sometimes evidence came to light that rumors were spread deliberately, whether they were true or not. The sisters of François Torlotin did not want him to marry Marie Croissant, so they spread rumors about her at the Christofle factory where they worked in St. Denis, saying that she went to public balls with other men.[72] Louis Jouault told people that his wife was having an affair, but he was not taken seriously since the alleged lover was a man twenty years her junior.[73] Jean Vigineix, however, managed to convince some of his neighbors that his wife was having an affair, though other witnesses vigorously contested it in their depositions. "If the neighbors say it, it's because they were tricked by him," his wife insisted, and the investigating magistrate, at least, was convinced of her innocence. "Public opinion, led astray by the defamatory propositions of the husband, seems to believe in the misconduct of the wife," he wrote in the official indictment. "But the investigation searched in vain for proofs that could justify such an accusation, against which la femme Vigineix has always protested with the greatest energy. The people who were within closest range to know and evaluate this woman portray her as a hardworking housewife dedicated to her duties."[74]

In the bourgeois household of the Duc couple, it was not thin walls but the initiative of a domestic servant that facilitated the spread of knowledge about the couple. Their maid Marie Raulin was particularly active in spreading information about the wife's infidelities, ultimately choosing to deliver a letter addressed to the wife's lover to her husband instead. Before this dramatic revelation, she had communicated notably with the concierge and other domestic servants in the building about the men who visited Madame Duc in her husband's absence. An upstairs neighbor seems to have taken an interest in the Duc household only after he heard about the wife's misconduct from his own maid:

Until 1873, I never heard anything about this household, which I believed to be excellent. But last November, I learned from my domestic that Madame Duc had a lover. She had it from Madame Duc's maid, and she gave me precise enough information for me to be assured of the accuracy of the fact myself. I searched out the means to tell her that I was aware of her intrigues, but this didn't hinder her from continuing. According to the word around the house, the lover came to Madame Duc's place, living at 68 rue Saint Denis... I heard it said in the house that Madame Duc had other lovers.[75]

Domestic servants employed by different households in the same building had evidently created a network of their own, sharing information among themselves and a few of their employers. It is unclear what their motives were in this case, however—whether they were maliciously trying to destroy Madame Duc's reputation or trying to sanction her behavior before her husband discovered her affair.

As possessors of detailed knowledge about one another's lives, neighbors had the responsibility of deciding what use to make of it. Indeed, this knowledge gave them a great deal of power, and not only when telling their tales in the courtroom. Neighbors could exchange information, spreading stories and rumors that could enhance or destroy a person's reputation. Quite literally, a decision by a neighbor to intervene or not in a violent situation could mean the difference between life and death for a victim. Exercising surveillance both benevolent and despotic, neighbors were actively involved in each other's domestic disputes, and evidence of neighbors who refused to get involved was rare.

For a person in danger, the first step in acquiring assistance was to spread the knowledge of her (or his) plight as much as possible, thereby creating a pool of informed potential allies. Julie Hardwick has found abundant evidence of this strategy among battered wives in the seventeenth century, as has Mary Trouille for the eighteenth.[76] Leslie Page Moch and Rachel Fuchs have emphasized the importance of female neighbors and kin in assisting poor women in nineteenth-century Paris.[77] Also, as Roderick Phillips concluded in his study of late eighteenth-century divorce cases in Rouen, women were far more likely than men to call on friends for assistance in times of crisis, while for an abusive man it was strategically wise to limit knowledge of his violence and prevent its exposure to the judgment of the community.[78] Indeed, the fewer allies a woman had, the easier it was for her abuser to control her. In the close quarters of lower-class Parisian housing, it was almost inevitable that neighbors would become aware of violent relationships, although there is also evidence that women purposefully exposed their griefs and wounds to other community members. The few women who did choose to keep an abusive relationship secret usually expressed their regret at having done so. Mélanie Lerondeau, for one, was unable to convince the court that it had been she, not her husband, who was the victim of abuse before his death. "He was the one who used to beat me," she stated. "I was wrong not to show the blows he gave me." She had no proof beyond her word, however, and no witnesses would corroborate her statement.[79]

The strategy outlined by a laundress named Marie Rault was much more typical. Far from seeking to hide her husband's violence (before she murdered him), she spread information about it as widely as possible. Her case is worth examining at length to evaluate the effects of this strategy. "I only have one means to avenge myself," she told her friend Isabelle Bruneau. "It is to tell the world what he does to me."[80] Bruneau specified that Marie Rault "reminded him in front of everybody of all the low blows he did to her, and she notably reproached him for having killed all her children when they were in her belly." For Marie Rault, publicizing her husband's abuses was an explicitly articulated strategy that she knew would be damaging to him, although it was not without cost to herself as well. One day when she and her friend Madame Bruneau had planned to go looking for work together doing laundry or ironing, Marie told her friend in her husband's presence, "Madame Bruneau, aren't I just as miserable as ever? He beat me again last night." Bruneau described the scene: "At the same time she showed me her hands, one of which was greatly swollen. At this, Rault began to grind his teeth, which was his habit when he got angry, and threw his wife a punch that did not reach her." Later in the day, Marie Rault came to Bruneau's apartment in tears, followed by her husband, claiming that he had tried to strangle her. He knocked her down and then left.

Anna Corryer, a neighbor, expressed her belief that the wife's complaints of mistreatment provoked more beatings. "La femme Rault must have bothered her husband by constantly complaining in front of everybody of being beaten by him," she said. Corryer's lover Jules Ouziaux, a friend of le sieur Rault, described one such incident when the two men were drinking together the day before the crime. "At this moment, la femme Rault arrived. She appeared very agitated; she called her husband lazy and told him to return to the house. As for him, he responded nicely that she should go do her housework or at least she should shut up on the pain of receiving some slaps. He added, 'If you have some observations to make to me, you will do it at our place. This isn't done in company, at the wineshop.' She persisted obstinately to yell, and he threw her a slap. An instant later she began her reproaches again, and her husband slapped her again, after which she went away, while her husband fell asleep on the table." It seems that Jules Ouziaux agreed with Rault that his wife should not be exposing their conflicts to the world, but she persisted in publicizing her troubles, even at the price of more violence. While the men in this case wished to keep personal conflicts private, Marie Rault insisted on displaying them for public consideration.

Nonetheless, although he professed the desire to keep their disputes out of the public eye, Rault's own behavior often made a public spectacle of their fights. The seventy-five-year-old woman who owned a building where they had once lived described the frequent scenes he caused. "Rault was a bad guy," she declared. "Many times, when Rault was drunk, he gathered the public in the street and the police officers had to intervene. He beat his wife on any occasion, and it was she herself who told me that. Often when the noise became too loud, I had to go down to intervene myself." The cabaret owner across the street from her building was also involved in monitoring their conflicts. "At every instant the public was amassed in the street for the scenes of dispute between the two spouses and the police would intervene. Often la femme Rault came to take refuge at my place, and her husband came after and threatened to break everything in my place if I was hiding his wife. I have seen him dragging his wife on the ground by the hair and hitting her with punches and kicks on every part of her body." Knowledge of the Raults' abusive relationship was thus widespread among their neighbors, thanks not only to the wife's efforts to publicize it but also to the husband's disruptive behavior. He may have claimed that he did not want their disputes to be made public, but he did little to conceal them.

As the cabaret owner's testimony indicates, however, people who chose to help Marie Rault were taking a calculated risk that they could limit the husband's violence without incurring harm themselves. Clémentine Trouvé, a ragpicker, often helped Marie Rault when her husband turned violent. She stated:

> I have known the Rault couple for five or six years. But I had a neighborly relationship with them principally when they lived at 33, Place Duplein, where I used to have my rag shop. Le sieur Rault was a drunkard who made his wife endure all sorts of mistreatments. Lots of times, in my presence, he tried to hit her, and threatened her, and I had to take her to my place, where she was safe, to keep her from receiving bad blows... La femme Rault came many times around eleven o'clock in the evening to ask me for shelter, since her husband had kicked her out... A number of times, I noticed on her body the traces of blows that she received... In sum, le sieur Rault was a sorry individual. Nobody dared to put themselves between him and his wife, and I am sure that if he had learned that his wife

came to my place when he kicked her out, I would have had to repent of my helpfulness for her.

Apparently, like the cabaret owner, Trouvé was able to keep this place of refuge secret, since neither one of them suffered any ill consequences at Rault's hands for helping his wife.

This was not possible for Rault's former employer in Versailles, a shoemaker, who registered his disapproval of Rault's behavior toward his wife by firing him. "I can affirm that Rault got drunk daily and mistreated his wife, a weak creature, defenseless against a man endowed with great strength who had fits like a ferocious beast. These daily scenes made me decide to fire him. I had loaned a table and some chairs to the young household, so I went one day to get back from Rault what belonged to me." Instead of thanking him for the loan, however, Rault beat him up, and the shoemaker chose not to file a complaint with the police for fear of reprisals. Once, the wife's half-sister tried to negotiate a truce between the couple on an occasion when Rault had kicked her out but was frightened away by his temper. Likewise, Marie's sister and brother agreed that intervention was risky. Her brother testified, "More than thirty times I witnessed scenes of dispute and violence between the two spouses. Rault, when he had been drinking, constantly hit my sister. If I wanted to intervene to protect her, he turned on me, hit me in my turn, and I was obliged to give in to him. Rault was stronger than me." The sister concurred, "He beat the living daylights out of her... Rault had extraordinary strength, and when he was angry, everyone ran away from him. My sister, on the contrary, was of a rather weak constitution, and all the fights and blows provoked the miscarriages. [They] left her interior wounds from which she will never be healed." In the end, it was Marie Rault who helped herself most decisively, since she finally stabbed her husband to death. She was convicted on a reduced charge of assault and given a short prison sentence.

Her bold revelations of her husband's abuse did help Marie Rault recruit some allies among her neighbors. That they knew about the violence, however, did not necessarily mean that they were willing to do anything to stop it. They helped her hide from her husband, but their fear of him kept them from doing more. Rault's threats against his wife's helpers were nearly as compelling as her claims against him: the neighbors helped her, but only when the coast was clear and an attack was over. Public knowledge thus appears to have been a necessary but sometimes insufficient step toward disrupting the dynamics of an abusive relationship, for the violence could only be stopped when the woman successfully left or when one partner was killed.

Marie Rault had an extensive network in her neighborhood, yet even a woman in a transient position could garner assistance. As she traveled through Marseilles, Lyon, Nice, and Monaco with her increasingly violent lover Jean-Baptiste Bernou, Anaïs Sauvan was cut off from a stable network of acquaintances. Some friends in her hometown of Guillestre (Hautes Alpes) had cut ties with her decisively when her illicit affair was exposed. Nonetheless, she managed to keep people around her aware of the dangerous situation she was in, recruiting allies among the restaurateurs and servants she met. During their stay in Monaco, in June and July of 1871, Anaïs Sauvan cultivated the friendship of Catherine Marquetti, who ran the restaurant where the couple habitually took their meals. Testifying for a *juge d'instruction* in Monaco, Marquetti reported that Sauvan had requested that her meals be sent to her room for a period of about two weeks because she was "indisposed." When she returned to the restaurant, she showed Marquetti traces of the wounds that had kept her confined for so long. "She had one side of her face all blackened from the scalp to the bottom of the face. She then admitted to me that her whole body was bruised from the blows that she had received. She showed me her leg, her thighs, and the length of her body up to the arm, which were black and yellow from blows on the same side as the cheek."[81] Considering the difficulty of removing enough clothes to show so much of her body, this must have been no casual demonstration on Sauvan's part but rather a purposeful revelation, and her efforts won her an ally. When Bernou showed up at the restaurant and tried to force Sauvan to leave with him, the *restauratrice* declared to him that, "at my place he would not beat that woman." Once, Sauvan gave Marquetti a trunk and an overnight bag for safekeeping when she was planning an unsuccessful getaway. Later, at the hotel in Monaco, Sauvan enlisted the help of a young man who was a servant there, who helped her hide in the basement and then escape through the window to get away from Bernou. Then in Monte Carlo, she confided to another *restauratrice* that she feared Bernou would kill her one day. An old family friend living in Menton finally loaned her the money to travel alone to Paris, after an unsuccessful attempt to flee to Italy. Bernou ultimately found her and killed her in Paris. Still, even if Sauvan's resourcefulness in purposefully publicizing her troubles and injuries did not save her, they did leave a record of Bernou's abuse that would help condemn him to twenty years of forced labor following her murder. Since Anaïs Sauvan had convinced other people of the injustice of her plight during her lifetime, they could help defend her cause after her death.

Ordinary residents of Paris, however, had a potential ally right at their front doors: the concierge. The concierge typically lived in a room (the *loge*) near the entrance to an apartment building, noted the coming and going of all residents, and controlled access to the building. It was quite literally the job of the concierge to know everybody's business, and therefore he or she was a frequent and well-informed witness in criminal cases. Usually, the investigating magistrate (if not also the police) interviewed the concierges from every house where the couple had resided in recent years. Even if very few witnesses were interviewed, the concierge always figured among them.[82] Sometimes this source yielded information that could be obtained nowhere else. For instance, the concierge Antoinette Bertin was the only person who was aware of the long-term affair between her tenant Louis Cousin and his employer, Estelle Pluchet. She saw Pluchet arrive on Sunday and Thursday evenings, disguised with a veil. In the mornings, the concierge cleaned the room and was entitled to the leftovers from their supper.[83] Another concierge who kept her tenant's secret was Louise Thierry. She appears to have been a personal friend of Louise Robert, who maintained an address in Paris while she pursued a singing career in Blois and elsewhere. Her husband Barthélemy Robert had traveled to La Plata to find his fortune, while in his absence she sang in cabarets and had at least two affairs. When a friend told her of his return to Paris, Louise Robert enlisted the aid of her concierge to keep him ignorant of her whereabouts. She wrote her from Blois:

> Dear madame, Jeanne writes me that my husband has been standing guard at her door for two days. So have you seen him, have you told him I am working? I am afraid, Madame Thierry, what should be done, above all don't tell him that I am in Blois. I beg you, he would come here, my God, what to do I don't know what to decide. Perhaps I would do well to leave right away. Finally, I don't know, but I'm crazy, I don't know what to do. Pity me, I know what awaits me, either he will kill me or he will force me to live with him. Never... and I don't want to die. Finally, guard my address well and say nothing I beg you I thank you I am crazy [signed] L Robert... Say simply that you do not know where I am.[84]

Thierry wrote back to say that Louise's husband was looking for her and that he said he would get the police to find her. "In this circumstance it is too delicate one cannot permit oneself to give advice," she wrote, signing her name, "your completely devoted." All the same, she obeyed her friend's request for secrecy, and it was only by chance that Robert and his wife finally met each other in the street, and he shot her. As a concierge, Louise Thierry would have been a likely source of information for the husband and the police, but as la femme Robert's friend, she was a trustworthy ally.

Depositions from concierges revealed them to be frequent arbiters in domestic disputes. Not only was the *loge* near the building entrance, and therefore on virtually any escape route, but the concierge, male or female, also had a certain status. They were not the buildings' proprietors, but concierges had the power to accept or expel residents and to be lenient or strict in cases of unpaid rent. Their esteem or sympathy was thus a valuable asset to gain for many reasons. Marie Louise Mellet ran to her concierge, la femme Dubois, for refuge when her angry lover pursued her; la femme Dubois interposed herself between the two and made the attacker leave.[85] The concierge in the building where the Kemps couple resided frequently gave refuge to her tenant:

> On this same Tuesday, Kemps returned around eight in the evening, still drunk. A few minutes later, his wife came down to me, saying, "My husband is on a binge. I want to give him time to go to bed—I'll go up soon when he'll be asleep."... She went up to her place, but very quickly she came back. "My husband," she told me, "is not in bed. He is still drunk, and he is walking around in his shirt in his room." She waited a few moments again, then she finally went up to her apartment for good.[86]

Marguerite Lebel's *loge* was also a refuge for Annette Clément, who lived in her building for less than a year, and she showed Lebel the traces of the abuse she suffered from her husband. "She wanted to leave him, she used to say, and everybody in the house counseled her to do it and to return to her father because she was too unhappy... I had to intervene many times to put an end to the commotion they made in their place."[87] The husband blamed her for giving his wife such advice. "The concierge is not telling the truth," he protested to the *juge d'instruction*. "She is the one who made trouble in my household by always advising my wife to leave me. I might have given a few slaps to my wife, but I never abused her, as you have been told."

The trial of Pierre-Auguste Perney included depositions from five concierges who had managed various buildings where he and his wife had lived. One of them, Aurélie Paquet, testified to the frequent abuse her former tenant Ernestine Perney used to suffer from her husband:

I did not see him hit her myself, but I heard the cries that she and not her husband made. Once I saw the wife all bruised. Her eyes were all blackened from blows. She showed me her arm in a frightful state. You would have said she had been bitten. She showed me her bruised breasts... Another time—it was a little before New Year's last year—her husband kicked her out in the middle of the night, in her slip and barefoot. She came all disheveled to ask me for help. [When I spoke to him] the husband responded that she was crazy and that he had not touched her... In my opinion, all the wrongs were on the side of the husband, who is no good.[88]

It was not easy to dispute such specific testimony from a person of a position of authority in the community. In this context, any concierge who claimed to be unaware of a situation with which others were well acquainted lacked credibility. In the trial of Godefroid Tiétard the professed ignorance of the concierge was not quite credible in the face of detailed information supplied by other witnesses. The concierge, la femme Andrès, would only say, "The evening of the event, from my *loge* I heard someone yell, 'Help! Oh! The brigand! I'm being murdered!' I went out. I saw Madame covered with blood. Before, I didn't know anything, and I didn't hear anything." The sarcasm of the presiding judge was quite apparent when he replied, "You are a discreet concierge."[89] When the tables were turned, however, and it was a couple of concierges who were on trial, their tenants came forward with many details about their private lives, showing that the flow of information went both ways. The Guerriers, for instance, both concierges, had more than two dozen witnesses—neighbors, coworkers, and relatives, but mostly tenants—testify in their case.[90]

Knowing about a violent relationship usually entailed doing something about it. Networks of knowledge were also networks of assistance. Help could come in many forms, from food and shelter, to diplomatic intervention, to physical assistance during an attack. Juliette Legrand was fed every meal by her long-term friends and neighbors the Mornets, who also escorted her to and from work daily to protect her from her husband. Ultimately, the husband shot at his wife and la femme Mornet, whom he blamed for his wife's alleged misconduct.[91] A young laundress testified in court about how she had repeatedly aided a neighbor who was often beaten by her husband. "I live on the same landing as monsieur. On Sunday evening, monsieur beat his wife and kicked her out. The next day, he beat her and put her in shreds. In the evening, he was drunk and hit her again... He chased her with a hammer in his hand. She got away in her slip. I was obliged to lend her a camisole. He left. So I said to his wife, 'Unhappy woman, how can you stay with him?'... I was afraid for her, justifiably so."[92] In a rare instance of men protecting each other from an attack, Charles Roché was escorted to and from work daily by a friend who was also his lodger.[93] Adelphine Odet, a woman who lived in the same building as la femme Kemps, described how she offered a sympathetic ear and material assistance. "I almost became her friend, and for six months, I saw her frequently. She told me many times about the brutalities that she [suffered] from her husband, telling me how unhappy she was." Odet heard a cry one Sunday night, and then,

> the next day Monday, she came to find me. She was walking with difficulty, and she on the side of her right eye, had received a blow that had swollen this whole part of her face. She had her head wrapped in a handkerchief. On her neck, she had bluish marks, and I was frightened of what I saw. "I have [bruises] like this," she told me, "all over my body." The pains that she felt made walking difficult. I went out for her, and I brought her back something to eat. On Tuesday, she could go get provisions "by bandaging her head well," she said. "Tonight, my husband will come home drunk again," she added. "How am I going to sleep tonight?" "If there is the least thing," I added, "call us." I have not seen her since. During that night, I lent an ear, for fear that la femme Kemps might call for help, but I didn't hear anything, and the thing that appeared strange to me—since it was unusual—I didn't even see light at her place.[94]

Adelphine Odet, who characterized her acquaintance with la femme Kemps as "almost" a friendship, still cared enough about her welfare to help her take care of herself and monitor her situation closely. Neighbors like her were moved by their knowledge of such victims' plight to act in giving them whatever assistance they could.

Women as well as men intervened during an attack to protect the victims of violence. Stéphanie Micholet held onto the jacket of her friend's attacker long enough to delay his pursuit and for him to throw her a punch.[95] Three men who were friends of Hippolyte Richard testified that they had stopped more than one serious attack against Marie Daouze before she stabbed her lover. Among them, François Gnad stated, "They both got drunk constantly, and many times I was there when they came to blows. Richard used to hit la fille Daouze, and she would strike back as she was able. Once, at the Hôtel des Deux Hemisphères, Richard had thrown his mistress to the floor and was holding her under him and hitting her head against the floor. I was the one who had to pull him off of her."[96] Désirée Solhart also received timely assistance from her neighbors.

She describes the attack, where her husband was beating her with a chair: "From the beginning of this scene, I felt so very dizzy and my blood had spurted from the wounds on my head with such abundance that it was impossible for me to make the least resistance against my aggressor. However, I called the neighbors to help me, and I had succeeded in breaking a part of the window to make them understand the danger I was in."[97] When their seventeen-year-old neighbor Henri Sangerou finally kicked in the door, her husband was trying to push her out the window. "If he was unable to succeed, it was thanks to the energy with which I clung to the window ledge," declared Solhart. She credited her own tenacity for her survival but did not discount the arrival of the neighbors, which caused her husband to stop his attack.

Other neighbors, paralyzed by fear, preferred not to intervene in dangerous situations. One woman who heard the sound of blows coming from the next room was afraid to intervene herself but sent her daughter to find the victim's adult children for help. "If my husband had been there, he would have broken down the door, but I was alone and I did not dare go help," she testified.[98] When a woman down the hall from the Herbellot couple heard a commotion between them, she was too frightened to try to help: "Nailed to the spot by fear, I did not dare leave my lodging. I did not go out until I heard the police arrive."[99] In the case of the Jacobs, the neighbors not only feared the husband's potential reprisals but also were so accustomed to his violence that it seemed almost routine. "Rather regularly, once a week, Jacob returned around ten or eleven o'clock in a state of drunkenness, then brutalized his wife, whose cries I heard," explained a nineteen-year-old man. He continued,

> One time among others the racket lasted longer than ordinary, and the whole house was upset by the screams that the unhappy femme Jacob made. It was around last July; the windows of the Jacob couple were open, ours too. I got up to go help the poor woman. But my parents, fearing that I would receive a bad blow from the husband, forbade me to go out. I went to the window, and I yelled to Jacob, "Will you finish soon, or I'm going to come up." From the window, he answered with a menacing tone, "Come then, if you have the courage."[100]

He did not have the courage, and neither did any of the other neighbors, though that was the night Jacob finally killed his wife. As one neighbor explained, "I was quite used to the noise of the scenes that frequently took place in the Jacob household."

The Jacobs were not unique in this respect. If a couple fought continually, neighbors could grow accustomed to the racket and not intervene—screams and cries for help became ordinary events and did not appear to designate anything unusually dangerous in the household. In such cases, it seems that the witnesses either believed that their intervention could not improve the situation (and might only put them in harm's way) or that the danger to the victim was not very great. They were desensitized to the violence. It is impossible to know how common such noisy, violent arguments were, outside of the couples that went to court. However, the simple fact that neighbors could become accustomed to it, to the point of not bothering to respond to cries for help, suggests that it was not an alarmingly unusual phenomenon in itself. For instance, Hortense Rouillier, a concierge, all but ignored the sounds of a murder taking place in a nearby room. "Around 10:30, I heard a woman's screams coming from la femme Cosson's room, three or four cries at the most—I didn't pay attention to it." The investigating magistrate summed up, "Nobody was worried; one was so accustomed to the scenes of this irregular household."[101] The concierge of the building where the Teste couple lived was so inured to hearing about threats and violence that he refused to take seriously the warning signs on the day that Ernest Teste shot his wife. "The morning of the crime, around a quarter to twelve, Madame Teste came to the *loge* a little more frightened and distracted than usual. 'Can you imagine,' she said, 'that my husband has sent away the workers, and he said he is going to kill me.' Since I was used to this situation, I didn't believe it."[102] He answered her, "You're not going to make us run every day [to help you]." He believed she was only crying wolf. Then after lunch, when the Testes' maid came to say that the husband had killed the wife, the concierge refused to believe her and told her to leave him alone. In these instances of nonintervention, neighbors did not offer assistance because the violence was so habitual that it no longer appeared to be an urgent crisis.

Occasionally, people did not explain their decision not to intervene in disputes.[103] Such unexplained noninvolvement, however, was the exception rather than the rule. In the case of the Guillots, out of twenty-five neighbors, employees, and family members who testified, only two neighbors asserted that they heard fights but did not wish to become involved. The others witnesses not only knew about the violence but tried to stop it in various ways. At the time of the attack, the wife had just filed for a legal separation and had opened a new store of her own after the grocery store the couple ran together went bankrupt. One woman who lived across the street stated, "At the moment of the crime, numerous quarrels existed in this household. I did not get mixed up in it, not wanting to take sides."[104] Another woman asserted, "I live in the same house as the Guillots. I have never wanted to go into their place because they argued often, and I did not want to get mixed up in their quarrels. But involuntarily I was present for scenes when they happened outside or in the stairways." Nonetheless, she had gathered a certain amount of information about the couple and rendered an opinion for the *juge d'instruction*: "I never saw Guillot use violence against either his wife or his mother-in-law. I saw on the contrary these women hit him, pull out his beard, and insult him. He responded with insults and not with blows. He accused his mother-in-law of being the cause of his bad household. I saw him drunk sometimes." The *juge d'instruction* asked her who she thought was usually right in those quarrels, and she replied, "I thought everybody was wrong." Whether she wished it or not, she was still privy to information about their relationship and was able to form a judgment about it.

In a handful of cases, witnesses stated that they did not choose to intervene because they did not think the conflict was anyone's business but the couple's, laying claim to a kind of privacy that did not in fact exist. Jean Boursault, who was on friendly terms with Alexandre Larue and his partner Mathilde Bourdeaux, refused to comment about their relationship. "I can't say what happened between them, because seeing them quarrel, I went away. I believed they were husband and wife, and I didn't want to get mixed up in their business."[105] In another case, assertions about the privacy of a couple's relationship do not seem credible at all. Two neighbors who were otherwise familiar with the troubles of the Biver household insisted, "I don't concern myself with the affairs of others," and "I am not concerned with such things" when they were interrogated about Biver's mistress.[106] One was a woman who worked as a maid in the house next door, and the other was a man who was a friend of Biver's. However, other testimony in the dossier describes the noisy conflicts between Biver, his wife, and his former mistress (who wanted to reclaim the savings she had invested in his wineshop) as a theatrical event. His former mistress Marie Fournet would stand outside the establishment in the evening, shouting at him for all to hear, while people gathered outside to watch and drink. The wine seller next door testified, "These scenes generally took place around ten in the evening, and they were so habitual that my clients said one time that it was not necessary to go to the theater because we had a spectacle on the boulevard." The night that Fournet shot Biver, the crowd that gathered for the usual show was so surprised when the conflict suddenly turned deadly that "nobody had the idea to intervene." Why other witnesses refused to discuss a "private" conflict that was so evidently public is unclear. Aside from these rare and not very credible assertions that a couple's relationship should be private, it was a matter of course that neighbors knew all about each other's lives and readily intervened in them.

That intimate knowledge of other people's relationships could be used to help or to harm the individuals involved might have provided incentive for people to stay on good terms with their neighbors, if not stay on their best behavior. In one case, a couple tattled on their adulterous neighbor in retaliation for an insult. Ernest Dameron explained, "Madame De Verneuil went around saying that my wife was a procuress. She even said to her husband that my wife wanted to procure men for her. It was to avenge ourselves for these mean words and also out of friendship for De Verneuil that I wrote him the letter" revealing his wife's infidelity. The couple also took De Verneuil to witness an encounter between his wife and her lover at the Cirque d'hiver, where he stabbed both of them, killing the lover. "Your behavior and that of your wife in this whole affair have been the most reprehensible, and one is in the right to impute to you the moral responsibility for the death of le sieur Brelle," scolded the *juge d'instruction* at their deposition. "If I could have foreseen this outcome, I would not have done what I did," replied the husband. His wife tried to excuse their intervention by claiming that they had followed De Verneuil to the Cirque d'hiver "to keep him from beating his wife too much." She continued, "If I could have foreseen the fury of Monsieur de Verneuil, I would have killed myself, but I was irritated at being called a *procureuse*." Their plans to punish their neighbor for her insults went further than they had intended, but their weapon was their knowledge of their neighbor's illicit affair.

These people took an unusually active role in promoting discord, if not violence, between a couple they knew. However, their actions were not out of line with the general system of mutual monitoring in urban neighborhoods of the laboring poor. In domestic disputes, members of the local community were both party and judge to questions about proper behavior for men and women and the legitimate uses of violence, for they could be held to the same standards that they helped enforce or undermine. Everyone had a stake in the system for the same standards could be applied to them in their turn. Family members and acquaintances in the *pays* were also implicated because an individual's behavior reflected on them as well. Thus the ongoing observation and interpretation of a couple's actions, and the resulting judgments about right and wrong or intervention or nonintervention, played a dynamic role in the maintenance and modification of relatively consistent roles for men and women. In this way, the community monitoring of violence in intimate relationships allows insight into how gender was constructed through practices of everyday life. Without expressing explicit awareness of the systems of social organization in which they participated, the actions and judgments of individual women and men nonetheless simultaneously constructed and were constructed by those systems.

In the immediate context of assize court trials, community members' judgment was crucial. A lone voice could not make a persuasive argument about how a given act should be interpreted; it took a chorus of neighbors and family members in agreement to corroborate the statement of an individual on the stand. A person who failed to win allies among his or her community could find his or her credibility seriously damaged in court. Members of an urban neighborhood thus depended on each other in creating favorable and compelling interpretations of their actions. Status or reputation depended not only on individuals' actions—and the community's interpretations and judgments regarding those actions—but also on their partners' actions and how they, in turn, were interpreted and judged. When neighbors witnessed, discussed, and judged each other's behavior, they formed the values of their community and the social ties that held it together. But this kind of interdependence was also the basis of a great deal of conflict, as individuals sought to control or punish their partners' behavior when they failed to conform to the community's standards. As the next chapter explains, it was precisely this system of mutual obligation that defined the limits of legitimate violence between domestic partners.

CHAPTER 4

Reciprocity and Retribution

"*Kill her!*" Thus Alexandre Dumas fils concluded his infamous 1872 essay, *L'Homme-femme*, on what a husband should do to his adulterous wife.[1] His was the most famous publication in a debate on adultery and the legitimacy of violence, prompted by the notorious case of an aristocrat named Charles-Arthur Leroy du Bourg. He had surprised his wife and her lover half-dressed in a room on the rue des Écoles in Paris. While the lover escaped over the rooftops, du Bourg beat and stabbed his wife so severely that she died three days later—but not before signing a declaration that her husband was right to try to kill her and that she deserved her fate.[2] Although he was accused of murder, du Bourg's sensational trial resulted in his conviction for manslaughter, with extenuating circumstances, and a relatively light sentence of five years in prison.

Across the political spectrum, arguments proliferated over whether he should have been convicted at all. The du Bourg verdict was taken as evidence of the inadequacies of the state system of justice in regulating family conflicts—some believed it was too inflexible in not absolving an understandable crime while others decried its failure to protect women from violent men. Indeed, Alexandre Dumas wrote his article in response to one by Henry d'Ideville, who recommended that a husband should pardon his faithless wife and seek to correct her behavior without violence. But it was Dumas's bold approval of deadly violence that seized the public's interest, and his article, originally published in *L'Opinion*, sold more than fifty thousand copies as a pamphlet in the first three months after its appearance.[3] For years after its original publication, references to the article appeared again and again in newspaper accounts of crimes of passion.[4] It is frequently cited, even now, as an example of the worst kind of antifeminism, and its popularity has been ascribed to various fin-de-siècle anxieties about gender and power.[5]

Dumas's piece sparked an intense public debate about the use of violence in intimate relationships and husbands' authority in marriage. Catholic authors pointed out that Jesus had been more forgiving of adulterous women than Dumas.[6] Louis Blanc endorsed a tract arguing that such dramas would be averted by equal civil rights and better education for women, as well as legal divorce.[7] Feminists seized the occasion to criticize inequalities between husbands and wives.[8] Hermance Lesguillon, prolific author of novels, poetry, and studies of women in society, penned a study of *L'Homme-femme* set in the imaginary salon of one Madame de Montulé. Here, a gathering of educated European women read and criticize Dumas's text together, dissecting his logic and offering their own critique of marriage. The characters specifically defend the right to legal separation to protect battered wives and applaud the leniency of judgments in infanticide cases where the mother had been seduced and abandoned.[9] The book ends with the arrival of a young society girl named Alice, who has just broken off her engagement after reading Dumas's book. "That 'Kill her! Kill her!' kept ringing in my ears, and I was afraid," she tells the assembled ladies. "How can one promise to be constant forever, when you lose your free will, since you depend on someone else? In marriage, if I answer for myself, for my sweetness, my resignation, my fidelity, can I answer for the character of the man to whom I am eternally chained? Can I swear that I will love only him, and if he becomes detestable in his feelings, if he is violent, arbitrary, despotic, can I promise to be imperturbably patient? Can I love him, if he become antipathetic to me?"[10] In her estimation, as a wife her continued love for her husband would depend on his continuing to treat her well and love her in return, and yet there was no guarantee of his constancy in a relationship where he was legally her superior.

More notably, in *Ève contre monsieur Dumas fils*, Maria Deraismes turned the tables against irresponsible husbands. Imagining herself giving advice to a young woman, she mirrored Dumas's advice to a young man and declared:

> Do not forget, you who are young, beautiful, educated, you who have talent and virtues, that if this gentleman who appropriates all that and in addition takes your dowry, your fortune, in order to make himself a notary, a stockbroker, or a deputy... if he supports bad actresses and floozies... if he ruins you, if he even manages to corrupt the purity of your blood, do not forget that this man *sullies the primoridal plan, the divine idea*... it is the ape that Darwin spoke of, it is Cain in person; KILL HIM, do not hesitate.[11]

Women and men, she insisted, share the same moral code because they are essentially the same, except for their bodies. "Nature, which has infinitely more intelligence and wisdom than all the poets, all the novelists, and all the playwrights together, has created reciprocal attractions where she wanted to create alliance and union;... she gave passion in equal measures to the two sexes; but in their consciences she has made manifest the morality that regularizes, that finds equilibrium: sensations, affections, desires, are subordinated to duty and morality, one, indivisible, unchangeable law." As for adultery, Deraismes notes that it occurs when the ultimate purpose of marriage, the propagation of the species, has not been attained. "It is understandable that when one of the two partners escapes his obligations, the other is authorized to commit adultery... Thus the case of adultery is always complex... When you touch on the wife's infidelity, you also touch upon the husband's conduct." Husbands, she contended, are often the first to be guilty, which means they are unfit to judge their wives' misbehavior: "When you lack virtue yourself, you lose the right to require it of another."[12] In effect, Deraismes claimed for women the right to sexual satisfaction in marriage and argued that wives were not to be blamed for seeking it elsewhere if their husbands deprived them of it. To be sure, Deraismes demurred that her advice to kill a bad husband was only a joke. What she hoped for was a more harmonious future, when marriage laws as well as moral codes would reflect the natural equality of women and men. Nonetheless, her articulation of the mutual needs and obligations of spouses would have resonated with many witnesses in the *cour d'assises*; only an innocent spouse could justly accuse his (or her) partner of misconduct.

In general, French feminists did not make marital violence a focus of their activism in the fin de siècle, in contrast to British and American feminists in the same era. Except for response to a specific event like the du Bourg trial, feminist critiques of violence were rare.[13] However, at the International Congress on the Condition and Rights of Women, held in conjunction with the Universal Exposition in 1900, attendees voted unanimously to eliminate the legal excuse for the husband's murder of his adulterous wife in Article 324 of the penal code. This occurred within a larger discussion of women's rights in marriage, including control of wages and property. As René Viviani asserted at the conference, marriage should be a relationship of equals, with equal rights.[14] This legal condition, however, was still generations from being realized, although the legal excuse of spousal murder was eliminated in 1907.

In the fin de siècle, Dumas was far from alone in his contention that violence could be a legitimate means of punishing bad behavior on the part of a spouse. G.-M. Ragonod, a Catholic priest who published a tract on the dire state of marriage in the 1890s, shared similar sentiments. He described, in a vivid fantasy of a higher-class male observing working-class life, the consequences for wives who did not attend to their duties:

> Go to their place when you want—the morning, the evening, during the week, on Sunday—it's always the same disorder, to say the least. The beds are not made, or only made with blows of a fist; the chamber is not aired; an acrid closed-in odor takes you by the throat from the doorstep; on the floor, dirty dishes, clothing, shoes, brushes, brooms, and all the rest lying pell-mell in the dust... The children are badly washed, badly combed, snot-nosed, dressed in rags like bohemians... The husband comes home angry and tired, reproaches his wife for the mess, and then she reproaches him for drinking his pay. "Go on, drink, you drunkard, go drink your children's bread!—Of course I'm going! Can I stay in a room kept worse than a stable!... And the quarrel becomes envenomed, foul words are added to bitter words, insults, and as usual, the argument finishes with a good whipping for madame: pif! paf! and there are screams, tears. The terrified children have taken refuge, hiding in a corner; the husband has gone in a rage to find a table at the neighboring inn, and the wife, red with powerless rage, goes to complain here and there of having a bad husband who insults and beats her. He did well, madame, he did well! And I hope that tomorrow if he finds his house in the same state of negligence, he will begin again and do it right this time.[15]

Ragonod's sarcastic comments extended beyond the lower classes: "And if in less rough milieus, one is not given to such violence, unworthy of well brought-up people, if one neglects this conjugal gymnastic, do we not see the same causes bring the same effects?"[16] In this account, the wife's failure to create a clean, orderly home directly led to her husband's drunkenness, violence, and abandonment. Indeed, Ragonod's complaints of wifely neglect oscillate between the idle bourgeoise, who fails to direct her household because she is too busy trying on new clothes and visiting her friends, and the slovenly poor woman, who doesn't bother to sweep up. In both cases, he recommends that firmer direction by the husband would result in a more orderly household, for as the family chief, he is responsible for the conduct of all his subordinates. A wife's failure was also her husband's. Ragonod and Dumas shared an understanding not only of the legitimate use of violence in marital disputes but also of the mutual dependence and obligations of husbands and wives.

Testimony from participants in assize court trials also confirms this notion that the use of violence functioned within an encompassing ethic of reciprocity. Along a continuum of possible strategies in household conflict lay a whole range of possibilities, from passive acquiescence, to arguing and insults, to withholding sex or household services, to leaving the relationship. From slaps and shoves to shootings and beatings, the use of violence too corresponded to escalating levels of conflict, and it was considered a legitimate tool in resolving conflicts. Practices of violence between domestic partners took place in specific social and material contexts that helped establish the range of possible interpretations available.

The cases that came to the assize court usually concerned extreme acts of violence, but they typically occurred as a result of long-term conflicts between domestic partners, which often involved less severe acts of violence along the way. The use of violence in itself was not generally shocking. It was neither hidden nor rare, as is shown in chapter 3, which examines networks of knowledge among neighbors and family members. However, within the system of mutual obligations that defined domestic partnerships among the laboring poor, the use of violence could only be considered legitimate if it performed a punitive or retributive function. This judgment depended on the relative positions of victim and attacker, the reputation they had earned, and, subsequently, the credibility of their interpretations of their conflict among other community members.

The precise obligations that domestic partners owed one another were constantly under negotiation, if not challenge. Acts of intimate violence entered into this ongoing process of negotiation, marking points of dispute about sexuality, getting and spending material resources, and other household concerns.

Sometimes attackers described a breach of the domestic bargain as an offense against their honor. An act of violence could be a decisive statement asserting the attacker's perspective over the victim—indeed, if the attack resulted in murder, the opposing point of view was quite literally annihilated. Yet the meaning of the act of violence also remained under negotiation, subject to the interpretations not only of the couple involved but also of their families and community, as well as the agents of the police and judiciary.

Most often, intimate violence meant that a man was attempting to assert or reassert control over a woman, for men outnumbered women three to one as attackers in this sample of assize court trials. This imbalance may be accounted for partly by the fact that the system of domestic obligations was inherently disadvantageous to women. While both men and women worked for wages, women also were expected to maintain the household and care for children, if the couple had any, creating the familiar double burden so frequently described by feminist scholars. Economically, women's lower wages, which were founded on the assumption of their dependency on men, reinscribed that dependence. Furthermore, women owed men a more exacting standard of sexual fidelity than they were owed in return. In effect, this domestic bargain meant that a broader range of women's behavior was potentially under the purview of their male partners. This arrangement created more opportunities for women's failure—or calculated resistance—and therefore more opportunities for men to attempt to bring them back in line.

Without doubt, when men asserted control of women's behavior, through violence or other means, they were enforcing a system of male domination. Nonetheless, women were far from being powerless in this context. In fact, their greater obligations within the household gave them better access to neighborhood networks of knowledge and assistance that could offer them crucial support in times of trouble. Small acts of collaboration and social exchange in the performance of tasks like washing, shopping, and borrowing could add up to a powerful network of allies. Moreover, community solidarity was not women's only resource, for they could use violence as legitimately as men did. That their conduct was more widely scrutinized than men's, however, may help explain why women were more frequently the targets rather than the perpetrators of violence. If the only kind of legitimate violence was retributive, and cases of violence tried in the *cour d'assises* were more frequently being judged to be legitimate, then many women (and some men) were being judged worthy of punishment. By the same token, many men (and some women) were deemed worthy of administering it, suggesting that the capacity to use violence under certain circumstances was a component of their gender identity.

Analyses of practices of intimate violence by present-day social scientists generally address issues related to the individual perpetrator, such as his psychological development or past experiences of trauma, or else issues related to a structural, social, or cultural analysis of the perpetrator's community. The analysis in this study falls in the latter category, evaluating accounts given by attackers, victims, and witnesses as valid possibilities in the competition to establish meanings for violent acts. To be sure, the historical record does not permit an in-depth psychological evaluation of an individual attacker's motives. What it does permit, however, is a conclusion that, regardless of the claim's veracity, if a man claimed he killed his wife because she was unfaithful, he acted as if he believed it were true and tried to persuade other people that this was the case. Explanations in the *cour d'assises* thus offer a great deal of evidence about what might have counted as acceptable uses of violence among the working people of fin-de-siècle Paris.

Practices of Violence

Most attacks recorded in the trial dossiers occurred not in some dramatically staged confrontation but in the course of mundane activities. Many were facilitated by the predictable rhythms of daily life. A detailed knowledge of the victim's work routine, for instance, could enable the attacker to plan the time and place of the assault. The early morning was a likely time for attacks of this kind because relatively few people were out on the streets, and the victim was typically running essential errands or traveling to work. Louis Périchon stabbed his estranged lover early one morning outside her door. "I will wait for her at the time she goes to fetch her milk," he had told a witness before the crime.[17] Similarly, when Marie Laforest answered the door one morning around 9:30, she and her daughter both expected it to be the milk carrier, but instead it was her daughter's estranged husband, who bluffed his way into the apartment and shot her.[18] Marie Rochat shot her husband around 6:00 A.M. in front of the creamery where he always had a glass of milk before beginning his work as a masseur at a nearby bathhouse.[19]

If violence erupted in the midst of daily routines, it could also be fashioned out of the trappings of daily life. While some attackers purchased weapons for the express purpose of committing a crime, in many cases objects or substances that were ordinarily used for benign purposes could be seized in a moment of anger and used to harm another person. Blades and awls used in various professions were frequently employed as improvised weapons. Charles Dabon stabbed his lover with the knife she habitually carried in her basket to use in her work as a fishmonger.[20] Jean Durban used his masonry compass, while Jean Giacardo and Marie Rault stabbed their partners with shoemaker's blades.[21] During mealtimes, knives were easily accessible. Thus Jean-Baptiste Bernou stabbed his mistress with a knife he had just been using to eat a pear.[22] When an argument erupted between Marie Gadel and her lover while she was chopping meat, she knifed him in the back.[23] Other household goods were ready at hand in domestic disputes. In cases where men beat women, any heavy object would do for a weapon. Georges Solhart beat his mistress with a carafe, a heavy crystal cup, and a chair before finally trying to push her out the window.[24]

Among household goods handy as weapons, sulfuric acid (also called vitriol) was privileged by female attackers. It was used for household chores ordinarily performed by women, such as polishing metal pots, and it was also extremely cheap: Marie Cotard said she purchased a flask of sulfuric acid for only thirty centimes.[25] Furthermore, throwing acid on somebody did not require a significant amount of strength or skill, nor did it require the attacker to get very close to the intended victim. All of these factors made it an eminently practical weapon for women, who, as Ann-Louise Shapiro has explained, entered the iconography of fin-de-siècle crime as *vitrioleuses*.[26]

Although guns were relatively expensive, men and women alike used them in attacks. They could be purchased from a gunsmith or even a department store like the Bazaar de l'Hôtel de Ville, where Désirée Valadon bought her revolver.[27] A couple of attackers reported that they purchased guns for less than ten francs, but the usual price was around twelve to fifteen francs, and one might pay as much as twenty-five francs for a twelve-caliber "Bull-Dog" model. Marie Fournet purchased one of these, trading in a smaller revolver on the pretext that she was going to travel to Nice to visit her uncle and wanted the gun for protection.[28] Besides their higher price, guns required at least a minimal knowledge of their mechanism to be used effectively. Men may have had training in the use of guns through military service or professions associated with law enforcement. "I didn't need to practice shooting a revolver," insisted Alexandre Larue. "I was attached to the security forces for two years in Mexico. I was part of the seventh battalion of chasseurs. I know very well how to use one."[29] Likewise, two patrol officers used their service revolvers to shoot at their wives.[30] Other people claimed, like Marie Fournet, to have purchased guns prior to the crimes for the purpose of their own protection. Louis Jouault, for instance, had purchased his gun during the Commune.[31] Alphonsine Ancel, who ran a brasserie on the rue du Temple, kept a loaded revolver in her cash drawer for security. Her lover used it to threaten her before finally shooting her with his own gun.[32] And Alexine Chalandre explained, "Living alone, I thought it prudent to have [the gun] at my place," though it seemed like a suspicious coincidence that she had it with her the day she confronted her estranged lover and shot at him. When the investigating magistrate suggested that she did not really know how to use the weapon, she replied, "If I had wanted to kill him, nothing would have been easier for me, since I still had five bullets in my revolver... Assuredly, if I had wanted to, I would have achieved my goal."[33] She was confident in her ability to use the weapon.

As these brief stories indicate, violence was not a male monopoly. Although direct statements about men's entitlement to use violence were fairly rare, a few men did articulate the belief that they had a right to use violence because they were men. Nobody made parallel statements about wives' or women's entitlement to use violence. So, while not exclusive to men, violence could be understood as a tool for enforcing male privilege, if not as a privilege of masculinity itself. Georges Koenig, for one, described his use of violence against his wife as an entitlement and an obligation. After stabbing his unfaithful wife, he confronted her in the presence of the *juge d'instruction*. When his wife mentioned a previous attack that had taken place before they moved to Paris, he replied indignantly, "You have the audacity to recall what happened in Montbéliard. I would have liked to have hidden it. I knew that you were seeing military men; I struck you. It was my right; it was my duty."[34] Apparently the court agreed with him, since he was treated leniently throughout the trial and acquitted outright of harming his wife, though it took her three weeks to recover from her stab wounds. Koenig acted in direct defense of his entitlement to his wife's sexual fidelity; indeed, he felt obliged to do so, and his actions were judged to be legitimate. It was his proper role to discipline his wife. Auguste Vallaud expressed an equally inflexible attitude toward his lover Marie Mellet when she tried to leave him. "I am your lover; you will do my will," he declared to her, and, "You must come back to me; it is my will."[35] However, Vallaud was her pimp, not her husband, and he was condemned for trying to kill her. While both men defended their use of violence by referring to their privilege or obligation to control their female partners' sexuality, this defense was only successful in a relationship not explicitly based on economic exchange. Where the man was not perceived to be fulfilling his proper duties as a man, punishing his partner for not fulfilling hers as a woman was disallowed. If a man claimed to be defending his manhood by punishing his partner, he had to have a manhood that was intact and worth defending.

That the masculine prerogative to discipline an errant partner was not license for unfettered violence is further illustrated by the case of Jean-Jacques De Moor. When he described the scene during which he killed his wife, De Moor claimed they argued all night about her infidelity and then she literally invited him to stab her. Seeing that he had picked up a knife, he claimed that she opened her clothing to reveal her chest and said, "If you do not strike, you have no heart, you are not a man." He continued, "At this moment, my wife was lying on her back, her bosom exposed, her arms crossed, and she threw herself back as though she were awaiting the blow. I held the knife—it was like I was drawn... I cut my wife's throat in a single movement... It was my left hand that acted... I heard no cry."[36] Since other witnesses totally contradicted the allegation that Catherine De Moor had a lover, and that she and her husband had argued before he attacked her, it appears unbelievable that she would invite her husband to stab her. Nonetheless, De Moor created quite an elaborate scenario to support his story: his wife challenged his manhood, and he reacted automatically, irresistibly, as if exacting violent retribution was not an entitlement but a reflex. However, the privilege of punishing his wife was not as straightforward as he imagined. Since his wife was in fact innocent of infidelity, and he himself was reputed to be a lazy, exploitative man, De Moor's claim that he was acting in just defense of his manhood was discounted by the witnesses and the court, and he was convicted of murder. The person who used violence as a punishment had to be worthy of administering it.

On the other side of the equation, for violence to be legitimate, the object of punishment had to have done something that required correction. Witnesses did not always agree, however, on the relative positions of the two people involved. François Corlieux, a former employee at the grocery run by the Guillot couple, argued that it was unjust for Guillot, a lazy man, to beat his industrious wife. He described his intervention in a fight as follows: "I was notified by an employee that he was in the middle of beating her; I was indignant and I lost patience. I went down to the basement to stop him, and I permitted myself to tell him that it was shameful for him who did nothing to beat a woman that way who did everything she could from morning to evening to run the shop. He told me it was none of my business, without showing any anger." In Corlieux's explanation, Guillot was trying to exercise power without fulfilling any of the responsibilities that would have entitled him to it. "He would have liked to be everything in the house, without giving himself any pains, without working. He was, as I have said, lazy and gluttonous; his wife, on the contrary, was very industrious. She had taken charge and set herself to ordering the employees. With his laziness and his habits of drink, he was beyond giving orders himself. Nobody gave a darn about him. For me, that's the explanation of his character; that's why he had fits of anger when he had been drinking."[37]

Guillot's sister, however, had another interpretation of the frequent beatings. "Perhaps his wife has some very good qualities, but she did not know how to handle her husband. Instead of treating him with gentleness, she reproached him, she gave him orders, and she wore him out." In short, it was Guillot's wife who drove him to violence. Although this opinion was in the minority in this case, the allegation that women brought violence on themselves by mishandling their partners was not unique. "The wife never ceased making scenes of jealousy with her husband and, losing patience, [he] finally brutalized her," declared a landlady regarding her former tenants, the Gys.[38] In another case, Dominque Millim insisted that he would not have stabbed his lover had she not been nagging him about drinking: "Without doubt, she reproached me for being drunk. She did it often. This made me angry. As I often used to tell her, it's when I'm sober that these reproaches should be made to me. I threatened her with a slap; she irritated me more. Unhappily, I had my knife in my hand, being in the middle of eating; I gave her a blow with it on the left thigh."[39]

If women could provoke violence by scolding or nagging men, they could also provoke it by committing violence themselves. One man described his mistress's provocations in these terms: "Esther insulted me, calling me a bastard and a coward, and at the same time she threw me a kick in the privates, which hit me, but without hurting me much. I was then next to the stairway. La fille Bonjour tried to give me another kick, but I gave her a slap myself, and mad with anger, since she was defending herself, I drew my knife, and I struck her."[40] Jean-Baptiste Santin also claimed he was enraged by his wife kicking him in the groin, much to the disbelief of the investigating magistrate. "Everyone agrees in saying that your wife was very sweet. You are also of this opinion. In these circumstances, doesn't it seem very difficult to believe, as you allege, that she kicked you in the privates?" the *juge d'instruction* asked in Santin's final interrogation. "However, that's what she did," he replied, "and it's a great misfortune, since without this kick, I would not have committed the crime. But the blow hurt me. I was already angry. I lost my head, and noticing the hammer within my reach, I grabbed it, and without thinking, I struck."[41] Whether or not Santin's wife really kicked him, his explanation depends on the assumption that such an act would understandably have provoked a violent response on his part. Georges Guerrier described a similar scenario leading up to his shooting at his wife: "I was furious to hear the stupid things that she said to me in front of everybody. I begged her to shut up, but it was only when she slapped me in the face that anger carried me away, and the revolver went off in my hands... I had told her, 'Shut up, I beg you, you'll make something bad happen.' I only wanted to make her be quiet, but she continued. It was only when she scratched my face and punched me in the head that I fired. I didn't want to hurt her."[42] By transferring the blame to their partners, these men distanced themselves from their own choices to use violence, as if, once set in motion, a reciprocal exchange of violence could not be stopped.

On a legal level, the question of provocation could be posed formally during a trial by the defense as "provocation by blows or serious violent acts towards one's person" (*provocation par coups ou violences graves envers sa personne*). Provocation would limit the gravity of the crime in the case of conviction, but it was rarely suggested in cases of domestic disputes, much less admitted. In the case of Jean Louis Degrange, for instance, the jury found that the one punch his wife threw before he beat her unconscious did not constitute a serious threat to him.[43] Provocation was similarly refused in the case of Jules Alphonse Michel, where a doctor testified that the cuts on his hands must have come from the struggle as he stabbed his mistress with a razor. (He had told a neighbor immediately after the crime that he had cut himself while preparing to eat a chicken purchased from a street vendor.)[44]

Still, as these cases suggest, it was not rare for women to fight physically with their domestic partners. "In the first days of my marriage, I allowed myself to be hit," explained Marie Rault, "but I swear that in recent times, because of having been mistreated so much, I had become less patient. When he used to hit me, I would defend myself as I was able, and I threw at my husband's head anything that fell under my hand. But the match was not even, since he was tall and robust, while I am short and weak."[45] A few men expressed their disapproval of her fighting back, accusing her of beating her husband. François Besson, who rented a room to the husband, blamed the wife for the violence in their household. "He drank a lot and instead of leaving him alone when he had been drinking, his wife got him worked up by scolding him. He and his wife fought each other constantly. The man's only fault was drunkenness. The wife drank too, and when she was drunk she used to hit her husband, like her husband used to hit her. Many times, I saw on Rault's face the trace of his wife's fingernails."

Rault, however, never admitted that he did more than shove her. In a hospital interview with the investigating magistrate the day after she stabbed him, he boldly declared, "When she bothered me, since I am a little quick-tempered, I sent her out walking. I even pushed her a couple of times, but I never struck her. As for her, she hit me many times. When she was angry, she broke everything." Many witnesses directly contradicted Rault's testimony. Given the volume of the testimony against him, it appears likely that Rault was lying in order to make his wife look as bad as possible and minimize the violence that he himself committed. It may well be true that she fought back or even instigated fights by criticizing him in public, but on balance, the physical harm he inflicted on her was far more severe than the harm she inflicted on him, until the moment when she stabbed him.

On the night of the murder, Rault had been brought home drunk by some comrades and had gone to sleep. His wife woke him up while trying to make room for herself to lie down in the bed. She described what happened next. "He looked at me, ground his teeth, and said, 'Now you're going to pay for that; you must die.'" He started to get out of bed, and she panicked, grabbed his shoemaker's blade and stabbed him in the belly. He died from peritonitis two days later. "I don't believe that another woman was tortured like I was tortured. I was beaten, kicked out at night in all weather, and sometimes deprived of food," she explained to the *juge d'instruction*. "My husband, however, had nothing to reproach me for. I was married a virgin, and I never belonged to anyone but him. I have always worked according to my strength and in spite of what I did in a moment of despair, I must not be a really bad woman to have endured such suffering for so long." Thus she emphasized her sexual fidelity, her work record, and his excessive violence, hoping to justify her actions to the investigator.

In a later interrogation, the *juge d'instruction* reviewed an occasion when she had pursued her husband with a blade and another when she fired at him a gun loaded only with powder. The investigating magistrate then pointed out that she was not in a position of legitimate self-defense when she stabbed her husband, since she could have escaped the particular situation where the attack occurred. At this, she seemed to lose some confidence, since pauses between each of her sentences are recorded in the transcript: "It is certain that I could have saved myself... I would have gotten away with spending one more night outside, and I would not have had the death of my husband to reproach myself for. It was anger that carried me away... He mistreated me too much at the end, too. In spite of everything, I regret what I did, because in spite of everything, I loved my husband." What can be recovered from this account of the crime is the interplay of the couple's mutual obligations and conflicts. Although originally charged with murder (*homicide volontaire*), Marie Rault was only convicted of inflicting one blow and wound (*coup et blessure*), causing unintentional death. The jury admitted extenuating circumstances. This was the lightest judgment she could receive and still be held responsible for a death. Her sentence was three years in prison—again, a relatively mild punishment, though it is tempting to speculate that had she been a more passive victim, rather than one who fought back continuously, she might have been acquitted altogether.

However, other women affirmed their prerogative to defend themselves physically from attack. Eulalie Jean, accused of having thrown a blade at her husband's head, explained, "It was my husband who had beaten me, I was certainly obliged to defend myself." She would go to trial for shooting at him, but their relationship was a long tale of mutual violence. Her husband echoed her words in his own deposition: "When she struck me either with a hand or the broomstick, I was certainly obliged to defend myself."[46] Violence invited the return of violence, from women and men alike. According to a neighbor who lived on the same landing, Augustine Catherine was always the one who threw the first punch when she and her husband fought.[47] "He gave me a blow, and I gave him back another," explained Marie Daouze after she stabbed her lover. Witnesses in her case placed the blame for the couple's frequent, violent arguments on both sides. Their maid said, "la fille Daouze was much more mean and more violent than he. I was present at many scenes where they beat each other and threw glasses at each other's heads. She was always the one who started it." A friend of theirs tended to blame the man more: "Richard used to hit la fille Daouze, and [she] retaliated as she was able... She used to say to Richard sometimes, 'I'll break your face.'" Another friend once saw Richard with a bloody nose.[48]

And yet, the match was never even between men and women. Most of the cases in which a woman fought back, or allegedly provoked violence through her words or actions, ended with the woman seriously hurt and the man on trial. After all, men were generally larger and stronger than women, if not more willing to use violence. When Philiberte Brossier scratched her husband's face in a fight, he responded by shooting her in the arm.[49] Like the widow Rault, who stabbed her husband in the belly, a few women responded to blows with lethal violence. Charlotte Gérard stabbed her lover in the chest with a pair of scissors after he hit her, though a neighbor woman said that she had never seen her defend herself before when her lover beat her.[50] Marie Gadel often fought physically with her lover, and she stabbed him in the heat of an argument. "What do you want?" she asked her maid after the crime. "He was beating me—I defended myself as I could. I had a knife in my hand, and he received a blow from it."[51] These explanations of self-defense and retaliation in the midst of a fight underscore the ethic of reciprocity: one partner injured the other, who in turn fought back.

Violence was never considered legitimate if it was committed randomly or out of causes unrelated to the person who was its object. When witnesses criticized violence, they pointed out that it was undeserved. Pauline Geoffroy witnessed an episode in her newspaper shop where Charles Chapuis twice slapped his pregnant former mistress. She testified, "I had the opportunity, later, to reproach him for his conduct towards Rosa Velay, who is a diligent worker and who truly did not deserve what happened to her," that is, to be abandoned and abused by him.[52] Complaining to a neighbor as they both got water from the common faucet on their landing, Clarisse Denis stated, "Believe me, it's not great to have a pig of a man like that one! To come back from your work at 6:30 and be beaten, mistreated!"[53] She was doing everything she was supposed to, working hard all day, preparing the evening meal, and if her husband beat her, she felt it was through no fault of her own and therefore unjust. When Victorine Lelong went looking for her former lover after the death of their child, she said he pushed her onto a chair and tried to slap her. "If you believe that I deserve to be hit, [then] hit, I permit you," she said she told him. "He answered me that he knew very well that I did not deserve it."[54] Perhaps the assumption that proper behavior should offer immunity from violence was an additional incentive for women to stay in line.

Whether their explanations were convincing to the witnesses and the court or not, the vast majority of the people tried in the assize court claimed that they used violence against their partners in order to punish them. Summing up his opinion of Jean Brudieux's defense for shooting at his wife, the investigating magistrate declared, "He intended, he says, to punish her misconduct. But this system of defense cannot be accepted along with the good information furnished on the morality of la femme Brudieux."[55] When Alphonse Catelier was arrested for strangling his wife, he proclaimed, "She deserved correction. I gave it to her!" Her reputation, however, proved to be excellent.[56] Interrogated as to why he shot his wife, Eugène Levielle reported, "Because she did not come home that night, because for a long time she had been living a depraved life, because she goes to the brasseries on Grenelle, to the ball. Because men escort her up to the door." He suspected her of loose living and adultery, so he felt justified in trying to kill her.[57] Charles Gaudot, admitting that he had given his mistress the poison that killed her, declared, "I only wanted to make her very sick to teach her a good lesson."[58]

Accused of frequently beating his mistress before he stabbed her, Gaspard Keiffer affirmed, "If I had to punish her many times, it was because she conducted herself badly." And yet she was reputed to be a hardworking woman who supported him.[59] Asked about his own poor behavior, Ernest Cotard admitted having an affair, and, he said, "I sometimes slapped [my wife] because I believed she was behaving badly, but I never punched her or kicked her." His violence toward her, he claimed, was not only justified but mild.[60] Nicolas Jacob offered a similar explanation. Although he denied that he had seriously injured his wife, he admitted that he hit her sometimes. "She constantly made scenes with me when I came home on the pretext that I did not bring back enough money. Hence, the disputes. But I did not beat my wife, and if it happened that I hit her once or twice, it was very legitimate on my part, and these acts have nothing to do with the so-called habitual brutalities of which I am accused."[61] His idea of what constituted a legitimate use of violence was consistent with the judgments of the *cour d'assises*. Occasional blows administered as justly deserved punishment were one thing; violence without a cause was another. The question then became whether or not the degree of violence was appropriate to the victim's offense, if one existed.

Although men could legitimately use violence to keep their partners in line, a few men proved unwilling to hit their partners even when others urged them to do so. In spite of numerous recommendations to the contrary, François Lerondeau refused to beat his wife to gain her submission. His friend Antoine Pelletier advised him on how to handle her: "Several times, when I had heard the noise of fighting... I would say to Lerondeau, 'Well then, you've had something again!' And I counseled him to make himself master at home, even by force." His second cousin explained, "He only responded to his wife's insults with pleading. Many people, witnesses of la femme Lerondeau's malevolence, advised the husband to set her straight, but he always answered that it would be impossible for him to lay a hand on a woman."[62] Although some of the men in his community clearly disagreed, Lerondeau believed it was inappropriate for a man to beat a woman under any circumstances.

Investigating magistrates readily shared this point of view. The *juge d'instruction* Atthalin scolded Louis Badran for beating his mistress, suggesting that it would have been more appropriate for him to fight with her brother, who was advising her to leave him: "Is it because Blanche was weak, defenseless, that you... took out your anger on her?" Badran replied that he stabbed her because she appeared to be on the verge of taking her brother's advice.[63] This less tolerant attitude toward the use of violence may be related to the higher social standing of the men who worked as investigating magistrates, for there was a sharp class divide over the use of violence in intimate relationships.

In distinct contrast to the complex negotiations regarding the legitimacy of violence that took place among working people, the few upper-class couples who appeared in court expressed an unambiguously negative attitude toward violence between men and women—except, of course, for the potentially lethal violence of a crime of passion. Alexandrine Duc brought a dowry valued at thirty thousand francs when she married François Duc, a physician twenty-eight years her senior. They would come to the *cour d'assises* after he shot her for having an affair. Madame Duc complained that her husband had left her alone too often and that he had slapped her twice. One of these occasions had occurred ten years earlier, "but in that circumstance, I was in the wrong," she said. The other incident had happened just the year before the crime, apparently around the time that she began her affair. "He was punishing my oldest son. I wanted to hold back his hands, and in his anger, he threw me a slap," she explained. Her husband elaborated that the slap was accidental but that it made his wife very upset: "She was resentful toward me and told me that I would pay for it and that she would never forgive me."[64] Two slaps, separated by ten years, would have been considered minor mistreatment in a less privileged social milieu, but Madame Duc considered them to be a major transgression on her husband's part. Indeed, her husband's remarks imply that he believed she embarked on an affair in retaliation for those blows.

Similarly, Emilie Muller, wife of the aristocrat Edouard Genuyt de Beaulieu, was shocked the first and only time her husband used physical force with her. In a struggle over letters regarding his infidelity that she had planned to send to some lawyers, he said, "I was obliged to use violence. I did not want to lay a hand on her, and I used only one hand to push her away. I had the other hand in my pants pocket." Blanche Piot, a domestic servant who witnessed the fight over the letters, went into more detail. "Madame said to him, 'You are a miserable man to act this way with a woman'... She tried to take back her letters. Monsieur, to make her let go, hit her on the hands and on the arms. Several times he threw her backward onto the furniture, on the bed. Once he took her by the neck and squeezed it so hard that she started to cry out and could not finish... She was crying. I was crying with her." The husband won the struggle for the letters and took them to his solicitor, but the wife shot him that afternoon as he sat at his desk, writing to his mistress. "These acts of violence, the first that had been exercised against me, had troubled me profoundly," she explained.[65]

The case of Georges Langlois suggests other ways in which an upper-class man could control his wife without resorting to violence. Once the proprietor of a waxed cloth factory, Langlois could have been prosperous had he not squandered so much money on prostitutes and high living, including the twenty thousand francs his wife inherited from an uncle. He never physically abused his wife—until he shot her, that is—but through depriving her of money, proposing that she use her looks to get him more credit with potential business partners, and carrying on with other women, he caused her a great deal of distress. She had moved in with her mother, taken a job as a cashier, and undertaken divorce procedures when he bluffed his way into her apartment and shot her. She had been reduced to working to support herself, and it seems clear that it was only the unswerving support of her brother and mother that enabled her attempt to extricate herself from her marriage. When she rejected his final demands to take him back, he said, "I saw, as in a dream, the woman I loved in the arms of another man that my children would call their father... I saw red. I took the revolver out of my coat pocket, and I fired."[66] It was only at the point when she seemed finally to be on the verge of escaping his control definitively, through divorce, that Langlois resorted to physical violence; all other means had failed. No doubt because he had been such a failure as a man, he was convicted of murder and sentenced to forced labor for life.

One notable feature of the Langlois, Genuyt, and Duc cases, all concerning well-to-do couples, is that they contain depositions only from family members and servants, not the usual network of friends, neighbors, and coworkers that are so numerous in most cases in the *cour d'assises* records. The spacious, solidly built housing that wealthier people enjoyed was purposefully designed to protect their privacy, shielding from public view what transpired in the bosom of the family. Because the number of people who knew what went on in their domestic interiors was so limited, it is difficult to gauge how much physical violence actually took place among the upper classes, in spite of professed ideals rejecting it. Nonetheless, the outrage expressed by upper-class people about relatively minor incidents—a few slaps, or a struggle resulting in some bruises—supports the idea that violence was not, or was not meant to be, an ordinary feature of upper-class relationships between men and women, as it was among working people. The use of violence in intimate relationships thus could be an important distinction between these two broad social strata.

Honor and Reputation

The other salient division between cases of higher- and lower-class couples in the *cour d'assises* is their different uses of the concepts of honor and shame. Higher-class couples were more likely to use the vocabulary of honor and shame to articulate the mutual dependence and reciprocal obligations that characterized their intimate relationships, but they did not have a monopoly on these terms. When lower-class people invoked the terms of honor and shame—as they did more frequently in court than in pretrial depositions—they meant something different than did members of the higher class. The parallels, however, are significant. Evidence suggests that the lower-class system of honor and shame is best understood as a subset of the broader ethic of reciprocity that pervaded the social interactions of couples and community members.

In his classic study of male bourgeois honorability, Robert Nye argued that the bourgeoisie developed a code of honor to distinguish itself from other social groups, creating an exclusive, cohesive class. Like the aristocrats who preceded them, Nye wrote, bourgeois men were concerned with producing heirs to maintain their patrimony, but they focused on the values of moral discipline and inner values, rather than relying on the privilege of birth. They adopted elements of the old chivalric code, most notably a concern for rules of politesse and the stylized conflicts of the duel, thus identifying themselves as legitimate political heirs to France's feudal past. Nye emphasized that male honor required constant protection; honor was subject to attack at any moment, and a man had to be ready to defend it. Relying on Ruth Harris's work on crimes of passion, he suggested that the need to defend one's honor was a concern for bourgeois men, not others. In trials for crimes of passion, he wrote, "It seems that the 'honor defense,' like the duel, was more or less restricted to bourgeois milieux or above. Working-class men seem to have preferred to defend themselves by appeal to extreme states of passion; or it may be that—a more subtle point— they realized that magistrates would find the language of honor inappropriate to them."[67] The present analysis of trial transcripts confirms Nye's suspicion of a distinction between bourgeois and working-class male honor, although on different grounds than he suspected. Claims about honor and extreme states of emotion were not mutually exclusive for men (and women) of all social levels.

William Reddy, too, has found "plentiful evidence of a popular sense of honor" in his analysis of dossiers for cases of legal separation in the Tribunal civil de Versailles in the early decades of the nineteenth century.[68] Also drawing on separation cases reported in the *Gazette des Tribunaux* during the first half of the nineteenth century, Reddy has argued that maintaining one's honor in a familial setting required a particular concern for appearances. For women, any appearance of impropriety, especially with regard to dress and conduct with men, could jeopardize their reputation for sexual purity. In addition, it was important for men and women alike to conceal anything in their household that might impinge upon their honor, whether inappropriate sentiments or deeds. Although the litigants and witnesses in Reddy's sample seem generally much more wary of public exposure and much less willing to intervene in each other's household affairs than would the working people of Paris a few decades later, the two groups shared a consistent concern for how they appeared in the eyes of their community. Around the beginning of the century, people involved in domestic disputes feared the exposure of their conflicts, and toward the end of the century, the same kind of people strategically spread knowledge of their difficulties among their neighbors and extended family—nonetheless, the critical concern about the judgment of the community remained constant. One's honor or reputation, the reservoir of deeds and characteristics on which the community passed judgment, was a precious resource for all.

The few upper-class defendants who appeared in court consistently invoked their honor in their defense. François Duc told the investigating magistrate that when he learned of his wife's infidelity and shot her, "I acted under the influence of sentiment that you must understand and of which a man so seriously wounded in his honor is not always the master."[69] Auguste-Frédéric Smeyers, a furniture dealer, shot his wife's lover after challenging him to a duel. "He had destroyed my honor. He had dishonored me in a cowardly way," Smeyers declared. "All this passed through my head, and I could not hold myself back."[70] According to these statements, the need to avenge one's honor was so strong as to be irresistible, and it was also assumed to be an urge that listening jurists would understand themselves. Likewise, Charles-Arthur du Bourg (the subject of Dumas's *Tue-la!*) claimed he was perfectly justified in stabbing his adulterous wife. With a vivid elision of manliness and barbarity, du Bourg asserted during his trial, "I was a savage beast when my honor was attacked. I can certainly be a man to defend myself."[71] As his lawyer M. Carraby argued, du Bourg's family had "amassed a capital of honor as others amassed a capital of money." What the wife should be to her husband was "the depository of his honor, of his secrets, of his name." As for du Bourg himself, Carraby said, "He is the husband, therefore he is the great judge [*grand justicier*] of his honor."[72] By this logic, the violation of a man's honor—which was the hallmark of his social status—gave him license to kill. The proper use of violence was an integral component of masculine honorability.

Not all men who invoked their violated honor as an excuse for their actions could make the claim successfully. In some cases, professional jurists disagreed sharply with the concept of violated honor that lower-class men on trial claimed as their motivation. A foreman at a printshop, Camille-Eugène Daly testified that it was in defense of his honor that he beat his wife (whom he believed was unfaithful) to death with a heavy candlestick. The presiding magistrate did not find his claim to honor credible. He observed, "When an individual kills to avenge his honor, he says it. He shouts it. He goes to the police captain to make himself a prisoner. You did not do any of this—on the contrary."[73] If one's actions were blameless, there would be no reason to hide, the magistrate suggested; in fact an honorable man would proclaim his vindication. Turning oneself in was itself a claim to the legitimacy of one's actions.[74] The jury rejected Daly's claim to a legitimate use of violence, and he was condemned to forced labor for life.

Eudoxe de Verneuil, a clockmaker, also did not meet the standards of the investigating magistrate when he attacked his allegedly unfaithful wife. He had received a letter from some malicious friends accusing her of infidelity, and he attacked her and her lover when he found them walking in the street together. "You were not only not in a case of legal excuse, but not even in one of those cases where a man has no more possible doubt on his dishonor," scolded the *juge d'instruction*. "You should not have trusted words alone, inspired by meanness, and killed a man because you met him lending his arm to your wife." But de Verneuil replied, "I was very excited, I admit, but I was mad, I had lost my head seeing myself publicly dishonored."[75] The magistrates reproached De Verneuil and Daly for not being sufficiently certain that their honor had really been violated, although the men felt sure enough.

Still, attacking one's unfaithful partner was not the only option for mending one's damaged honor. One could also instigate a duel. The terms of such duels among members of the lower classes, however, did not reflect a perfect translation of the values of the upper classes who invented such trials. In a case involving rival lovers, Charles Balade once showed his revolver to Rodolphe Salis, to whom he had lost his mistress. "I asked him what he was going to do with it," Salis reported. "He said, 'If you want to buy one, we will go into the woods to shoot at each other.'"[76] Balade's idea of a duel may have needed some explanation, but his proposal of a formal fight retained only the barest outline of the form studied by Nye among the bourgeoisie. In another twist on the usual pattern, Charles Joulain wrote his lover's husband to demand a duel when she threatened to return home to him.[77] There was other evidence that people who were not domestic partners settled disputes through fights that were less ritualized than duels but more formal than impromptu fistfights. When François Corlieux reproached his employer Modeste Guillot for beating his hard-working wife, Guillot told him that they had an account to settle. "I asked him if this concerned firing me or fighting each other," Corlieux recounted, and Guillot said it was fighting. He then pulled out a gun, which would not fire, and Corlieux quit his job.[78]

Such dissonant or incomplete comprehension of the proper way to defend one's honor in a duel highlights the different conceptions of honor held by magistrates and the lower-class people who testified before them, but magistrates and witnesses did find common ground. Most frequently, honor was used in the official indictment or the interrogation of the accused as a kind of shorthand to say that someone belonged to a good family—at least a family of people who worked hard and had not previously been entangled with the law. In his indictment, Hillairin de Saint-Priest was described as being from "an honorable family but without fortune."[79] In the trial of Louis Anatole Léon Barbot, the investigating magistrate asserted, "The accused could not have entered into a more honorable family" through marriage.[80] Occasionally, the investigating magistrates' use of the concept of honor was more nuanced. One *juge d'instruction* scolded Simon Richelet for pursuing his wife after she left him: "Knowing that she lived at M. Marius Lalet's place, where she has an honorable refuge, you caused her to be kicked out because of the scenes that you came to make with her. She was working honorably at M. Marbiot's place; you came to threaten her,"[81] and she lost her job. Apparently, this investigating magistrate believed that even a woman who had left her husband could put herself in an honorable situation. The magistrate investigating the case of an abandoned mother who tried to shoot her husband also spoke sympathetically of her actions: "The abandoned wife, deprived of her children, would have avenged her own dignity and her honor as an offended mother."[82] These references to honor are not detailed or numerous enough to support an analysis of precisely what the investigating magistrates as a group thought about the honorability of the ordinary people on trial. Yet they do permit the conclusion that working people were not a priori excluded from honorability by their social superiors, even if their understanding of the concept differed.

About half a dozen working people whose cases were examined in this study used the vocabulary of honor to describe themselves. Henri Béziade called himself "an honorable man" in a letter to the investigating magistrate, even though he did not dispute that he had seduced a woman with false promises of marriage.[83] The brother of Adèle Pautard, a woman tried for disfiguring her rival with acid, wrote the investigating magistrate to insist that "our family is honorable" and to express the hope that the case might be dismissed, as though an honorable family should be shielded from such public exposure as an assize court trial.[84] A few months after he shot his estranged wife, Charles Duchêne begged her to take him back. "I give you my word of Honor," he wrote, "that I will work and will keep my word... On my life I swear it and make the oath before God to be a serious man in the future Who will make you Happy. And will do Honor to my business. Your husband who loves you and kisses you with his whole heart. Give me your word of honor that you will return. Keep your word and I will keep mine."[85] Here, the invocation of honor appears to have been occasioned by the gravity of Duchêne's proposition, intended to enforce his credibility or sincerity. He offers his honor as the guarantee of a new bargain; if his wife does her part, he will undertake to do his.

The case of the Richelet couple offers a glimpse of a more sophisticated understanding of honor.[86] After several attempts at reconciliation, the husband shot and seriously wounded his wife. She had been unfaithful, briefly cohabiting with another man, although some witnesses claimed that her husband drove her to it. Her brother, a patrolman named Alexis Leca, was not so forgiving. He presented himself on his own initiative to the police commissioner and gave detailed and negative testimony concerning his sister's honor, which he felt reflected on the whole family. After she left her husband, he said, her conduct became "disgusting." He continued, "I was revolted by it, and I believe that if I had not been the father of a family, I would have intervened myself, violently, to put an end to this state of things that had become a dishonor for me, for my four brothers, and for our whole family. All of us, in varying degrees of fortune, some comfortable, others almost rich, we are honorable. There is only that one who turned out badly." He said that he once slapped his sister and kicked her lover in the derrière when he met them in the street, and he went on to explain why he was so intensely disturbed by the situation: "She used to be what one calls a good woman, very submissive to her elders. I would even say that like all Corsican women, she was sensitive about anything that could touch her honor or her morality." In her brother's account, his sister's downfall was due to the corruption of her morality as a good Corsican woman, which ultimately discredited her and their whole family. "I blush for her, and I pity her unfortunate, arrested husband," he concluded. His more keenly developed sense of honor may well have sprung from his cultural roots, since in the Mediterranean islands a code of honor and shame has persisted vigorously even through the end of the twentieth century.[87] Richelet was acquitted of attempted murder.

As in the unhappy case of Rose Richelet, a woman's honor was primarily defined by her sexual conduct. Decrying her former lover, who had abandoned her and her child, Désirée Zéphirine Valadon said, "He took me as a virgin [*sage*] and stole my honor... he ruined my position for ten years." The lover did not dispute the terms, "She wanted me to marry her to return her honor to her."[88] Marie Féral attacked the lover who abandoned her when she became pregnant. "He dishonored me and dishonored my family," she declared.[89] Marie Croissant, also abandoned with a child, confessed, "My intention was to kill him, since he dishonored me."[90] Marie Fournet did not know her lover was already married when they opened a wineshop together. "He had taken my honor and my money," she explained. "I was furious to see that all my savings were lost and that I had been duped by Biver, and that is why I killed him."[91] In all of these cases, it appears that the woman attributed her own dishonor not to the fact that she had sex with a man to whom she was not married but rather that the relationship did not result in marriage or the establishment of a permanent relationship. All of these women were left with children or, in the case of Marie Fournet, with a significant financial loss. And all of these women chose to use violence only after repeated attempts at reconciliation, unlike many men, who tended to use increasingly harsh violent measures leading up to an extreme final attack. These women waited until the relative merits of their position were in the ascendance, and then they used violence to enforce their claims. Their sexual relationships only became dishonorable when followed by betrayal on the part of their lovers, and the court confirmed their point of view: Valadon, Féral, Croissant, and Fournet were all acquitted of murder or attempted murder. For these women, using violence in defense of their honor was legitimate.[92]

Sexuality was not the sole arena where honor came into play, for women as for men. Honor was also at stake in business dealings, as in the case of Jean Vigineix-Roche, who flew into a rage when his estranged wife said he had dishonored himself by declaring their umbrella store bankrupt.[93] In another case, the very fact of going to court was considered shameful. Georges Langlois's wealthy father testified against his son, but during his pretrial deposition he begged, "If it is possible, spare me the shame and pain of deposing in public before the *cour d'assises*."[94] The misuse of violence was also sometimes described as dishonorable or shameful. Armand Massacry testified that his sister's face was so badly bruised from her husband's beatings that he was "ashamed" to go out with her in the street.[95] Was he ashamed because he did not prevent his sister's beating? Was he ashamed because people might assume that he had caused the bruises himself? Or was it simply that a woman with visible bruises was a sign of shamefully excessive mistreatment, no matter the cause? He did not elaborate. All the same, these diverse examples reinforce the idea that honor depended on the relative positions of the people involved in a dispute, and the connections and obligations among them.

Siblings and parents sometimes felt that a relative's misconduct had injured their honor or family name. Before his murder trial, Georges Koenig received a letter from his brother in Besançon, despairing of the "shame that had spread over the whole family."[96] Guillaume Malmézac's brother and sister both testified that their brother's trial ended a history of two hundred years of good conduct by the family.[97] Writing her brother for help, Adèle Pautard reported her husband's infidelity and abandonment, saying with bitter irony, "He is dragging his name in the mud; his family should be proud of him."[98] Sympathizing with Legrand's decision to attack his unfaithful wife, a female neighbor said, "He could not tolerate his wife dragging his name through the mud any longer."[99] According to Rosine Langlois's brother, she feared that if she did not divorce her husband, her husband would "dishonor the name of her children by his indelicacies and frauds."[100] The public exposure of a member's misconduct was most damaging to the family's collective reputation.[101]

Precisely because of these close interconnections between the honor of an individual and that of his or her family, third parties could intervene in a couple's dispute. If an offense against one person constituted an offense against that person's family, then family members were in a position to retaliate. Thus, François Marambat was acquitted for stabbing his pregnant daughter's lover when he refused to marry her.[102] In another case, a woman demanded that a third party seek vengeance for her death not through violence but though exposing the murderers. Clarisse Denis, age fifteen and a half, wrote to the investigating magistrate to demand the chance to testify after her mother's death. She gave a negative account of her stepfather and claimed that just a week before the crime, her mother had demanded that she speak out: "If he kills me," she had said, "you will tell all the harm that he has done to me and all his threats of death."[103] Denis's testimony and that of her sister doubtless contributed to the stepfather's conviction.

Whether vengeance was exacted through violence or through words, it could only be legitimate in response to a prior offense, real or imagined. The relation of a man's honor to his partner's sexual fidelity illustrates this point. As his honor was tied in with his prerogative to maintain exclusive sexual access to one woman, if a man failed to control his partner's sexual activity, it reflected badly on him as well as on her. In many cases, the equation seemed simple—a partner's infidelity required violent retribution. In the words of Jean Legrand, who would be acquitted of murdering his unfaithful wife, "She dishonored me. My only desire was that she be dead."[104] To Legrand and many others, violence was a means of asserting control that had previously been lost. He had to act to assert his power precisely because his power had already been undermined. In the constant negotiation of meaning that attended every action in a couple's conflict, the use of violence may be seen as an effort to make one interpretation finally stick. Although killing his wife may have destroyed the most potent sign of Legrand's failure, however, it could not restore her fidelity.

By choosing to have sex with another man, Legrand's wife had betrayed one of the fundamental elements of the implicit bargain at the foundation of their domestic partnership. According to the evidence of her actions, the deal was already off, or at least its original terms had been canceled. Legrand could choose to accept the new conditions of their relationship (that she could continue to have sex with other men), or he could act, as he did, decisively in favor of the old conditions. Following a challenge to the status quo, a partner had the choice to permit change or to fight to reinstate the boundaries being challenged. In this milieu, this could entail a legitimate use of violence.

The most dramatic incidents of this sequence of challenge and defense occurred in cases where one partner had left, or was threatening to leave, the other. In fact, this was the most frequent single circumstance common to cases of intimate violence in the *cour d'assises*, affecting more than one-quarter of the total number. In these cases, the partners who left were insisting that the deal really was off. They took away all the sexual, emotional, and financial services that they had provided their partner, in addition to whatever status accrued to the fact of having a partner at all. In fin-de-siècle Paris, it was relatively easy for the working poor to find new jobs and new housing in the city or even travel to a different region altogether. Many women were able to support themselves financially and usually were not encumbered with numerous children. Together with the closely knit networks that characterized urban neighborhoods, these factors made it possible for people to physically leave partners with whom they were dissatisfied. Few forces beyond emotional preference existed to keep a couple together: the relationship was not necessarily maintained by economic necessity nor by a belief that unions had to be permanent. It is therefore possible that the conflicts brought to the *cour d'assises* were evidence of a growing insecurity in domestic partnerships. Retributive violence frequently marked relationships that had already broken down.

As a model of justice, retributive violence is about inflicting harm commensurate with harm: an eye for an eye—or perhaps a black eye for a transgression of the domestic contract. What retributive violence cannot do is to reform or rehabilitate its object. What it can do is police the boundaries of acceptable behavior. It promises that more violence may be forthcoming if the line is crossed again, and in that sense, it can function as a deterrent against testing the boundaries. It can reinforce the terms of the reciprocal obligations between domestic partners. Strictly speaking, retributive violence was extralegal in the fin de siècle, but it also served to regulate relationships between cohabiting couples that fell outside the legal contract of marriage.

By the end of the nineteenth century, this community-based, retributive model of justice was out of sync with the judicial apparatus of the state, which sought legitimacy in utilitarian models of justice.[105] The regime of prisons and penitentiaries was intended to bring about the reform and rehabilitation of the criminal.[106] The offender was to be remade into a fit member of society, not just harmed in retaliation for his misdeeds. After all, social control is more efficient when the individuals police themselves and never dare to test the boundaries in the first place than when they are monitored and punished by other agents. Nonetheless, the French judicial system did not succeed in either punishing or reforming many offenders accused of intimate violence. The key to this paradox lies in the interaction between the courts and the local communities where the violence occurred, which is analyzed in the next chapter.

CHAPTER 5

Local Knowledge and State Power

In 1894, a top statistician from the French Ministry of Justice exposed a shocking increase in the rate of acquittal for cases tried by jury in French assize courts. Emile Yvernès reported that acquittals for serious assault (*coups et blessures graves*) rose from 27 to 78 percent between 1860 and 1890, acquittals for murder grew from 15 to 34 percent, and the rate of acquittal for homicide increased from 16 to 24 percent. By contrast, acquittals in crimes against property rose only slightly during the same period, from 17 to 19 percent. Like many of his peers, Yvernès was particularly worried by the high rate of acquittal for so-called crimes of passion committed between lovers or spouses. He contended that "these misdeeds, often inspired by passion, hate, or vengeance, more and more often find with the jury not only indulgence, but absolution." Jurors acquitted criminals, he argued, because they believed the punishments provided by law were too harsh. "If these negative verdicts from the jury were always founded on the real absence of guilt of the presumed authors of the crimes," Yvernès observed, "we could perhaps congratulate ourselves for meeting so many innocent men, and we would have nothing to do but to deplore the lack of clairvoyance of the judicial investigation." But the truth of the matter must not be hidden, he wrote. "The moment has come to put an end to arbitrary [judgment] and to fictions," he declared. "Everything by the law and nothing but by the law."[1]

Yvernès was right. The seemingly erratic verdicts of the juries meant that the law was not applied equitably to all defendants. Raoul De la Grassière, a sociologist and *docteur en droit*, also believed jurors' misjudgment was at its worst regarding crimes of passion. "Today, [they] form a class apart, even in the minds of jurists," he wrote. "This development is the work of the jury, which has been developing it for a long time. It appreciates the subjective element and with it the motives. The motive can be so strong that it justifies the act. [The jury] finally comes to place itself above the law and to break it, arrogating to itself supreme sovereignty... So making for itself a special conscience, it believes itself authorized to lie and to declare that the infraction does not exist, and it acquits. It acquits in spite of the confessions of the accused, and there are cries of scandal, the violation of the law!"[2] But what can account for this high rate of acquittal? If the law did not hold sway in jury trials for crimes of passion, what did? If the jurors were merely incompetent, as Yvernès and many of his contemporaries believed, then it would be reasonable to expect their incompetence to manifest itself in all kinds of cases. Yet such frequent acquittals occurred only in cases of crimes against persons, rather than crimes against property or even the legally more complex cases of fraud and libel tried in the assize court. If jurors were subverting the system, they did so in predictable and consistent ways. This regularity suggests that in their decisions jurors applied standards regarding the use of violence other than those dictated by the law. Indeed, a close analysis of trial dossiers in cases of intimate violence reveals that juries' verdicts were not capricious but coincided with the implicit judgments of guilt or innocence articulated in witnesses' testimony.

This study contends that the processes of criminal investigation and trial worked to privilege the stories, knowledge, and judgment of the witnesses and defendants in the assize court and thus effectively facilitated the transfer of a popular system of retributive justice into the verdict of the court. Unlike the utilitarian state system of justice, this popular system of retributive justice was personal and subjective. It validated the use of violence in disputes between domestic partners where violence was used to punish a previous wrong—the reciprocal exchange of harm commensurate with harm. The perplexing issue of acquittals in the fin-de-siècle assize court was nothing less than the failure of the state system of justice to displace a popular system of justice. Rather than the state grafting an alien code of behavior onto an acquiescent population, the people co-opted the state system for their own objectives.

How this transfer could occur is only apparent with a clear understanding of legal procedures under the Third Republic, together with an evaluation of witnesses' testimony and trial outcomes. According to trial dossiers, as well as accounts of trials reported in the popular press, it is evident that court proceedings almost never concerned the bare "facts" of the crime alone. The French judicial system actually permitted witnesses a great deal of freedom to craft their depositions as they chose. While the accused almost invariably admitted his or her deed, the witnesses who testified in any given case focused little attention on the act of violence itself. Instead, they spoke at length about the circumstances surrounding the crime: the couple's relationship, the partners' reputations, and whether, in short, the victim deserved violent punishment. It was thus not the act of violence but its legitimacy that was in question in witnesses' testimony. From this perspective, it becomes clear that court verdicts are best understood not as the result of an application or rejection of rules of law but rather as the outcome of a complex process of social interaction, where multiple systems of standards of behavior and judgment came into play.[3] This approach assumes that witnesses and defendants in court have a certain knowledge of the social structures and institutions in which they participate and are capable of strategizing within them. In Pierre Bourdieu's terms, they have a "feel for the game"; they are not dupes of culture who can only say yes or no to the powers that constrain their lives.[4]

It may seem surprising that even in the late nineteenth century, the French judicial system provided a structure on which ordinary people could have an impact. Historians and social scientists have widely regarded modern criminal justice systems as a tool to homogenize local customs of justice and to arrogate to the centralized state the exclusive functions of violence and punishment. A traditional Marxist analysis of this process would cast the police and judiciary as tools of the ruling class—the laws and procedures that governed would only be perceived as legitimate as long as they maintained at least a semblance of justice, that is, as long as their true purpose of controlling the laboring classes was masked by (apparently) higher ideals.[5] For Norbert Elias, this process led to nothing less than the creation of the superego and modern subjectivity.[6] In Michel Foucault's analysis, it resulted in new, internalized controls of body and mind.[7] Although abundant documentary evidence describes the apparatus of the state and the values of the elites who created them, evidence about the effect of state-sponsored systems of control on ordinary people is much scarcer.[8] The method here is to analyze what happened in the Parisian assize courts from a dual perspective, in terms of the formal procedures of the court and the interests of the state on the one hand, and the use that ordinary people made of them on the other.

Interactions between ordinary fin-de-siècle Parisians and the police and judiciary do not reveal that these institutions were able to impose social controls alien to those of the local community. In some contexts, historians have found that jurists were successful in imposing their values over and against more permissive community standards for violence against wives, effectively using the state to limit the power of husbands within the family.[9] In other contexts, research demonstrates that battered women were able to find some protection by playing off one patriarchal institution (the state judicial system) against another (their families), in a strategy that Steve Stern has dubbed "pluralizing patriarchies."[10] By contrast, in fin-de-siècle Paris, state and local systems of social control effectively worked together. The formal structures of the police and the court system helped them function as extensions of community systems for arbitrating and resolving disputes. Neighborhood patrolmen, especially the *commissaire*, were cultivated as allies in domestic conflicts and were sought out as informal arbiters. When a case went to court, the process of investigation, together with the nature of the evidence admitted in court, served to foreground the information and interpretations put forward by witnesses from the community, which would serve as the basis for the jury's verdict. Just as the elites in the government and judiciary feared, decisions in jury trials rejected the impersonal rule of law in favor of an ethical system based on contextual and subjective interpretation of the individual crimes.

In order to explain the peculiarities of the fin-de-siècle criminal jury trial, and modern French legal method more generally, it is necessary to understand their revolutionary origins. Seeking to complete the long process of standardization and centralization that had defined the growth of the French judicial system for centuries, the revolutionaries (like the eventual authors of the 1804 civil code and 1810 criminal code) sought to amend the worst abuses—and most confusing features—of Old Regime law and judicial procedure.[11] Like all classical law codes, the new French code emphasized the nature of the crime, not the criminal. A crime was defined as an offense against the state, a violation of the social contract, to which the state responded with measures intended not merely to punish but to rehabilitate the offender, remaking him a fit member of society. Judgment was to be based on the impartial application of the law, with strict correlations between certain crimes and punishments, independent of the social status of the accused or the whims of his judges.

Implementing this utilitarian approach to justice required a neutral magistracy, whose powers would be more limited than they had been in the Old Regime. The revolutionaries were particularly concerned to ensure the separation of judicial and legislative powers. During the Old Regime, law could originate either with the king or the *parlements*, which could issue *arrêts de réglement* that would apply to future cases in their own jurisdiction. The law of 16–24 August 1790 prevented the courts from participating in creating law as the old regime *parlements* once did.[12] Broadly, this exclusion explains the absence of *stare decisis* in French law that persists to this day: if a judicial ruling were to set a binding precedent for future cases, a magistrate would in effect be creating a kind of law. Thus decisions rendered by professional judges must be based on the letter of the law, not judicial precedent. As defined in the early nineteenth-century law codes, the judge's role was to apply the rules outlined in the law codes—not to interpret them creatively or flexibly but to render syllogistic decisions that apply only to the facts of the case before him.

The establishment of criminal jury trials in 1791 further limited the power of professional magistrates. In contrast to Old Regime procedures in which professional judges studied written evidence to create written rulings through a process of logical reasoning, jury trials were designed to respond to the historical contingency of the moment. Witnesses would depose orally, as freely as possible, in the presence of the jury, a panel of professional judges, and a public audience. Jurors would then base their decisions on their own sense of justice, their "*conviction intime.*"[13] Recent work by Laura Mason has highlighted the new and significant value placed on oral testimony by the revolutionaries who introduced criminal jury trials. "Rejecting the primacy of the text in the courtroom, the Constituent Assembly asserted that oral testimony was indispensable to the proper functioning of the jury. Imagining juries that were imbued with *sensibilité* and organically linked to the public from which they were drawn, legislators agreed that witnesses' spoken testimony was the single most important feature of the criminal trial necessary to sustain both qualities."[14] As Mason contends, jury trials were explicitly designed to be responsive to public opinion.

These legacies from the revolutionary era—the magistracy's commitment to the rigid application of the law code, together with jury trials whose verdicts were to be based on the flexible and contingent standards of jurors' own moral compasses—still prevailed in the Third Republic, establishing the conditions for the dilemma outlined by Yvernès. A professional magistracy trained in syllogism and deductive reasoning, dedicated to the strict application of a set of rules enumerated in the legal codes, confronted a rising number of verdicts rendered by jurors whose *conviction intime* seemed to disregard not only the letter but the spirit of the law. It was difficult to justify the efficacy of jury trials when the people seemed to be doing such a bad job rendering justice.

Yvernès and his republican peers struggled with the inherent contradictions of jury trials, applauding the role of the people in the judicial system but deploring the results of their lenient judgments. The jury trial was supposed to enact and instill the ideals of the new regime, reinforcing the ideas of equality under the law and the importance of citizens' participation in the business of the state. With the exception of a short-lived reform during the Commune, the system that obtained during the Third Republic was the most egalitarian standard yet applied to jury service. The Dufaure law of 21 November 1872 in principle extended eligibility for jury service to any man over thirty who enjoyed full political and civil rights. However, as the century drew to a close, it became increasingly apparent that jury trials in the assize courts were not administering justice successfully, given the increasingly high rates of acquittal for crimes against persons, especially crimes of passion. In a flurry of publications at the end of the nineteenth century, contemporary observers articulated a variety of explanations for this perplexing and distressing trend, suggesting that jurors were insufficiently educated to understand the law, that they were befuddled and intimidated by the dramatic trappings of the court, or even that they understood judicial proceedings but willfully chose to disregard the law.[15] The consequences of the jurors' apparent inability to render justice were grave, for it cast doubt on the cornerstone of republican justice, highlighting the precarious foundations of the Republic itself.

The problem was magnified by the extensive coverage of crimes of passion in the burgeoning popular press, which frequently published sensationalized accounts of gory murders and dramatic trials.[16] Many of these well-publicized cases were the kind popularly known as crimes of passion. Stereotypically, such crimes were precipitated by abandonment or infidelity and carried out in a fit of madness or overwhelming emotion. Crimes of passion were not defined as a separate legal category under French law, and so it is not possible to reconstruct precise statistics for the rate of acquittal in such cases, but it is certain that they were much higher than for other kinds of crimes. The overall rate of acquittal for all cases tried in the assize courts during the Third Republic was around 28 percent,[17] but acquittal rates for crimes against persons were significantly higher than this average and rose during the last decades of the nineteenth century. Women were even more likely to be acquitted than men. By contrast, the rate of acquittal in correctional court, where a panel of professional judges tried lesser crimes, was around 10 percent. The problem of acquittal thus was not merely a matter of perception on the part of anxious politicians and social critics but was in fact statistically significant.

In seeking to explain the high rate of acquittal for crimes of passion, recent historians have not focused on the specific judicial context of fin-de-siècle jury trials, and yet closer attention to the judicial process can help illuminate the social and cultural problems these historians have addressed. Notably, Joëlle Guillais has analyzed crimes of passion in terms of a contest between the normalizing, oppressive forces of the state and the marginal, subversive culture of the lower-class people who committed the crimes. Reproducing numerous letters and depositions from defendants, she reads their statements as evidence of (ultimately futile) resistance to the control of the dominant classes. In her analysis, defendants and witnesses are on the losing end in court: "Their powerlessness is real; conscious of cultural differences, they attempt to adjust their language and their comportment to that of their judges."[18] They are literally at the mercy of cultural and discursive forms not of their own making, and only by successfully adopting those alien forms can they hope to escape conviction.

On the contrary, a more detailed analysis of the process of investigation and trial makes clear that crime stories recounted in the official indictment or even in press accounts depended on the knowledge of the witnesses in the case. Far from being forced by the agents of state power to conform to existing narrative structures, such as melodrama, witnesses had surprisingly wide latitude to tell their own stories. People who testified in fin-de-siècle courts were not immune to the influences of certain narrative conventions, but they crafted their own narratives within contexts that were not only discursive but social. Whether or not a murderous cuckolded husband could make his story conform to the expectations of a jury versed in the plots and characters of melodrama, his story could only appear credible to the jurors if it were reinforced by a chorus of witnesses who supported his claims about his relationship with his wife, his virtues as a husband, and her failures as a wife. Stories of crimes of passion were rendered "true" or compelling in court through reference to the social world out of which they grew. And that social world only became visible in court through specific procedures of the French criminal jury trial.

Ann-Louise Shapiro has explored how female criminals were implicated in fin-de-siècle discourses about criminality, insanity, bourgeois family norms, and politics. In *Breaking the Codes*, Shapiro imparts a strong sense of the feelings of crisis and anxiety that pervaded the publications of many bourgeois social commentators during this era. Although Shapiro aims "to discover how ordinary men and women interpreted and responded to this material," her analysis of the dynamics of assize court trials rarely ventures into the complexities of the cases. Instead, Shapiro focuses on the confrontations between the accused and the magistrates, disregarding the testimony of other witnesses. For instance, Shapiro describes the case of Marie Fournet, who was eventually acquitted of killing her former lover and wounding his wife, as "exemplary" of the impact that "the construct of Woman defined by love" had on stories told in court.[19] Shapiro limits herself to discussing two exchanges between Fournet and the investigating and presiding magistrates in her trial, together with an anonymous commentary from the pages of the *Gazette des Tribunaux*. These sources certainly support Shapiro's contention that Fournet sought to explain her crime in different terms than the jurists: Fournet insisted she was angry not only because he misled her about being married but because her lover had dissipated her savings in a bad business deal, while the magistrates insisted her disappointment in love must be her primary motivation.

Shapiro leaves the bulk of the evidence preserved in the trial dossier unexplored, including testimony from more than a dozen witnesses, numerous letters, and a long confrontation between Fournet and the surviving victim, her lover's wife.[20] In choosing to focus only on the confrontations between the accused and the agents of the professional judiciary, Shapiro misses a lot of detail that could add nuance to her analysis, for the other witnesses testified at length about the complicated relationships among Fournet, her lover, and his wife and their interactions with other people in their neighborhood. Instead Shapiro finds dissonance and silences in court testimony, and she concludes: "Alternative meanings were literally expunged, preserving intact the woman-in-love."[21] Shapiro's interpretation is compelling as far as it concerns the creation of the official indictment written by the investigating magistrate. Yet in court there was not simply a two-way opposition between the magistrate and the defendant—whether male or female. Rather, many witnesses told competing stories that may or may not have coincided with the magistrate's version. It seems unlikely that the jurors would ignore all the testimony from Fournet and other witnesses in court about her bad business deal with her lover and his frequent violence toward her and his wife. That Fournet was acquitted of murdering her lover but required to pay his widow five thousand francs in damages (exactly the price of the establishment Fournet and her lover had purchased together a year earlier) suggests that the court was not insensitive to the business conflict Fournet emphasized.

Ruth Harris also analyzes assize court defendants as the objects of normalizing discourses. In her book *Murders and Madness*, she studies crimes of passion through the lens of the professional discourses of law and psychology.[22] Harris contends that it was the medicalization of crime, and more specifically the diagnosis of sudden madness in crimes of passion, that led to such frequent acquittals. However, analysis of a larger sample of cases suggests that Harris's explanation can only account for the outcome in a small number of trials involving crimes of passion. All told, only 28 of the defendants among the 264 in the present study underwent psychological evaluation (including those in all of the relevant cases studied by Harris). Of these, only nine—five men and four women—were deemed by the medical professionals to have any kind of mental disorder. Furthermore, juries were remarkably inconsistent in their responses to the alienists' diagnoses. Of those nine who doctors deemed mentally ill, and therefore potentially not responsible for their deeds, four were convicted by the juries. By the same token, ten defendants who doctors judged to be sane and responsible for the violent deeds that they indisputably committed were nonetheless acquitted. These numbers are persuasive evidence that the juries were using standards other than those of medical experts when they judged a case.

Indeed, as Harris's work illustrates, the medical professionals themselves were in the process of establishing standards for mental competence in this era. Here, for example, is the rather ambiguous diagnosis written by Auguste Voisin, a doctor at the Salpêtrière, for Nicholas Magerus: "We think that at this moment Magerus presents no disturbance of his mind, no delirium that could push him to this criminal act, but that passionate motives of a jealous nature are the determining cause, along with the abuse of alcoholic beverages of which he made use during the hours that preceded the crime. But, if the responsibility for the act can be diminished by this latter cause, the attenuation must be reduced to a small thing if one recalls that Magerus made use of an accomplice, [and] hid behind him to strike his wife more easily."[23] In Dr. Voisin's analysis, passion and jealousy were not signs of mental illness, and even the alcohol Magerus consumed did not significantly impair his rational capacity. Yet the jury surely did not share Dr. Voisin's logic, since they acquitted Magerus of stabbing his wife, while convicting him of stabbing one of her relatives who attempted to intervene in the conflict. Whatever his mental state may have been, the jury condoned (only) the violence against his wife. Jurors apparently believed that expressing emotions through violent behavior was legitimate in certain situations, so once again it is necessary to turn to the social context of those emotions and actions to understand why this was the case.

It is incontestable that the bourgeois jurists, journalists, and medical professionals who are the focus of Shapiro's and Harris's studies were alarmed by the disorder demonstrated in crimes of passion and that those anxieties were deeply implicated in their understandings of gender, madness, and criminal responsibility. However, it is another step entirely to say that the jurors shared these professionals' preoccupations. If jurors were so concerned about female disorder or so threatened by the specter of madmen murdering their family members, then why would they acquit so many authors of such violent deeds? It is not enough to say that professional discourses seeped into jurors' consciousness and informed their decisions, when there is so little evidence that those discourses were articulated during trials. To discover what actually motivated their decisions requires the historian to triangulate among different kinds of evidence, for jurors were (and are) forbidden by law to comment on their verdicts in any way beyond the "yes" or "no" they wrote on their ballots. We may assume, along with Guillais and Shapiro, that they read crime reports in the popular press along with melodramatic love stories. Like Harris, we may expect that many of them were aware of medical theories about criminal responsibility. Yet we must also consider carefully the primary sources of information in any trial—witnesses who talked about intimate violence because they had experienced it in their own lives. It is entirely possible that jurors listened to the evidence presented to them during the trial itself and made sense of it in a coherent manner reflecting the standards of their communities.

Jurors came from a distinctive socioeconomic group that overlapped very little with the kinds of people who usually were defendants and witnesses. Despite the democratic spirit behind the Dufaure law liberalizing eligibility, in practice jurors came from a limited group that was largely bourgeois. It is therefore not obvious that they would have been particularly sympathetic to the people on trial, who were primarily wage earners. While Article 1 of the Dufaure law affirmed the principle that any man over thirty who enjoyed political, civil, and familial rights could serve as a juror, the articles that followed limited the criteria for eligibility considerably. Among the excluded were convicts, the insane, the deaf, the blind, servants, and those illiterate in French. Article 5 gave further dispensation to men "who need their daily manual labor to live." Effectively, this last dispensation meant an outright ban of working people from the lists of potential jurors. Since jurors were not remunerated for their services, except for the cost of traveling to court in the provinces, service by a man who depended on a daily wage truly would have been a hardship.

Indeed, the names of working men virtually never appeared on lists of potential jurors. The process of selecting pools of potential jurors remained closely controlled by the magistracy, who compiled annual lists of eligible jurors in a two-step process. In the department of the Seine, the annual list included three thousand potential jurors, although the population of Paris exceeded 2 million by the last decades of the nineteenth century.[24] Names of eligible jurors were drawn at random from an urn before each session of the assize court, and the presiding judge could also select replacements directly from the master list if too few citizens appeared for duty on the appointed day. Thus, although the initial principle of the Dufaure law was that any man enjoying full political and civil rights could be a juror, the actual pool of jurors was carefully limited.

Proponents of the jury system in this era congratulated themselves on the class composition of jury lists. "Emanating from the people, the jury is the representation of the public conscience," wrote André Bougon, a barrister at the Paris appeals court. "It effects judgment by peers as much as is possible, because it is always taken from the middle class: small tradesmen, *rentiers*. Without doubt these men are of a social level superior to the accused. Not a lot, however. They live very near to this popular class where nine-tenths of the criminals are recruited; they know better the struggles, the sufferings, the compulsions, the excuses. There is a guarantee of the first order for the accused: being better understood, they are more impartially judged."[25]

Bougon was correct that juries were primarily middle class, but his assertion that they were "near" the "popular class" on trial is rather overdrawn. A brief survey of jury lists drawn up for sessions of the Cour d'assises de la Seine throughout the fin de siècle reveals a preponderance of men from comfortable economic backgrounds. For example, the jury list for the trial of Emile Michaud on 25 January 1875 included the following professions: property owner (9), *rentier* (3), bailiff, hardware vendor, wallpaper manufacturer (2), vendor of fashion accessories, printer of fabric, professor at Louis le Grand, grocer, plumber, pharmacist, engineer, and clerk at the Ministry of Foreign Affairs.[26] Similarly, two decades later, for the trial of Marie Claire Rochat, held on 6 January 1892, the jurors' professions included architect (2), property owner (2), manufacturer of carbonated beverages, wholesale merchant (3), furniture maker, doctor or medical doctor (5), mining engineer, restaurateur, veterinarian, printer specializing in geography, clockmaker, and retired army officer.[27] Overall, it is a mixture of businessmen, artisans, white-collar employees, and members of the liberal professions, with only the occasional appearance of a man from a higher socioeconomic position.

By contrast, most of the defendants who appeared in the assize court were from decidedly lower strata, members of the economic majority. They were the working people of Paris, who owned little or no real property and whose economic security was precarious at best.[28] It is not self-evident that these two distinct socioeconomic groups—the people on trial and the people who judged them—would be in sympathy on issues like the use of violence in intimate relationships or the boundaries of proper behavior for women and men, which were the focus of assize court trials for crimes of passion. Indeed, the usual assumptions of social and cultural history suggest the contrary. The middle-class jurors would seem to be precisely the class that would be most interested in enforcing a strict application of the law and their own rigorous standards of personal conduct. Yet this did not occur.

The Police

Many who appeared in the assize court were not strangers to the judicial apparatus of the state and in fact had already sought assistance from the front-line agents of state control, the police. In about one-quarter of the cases in this study, couples who ultimately reached the assize court had had previous interactions with the police in the course of their domestic disputes. Throughout the nineteenth century, the Paris Prefecture of Police conformed to the structure Napoleon had established for it in 1800.[29] Broadly, the police was divided into two branches, the *Police Municipale*, which included all patrolmen, and the *Police Judiciare*, better known as the *Sûreté*, which included the morals brigade and detectives. While the *Sûreté* was centrally located on the rue des Saussaies just north of the Palais de l'Elysée, the *Police Municipale* reached into every corner of the city. Each arrondissement had its own hierarchy of police administration, headed by a police captain, called the *commissaire*. Geographically, each arrondissement was divided into four *quartiers* (comparable to precincts), one of which was the *commissariat*, or central post. The number of men serving in the *Police Municipale* doubled during the last half of the nineteenth century. By 1896 they numbered just over eight thousand, walking the beat in eye-catching blue uniforms, carrying standard-issue revolvers.[30] Most of the rank and file of the police—patrolmen called *gardiens de la paix*—were former soldiers, whose background and salary did not raise them above the socioeconomic level of the average Parisian worker. Although their ubiquitous presence throughout the city could be interpreted as a symptom of the growing reach of the state into the lives of individual citizens, evidence from trial dossiers suggests that people reached out to the police as well.

Far from simply being instruments of repression, imposing the law with an iron fist on an unruly population, the Parisian police played a much more flexible role, and their intervention usually took place at the invitation of the people involved in a dispute. In this sense, they were continuing the habits of eighteenth-century Parisians (analyzed by Arlette Farge), who readily involved the police in their domestic disputes, including episodes of violence against women.[31] People turned to the police for arbitration of disputes, protection, advice, and intervention. Nothing obliged them to use the police force in these ways, and, strictly speaking, the police were not obliged to assist people in resolving domestic disputes, either.[32]

In particular, people who felt they had been wronged by their partners often turned to the local *commissaire* for advice or protection, mobilizing one of many potential resources for their aid. With the *commissaire*'s support, individuals could enforce their claims against their partners, even if they lacked other means to do so. In her 1872 letter to the state prosecutor requesting a legal separation, a bread carrier named Virginie Jouault revealed that she had first enlisted the *commissaire* to try to reform her husband's ways. "My husband doesn't even pretend to do anything, and wants to be fed, lodged, and clothed with my poor salary or I will be beaten up; that is what happened day before yesterday before eight in the evening and obliged me to place myself under the protection of *Monsieur le commissaire de police* of the quarter who had my husband summoned to tell him that his conduct toward me could call upon him the severities of the law."[33] Likewise, Jeanne Vigineix placed herself under police protection twice before she finally decided to seek a legal separation from her violent husband.[34] A *commissaire* could also help arbitrate disputes, as in a conflict about property between Paul Pringuet and the mother of his child. When Pringuet stopped paying the cost of the wet nurse for his illegitimate daughter, his former lover took the child to his boss, who then placed her with the *commissaire de police*. The *commissaire* summoned Pringuet to his office and persuaded him to take the child back to his nurse and continue to pay for her care, "to avoid scandal," as Pringuet told it.[35] An implicit understanding that failure to conform to the *commissaire*'s instructions would result in a more formal and severe application of the law enforced his decision. While no law gave the *commissaire* the legal capacity to render judgments and punishments, his constant presence in Parisian neighborhoods made him an easily accessible surrogate judge.

In the eyes of some community members, arbitration by the *commissaire* was in itself an alternative to violence. "If I had followed the advice that the *commissaire de police* gave me one month before, to ask for my divorce, all this would never have happened," declared Emile Herbellot, who was convicted in the murder of his daughter and mother-in-law, and the attempted murder of his wife.[36] Even though he was the aggressor, he claimed that mediation through the judicial structure could have averted his violence. Eugénie Duchène also perceived the use of the police and judiciary as an alternative to violence. She testified that she went to the *commissaire de police* several times to tell him about her difficulties with her husband and to discuss the proper means to obtain a legal separation.[37] After several violent incidents, she declared, "I went to find the *commissaire de police* to tell him that I had resolved to pursue my separation and to ask him to show me what path to take... In order to assure my security, I believed I should go back to the *commissaire de police* again, and beg him to call in my husband to make all useful reproofs." Her husband refused to comply and tried to force her to live with him again. In response, she said, "I answered him to go find the *commissaire de police* and that I would see then what I should do. He left, saying that he did not need the *commissaire de police* and that he would know how to do me in and others." Clearly, Eugénie Duchène had been cultivating the *commissaire* as an ally, one with useful information about how to navigate the legal system and one whose protection could offer her physical safety from her husband. Her husband, however, rejected the *commissaire*'s authority. He did not need outside help to press his claims on his wife, for his strength came from the use of violence rather than the cultivation of allies.

As the more frequent victims of violence, women also appear to have been more likely to cultivate a relationship with the police than men were, as the case of the Duchène couple suggests. In this light, the police (and judiciary) appear as potential allies of the physically and economically weaker against the stronger.³⁸ When a victim of violence went to the police, it was often with the purpose of informing them about her partner's violence, not necessarily to file a formal complaint or to have the perpetrator arrested. People went to the *commissaire* seeking above all the strength of an ally rather than the mechanisms of the law and trying to establish a record of the violence they suffered, if not in the police ledgers then at least in the minds of the *commissaire* and his officers. When the violence became more severe, leading to a criminal investigation, or when the victim decided to seek a separation or divorce, police testimony could add weight to the victim's allegations. Since all criminal investigations began with the police, it could be extremely strategic to have cultivated them as allies in advance of a crisis.

The most immediate assistance that many women demanded from the police was physical protection from their attackers. Sometimes the police arrived on the scene quickly and effectively limited a violent conflict. When Augustine Gohin was stabbed by her former lover, her cries brought police from the *poste* right across the street.³⁹ When Jules Michel was drunk and threatening to beat his mistress, a friend of hers called for help out the window of their building to two passing policemen. The police restrained Michel (employed as a patrolman himself) until the woman was safely locked in her apartment.⁴⁰ While many women had confidence that the police could protect them, police were often unable to do so successfully. When her estranged husband stole money from her and bought a gun, Anne Brudière alerted the *commissaire* of her potential danger, but her husband shot at her that evening.⁴¹ Even when the police were vigilant in protecting a victim, their efforts were not fail-safe. Marie Breffeil had established an ongoing system of protection with the security guards (*gardiens des halles et marchés*) who patrolled the market at the Chateau d'eau where she sold fish.⁴² Whenever her husband entered the market hall, the guards hid her and forced him to leave the market. "He never caused any scenes with his wife," attested a fishmonger from a nearby stall, "because the guardian ran right away to set things straight." Marie Breffeil said she felt safe from her husband as long as she was at the market, because "the Inspector of the market forbade him to enter the pavilion, and pointed him out to the agents of the *Sûreté*" for surveillance. Beyond the reach of the market guards, however, she remained vulnerable, and her husband managed to stab her on her way to work one morning.

Nonetheless, the simple threat of police intervention could be sufficient to change a person's behavior—for better or for worse. Early one morning when his drunken father showed him the gun he intended to use to kill his mother,

Charles Jouault said, "I then threatened to have him arrested by a *gardien de la paix*, so then he softened," and put off his attack for another day.⁴³ After hearing Ernest Cotard's frequent quarrels with his wife and seeing the traces of his beatings on her body, Cotard's former employer confronted him about his behavior. He testified, "I threatened Cotard with denouncing him at the *gendarmerie*, and I ended up firing him."⁴⁴ While the threat to call the police appears to have been something of a deterrent in these cases, in one incident the threat of police intervention actually precipitated an attack. Célestine Trudersheim frequently took refuge from her abusive, neglectful husband back home with her mother and younger brothers. One day when her husband came to reproach her for leaving their apartment, he threatened to lock her out for good. "My mother answered him that she would have the door [to our apartment] opened and that she would have him put under surveillance by the police. She had barely pronounced these words when he turned on my mother; he knocked her over in the stairwell and seized her by the throat." The struggle ended when one of her brothers shot her husband in the head.⁴⁵

Legal Separation and Divorce

While the police were available to serve as informal judges in domestic disputes, couples also had the option go to civil court for a legal separation or divorce (newly legalized in 1884).⁴⁶ Seventeen couples in this study used the power of the state to attempt to resolve their conflicts in this way. Filing a court case entailed the risk of sparking a new attack. Louis Jouault shot his wife immediately after receiving a summons from the office of legal assistance indicating that she was instigating a case for separation. "I loaded [the gun] on Sunday morning as soon as I read that she wanted to plead for *séparation de corps*," he declared in his interrogation. Another witness in the case reported that he said, "My wife is attacking me in separation. I know well that I have lost before playing. I will do her in. I'll do myself in afterwards." The whalebones in her corset preserved her from serious injury, but Jouault was condemned to hard labor for life.⁴⁷ Georges Koenig would be acquitted for attacking his wife under similar circumstances. When he learned that she was preparing to file for a separation, witnesses said he attacked her with a knife, yelling, "Here is my request for separation!"⁴⁸ Like the men who declared their disdain for the intervention of the *commissaire de police*, these husbands used physical violence to counter their wives' use of the judicial process.

In other cases, the causal link between filing for separation and a violent attack was less explicitly stated but is still evident. Women who ended up in the *cour d'assises* told much the same story about their decisions to seek a legal break with their husbands. Often having endured a bad partnership for many years, they invariably complained that their husbands were lazy men who earned little or no money and beat them excessively or without provocation. These complaints are similar to those made by women requesting *lettres de cachet* against their husbands in the eighteenth century. In the sample compiled by Arlette Farge and Michel Foucault, three-quarters of the women complained of their husbands' excessive violence, and two-thirds described economic hardship.[49] Zoé Legrand may serve as a typical example here. She had been married for sixteen years before filing for divorce, citing her husband's laziness and abuse. Many witnesses agreed that by selling vegetables she alone earned the money to support the household and pay for boarding her six-year-old son, while her husband beat her if she denied him money to go drinking. He was evicted just a few days before he shot her, indicating that his need for her was as much financial as anything else.[50] Legrand's case and others like it illustrate that violence and civil action were not mutually exclusive options for resolving domestic conflicts. It also suggests that the choice between using violence or using the judiciary was often made on gendered ground: while men far outnumbered women as defendants in this sample of violent conflicts brought to the *cour d'assises*, women outnumbered men as litigants in cases for separation and divorce, just as they did in complaints to police. Thus women, more than men, sought to use the state's formidable powers to resolve their domestic conflicts.

The Assize Court

Whether or not an episode of violence would be prosecuted in the assize court depended on the processes of the state judicial system, not the preferences of the antagonists.[51] The *commissaire* reported serious incidents to the investigative branch of the police, the *Sûreté*. Agents from the *Sûreté* then conducted initial interviews with witnesses and sent a dossier of interview transcripts to the Paris *Parquet*, where a panel of judges would determine if a prosecutable felony had likely been committed and, if so, assign the case to an investigating magistrate, the *juge d'instruction*. The investigating magistrate had broad powers to interrogate witnesses and the accused, gather physical evidence, and hire experts to evaluate the crime scene, the weapons, and the mental and physical conditions of the victim and the accused. It is extremely significant that, given such broad freedom to investigate cases as they saw fit, the investigating magistrates virtually always focused their efforts on collecting testimony from nonexpert witnesses. They always began their investigations by deposing the same people who had been interviewed by the agents from the *Sûreté*. These included not only eyewitnesses to the crime, if there were any, but also family members, neighbors, friends, co-workers, and employers of the victim and the accused. Their words and, occasionally, the magistrate's questions were recorded by a clerk in the magistrate's office. Witnesses read and signed these documents to confirm their veracity, and the accused, whose comments were sometimes recorded as well, also read and signed them.[52] Out-of-town witnesses, such as relatives in the defendant's region of origin, gave their depositions to local police or magistrates, who mailed their statements to Paris. Altogether, these depositions comprise the bulk of the existing case dossiers.

To be sure, witnesses' depositions were crafted to suit the rhetorical occasions of the investigation and trial. Their testimonies were strategic interventions to "fix" the meaning of a violent act, with the ultimate result that it would be judged criminal or legitimate. These accounts served largely as the foundation for the official indictment (*acte d'accusation*) that the investigating magistrate prepared for the court, even to the extent that direct but unattributed quotes from witnesses' testimony sometimes appeared in them.[53] The *acte d'accusation*, in turn, was frequently reproduced in the press accounts of trials, though without being identified as such. Any reader who had not heard the indictment read aloud in court would have no way of knowing that what he read in the newspaper was not composed by a journalist.[54] Thus, quite literally, local knowledge often came to constitute official knowledge about the case.

The purpose of the *acte d'accusation* was to define the case for the state. Once the indictment was prepared, a panel of judges (in the *chambre des mises en accusation*) ruled on whether to direct the case to the assize court, where it would be tried as a felony, or to correctional court, where it would be tried as a lesser offense.[55] Assize court cases began with a reading of the *acte d'accusation* immediately after court was convened and the jury was sworn in.[56] The presiding magistrate (*président*) then directed the witnesses to leave the courtroom until it was their turn to testify, so that they would not be influenced by each other's testimony. His next order of business was to interrogate the accused. The accused and the witnesses were each permitted to make an uninterrupted initial statement before being questioned by the presiding magistrate, whose manner was usually accusatory and aggressive, strongly demonstrating his belief in the defendant's guilt. After the interrogation of the accused was complete, the witnesses were brought in one by one to testify. Following their testimony, they were not permitted to leave the courtroom again until the end of the trial, another rule designed to discourage collusion among the witnesses. They had to swear "to speak without hate or fear, to tell the whole truth, and nothing but the truth." After each deposition, the accused and the jurors were permitted to question the witness through the presiding magistrate, although it appears that jurors did not intervene frequently.

Only after all the nonprofessional witnesses were deposed could the prosecution and the defense introduce physical evidence or expert reports, as well as professionals to interpret them. These might include the doctor who performed the autopsy on a murder victim, alienists who evaluated the mental capacity of the accused, a chemist if the case involved poisoning, an architect who drew a plan of the crime scene, or an *expert arquebusier* who testified about the use of firearms. At last came the closing arguments. The prosecution repeated the terms of the indictment, the defense lawyer pled for acquittal, the jurors and the accused were given one last chance to intervene, and the presiding magistrate declared the session closed. For many years, the presiding magistrate gave a final summary of the accusation and the defense before the jurors were sent to deliberate, but in 1881 this step was eliminated in the interest of giving the defense the last word.

At this point the presiding magistrate gave the jury instructions before they left to deliberate in a separate room. All decisions were to be made with written ballots and with a simple majority of at least seven out of twelve voices. The questions the jury had to answer in their deliberations were not framed in terms of guilt or innocence, but rather as yes or no questions, such as: Did X commit murder on the person of his wife, Y? This statement does not invite a qualitative judgment about the legitimacy or culpability of the act, which makes the acquittal of defendants who confessed committing their crimes even more surprising. Jurors could not reveal the margin of their vote nor the reasons for their choice. In the event of conviction, the prosecution, the defense, and the accused had one last chance to speak, and then the presiding magistrate, together with two other judges (*assesseurs*), decided on the sentence.

Problematic Acquittals

Jurors were technically forbidden to consider the sentence as they deliberated, since it was entirely in the hands of the judges. However, short of outright acquittal, jurors could choose on their own initiative to convict with extenuating circumstances (*circonstances atténuantes*), a limiting factor applicable to all crimes in the Code Pénal (Article 463), thanks to a law promulgated on 28 June 1832.[57] They could not, however, offer any explanation about what the extenuating circumstances were or to what extent they thought the punishment should be mitigated. Rather, extenuating circumstances signaled the judges who decided the sentence that they should not apply the full measure of punishment provided for by law. To consider one salient example, according to the Code Pénal the prescribed punishment for *assassinat* (murder preceded by ambush or premeditation) was execution. Only the presiding judge could reduce the charge to a lesser offense during the hearing (from murder to accidental death through assault, for example). But conviction with extenuating circumstances could result in a lesser punishment of forced labor or prison.

There were four legal exceptions to the correlation between a murder conviction and a death sentence. Murder was excused but not absolved if the murder was provoked by serious violence toward the killer (Article 321) or if the victim was killed while breaking into an inhabited house (Article 322). The infamous Article 324 concerned spousal murder. It provided that a wife or a husband was excused for killing her or his spouse if the killer's life was in peril at the moment of the murder. A husband could also be excused for murdering or injuring his wife or her lover if he surprised them *en flagrant délit* in the conjugal abode, a configuration of circumstances that rarely coincided.[58] Article 326 made it perfectly clear, however, that an excusable crime was not to be confused with automatic acquittal. "Once the fact of excuse is proven," it read, "if it concerns a crime carrying the pain of death, or that of forced labor for life, or that of deportation [to a penal colony], the punishment will be reduced to an imprisonment of one to five years. If it concerns any other crime, it will be reduced to an imprisonment of six months to two years." The law, therefore, did not provide for outright acquittal in any case where a person actually committed the act of which he or she was accused.

Nonetheless, the provision for excusable crimes was widely misunderstood, and spouses were acquitted of attacking their unfaithful partners under a variety of circumstances, even if the infidelity was merely suspected. "Ask the first comer, even choose an educated man," challenged Paul Peyssonnié, a solicitor general speaking at the opening session of the *Cour d'appel d'Orléans* in 1897. "Ask him if, in France, the husband has the absolute right to kill, *en flagrant délit*, the adulterous wife or her accomplice, he will invariably answer that he has this right, and that, by law, such a murder is assured of impunity."[59] Yet even if the sexual misconduct of a woman in French society was considered more reprehensible than that of a man, Peyssonnié reasoned, the jealousy of a wife who discovers her husband's infidelity was just as extreme as his, so why would her murdering him not be excused? Would not lovers feel equal fury, even if they were not married? Would a drunken, brutal husband who had deserted his wife really be just as excusable if he later attacked her for infidelity? By raising these questions, Peyssonnié sought to demonstrate that Article 324 was not only illogical but barbaric in seeming to condone certain murders. It would be ridiculous to allow women to kill their husbands with impunity; therefore, he concluded, the logic of Article 324 had to be rejected entirely.

Voting to acquit in spite of irrefutable evidence that the accused had committed the deed clearly went contrary to the law. That jurors did so anyway was widely attributed to the perceived discrepancy between the magnitude of the crime and the magnitude of the punishment. Suggesting that it would be a greater evil than the crime on trial to allow a defendant to be punished too severely for his deed, the author of the *Carnet du juré d'assises* imagined that a juror would say to himself, "the legislators made a mistake, or they were too cruel; at this moment I can limit the effects of their error and their cruelty."[60] In this interpretation, voting to acquit was an effective protest against a rigid legal structure that was out of touch with the mores of the people. However, this was a minority opinion among professional jurists, who saw the jury overstepping its role by considering the penalties for conviction. One solicitor general gave a speech during the opening session of the *cour d'appel* in Grenoble in 1885 in which he decried jurors' speculation about punishments. "Let not the law trouble [the jurors'] conscience by severities that public opinion would not ratify," he proclaimed. "Otherwise, they will be driven almost fatally to perform an act of OMNIPOTENCE, in fixing, despite themselves, their thoughts on punishments which... would still remain for them out of proportion to the crimes committed."[61] To remedy the situation, Charmeil proposed informing the jury more fully about the punishments that certain crimes were likely to incur, sending more cases to correctional court and legislating more specific combinations of crime and punishment, so that the whole process would be more standardized and less arbitrary.

Frequent acquittals of manifestly guilty people disrupted the balance between the people's capacity to judge and the state's capacity to punish, and the proposed solutions to the problem proliferated as the rate of acquittal rose. "Jurors follow opinion more than they advance it," complained the investigating magistrate Adolphe Guillot. "If they judge badly, it is because the country thinks wrongly."[62] Raoul de la Grassière nonetheless decried the inadequate education of the typical juror. "He is unaware of the simplest laws of justice. He has never appeared in court, and the judicial apparatus disturbs him profoundly. He sits ill at ease, as uncomfortable as the defense lawyer or the guilty man. Thus, everything troubles him, the authority of the president, the vivacity of the prosecutor, the attacks of the lawyer; he is of the opinion of the one who spoke last, and what he would wish the most vigorously at the end of the debates would be not to have to decide; he is, in every sense of the word, a *forced* judge."[63] Adolphe Guillot, a *juge d'instruction* in Paris who investigated several of the cases in this study, concluded in his 1885 book *Le Jury et les moeurs* that proof of education and mental capacity should be required to qualify potential jurors. "How can society, which requires diplomas, internships on the part of its most minor agents, prove itself imprudent when it comes to the highest, the most awesome of all?" he wrote. Although requiring proof of competence "might ruffle [*froisser*] egalitarian ideas, it is the only way to save the jury."[64]

Short of requiring proof of previous education, a number of legal professionals took it upon themselves to instruct potential jurors on their duties through the publication of handbooks. One of the handbooks, written "by a lawyer" in 1883, was conveniently pocket sized and contained a summary of the procedures in the *cour d'assises*, in addition to a glossary of legal terms and a fold-out miniature reproduction of the verdict form.[65] Charles Berriat de Saint-Prix, a magistrate in the Parisian court, wrote a jury manual that was in its fifth edition by 1875.[66] Constant Fenet, former *avocat à la cour d'appel*, wrote several works meant to aid jurors, including a volume that reproduced the key articles of the *Code d'instruction criminelle* most relevant to trials in the assize court.[67] A quick education in jurisprudence was as near as the conscientious juror's local bookstore. Despite the frequency of their publication, it is impossible to determine what impact such jury manuals actually had on potential jurors.

Contemporary criticism of jury verdicts focused on the moment of choice when the jurors decided. Since the average juror lacked knowledge of the judicial process, argued a justice of the peace named Jules Lévy in 1875, he was likely to make troubling acquittals that were "less like judgments than letters of pardon." Lévy continued, "Certain assemblies, even while recognizing guilt, believe they must absolve. The accused admits the deed, but, it is said, he has already suffered preventative incarceration [before the trial]; another is guilty, it is recognized, but he is the only support of an honest family which a condemnation would reduce to misery and despair; a third is acquitted, because being young and ignorant of life, he succumbed in a moment of weakness or because the deed was not serious. One can do without other [examples]. But the jury does not have the right of pardon, it is a prerogative with which it is not invested."[68]

Lévy's illustration of the incongruity of the law's objective requirements and the jurors' subjective understanding provides a fine illustration of the conflict at the heart of the controversy over acquittals in jury trials—the confrontation between the rule of law and the vagaries of human relationships. In Lévy's examples, jurors were moved to leniency because they understood the situation of the foolish young man who had merely made a mistake he was unlikely to repeat or of the man who needed to support his family. Or perhaps they felt that the man who had been in prison awaiting trial had received punishment enough already. Jurors thus supposedly based their decision on pity and sympathy for the defendant.

It may well be that jurors felt an affinity for the accused, but this claim is difficult to prove in the absence of direct evidence from jurors beyond their verdicts. Other factors in the trial process itself, however, could heavily influence jurors to disregard the rigidity of the law. As noted above, jurors did not have to swear to uphold the law but rather to consider the interests of the accused and of society as a whole and to render their judgments according to their "conscience" and "inner conviction." Thus it is perhaps a moot point whether jurors understood the law or not, since they were not explicitly required to adhere to it, underscoring once again their nonprofessional status as temporary judges.

Furthermore, it was not simply at the point where the jury decided its verdict that the opposition between law and subjective judgment came into play; the opposition was inherent throughout the whole process of collecting and presenting evidence in assize court trials. Contrasting the procedures of the French assize court with Anglo-American traditions can help clarify this point. In American courts, where witnesses testify only through cross-examination by professional jurists, courtroom debate is quite largely shaped by the conventions of legal discourse. As some legal anthropologists have observed, testimony that does not speak directly to the requirements of the law seems irrelevant if not unintelligible in a courtroom. Witnesses who stray from the path directed by the lawyers' questions are immediately reprimanded by the judge, who instructs the jury to disregard the offending statement. Witnesses are not permitted to speculate, to offer their own interpretation of events, or to repeat hearsay. In short, they are not permitted to tell their own stories.[69]

The French assize court of the nineteenth century, in contrast, offered far more latitude to the people on the witness stand. While the presiding magistrate did have a dominant role in conducting the trial, he did not have the power to constrain witnesses' statements nearly to the extent that Anglo-American judges and lawyers do.[70] The French ideal, harkening back to the revolutionary era, was for the witness to give his own account without any prompting. Since the transcript of the deposition did not often include the magistrate's questions, the effect given was of a seamless narrative recounted by one person, not a statement delivered piecemeal through interrogation. Yet this impression was not merely an artifact of the recording secretary's style. By the time a witness took the stand in the assize court, he or she would have repeated the story several times: to the officers from the *Sûreté*, to the investigating magistrate, and doubtless several times to friends and family. In more than forty cases in this sample where it has been possible to compare the three written records of a witness's statement (from the police, the investigating magistrate, and the trial itself), little variation occurs among the different accounts. Witnesses did not change their accounts significantly as they repeated them in those different circumstances. And what they had to say, it must be emphasized, usually did not bear directly on the facts of the crime itself. Witnesses offered up rumor and hearsay, their own interpretations of events, perhaps even accounts that were not strictly truthful. Generally, their narrative strategy was inductive; they recounted anecdotes or made statements and assumed that the evidence they offered would speak for itself. If a witness testified that a woman used to have male visitors when her husband was away, for instance, the implication was that she was unfaithful and therefore that if her husband beat her, it was excusable. The testimony that witnesses gave in court reenacted the kind of tale telling, interpretation, and judgment that characterized neighborhood gossip. To compare it to gossip is not to trivialize it, however, for the constant circulation of news spun the web of connections that defined the local community.

Community Judgments and Court Verdicts

The 1881 case of Georges Koenig illustrates this dynamic.[71] He was acquitted of attempted murder, although there was never any doubt he had stabbed his wife Marie Tholomier, rendering her incapable of work for over three weeks. The dossier for his case includes depositions and reports from more than two dozen witnesses in Paris and another eight from the town of Besançon, where the couple had formerly resided. Georges was a former army officer and worked as a patrolman (*gardien de la paix*) in Lyon, Besançon, and Paris. Perhaps because of his profession, he proved himself to be particularly savvy about the judicial process and the expected outcome of his trial. He wrote to his brother Louis in Besançon, encouraging him to come to Paris to be entertained during his trial: "Since you have wanted to see Paris for a long time, please come without fail to my trial. You'll make me happy, and at the very least we can tour the city, since I'll have several days to myself." He also wrote to his wife's parents bragging that he was sure to be acquitted.

Georges's former supervisors in Besançon described him as hot tempered and pretentious, and they noted that his wife had been the subject of reports by the local vice squad. Marie's behavior was so notorious, one officer reported, that people would yell at her in the streets. Georges's brother and father testified that they had urged him not to marry Marie, given her loose reputation, and even her own mother admitted that Marie had had at least one lover before her marriage. After a stint in a convent to be treated for venereal disease, Marie joined her husband in Paris and continued her scandalous behavior. One concierge reported that she often chatted with men in a familiar manner and once was caught in bed with another resident of the building. When the concierge reproached her for her behavior, sarcastically telling her to take care to lock the door when she slept with other tenants, Marie calmly replied, "Very well, madam," refusing to demonstrate the shame or anger the concierge expected. The wife's sexual misconduct was therefore well known in two cities where the couple had lived, and the husband had been aware of it for quite some time.

Some witnesses suggested that he was partly to blame for his wife's poor behavior. "This child has a light character, but she isn't mean," Marie's mother testified, and "leading her with gentleness" would have improved her behavior. One of Georges's coworkers in Paris agreed that he was accountable for his wife's misconduct: "I urged him to be gentle, and to look after his wife in order to avoid a scandal; and since he told me that he took her to a low-class ball to entertain her, I made the observation that this was imprudent on his part." Georges's status as a man depended in part on his wife's fidelity, which he was responsible for enforcing.

What spurred the attack for which he stood trial, however, was not specifically her longstanding infidelity but rather what seemed a credible threat on her part to seek a legal separation. He had caught her talking with one of her alleged lovers and dragged her off to the police station; the following day she sought information about filing for separation. Although he seemed to support the idea at first, actually giving her twenty francs to rent a room of her own, he later got in an argument with her and stabbed her when she called him lazy (*fainéant*) and cowardly (*lâche*). "So it was to revenge yourself for an insult and not to punish her infidelities that you struck her?" inquired the investigating magistrate during one of Georges's interrogations. "Everything was muddled together in my mind. Once the insults were said, everything else came back to my memory," he replied. In some ways, Georges fit the stereotype of the outraged husband who commits a crime of passion against his faithless wife. But the details that emerged from the witnesses' testimony indicate that he had tolerated her infidelities for years and that he did not actually attack her in a fit of sudden, overwhelming emotion.

If he had been less than perfectly masterful as a husband, he at least was certain that her wrongs outweighed his. "Can you make a single reproach against me?" he demanded during a confrontation with his wife in the presence of the investigating magistrate. "Was I drunk? Did I behave badly? Did I run after women? Didn't I do every little thing for you? Didn't I take care of the household, wash your laundry along with mine, spare you anything that could tire you? Speak? Do you have anything to say against me?" His wife answered, "You have always behaved well. I can't say the contrary, but sometimes you beat me—notably, when we were at Montbéliard." He replied, "You have the audacity to recall what happened at Montbéliard. I would have liked to have hidden it. I knew that you were seeing soldiers. I hit you. It was my right. It was my duty." Here the transcript of the confrontation ends, so it is impossible to know how the investigating magistrate or Marie reacted to his claims. Georges's assertion that he did housework, sparing his wife such traditionally feminine chores as doing laundry, seemed to offer evidence of his exceptional devotion or even indulgence toward her. Yet this was balanced with what he saw as his masculine entitlement to use force to punish her infidelity. In his assessment, and that of the other witnesses in the case, his shortcomings as a husband were minor compared to hers as a wife.

"I acted in a moment of very legitimate fury," Georges insisted during his first interrogation. The history of his marriage and the circumstances that precipitated his attack legitimated, or indeed produced, the strong emotions that he felt during the attack. As his neighbors, family, and coworkers attested during his trial, Georges's use of violence was part of a long pattern of offense and retaliation in his relationship with his wife, not the sudden madness of a stereotypical crime of passion. It was the social context of his act that made his rage and his violence permissible, resulting in his acquittal.

Thus the process of judgment that took place among community members was transferred into the assize court, fostered by the official procedures of the criminal investigation and trial. The investigating magistrate invited witnesses to tell their stories, casting his net widely to include people connected to the accused through work, family, and neighborhood. Jurors thus heard a barrage of information that had little to do with the crime itself but instead illustrated community systems of mutual obligation between men and women, family members, coworkers, and neighbors. Although the trial was framed by the intervention of the presiding magistrate and the prosecution, who invariably argued loudly for guilt, jurors more and more frequently concurred with the testimony of the witnesses, who said that acts of violence were understandable, excusable, or even deserved.

The justice enacted in assize court trials was not therefore the utilitarian justice of the state, applied equally to all defendants for the good of society, but rather a popular system of retributive justice. Retribution is fundamentally an equation of inflicting harm commensurate with harm: the victim has merited the violence through his or her prior offenses, and the attacker is entitled to administer the violence by virtue of being the offended party. By contrast, the utilitarian approach to justice casts the crime as an offense against the state, a violation of the social contract, with the state therefore responsible for punishing the offense. Punishment, then, aimed to protect the state from future offenses by rehabilitating the criminal. In principle, at least, the public vengeance of trial and punishment was meant to take the place of private vengeance that individuals might pursue on their own, whether through the ritual violence of a duel or more spontaneous attacks.

Nonetheless, the verdicts in crimes of passion suggest that the state was not very effective in replacing private vengeance with public justice. Where the use of violence was judged legitimate by the local community and acquitted by the jury, the principle of retributive justice took precedence over the utilitarian model. It was not obvious that crimes of passion were offenses against the state or offenses that could be remedied through penitentiary punishment. Although the state certainly had an interest in maintaining order and harmony within families, the violence of crimes of passion could be understood to have resolved the need for punishment before state justice could intervene. The abandoned wife or the cuckolded husband struck against the faithless partner who had previously harmed her or him and thus closed the circle of offense and punishment. In such cases, jurors were faced with an ethical dilemma that pitted the strict application of the law against the utility of potential punishment. On the one hand, the law dictated that anyone who committed certain acts of violence must be punished in prescribed ways. But on the other hand, punishment could seem unnecessary because the attacker posed no further danger to society (having harmed his or her only likely victim) and was not in fact criminal or deviant (having acted in a way consistent with ordinary standards of behavior). If it was not necessary to reform the attacker through penal discipline, then it was not necessary to convict him or her. An acquittal in the assize court indicated that justice had already been served through the attacker's own violence.

Fin-de-siècle jurists and legislators worried that jury trials were escaping the rule of law, and they were correct, though perhaps for more profound reasons than they imagined. The problem went deeper than the jurors' incompetence or the undue harshness of the punishments prescribed by the penal code. Rather, by privileging witnesses' accounts and the implicit standards they contained, the process of criminal prosecution undermined the possibility of a straightforward application of the law. The lower-class people on trial were not colonized by bourgeois norms of propriety nor silenced by the strictures of legal discourse nor erased by the administrative requirements of the justice system. The process was not one where power and control flowed from the top down, from the representatives of state justice to individuals and their local communities. Instead, the flow of power was much more complex, and one system of justice was grafted onto the other.

Controversial acquittals in jury trials remained a problem for the French judicial system into the first decades of the twentieth century.[72] A 1908 law permitted the presiding magistrate to enter the chamber where the jurors deliberated in order to instruct them on the laws relevant to their decisions. Yet acquittals still remained high. A new law in 1932 enabled the jury to decide punishment, deliberating together with the three magistrates of the assize court after deciding alone on the question of guilt. In 1938, a project for reforming the Code of Criminal Instruction proposed instituting *échivenage*, where the jurors (as temporary judges, or *échevins*) would deliberate together with the court on both the verdict and the sentence. This proposal was put into effect with a decree of 25 November 1941 and was ensconced in the revised code of 1959. Although the impulse to limit the jury's power certainly meshed well with the agenda of the Vichy regime, legal scholars are unanimous in insisting that *échevinage* was not a product of the authoritarian regime but rather the result of an organic evolution of the French judicial system.[73] It is, moreover, a feature of the modern Italian and German judicial systems. Nonetheless, *échevinage* finally brought the jury under the control of the professional magistrates, and acquittals fell to only 8 percent after it was instituted in 1941.[74]

The extent to which this change in judicial procedure in the mid-twentieth century may have accompanied a shift in popular conceptions of justice and the legitimacy of intimate violence remains a subject for future study. However, the high rate of acquittal in cases of crimes of passion at the end of the nineteenth century indicates that instead of punishing private violence, the judicial apparatus was made to condone it, even in the heart of the family. With the unintended cooperation of the state, the use of violence in domestic conflicts between men and women was perpetuated.

Many scholars have constructed a persuasive picture of the fin-de-siècle preoccupation with crimes of passion and the disorder that they signified, documenting how journalists filled the pages of popular newspapers with crime stories, how legal and medical professionals deployed their skills to explain the causes of crime, and how bourgeois observers decried crime's effects on the security of the family. Along with this high tide of anxiety during the fin de siècle, however, jurors acquitted defendants of attacking their lovers and spouses, after listening to copious testimony in court about whether or not their use of violence was legitimate in the eyes of their community members. It is possible that the jurors, defendants, and witnesses also were concerned about the social disorder of which crimes of passion were a symptom. But it is also possible that they considered the retributive use of violence to be a legitimate way of reestablishing order. It is significant that women were acquitted more frequently than men, even if they were by far in the minority as defendants. Acquittals for crimes of passion cannot accurately be read *only* as a crackdown on female disorder, whether women were seen as subversive appropriators of masculine privilege or as victims worthy of punishment by male attackers. Juries condoned violence by (and against) both men and women. This phenomenon is evidence of a relatively permissive attitude toward intimate violence, which was not condoned by law. If French law had been applied strictly in these cases, as fin-de-siècle jurists desired, violence between domestic partners almost certainly would have been judged as harshly as any other kind of violence. It is only the flexibility in this era of the French criminal jury trial, with its inherent responsiveness to public opinion, that makes popular attitudes about the use of violence in intimate relationships visible.

CHAPTER 6

Reading and Writing Stories of Intimate Violence

In *Crime de Femme*, Lydia de Santorem and her confidence man debate the various ways of disposing of her rival for Roger de Merens's love.

"Vitriol!..." repeated the marquise softly.

"To begin with," continued Pioufle, without seeming to notice the interruption, "no matter how skilled the hand that wields it, one is not always sure of hitting the target precisely... One false move, caused by the slightest thing, and the attempt is botched!... In this case, three quarters of the time the aggressor is arrested... Jail, trial, scandal!... When the investigating magistrate sticks his nose into the affair, you are no longer assured of anyone's discretion... And then all dangers are to be feared."

"Oh!..." Lydia replied. "You are right."

"I would add that, even if the attempt succeeds, when you are dealing with sensitive people, with chivalric sentiments, with generous inclinations—and this seems to me to be the case!—You must fear the worst!... The soul is inspired by her sufferings... The heart softens... Medicine and especially surgery have progressed so far that one can no longer be sure of anything... Convalescence is rich in surprises; and one day, when the bandage falls and reveals the scarred face of the woman, it is so surprising to see the one that Love has placed on the eyes of the man is thicker and more solid than ever!"

"Let us give up this method..." she said. "... You must have some others."[1]

When an elaborate plan to convince Roger of his lover's infidelity does not work, Lydia takes matters into her own hands. She disguises herself as a man in order to gain entry to her rival's dressing room at the theater, where Lydia brutally stabs her to death. After nearly evading justice, Lydia's sister and husband compel her to commit suicide rather than besmirch their family's honor in the assize court. This murder case was not a real one but was imagined by one of the popular serialized novelists of the fin de siècle.[2] It was exactly the kind of story that worried social critics and criminologists of the day. Far from being mere entertainment, they believed it could inspire if not actually cause its readers to commit a crime of passion.

The representation of crimes of passion in the popular press has been well documented by several historians of fin-de-siècle France. Dominique Kalifa has situated accounts of crimes of passion within the framework of the history of the press, while Ann-Louise Shapiro has explored the mutually constructive relationship between representations of female criminals in the press and bourgeois notions about femininity.[3] Contemporary scholars agree that the burgeoning mass media must have had some power to shape popular perceptions of contemporary issues. It remains a challenge, however, to discover how the hundreds of thousands of readers of the popular daily press may have read and interpreted its stories of crimes of passion. By analyzing the press accounts of a crime of passion together with other kinds of evidence about popular responses to it garnered from the police and judicial archives, it becomes clear that readers did not passively absorb what they read in the newspapers. Instead, they actively integrated the stories they read in the press with the events of their own lives. Michel de Certeau has described this kind of active consumption of written texts as "poaching." "[The reader] takes neither the position of the author nor an author's position. He invents in texts something different from what they 'intended.'... He combines their fragments and creates something un-known in the space organized by their capacity for allowing an indefinite plurality of meanings."[4] Although people used stories from the press to make sense of events in their own lives, testimony given by working people in assize court trials for crimes of passion demonstrates that the discourses produced by the media, much less the professional elite, were far from hegemonic. Rather, defendants and victims created as well as consumed stories of crimes of passion, sometimes responding to published accounts and sometimes developing competing narratives of their own.

Nowhere is this creative engagement more vivid than in the sensational case of the woman cut in two. On 11 November 1876, *Le Petit National* broke the news that was to dominate the popular press for months: The body of a woman, severed at the waist, had been found floating in the Seine.[5] With her head shaved and her body eviscerated, packed with sawdust and paper, and bundled in pieces of a calico skirt, the victim was so disfigured that her identity remained a mystery for nearly two weeks. Hoping for a positive identification, the police distributed photographs of the victim in every quarter of Paris. They also sent them to major cities throughout France and had descriptions published in popular daily papers. In addition, they displayed the mutilated body at the morgue, where more than 100,000 people viewed the body (or, later, a wax replica of it) between 11 November and 15 December.[6]

The extent to which people willingly completed the mysteries in their own lives with the woman cut in two is nothing less than astonishing. Numerous (false) identifications were made on the spot, and dozens of letters and photographs from all over France poured in to the offices of the *Procureur de la République*, the police, and daily papers like *Le Petit Journal*.[7] It seems that the investigation occasioned a nationwide search for women who had disappeared under suspicious circumstances. The police compiled a list of "unidentified women" from such far-flung locations as Orléans, Dijon, Bordeaux, and Quimper, whose descriptions turned out not to match that of the victim. Another list detailed twenty-two other "found women" who were located after further investigations.

Speculation about the circumstances of the murder ran wild. Letters to daily papers and to the police suggested all kinds of possibilities. The victim was imagined to be a prostitute, a nun, the victim of a botched abortion; her murderer was a doctor, a sailor, or a jilted lover. The mystery inspired songs and souvenir portraits, hawked on the street for a few centimes. A police informant reported that in the workshops a rumor was circulating that the whole event had been staged by the government to divert the public's attention from political matters. It was supposed to be exactly like the Troppmann case of 1869, where a man murdered a family of eight in Pantin, near Paris—a crime rumored to have been fabricated by the government to distract the people from the tensions with Germany that would lead to the Franco-Prussian war.

At last, the vast publicity campaign worked, and it was revealed that the woman cut in two met her end under circumstances that were all too common. On 20 November, a number of regular patrons at the Café Charles on the boulevard Ornans obtained a photograph of the corpse and recognized the woman, who had been coming to the café for a year in the company of a former soldier known as "le Décoré." The proprietor asked around to find out the couple's real names, and two days later a group of the café patrons went to view the wax portrait at the morgue and make their statement to the police. The victim was a domestic servant named Jeanne Marie Le Manach, widow Bellengé, and her murderer was Sébastien-Joseph Billoir, a retired soldier. They had lived together for fourteen months while Billoir squandered the modest inheritance that Le Manach had received from her husband and she held fast to hopes that he would marry her. Apparently, she had run out of money and could not bring herself to leave him and place herself as a domestic; people who saw them in cafés remarked that he appeared irritated by her presence, while she seemed affectionate and submissive.

During his first interrogation, Billoir made a statement that would characterize his defense throughout the investigation and trial. He was "more unlucky than guilty," he claimed, since he had not intended to kill his mistress. Her death had been the accidental result of an ordinary fight. As he told it, she had returned home drunk and had broken a particular glass that he treasured. He kicked her in the belly as she stooped to clean it up, and much to his surprise, she died. Neighbors testified that they had in fact heard a fight on the night of 6 November but had not been alarmed enough to intervene. The next day they thought it was odd that Billoir went to the courtyard to draw water and empty the waste pail, since that was normally his mistress's chore. Later, the concierge (a woman) helped confirm Le Manach's identity by telling the police that the skirt wrapping the corpse's legs was one that Le Manach often wore during her menstrual period. Police took the skirt, along with another Le Manach had owned, to "one of the most important houses of couture in Paris," where two expert seamstresses confirmed that the same person had mended them both.

The combination of intimate knowledge and public spectacle that characterized the investigation continued during the trial, held 14 and 15 March 1877. The court was packed with spectators, as people who had read about the investigation in the papers and perhaps even viewed the corpse at the morgue, eagerly sought out the next installment of the drama. Billoir was found guilty of murder with premeditation and executed on 16 April. Read as a crime of passion, Billoir murdered his mistress in a fit of uncontrollable rage and entered the rogues' gallery of *faits divers* celebrities. Read as intimate violence, Le Manach's murder was the outcome of ongoing domestic conflict. Testimony from the couple's neighbors indicates that Billoir and Le Manach were neither isolated nor marginal. What was unusual about the crime was that the identity of the victim and the attacker had remained a mystery so long and, of course, that the body was disposed of in such a strange way, but the fate of Jeanne Le Manach was the result of the type of violent domestic conflict that was well known to her neighbors.

The legacy of the woman cut in two continued to resonate in accounts of crimes for at least the next two decades. When another woman cut into pieces was discovered in a sack at a Parisian construction site in November 1892, *Le Petit Journal Supplément Littéraire* recalled all the details of Billoir's crime.[8] The story of the woman also lived on in the work of fin-de-siècle criminologists, jurists, and social commentators, who were alarmed by the wide publicity such crimes received in the press. "At one moment, a woman is cut in two," wrote Dr. Séverin Icard. "One goes back twenty years, fifty years, a century, several centuries beyond that, [there is] no similar example; one goes forward a few years toward us, and one cannot count the number of cases of men and women that were cut into pieces, they are so numerous."[9]

Out of Control: Violence and Irrationality

As Icard's statement suggests, elite discourses about crimes of passion consistently ignored how such crimes grew out of ongoing domestic conflicts, defining them instead as aberrant emotional explosions caused by the passive absorption of suggestive images. A broad range of social observers agreed that some people who saw vivid accounts of crimes in the papers would be inspired to imitate them. This assertion depended on certain ideas about the nature of cognitive function and social behavior that gained ascendancy as the century drew to a close. French medical psychologists like Jean-Martin Charcot and Hippolyte Bernheim were instrumental in developing theories about mental processes that privileged the visual, nonverbal, and nonrational functions of the brain, especially through their experiments with hypnosis. As art historian Deborah Silverman has explained, "Images were discovered as an irresistible outer force in the thought process, permeating the brain directly from the outer world, and projected outward as if to shape the world in accord with inner visions, unmediated by rational discretion."[10] Scientists who studied the brain, whether as neurologists or psychiatrists, agreed that images could enter the brain and influence behavior without the intervention of the rational mind. Dr. Icard described this new understanding of the brain in terms of another great nineteenth-century discovery, photography: "The brain is a perfect recording instrument: all sensations perceived, whether weak or strong, whether conscious or unconscious, leave their imprint there as on a photographic plate. These cerebral impressions are indelible, *they are potential acts, acts in the latent state*, and an insignificant circumstance suffices to make them pass into the active state, even though everything seemed to be forgotten or even though there was never any memory of the thing."[11] Images were absorbed automatically by the brain only to resurface in unpredictable and ungoverned ways. An individual's actions, therefore, were not entirely under his or her control, for perception and action could take place without the intervention of the rational self; indeed, this finding made the self seem to be a more unstable entity than ever before.

Several historians have explored the impact of theories of irrationality on criminology and jurisprudence in the fin de siècle.[12] Still, it is well worth noting that the most influential contemporary experts primarily chose depictions of crimes of passion in the press to explain the dangerous effects of modern media on the mind. To the eminent criminal anthropologist Dr. Paul Aubry, the popular press was a major agent of criminal inspiration in the modern world because its grisly images of crime transmitted the idea of murder to the masses. According to Aubry, the moral shock caused by reading about a horrific crime in the press, "was like the action of the planter that sows the seed and makes it germinate."[13] He continued,

> The idea sown by chance would continue to be consolidated [in the mind of a susceptible individual], even more so since it would be reinforced everyday by the new stories of crimes presented with an unheard of luxury of details. For some years it has been considered useful to add drawings... to these remarkable descriptions, so that to learn to commit a crime, it is no longer even necessary to give oneself the trouble of reading long articles, a glance suffices, thanks to *Le Petit Journal* and *L'Intransigeant* (I am only citing two of the main ones) which, each week, have posted in every kiosk and boutique an engraving representing the crime of the day. In the street you cannot escape this suggestion, much more dangerous that that of pornographic images; it pursues you everywhere: the victim is stretched out in a sea of blood, very red and very large, and the assassin is just finishing his work.[14]

The effect of seeing a depiction of a crime in the press was what the Lyonnais doctor Armand Corre called an "imitative suggestion." Prior to reading about a crime or suicide, a person may have shown no character flaws at all, but after receiving the idea, he or she would suddenly feel compelled to imitate it.[15] Corre was explicitly building on the ideas of Gabriel Tarde, who theorized that imitation was the primary means through which society replicated itself. Enormously influential among fin-de-siècle criminologists and sociologists, Tarde also worked as Director of Criminal Statistics in the justice ministry. According to Tarde, a social group was defined as "a collection of beings in as much as they are in the process of imitating each other, or in as much as, without actually imitating each other, they resemble each other and their common traits are ancient copies of a single model."[16] Imitation could be conscious or unconscious, voluntary or involuntary, but he considered these distinctions less interesting than their result on a grand scale, which was nothing less than the creation of civilization.[17] "The social state, like the hypnotic state, is only a kind of dream, a dream of command and a dream of action. To have nothing but suggested ideas and to believe them to be spontaneous: such is the illusion proper to the somnambulist, and just as well to social man."[18]

Some historians of fin-de-siècle criminology have emphasized the notion that certain people were rendered more vulnerable to the power of suggestion by their age, education, class, and especially their gender. Ann-Louise Shapiro has argued that female criminality, above all, "became the material and discursive site where bourgeois authorities could attempt to address the problem of mass culture as they sought to secure their professional authority and cure the syndrome of modernity."[19] Even if women were understood to be more susceptible to irrational forces, however, contemporary criminologists agreed that men were far from immune. In Dr. Aubry's words, "the most virtuous being encloses a sleeping criminal; it suffices for a bolt of lightning shot from the atmosphere to separate the until-then flawless self, from the rapist, murderer, incendiary self."[20] It was impossible to know who might succumb to a sudden stimulus, for, as Proal observed, "The normal man can resist his passions. But by what physical signs can the normal man be distinguished from the degenerate? In spite of the work of contemporary physiologists and alienists, nothing is more obscure than the knowledge of man."[21] The bolt from the blue could shatter the thin veneer of civilization that ordinarily kept criminal urges in check. Dr. Hélie Courtois, in his doctoral thesis in psychiatry, explained, "The first impulse of a betrayed husband, a discarded lover, a slapped man, is to kill, it is a primitive gesture whose violence civilization has diminished without eliminating it."[22] Violence appeared as the inevitable result of the disjuncture between instinct and reason, and crimes of passion perfectly illustrated the fragility of civilization.

These theories on the causes of criminal behavior had potentially grave consequences for the state-sponsored system of justice. Rooted in Enlightenment theory, the justice system assumed that the criminal was a rational actor, who weighed the possible consequences of his action, chose to commit his crime, and was therefore responsible for his deed.[23] The possibility that attackers were helpless to resist the power of their emotions or some temporary madness that paralyzed their rational powers posed a serious problem for the legal system. But if criminals did not will their actions through rational choice, if their acts were flukes, entirely dependent on outside forces and internal brain processes over which they had no control, then neither reform nor retribution would be appropriate. Jurists wrestled with the implications of this conclusion, for it would negate the function of the judicial system altogether. Anatole Bérard des Glajeux, longtime *président* in the Cour d'assises de la Seine, insisted in 1892 that rationality, and therefore responsibility, could still be found just prior to the moment when the criminal succumbed to his urges. "The man who commits a crime was beside himself [*sorti de lui-même*]," wrote Bérard des Glajeux. "He acted under the empire of a violent passion; he has simulated and dissimulated; of all the precautions that human prudence suggests, none was forgotten by him in the cold-blooded moment that is almost always placed between the hesitations of the conscience before acting and the *fait accompli*."[24] In Bérard des Glajeux's analysis, authors of crimes of passion were particularly slippery on this point. "He who takes vengeance says that a mysterious force armed his hand and pushed him in spite of himself to do justice himself: whoever can use love for his defense pretends to have been carried away without being able to hold himself back through the impetuosity of his passion; one invokes the madness of pain if nothing else; no one says he is mad with pride, and this is however the most frequent case. In reality, these so-called madmen are very well-behaved [*sage*] people, who, having gotten themselves into a bad business, take the positions most favorable to liquidate their responsibilities."[25] The task of the judicial investigation, Bérard des Glajeux continued, was to unmask such false pretenses and lay blame where it was due. Louis Holtz amplified this same position a decade later. "The psychological problem is complicated by a moral problem: if passion can thus deprive an individual of his will, to the point of acting, in some sort, in his place—*non agit sed agitur*—is it not by the fault of this man?"[26] Because he allowed his passion to take over, the criminal should thus be punished for his moral weakness, if not his moral responsibility.

Alcohol also could weaken the individual's control of his passions. Indeed, passion and drunkenness were often equated on more than a strictly metaphorical level, as in the work of the influential physiologist and professor of medical jurisprudence Henry Maudsley, who stated that love was an "intoxication."[27] Proal affirmed that alcohol and literature were equally harmful: "Literary intoxication by bad novels is as fatal as intoxication by alcohol."[28] Strong emotions and alcohol alike posed dangerous threats to the equilibrium of the mind and thus to the social order. During the second half of the nineteenth century, alcohol consumption in France increased dramatically, along with a new intolerance for drinking in certain circles. According to historian Didier Nourrisson, France led the world in per capita consumption of alcohol by the 1890s, thanks to improvements in methods of production and distribution and a rise in discretionary income for working people.[29]

Some social critics linked rising alcohol consumption to the incidence of crimes of passion. In 1887, supported by the Société Française de Tempérance, a financial officer at the Sainte-Pélagie prison in Paris named Marambat published what he claimed was the first study directly linking the influence of alcohol on criminality. Marambat argued that 50 to 100 percent of those committing all kinds of crime were habitually excessive drinkers.[30] The examples he gave to illustrate the dangers of drink are telling, since they focus disproportionately on violence in the family: "first a man aged 41, who strangled his wife, drunk from drinking three-quarters of a bottle of eau-de-vie...Then, there is another who beat his mother to have money for drinking...Another attaches his child of five years to a clothes line, drags his wife in the direction of a pond to drown her, bites a neighbor who intervened on the arm."[31] After citing these sad cases, Marambat compared alcohol consumption and rates of crime throughout France, charted the professions of convicted criminals and their drinking habits, and concluded, "There is, furthermore, one undeniable fact: that the passion of drunkenness spreads itself more easily among the working class than any other."[32] Likewise, in Louis Holtz's opinion, alcoholism was the primary cause of crimes of passion among the lower classes. "Not only does it often happen that the jealousy of the man of the people explodes during his drunkenness, but the mere usage of alcohol makes the character more irritable and violent, and consequently predisposes him to acts of violence and vengeance."[33]

Given this strong correlation between alcohol and domestic disorder, it is surprising that alcohol was rarely cited as a cause of attack in cases of violence between domestic partners brought to the assize court. Certainly, there was plenty of evidence that the people involved in these cases drank, perhaps excessively. For example, Simon Richelet "used to drink a lot sometimes," in the words of his concierge, "but not heavily for a worker."[34] In another case, a witness was careful to downplay his old friend's habitual drinking: "I have always known Legrand for an honest man, helpful and hardworking. Only on payday he used to drink liquors, and his wife had the fault of sharing this kind of satisfaction."[35] Nonetheless, information about drinking habits was given to illustrate people's performance as workers and domestic partners. It was more relevant to determining a person's character than to determining the specifics of an attack. Comments on excessive drinking went hand in hand with descriptions of people who squandered their money and failed to work steadily. Louis Barbier's concierge had an especially low opinion of him: "He was brutal, jealous, a womanizer, a drunk. He consumed his pay at the cabaret with girls of ill repute and came back almost every night in a state of drunkenness, when he didn't sleep away."[36] Pierre-Auguste Perney's brother-in-law asserted, "From the day of his marriage, Perney stopped working completely. He didn't do anything but live off of the money belonging to my sister; he never sobered up."[37]

Nonetheless, only one defendant claimed that he was carried away in a drunken fit and did not know what he was doing, as he may have claimed that he was carried away by rage or jealousy.[38] Even in four cases where the attackers were diagnosed as having clinical problems with alcohol, the men were still convicted and given stiff sentences.[39] A few people admitted they had a few drinks to get their courage up before an attack, like Louis Martinière, who had some absinthe before he shot at his mistress.[40] Thus in the explanations that people gave in court for their behavior and the behavior of their peers, the use of alcohol was neither offered nor accepted as an excuse for intimate violence.[41]

Whether spurred by images in the media, overwhelming emotions, or the effects of alcohol, elite discourses constructed crimes of passion as being about the loss of control. A major group of social scientists found in crimes of passion evidence that atavistic passions and irresistible urges were all too easily loosed from the inadequate controls of civilization and the individual's own rational will.[42] Given their understanding of nonrational cognitive function, these social scientists linked frequent media depictions of violence, especially crimes of passion, with the incidence of crime. Yet social scientists were not the only ones to offer explanations about the causes of such crimes. While the professionals theorized that they were passive in their responses to depictions of crimes of passion, defendants, victims, and witnesses in assize court trials also articulated their own, competing understandings of these acts of violence. Although their popular discourses about crimes of passion intersect in superficial ways with the professional discourse, they ultimately reveal an entirely different understanding of the phenomenon.

Popular Engagement with Discourses on Crimes of Passion

As the criminologists predicted, a few authors of crimes of passion did claim to have been inspired by the media to commit their crimes, and famous assassins indeed had their imitators. A certain Pierre Lachaize, frustrated that he could not marry his employer, the widow Lequier, tried to kill her and her children, declaring, "I want to do like Troppmann."[43] On several occasions, Denis Roulland threatened his estranged wife with violence, saying that he would "clean house" like Troppmann did.[44] Both of these cases attest to the durability of the Troppmann story—more than a decade after the crime took place, these two attackers still found it compelling enough to use it in describing their own desires and deeds. Newspaper accounts of less notorious cases could also provide inspiration for potential attackers. A lodger testified that she had often heard Guillaume Malmézac speak approvingly of stories about people using revolvers, before he shot at his employer, a woman he had hoped to make his mistress.[45] In another case, although Angélina Merle admitted threatening to kill her lover if he refused to marry her after they had sex, she was surprised and distressed that her sulfuric acid attack had injured him so badly. The investigating magistrate found her attitude disingenuous: "How could you not know that vitriol is frequently used by women who want to avenge themselves! That it is one of the most powerful corrosives, whose contact causes the most serious wounds?" Merle answered, "Not at all, monsieur. I had read about such things in the papers, but I didn't know any more."[46] Her crime may have been inspired, if not accurately informed, by crime stories in the newspapers.

Other attackers may not have found inspiration in the press, but they took delight in numbering their exploits among those that appeared in the papers. They articulated the desire that their deeds make headlines, situating their own actions within the realm of crime stories in the press. Louis Jouault, for one, declared that he would give his wife such a blow "to have it put in the papers," and he succeeded.⁴⁷ Victims, too, occasionally seemed to relish ranking their cases among those worthy of report in print. Writing from the Hôtel Dieu to a friend in her native region, Marie Thiérion remarked, "I hope that even though Paris talks of nothing but me you are not entirely in the dark. Get yourself the newspaper from Sunday 22 December or the twenty-third of this month, do everything possible to read them [sic], you will see my family name and his."⁴⁸ In another case, Henriette Damotte, fearing her ex-lover's violence, told her sisters that "one of these days there will be talk about the drama of the rue du Petit Pont."⁴⁹ That phrase could easily have been the headline under which her murder was reported in the popular press. Thus, some people willingly projected the events of their lives onto the pages of the daily paper. They were savvy about the conventions of media reports on crimes of passion and about how their own experiences might figure among them.

Sometimes, stories in the press did not merely hold up a mirror, reflecting or replicating crime stories, but actually played an active role in the unfolding drama of a criminal investigation. The case of the woman cut in two is a fine example of this influence; the publicity in the press helped lead to the identification of the victim and the murderer.⁵⁰ In about a dozen other cases in this study, family members or friends of the accused and the victim (living as far away as Belgium) learned of an attack through accounts in the press and then wrote to the investigating magistrate offering whatever information they had about the couple. Quite remarkably, in one case the attacker himself only learned about the injuries that he had committed through a popular daily paper. Louis Périchon explained in a letter to the investigating magistrate that he had not realized at first how badly he had hurt his lover. He happened to run into his cousin the next day, Périchon wrote, who told him that he had read all about the attack in *La Lanterne*. Périchon hurried to buy the paper himself. He read about his crime and then immediately contacted the chief of police to turn himself in.⁵¹ More typical was the case of Eugène Henry, the author of an unsuccessful murder-suicide. The man who had been his schoolteacher in Blargies (Oise) wrote Henry's lawyer to tell what he knew about Henry's character: "As soon as I learned from *Le Petit Parisien* what my former student Henry had just done, I was not surprised, since at my school he had always shown the greatest taste for reading. He had run through almost all of the books of the Bibliothèque Scolaire, but the books that he greedily sought out were above all novels." He went on to speculate that this terrible taste for novels contributed "not a little" to the crime.⁵²

While only a handful of people who appeared in the *cour d'assises* were illiterate to the point of being unable even to sign their names on the transcripts of their testimony, on the other end of the spectrum, those who read a great deal were suspected of being up to no good. People who spent all their time reading were probably neglecting the work and obligations they should have been attending to. Consequently, François Schenk and his neighbors condemned his wife for reading novels all day instead of maintaining her household.[53] Similarly, Jean Delthil scandalized his neighbors when he quit his job, moved in with his mistress, and did nothing but write letters and read novels.[54] In a milieu where everyone worked for a living, the general assumption seemed to be that anyone who spent a great deal of time reading and writing was not only shirking their responsibilities but also undergoing some kind of unhealthy influence that could lead them to crime.

Altogether, the connection between crimes of passion and the popular press and literature did exist in practice. Although the links are explicit in only a few assize court cases (one-sixth of the cases in this study), the relationship was not just a phantasm of the educated elite's imagination. Ordinary people identified their predicaments with crimes they read about in the papers, and they willingly situated themselves and their deeds among the stories they read. But this apparent similarity among the professional discourses on the causes of violence and the explanations offered by defendants in the assize court requires further scrutiny. Did the defendants understand themselves to be irresistibly inspired by media representations? Were they "out of control" in the ways the criminologists theorized? Many defendants in the assize court did claim that they were overcome by emotion or irrationality at the moment when they committed their attack. Men and women alike spoke of anger, fury, despair, chagrin, jealousy, and exasperation—emotions that were too strong for them to resist. "I gave in to a violent wave of anger."[55] "At the last minute, anger blinded me."[56] Furthermore, the vocabulary of emotion was often paired with the vocabulary of madness. "My actions were faster than my thoughts; I can't explain them except by a wave of furious jealousy... I lost my head."[57] "I no longer knew what I was doing—I was like a madman."[58] Frequently, an attacker made such statements during the first, brief interrogation when he or she was informed of the criminal charges in the case. Accused attackers might have had many reasons for claiming their actions resulted from something besides rational calculation. Most simply, it is entirely plausible that the attacker's emotions were indeed very strong at the time of the attack.

On a more complex level, the accused might have known that the consequences for a premeditated crime were legally more serious than for an act committed on the spur of the moment, and claiming a sudden rush of emotion could have seemed like a good alibi. However, no correlation exists between such claims of spontaneous action and lesser sentences—nor, for that matter, is there a correlation between admitted premeditation and harsher sentences. Alternatively, the use of vocabulary describing madness could indicate that the accused was strategically invoking the latest psychological theories in defense of his or her innocence. Yet the intervention of medical professionals had little impact on trial outcomes.[59] Furthermore, in spite of their rhetoric of emotion and madness, it is well worth noting that no defendant in this study ever described himself or herself as a *criminel(le) passionnel(le)*, nor did any defendant describe his or her deed as a *crime passionnel*. Indeed, the word *passion* was hardly ever used in court at all, except occasionally to describe excessive love.

Even if traces of professional discourses on crimes of passion can be found in assize court testimony, however, they appear within the context of an entirely different, popular discourse about the legitimacy of the use of violence in intimate relationships. Where a defendant's claims about emotion and madness in court mattered most was in their relationship to the rest of the information presented in the case. To say one is carried away, overcome, or beside oneself with emotion is to imply that such is not the case in ordinary circumstances. In simultaneously admitting the crime and claiming disempowerment, the accused was saying in effect, "Yes, I committed this act of violence. But I was not my usual, rational self. Only some extraordinary force could have made me do this." If the other witnesses in the case concurred that the accused was a respectable, hardworking individual—and better yet, that the victim was deserving of punishment—then the defendant's claim would stick. The defendant's excessive emotion, and the violence it inspired, would be condoned. The defendant would not be convicted as a criminal but instead would be judged to be a good man or woman, whose extraordinary action was understandable and excusable. In short, the author of the crime would not be held responsible. This kind of judgment did not depend on the terms of elite discourses about crimes of passion but rather on information about the couple's conduct and reputation.

Popular Literary Practices

Furthermore, participants in assize court trials were not only consumers of journalists' or criminologists' discourses of crimes of passion, they were also producers of written accounts of their love affairs and conflicts. The investigating magistrate was legally authorized to seize virtually any kind of physical evidence during the course of his investigation, including private correspondence.[60] In addition, people involved in the cases wrote letters specifically addressed to the investigating magistrates, giving their accounts of the crime. About sixty dossiers in this study contain letters collected during the investigation; twenty of these include letters exchanged between lovers or spouses.[61] "These letters were my only consolation. I couldn't do without them. I read and reread them constantly." Thus Louis Parrain, a cooper, described love letters from his former mistress Jeanne Bonnefoy, a seamstress, during his investigation for her attempted murder in 1888. Before the lovers' correspondence became evidence for the prosecution, however, these letters had circulated for quite different purposes among Parrain, Bonnefoy, and her husband. The archives of the assize court of the Seine may seem like a surprising source for evidence of popular literacy, but documents like those preserved in the Parrain case provide a rare glimpse into the writing and reading practices of working people in fin-de-siècle Paris. Historians know that ordinary Parisians were avid consumers of the popular press in this era but have little addressed their activities as authors, especially outside the political sphere. Shifting the focus from consumption to production and from public to private practices of literacy, love letters preserved in trial dossiers reveal a variety of popular literacy practices. Writing letters was not only a means for the author to construct a certain representation of him- or herself but also one way through which people used their often imperfect literary skills to engage with the judicial apparatus of the state.

Is it possible to verify the authorship of all the documents? After making their depositions to the investigating magistrate, witnesses were legally required to sign the transcribed version of their testimony to certify that it was an accurate rendition of what they had said. Only a tiny minority of witnesses in this study were unable to do this. However, as several scholars have noted within the past decade, assessing literacy based on signatures has its limitations—people who can sign their name might not be able to read, and vice versa, and the skills required to compose and record original texts are a different order of literacy entirely from being able to write one's name.[62] It is therefore not safe to assume that the person whose name was signed at the bottom of a letter was actually the author. In a handful of cases, the intervention of third parties in the exchange of letters between lovers was openly acknowledged. A day laborer named Charles Gaudot testified that he wrote two letters to his mistress after his arrest but had a fellow prisoner write another.⁶³ Eugène Thauvin, a poultry seller, was able to sign his name, but he had a friend write two love letters to his supposed mistress, a wine seller.⁶⁴ That in these few cases people went out of their way to describe particular arrangements suggests that they were indeed unusual.

However, it seems possible that letters written after the crime, especially those addressed to the investigating magistrate, may have been influenced by the intervention of some kind of professional, especially the defendant's lawyer. For instance, Victorine Lelong's six-page letter (written front and back) about her unhappy marriage seems to be far too full of ornate phrasing and the subjunctive mood, and written far too neatly, to be the work of a domestic servant by herself.⁶⁵ In another case, a remark by the investigating magistrate during the interrogation of Jean Legrand, a mechanic, implied that Legrand had sent his life story to the investigator on his lawyer's advice. The scrawled handwriting and poor grammar and punctuation of the letter in his dossier, however, suggest only minimal intervention by a highly educated professional in the actual composition of the document.⁶⁶ Most letters in these cases demonstrate a competent, but flawed, level of writing skill. Absent any clues to the contrary, there is no compelling reason to doubt the authenticity of their authorship.

Historians know little about the epistolary habits of such imperfectly literate workers, though an important body of scholarship has investigated the letter-writing practices of bourgeois families. Most notably, the team of historians that produced *Ces Bonnes lettres* has analyzed the exchange of letters among the members of one elite family throughout the "long" nineteenth century. Focusing on the practices of exchanging letters rather than their content, the authors contend that the rituals of correspondence worked to create "the written production of [the family's] social identity."⁶⁷ At the same time, letter writers positioned themselves as wives and mothers, husbands and fathers, within the larger framework of the family, thus simultaneously constituting individual social identities within the family group. This approach is particularly apt for understanding love letters, where authors construct a certain presentation of themselves and of the couple. Such letters are at once imaginative and instrumental; among the desired effects of a love letter is surely the acceptance by the recipient not only of the letter but of the relationship it helps constitute.

The authors of *Ces Bonnes lettres* further develop the reciprocal relationship between letter writers and recipients with their notion of the "epistolary pact" that governs their exchange. In the epistolary pact, they explain, authors deploy certain rhetorical tools to create the desired rapport with the reader.⁶⁸ Many of these effects are achieved through the author's use of ritual gestures, like noting the date and place of composition at the top of the first page and utilizing specific forms of address in the opening and closing. Through these devices, the author marks his or her temporal and spatial separation from the addressee, while also invoking the proximity of their affective and familial relationship.

Such attention to the form of letters permits even greater insight into how individuals manipulate conventional practices and expectations to create their own meanings and relationships. Yet the letter writers in this study typically did not observe the details of such ritual forms. Although they could well have been exposed to normative models of letters through letter-writing manuals or elementary education, they did not usually note the date and place of composition or use elaborate forms of address.[69] Only clerks and the few higher-class authors whose letters ended up in the trial dossiers did so. Otherwise, a brief phrase such as "my dear," or "dear Marie," or "to the investigating magistrate" usually sufficed for a salutation, and a simple signature was the only closing. The dossier concerning the murder of Léontine Puthomme contains three letters written to observe New Year's Day that she wrote her family from the Couvent du Bon Pasteur in St. Florent near Saumur, where she was a boarding student.[70] They are full of rhetorical flourishes, with impeccable spelling and grammar. "What a beautiful day is New Year's for a little girl, where I can tell you how happy I am to be able to wish you a happy new year and good health, and how much I love you," begins her letter from 1868, when she was only seven years old. It seems quite likely that she was copying a formula proposed by her teachers. Five years later, in a note thanking her father for some money and little gifts he sent her, she reassured him, "As for the letter, it was really me who wrote it," as if he had questioned whether a recent communication was beyond her abilities. Not surprisingly, the note she scrawled to her father in 1879 after drinking a glass of poison that her lover gave her was not nearly as polished (*"vien vite je ten suplie je ne voi plis je tremble je ves mourire je tembrasse de tou coeur ta fille qui est bien coupable"*). The extreme distress illustrated by her poor spelling and penmanship was not enough to move her father to come visit her in the hospital, even though he lived in Paris at the time. "When the heart is closed it cannot be opened," he told the investigating magistrate, who reproached him for ignoring her final plea.

Of course, it is separation that necessitates writing, but separation could be caused not only by military service, or migration to the city, or travel[71] but also merely by a few blocks or miles within the city of Paris.[72] Octavie Levielle, a laundress, sent a dozen letters to her husband Eugène during the months of September and October 1889, when he left Paris to convalesce with tuberculosis.[73] She complained in her first letter to him that his recent letter to her (which is not in the dossier) was not nearly as nice as one he sent her the last time he left town; he no longer addressed her as "his angel." Apparently, he pleased her better with his next effort, for she wrote: "I am responding to your letter which made me much happier than the last one[.] I saw that you remembered your charming words." This time, instead of just signing off as "your wife," she closed with: "Your little wife who loves you and adores you, a thousand kisses and take care of yourself." She decorated her next letter with a pink ribbon woven through chevron-shaped slits along the top and side of her paper, as well as a blossom that she described as being plucked from his rosebush. This one was signed with "100000000000 kisses to her beloved." But by the end of October, though, his requests for money and complaints about her handling of the household finances in his absence had irritated her considerably. "One might say that you don't know how to count," she complained. "I'm telling you that I'm not sending you any money because I don't have any You should have enough for your return I beg you to write me for Tuesday morning only so that I can go pick you up [at the station] nothing else to say to you." This packet of letters reads like bickering by post, where expressions of affection reinforcing the couple's emotional ties at a distance give way to disagreements about household finances.

A dozen dossiers contain evidence of more or less regular correspondence exchanged among family members living at a distance. Some were written only on formal occasions such as the New Year or to express condolences over a death,[74] but others suggest that parents back in the *pays* were regularly kept informed of ongoing events in the lives of their grown children in Paris. Eulalie Jean sent ten letters to her father in her hometown of Blanc (Indre), telling him about her unhappy marriage, even including a brief newspaper clipping of an article titled "A Difficult Wife," which reported how she had shot at her husband.[75]

In another case, Clarisse Denis, a maid, wrote her mother about a brutal attack by her husband (a delivery driver for a furniture store) and her fears for her life, which unfortunately would be realized in 1890.[76] This letter is worth reading closely for the evidence it suggests about attitudes toward the importance of distance between correspondents and the instrumentality of letters. It begins quite conventionally. "I am writing you two words to give you my news I am well for the moment." But then Clarisse introduces the possibility of her death as a potential interruption in the correspondence. "My dear mother I will tell you that yesterday I barely escaped never writing you again," and she goes on to describe her husband Clément's weekend drinking binge and his violence. She explained that she was writing in her husband's absence, without his knowledge, and twice she urged her mother not to write her back and not to mention the contents of the letter, in order to prevent her husband from knowing that she wrote it.[77] "I beg you to keep this letter because if anything happens to me you will show it," she admonished. After (what must have been) the shocking content of the letter, she closes it quite conventionally, sending kisses to the family and signing off, "your devoted daughter."[78] In writing this letter, Clarisse Denis was quite purposefully creating a record of her violent relationship, and indeed the letter did become evidence in her husband's trial for murdering her. In this case, the distance of her mother from Clarisse's household was important—the letter could be preserved where her husband could not find it. Clarisse also clearly understood that writing the letter was a way of preserving her words, her own version of the story, replacing her speech if she became no longer able to speak for herself. With this letter to her mother, Clarisse consciously created enduring evidence of a particular kind of relationship.

Love letters exchanged between partners could serve much the same purpose. Love letters were used in court as concrete proof of amorous relationships, and they were treated as such by the people who exchanged them. The assumption was that anyone who would accept and keep such a letter must be a lover. Jeanne Douët's former employer, a baker, testified that he first discovered her infidelity to his friend François Badault (day laborer) when a letter arranging a rendez-vous with another man (Augustin Froquières, a pallbearer) happened to fall out of her pocket. "I teased this girl on the content of these letters," he testified, "and she confessed that although Badault didn't know it, she was courted by Froquières."[79]

Continuing to exchange letters indicated the continuation of a relationship. Although she did not date her letters, it appears that Marie Fournet, a domestic, wrote her lover (who ran a wineshop) a couple of times after his wife came to Paris and kicked her out of the house. "I loved you too much, with too much respect, for you to mock me... For eight days I have been unable to eat every night I call for you, yet you see how I am tormented, my well-loved little Pierre one little word—I implore you, I beg you on two knees, write me a little word to tell me you are no longer angry with me."[80] (He never wrote, and she eventually shot him.) Louis Parrain, cited earlier, treasured the letters that his erstwhile mistress Jeanne Bonnefoy wrote him. He refused to give them back to her when she tried to end their relationship and asked for their return. In turn, Jeanne testified that he had threatened her with a saber and forced her to copy letters he had drafted that would expose their affair to her husband. "That's fiction," Parrain protested ("*Ça, c'est du roman*") when the investigating magistrate told him about her claim.

What was in those love letters that Parrain so fetishized? The dossier preserves several notes, usually quite short, often giving times for rendezvous and almost always written in baby talk, or what the investigating magistrate referred to as "*langage nègre*." Here is a sample: "*Moi bise bien toi moi aime toujours bien mon pauvre gros malade aimé que j'espère bien faire bise ce soir.*" (Translating these lines into English risks losing their distinctive flavor: "Me kiss you lots me still love lots my poor beloved sickie who I hope to kiss lots this evening.") But this childish language, which literally infantilizes her, is mingled with comments on the progress of her tasks as a seamstress. The same letter continues: "*Ta petite femme va encore bien vite après déjeuner partir travailler pour gagner ainsi sousous car elle en aura bien besoin pour terminer ti roe zolie.*" ("Your little wife is going to leave again very quickly after lunch to work to earn some pennies since she really needs them to finish purty lil' dress.") Just a couple of notes are written in a more straightforward, adult tone: "*Je te dirai mon mignon que cette semaine tous mes jours sont pris, j'ai deux robes à faire aux enfants j'ai une robe de fillette à livrer après demain pour pocher des sousous car j'en ai grand besoin j'ai à aller au lavoir à repasser et à faire mon ouvrage tu vois que je n'ai pas une minute à perdre maintenant.*" ("I'll tell you, sweetheart, that this week I am busy every day, I have two children's dresses to make, I have a little girl's dress to deliver the day after tomorrow to pocket some pennies because I really need them I have to go to the laundry, do the ironing, and do my work, you see that I don't have a minute to spare now.") In this note, in particular, it proves impossible for her to reconcile the image of herself as a childish dependent, always waiting for her lover's visit, with her hard work as a seamstress. Yet in spite of the infantile image she attempts to construct for herself in her love letters, Jeanne would be the one to tell Louis that their relationship was over. His attempts to counter her rejection through the power of words failed— he never dared send the incriminating notes to her husband, nor could he persuade her through arguments to take him back— and so perhaps it seemed logical to him to claim power over her through violence instead—threatening her with a sword, and then shooting her and himself in an unsuccessful murder-suicide.

Many other women presented themselves as weak and dependent in love letters to their partners or in love stories addressed to investigating magistrates. Thus, when Marie Sanglé, an embroiderer, composed a rambling account of her relationship with her husband, she emphasized her long, patient suffering. She was always scrambling to make ends meet, practically starving while her husband went out on the town with his friend Auguste Delinon.[81] "I love my husband so much, I put up with all the tortures I endured with him," she wrote. In such accounts as this, women often presented themselves as passively waiting—for their lovers, and for the attention and resources that their partners owed them. They almost never portray themselves as the active pursuers, which would be dissonant with the prevailing cultural expectations for a woman, or even a heroine in a melodramatic romance. And yet both of the women in these cases were resourceful and hardworking. Furthermore, Jeanne Bonnefoy seems to have called the shots about when and where the couple would meet, while Marie Sanglé took matters into her own hands and threw acid on her husband's friend Auguste, putting an end to their carousing in the cafés.

By contrast, men usually sought to present themselves as masterful and in control, even in situations where their economic and social status rendered this posture more or less fictional. Emile Perrin was a clerk who earned only one hundred francs a month—less than the average skilled male worker in his time and not enough to support a woman in comfort, as his former lover Marie Iltis observed.[82] After living with him for six months and sometimes going hungry, she took her sister's advice and found herself another man who could support her more generously. Emile, however, remained attached to her, and he eventually tracked her down at the Folies-Bergères, where he shot her in the head and himself in the chest, without either of them being seriously injured.

His trial dossier contains transcriptions of four letters written to her after the attack, together with a long document entitled, "My Life, from 10 December 1881 to 8 November 1882," which is an account of their love affair from their first meeting to the day of the attack. In this narrative, Perrin casts himself as his lover's savior, teaching her good manners along with good penmanship.[83] For Perrin, his literary accomplishments were clearly central to his sense of who he was. In his account of the affair, he sets himself up as an expert in reading and writing, and he explicitly links his mistress's acquisition of those skills to her acquisition of respectability, transforming her from harlot to housewife. He makes claims to even greater literary expertise in one letter, apparently written on the day of a confrontation between the ex-lovers in the presence of the investigating magistrate. At that time, Marie told him in no uncertain terms that she did not love him. He begins by describing his disturbed emotional state before launching into a poem that sounds very much inspired by Rimbaud's "Les Voyelles."[84] Even in the face of his mistress's ultimate rejection, his last letter to her (or at least, the last one in the dossier) continues his presentation of himself as a skilled and savvy writer: "I suffered so much that to persuade you of my love I sought all the most violent expressions that the poets used in the painting of passion!"[85]

What can we make of this would-be poet clerk? One response is to mock the pretensions of an autodidact. The investigating magistrate, for one, found Perrin's tale of passion to be unconvincing because of the social status of his mistress: "It is very difficult to admit that you conceived such a violent passion for this girl, who belonged to everyone," he remarked in an interrogation. He was unconvinced by Perrin's self-presentation as a great lover or a gatekeeper of literary culture. In his eyes Perrin was no more a master of language than he was of his woman. Another would-be poet, Georges Ducret, voluntarily turned himself in for the murder of a coachman's wife in 1887, asking only that he be permitted to continue to write during his imprisonment. The press had a field day with his literary pretensions. *Le Gaulois* regretted that his manuscripts had been seized as evidence in the case and could not be made known to the public, while an article in *La Patrie* speculated on the appeals of a penal colony to a poet. The latter article depicted Ducret walking to the police station, sniffing the spring air, occupied with pleasant thoughts of the tropics: "How sweet it must be, for a poet who asks only to be left alone to stroll at his leisure under real palm trees, in the middle of a real forest, on the banks of a real river, far from mocking boulevards and unfriendly editors!"[86]

These cases certainly demonstrate the contempt that professionals harbored towards the literary efforts of working people. But it does not follow that the highly educated elites in the judicial system automatically had the upper hand over lower-status defendants in the creation of compelling narratives. The vast bulk of the evidence presented in the assize court was not written. It was oral testimony given by witnesses—the friends, neighbors, coworkers, and family members of the couple involved in the case—and the verdicts rendered by the jury usually coincided with the judgments expressed by the witnesses. In this context, written evidence appeared to reinforce oral testimony. Crafting such written narratives must have required a fairly high degree of self-awareness, and the authors deployed certain personas that were deeply inflected by their class and gender status. Female authors tended to cast themselves as faithful, long-suffering martyrs, while male authors tended to present themselves as masterful, experienced lovers, although their positions were constrained by their material situations.

The spread of literacy has sometimes been viewed as a means through which the modern state could exercise increasingly strict social, political, and moral regularization over the people. But these Parisians whose domestic conflicts brought them under the purview of the courts wrote letters to magistrates and others in order to persuade them of their versions of the story and of their roles within it. Whatever the ultimate efficacy of their narratives, it seems clear that the authors *believed* that their writing could have power to affect the readers, and they seized that power for themselves. They were far from being the passive recipients of mass media representations of crimes of passion that contemporary social scientists theorized them to be. Not only did they respond creatively and imaginatively to accounts of crimes of passion in the popular press, interpolating newspaper stories with the events of their own lives, but they also actively produced their own written accounts of love stories and violent conflict. This agency demonstrates the limited power of elite discourses to constitute "crimes of passion" beyond professional circles. While social scientists theorized that ordinary people were "somnambulists" with minds like "photographic plates," responding to exterior stimuli that might cause them to lose rational control and commit violent acts, participants in assize court trials cast themselves in quite different roles. They did not adopt elite notions of the causes of violence any more than they responded unthinkingly to a murder case reported in *Le Petit Journal*. Rather, they made use of the stories in the press together with their own tools of literary production to explain, if not constitute, their own relationships and conflicts.

CONCLUSION

"Men Who Kill and Women Who Vote"

In 1880, Alexandre Dumas the younger revised his earlier stance on the implications of intimate violence with a new publication, *Les Femmes qui tuent et les femmes qui votent*.[1] He argued that women should be permitted to vote (but not to hold office) in order to change unjust laws concerning divorce, infidelity, and paternity suits. Women like Marie Bière, whose trial he had recently attended, had been left no other choice by the law than to use violence against their faithless lovers or husbands.[2] For Dumas, the fact that women committed murder and were acquitted by the courts and public opinion revealed the insufficiency of the law to protect the innocent. "In my opinion," he wrote, "women who kill lead to women who vote."[3] With greater political rights, women would make the law more just.

Although this publication heralded Dumas's endorsement of the feminist movement—he eventually joined Léon Richer's Ligue française pour le droit des femmes—his equivocal stance about the extent of women's rights did not go uncriticized.[4] Emile de Girardin, a politician and social reformer who had previously published a rebuttal to *L'Homme-femme*, objected that Dumas focused on the wrong kind of violence. A better title for Dumas's new book, he suggested, was "Les hommes qui tuent, et les femmes qui votent," because it was men's violence against women that better revealed women's lack of rights. Borrowing Dumas's terminology, he wrote, "When 'the feminine' becomes an elector, she will want to be eligible for office, and she will be right to want it, if for no other reason than to expunge Article 324 from the penal code, by virtue of which MEN WHO KILL are legally excused for killing their adulterous wives, this article of Roman law that perpetuates the vassalage of the wife and the lordship of the husband." If women could vote and hold office, de Girardin argued, they would not only reform laws concerning marriage and parental rights, they would also reform their intimate relationships. "Women will no longer want a coarse husband. Legally independent of him, she will no longer permit him to be brutal with her." What most interested him was "not the woman who kills the man, but the woman who kills the old moribund society."[5]

A century after de Girardin's optimistic prediction, French women with full political rights finally embarked on large-scale efforts to end intimate violence. In the mid-1970s, once the right to legal abortion had been obtained, violence became the primary focus of French feminist activism, according to historian Gill Allwood. In 1975, members of the Ligue du droit des femmes established a helpline for women who were survivors of male violence. Three years later, the same group established the first shelter for battered women in France, the Refuge Flora Tristan, in Clichy.[6] As their work with survivors expanded, feminists amplified their claims for better legal protection and social services, as well as their critique of violent masculinity. They also held demonstrations against domestic violence and rape throughout the 1970s. While the Mouvement de libération de femmes spoke out against domestic violence, public awareness was also raised by the trial of Alain Fischer in Strasbourg in 1976.[7] Similar to the du Bourg case in the nineteenth century, this sensational trial sparked a public debate about the legitimacy of violence in intimate relationships. Fischer was condemned to twenty years in prison for killing his wife, a sentence that some found to be excessive. In the summer of 1979, women from the group S.O.S. femmes battues began promoting a law that would expel violent partners from the home in order to protect survivors of abuse.[8]

More recently, demands for reform that originated with feminist activists have been ensconced in French law. As of 1992, the civil code designated the fact of being the *conjoint* or *concubin* of the victim as an aggravating factor in certain crimes.[9] It is notable that this was the first time the term *concubin* appeared in the penal code, defined as any union "characterized by a life in common, demonstrating a character of stability and continuity, between two people of different sexes or the same sexes, who live as a couple."[10] This broad term recognizes the diversity of intimate relationships in which violence might occur, not just legal marriage. However, the law of 4 April 2006, which implemented a number of reforms concerning violence within couples and violence against minors, went even further.[11] With this law, the fact of being in any way partnered with the victim of a crime or misdemeanor was made an aggravating circumstance.[12] Being an *ex-concubin* was also defined as an aggravating factor, in recognition of the numerous attacks that occur when one partner leaves the other.[13] At last the legacy of the old Article 324, where being a husband of the victim mitigated the attacker's guilt, was completely eliminated. The new law further provides that a judge may order the violent partner to be expelled from the conjugal abode, even if the conflict is between a married couple not involved in a legal separation or divorce.

These reforms of French law took place within the context of continuous feminist activism in France as well as the policies of the European Union. On 16 September 1997, the European Parliament resolved to promote "zero tolerance" of violence against women, building explicitly on human rights principles.[14] Toward that end, the European Council established the Daphne Programme, now the Daphne Initiative, under the auspices of Justice and Home Affairs. The Daphne Initiative has spent millions of euros funding projects to "prevent and combat violence against young children, young people, and women and to protect victims and groups at risk."[15] Numerous local organizations, including many in France, have benefited from the financial support as well as international networking facilitated by Daphne. Thus, efforts to spread awareness of intimate violence, to assist its victims, and to eliminate it now emanate from feminist organizations, the national government, and the supranational institutions of the European Union.

In the present day, a wide range of institutions and organizations in France actively campaign against intimate violence. Even though it still continues in practice, such violence is widely condemned as being entirely unacceptable and inexcusable. The law and public discourse are now firmly on the side of the victims, unlike in the late nineteenth century. Then, the primary site of a sustained critique of intimate violence was in crowded urban neighborhoods, where men and women monitored each other's behavior, their domestic partnerships, and the violence that marked them.

Practices of Violence in Fin-de-Siècle Paris

Violence was used to patrol the boundaries of acceptable behavior for men and women in domestic partnerships, functioning to help construct gender roles in the immediate and contingent context of daily life. In fin-de-siècle Paris, those roles were definitely open to negotiation; it was by no means preordained that old norms would continue to obtain. Couples often came to the city from other regions of France, and the economic and social situations that they encountered were unlike what they had known in their regions of origin. In Paris, women and men alike worked for wages, and the household was typically not a productive unit, as a household in a farming community might have been. Although many couples maintained important ties with their families in their hometowns, in Paris it was not so often family members as neighbors who involved themselves in monitoring a couple's relationship. Without the imperatives of economic survival or family ties to keep a couple together, personal considerations like emotional and sexual satisfaction could come to the fore as men and women sought partners or decided whether or not to stay with their current partners. In the city, the possibilities were great for leaving an unsatisfactory partner and finding a new one.

This potential mobility was the basis of a great deal of conflict as couples fought over not only the qualities that made a good man or a good woman but also the very prerogative for one partner to leave the other. The potential for separation was a major cause of domestic conflicts: couples would be more likely to resort to violence in the absence of other means of controlling their partners or compelling them to stay. Furthermore, the heightened importance of emotional and sexual satisfaction in the choice of a partner may also have contributed to increased violence in this context. Some historians have argued that the growing intensity of emotional relationships accounts for an increase in family violence in the modern era,[16] and it is true that some fin-de-siècle attackers claimed that the intensity of their emotions—love or jealousy—motivated if not validated their use of violence. But these claims were weighed by victims and witnesses who often found them insufficient and offered counterclaims about work and household obligations. The expectation of emotional and sexual satisfaction in a domestic partnership may well have exacerbated the disappointment individuals felt when it was not forthcoming. Yet it is clear that these expectations of intimacy were added to, but did not replace, practical and material household obligations.

By the same token, expectations of a certain kind of intimacy may have reduced the acceptability of certain kinds of violence—if not the extreme violence of the crime of passion, then perhaps the nonlethal blows that may have punctuated day-to-day conflicts. This assumption has informed certain "trickle-down" accounts of the history of domestic violence, in which the lower classes learn to imitate—or are colonized by—the more peaceful practices of the bourgeoisie. However, it is impossible to say for sure if the incidence of intimate violence increased or decreased during this era. Not only did the present-day category of "domestic violence" not exist, but even the unofficial category of "crimes of passion" was not systematically quantified.

Nonetheless, it is possible to learn a great deal about popular practices of intimate violence from existing sources. Testimony in assize court trials demonstrates that "crimes of passion" sprang from ongoing domestic disputes that were deeply implicated in the creation and maintenance of gender roles for women and men. In contrast, the constructions of crimes of passion in the press and in elite discourses worked to obscure the ways in which such acts grew out of normative uses of violence in ongoing domestic disputes. Defined as the result of uncontrollable emotion, crimes of passion were cast as problems of individual psychology, or a couple's unhappy love story, not gendered power struggles within the household.

The impact of these discourses about crimes of passion was limited, however. Attackers, victims, and witnesses in the assize court were far from being passive recipients of crime stories in the media, much less of professional discourses about crimes of passion. Instead, people who testified in court articulated the contours of a popular system of retributive justice within which violence was deployed and contested. The high rate of acquittal in such cases demonstrates the enduring power of popular justice, even within the state judicial system. Thus, multiple and intersecting systems of social control, not simply the repressive apparatus of the state or dominant classes, worked to legitimate certain uses of violence.

Violence and Gender

This insight has important implications for the history of violence and gender. Practices and attitudes concerning intimate violence do not necessarily correspond with trends in violence that typically occurs between men rather than between men and women. Norbert Elias's classic account of the state monopolization of violence is almost exclusively concerned with public expressions of violence—such as duels, feuds, brawls, and vendettas—that primarily occurred among men.[17] It seems clear that modern European states only began to try to control intimate violence (which is primarily but certainly not exclusively directed against women and children) in the nineteenth century, and then only in response to pressure from reformers interested in promoting women's rights and child welfare.[18] However, just as dueling remained an integral part of masculine honorability in nineteenth-century France, so too did the use of retributive violence in intimate relationships. Like du Bourg, who proclaimed, "I was a savage beast when my honor was attacked[;] I can certainly be a man to defend myself,"[19] knowing when to unleash lethal violence demonstrated one's manhood. While higher-class witnesses and jurists deplored the use of nonlethal violence in intimate relationships—the stereotypical, habitual abuse characteristic of partnerships among the lower classes—they also condoned the violence of a crime of passion, where a man attacked a woman who had sullied his honor, especially through infidelity. However, whether lethal or quotidian, violence could be deemed legitimate only as long as it performed a retributive function. Knowing how to use violence legitimately thus implied knowing how to make the proper judgments about the reciprocal obligations of men and women in a domestic partnership: the perpetrator was, in a real sense, the arbiter of proper comportment for women and men. Not only has he upheld his end of the domestic partnership, he has judged that his partner has not upheld hers. His capacity as a moral arbiter is thus part of his entitlement to use violence; his feel for the game enables him to make the right move.

In fin-de-siècle France, it appears that this elision of moral man and violent beast lay at the core of an embattled sense of masculinity. In her work *L'Identité masculine en crise*, Annelise Maugue has pointed out that in the forty-four years between the Franco-Prussian War and the First World War, French men were not called upon to fight in any major wars. Their work in industry and business became ever more passive, and they were haunted by the threat of being feminized, even to the point of doing household chores while their wives went out to work and supported them financially.[20] Wives who betrayed or abandoned their husbands, Maugue contends, were an obsessive theme of male writers who feared the loss of their traditionally dominant role.[21] The pervasive public discourse on degeneration and depopulation in this era suggests one reason why French men might have remained attached to the use of violence in intimate relationships.[22] As they feared losing status or control in other areas, they clung to the possibility of demonstrating their power in the household by using violence against their domestic partners.[23] Perhaps not surprisingly, Jean-Yves Le Naour has found that during the Great War, popular opinion as well as the courts were extremely forgiving toward soldiers home on leave who killed their adulterous wives.[24]

Nonetheless, during the fin de siècle the legitimate use of violence was not limited to men, as demonstrated by women's especially high rate of acquittal. Wielding a knife or a gun with lethal effectiveness is certainly at odds with the image of a submissive and loving wife. Yet women who were acquitted for crimes against their partners proved themselves to be exemplary in fulfilling their household duties—they were "good" women, whereas their erring partners had failed to live up to their obligations as men. In this sense, the legitimate use of violence by women was the mirror image of its use by men: both depended on the attacker's working knowledge of proper gendered behavior. Of course, when women used violence they were not reinforcing a system of female dominance—on the contrary. But women's use of violence against their domestic partners also fell within the long tradition of women's roles as moral arbiters in their local urban community. Women in unsatisfactory partnerships martialed the assistance of neighbors and family members against their men but they also could act as judge and executioner.

Even as community standards and the verdict of the courts worked to legitimate the use of violence by men and women in intimate relationships, however, they also worked to limit it. Such violence could be legitimate only if it performed a retributive function, and retribution is a kind of justice grounded in relationships, not individuals. When victims and witnesses objected to the use of violence, they did not articulate any notion of individual rights, such as the right to bodily integrity that would become common currency among liberal feminists in the twentieth century. Nor did they make prescriptive statements condemning the use of violence in general, under any circumstances, in an intimate relationship. Instead, they objected to the use of violence on the grounds that the victim had not deserved it. Because she (or more rarely he) had not deviated from the behaviors expected of her and had fulfilled her part of the implicit bargain of the domestic partnership, she did not deserve punishment.

It is undeniable that the unspoken terms of the domestic contract were inherently disadvantageous to women. Women had more responsibilities for maintaining the household and its symbolic capital than men did, more responsibilities for childcare, and stricter standards of sexual fidelity. They were far more frequently the victims of violence of all degrees than men were. And yet this system also held men accountable for their behavior. Men who squandered household resources, were bad workers, were sexually incontinent, or used violence excessively were seen as having lost the masculine privilege of disciplining their partners and could become legitimate targets of retributive violence themselves. Thus, practices of violence worked to promote a particular kind of intimate relationship, sustained through the fulfillment of mutual obligations. Men and women were not equals, but women's more limited "rights" within the relationship were taken seriously and were guaranteed by public scrutiny of the couple's behavior. Ultimately, in these domestic partnerships, the balance among emotional needs, sexual desires, financial resources, and household services privileged men over women, and yet masculine domination was neither absolute nor unquestioned. Through public networks of knowledge about a couple's behavior, women as well as men participated in defining and enforcing the mutual obligations between domestic partners.

The history of intimacy suggests that the eroticization of the couple coincides with the increased privacy of family life: the couple retreats to the home, disconnects from larger family networks, and turns in upon itself. This analysis of the intimate lives of the working people of Paris has demonstrated that many people valued and sought emotional and sexual satisfaction with their domestic partners, suggesting that the eroticization of the couple was indeed underway in this milieu. However, there is little evidence that these couples sought privacy or attempted to shield their intimate relationships from the knowledge and judgments of their neighbors. The publicity of their relationships clearly helped to limit the use of violence within them. It is therefore likely that increased privacy in intimate relationships would decrease women's protection from violence within them.[25] At the same time, the move toward privacy appears to correspond in the late twentieth and early twenty-first century with a shift from community to state-sponsored regulation of intimate violence.

Contrary to the old logic of the crime of passion, today French law directly punishes violence in intimate relationships. This resonates with the hopes of one author who responded to Dumas's "Kill her!" with the imperative, "Love!" Addressing Dumas directly, she wrote: "Destiny is calling you. Approach. Bring her the huge, blood-soaked stones from the ruins of the past, and help her to build this superb temple of the future, which will have but one word for law: *Love*."[26] This is a vision of love that no longer permits violence in its name but that serves as the foundation for a mutually respectful, intimate relationship between equals. Nineteenth-century French feminists saw the use of violence and the laws that condoned it as barriers to this kind of relationship. Witnesses in the assize court contended that violence in domestic partnerships should be limited; in a partnership where both people held up her or his end of the domestic bargain, there would be no legitimate reason for violence to occur. Such a vision of love without violence remains compelling. It was a goal, if not a reality, for some individuals in fin-de-siècle Paris, who sought to attain it through the complex interactions of personal desires, community standards, public discourses, and judicial processes.

Notes

INTRODUCTION. Problematizing Crimes of Passion

1. Archives de la Ville de Paris (hereafter AVP) D2U8/173, Maxant, 6 December 1884. All translations are by the author.
2. As legal scholar Louis Holtz wrote in 1904, crimes of passion are "caused by love, not motivated by financial interest, and only the violence of passion carried away a normally honest man" (*Les Crimes passionnels*, 11).
3. Ruth Harris claims that "literally hundreds" of defendants in *cour d'assises* cases claimed themselves to be "*criminels passionels*" (*Murders and Madness*, 210). Unfortunately, Ann-Louise Shapiro (*Breaking the Codes*, 90) and James F. McMillan (*France and Women*, 104) have repeated this claim. These scholars may have relied on earlier work by Joëlle Guillais, who reported that 735 crimes of passion were committed in France between 1871 and 1880 (*La Chair de l'autre*, 42). In my view, this number must be treated as a rough and uncertain estimate, since statistics on "crimes of passion" were not compiled by the judicial system. By comparing the categories in the *Comte général de l'administration de la justice criminelle en France*, which list adultery or jealousy as motives for crimes—presumably, crimes that could be construed to be crimes of passion—with surviving trial dossiers, it became clear that it is not possible to verify Guillais's calculations.
4. Benjamin F. Martin, *Crime and Criminal Justice under the Third Republic*, 4. Martin bases his estimate on the annual volumes of the *Compte général de l'administration de la justice criminelle*. By contrast, the rate of acquittal in correctional court, where a panel of judges decided lesser crimes, was around 10%.
5. Emile Yvernès, *Le Crime et le criminel devant le jury*, 14. Acquittal rates rose between 1860 and 1890 for aggravated assault (27–78%), homicide (16–24%), and crimes against property (17–19%).
6. Although Maxant's profession may have made him more aware of the conventions of criminal investigations, it was not unusual for defendants to participate as actively as he did in constructing his defense.
7. Articles 321–326 of the penal code defined the "excuses" that could reduce—but not eliminate—punishment for murder in cases where the murder was preceded by serious violence toward the murderer: where the victim was breaking into an inhabited house, where a husband or wife killed his or her spouse when his or her own life was in danger, and where a husband killed his wife or her lover when he surprised them *en flagrant délit* in the conjugal abode.
8. Arlette Farge, *La Vie fragile*, 11.
9. AVP, series D2U8, cartons 12 through 295. After 1892 no relevant dossiers have

been preserved, and in fact only a handful of dossiers from the assize court of the Seine have been preserved for many decades after that date.

10. The corresponding French legal terms are *coups et blessures, assassinat, tentative d'assassinat, meurte, tentative de meurtre,* and *empoisonnement*. Poisoning was a separate category in French criminal law.

11. Among the works of enduring value are Carlo Ginzburg, *The Cheese and the Worms*; Emmanuel Le Roy Ladurie, *Montaillou*; Natalie Zemon Davis, *Society and Culture in Early Modern France*.

12. Michel Foucault, *I, Pierre Rivière*.

13. Ginzberg, *The Cheese and the Worms*, xviii.

14. Harris, *Murders and Madness*.

15. Guilllais, *La Chair de l'autre*; Shapiro, *Breaking the Codes*.

16. My sample includes all the relevant cases studied by Guillais, Harris, and Shapiro, plus about 150 more.

17. Sherry Ortner, "Making Gender," 2.

18. Ibid., 12.

19. Pierre Bourdieu, *Distinction*.

20. Ortner, "Making Gender," 13.

21. Pierre Bourdieu, *The field of Cultural Production*, 258.

22. Leslie Page Moch, *Paths to the City*.

23. Martine Segalen, *Love and Power in the Peasant Family*.

24. Michèle Perrot, *Les Femmes ou les silences de l'histoire*, 223.

25. For a concise statement of this cornerstone of Weber's theory, see *Economy and Society*, 54–56. He writes: "The right of a father to discipline his children is recognized—a survival of the former independent authority of the head of a household, which in the right to use force has sometimes extended to a power of life and death over children and slaves. The claim of the modern state to monopolize the use of force is as essential to it as its character of compulsory jurisdiction and of continuous operation" (56). Although this passage proves that Weber included family violence in his theory of the monopolization of violence by the state, it is curious that he mentions only violence against children and slaves, not wives.

26. Norbert Elias, *The Civilizing Process*, 1:239.

27. In a recent survey informed by Elias's work, Julius Ruff briefly considers family violence (*Violence in Early Modern Europe*).

28. A classic example is Louise A. Tilly and Joan W. Scott, *Women, Work, and Family*. They write, "The important point is that the family or household is the unit of decision making for the activities of all its members" (6).

29. Frédéric Chauvaud, *Les Passions villageoises*.

30. Frédéric Chauvaud, *De Pierre Rivière à Landru*, 44.

31. For the seventeenth century, see Julie Hardwick, "Seeking Separation," "Early Modern Perspectives," and *Family Business*. On the eighteenth century, see Roderick Philips, "Gender Solidarities" and *Putting Asunder*, as well as Mary Trouille, *Wife-Abuse*, which focuses more on discursive analysis of legal texts and publications rather than social history.

32. Eugen Weber, *France: Fin-de-Siècle*, 84.

33. Ibid., 87.

34. Eugen Weber, *Peasants into Frenchmen*. Weber's mention of intimate violence in

this earlier work is rare. He cites a proverb against wife beating which he describes as "seldom heeded" (170) and recounts the lurid tale of a woman who injured her husband by dragging him by his penis (173), but he does not mention wife beating in his lengthy discussion of charivaris, except in a footnote on Natalie Zemon Davis's work (558, n. 1). Weber is not alone in this assessment, however. Nancy Tomes, who is often quoted in more recent studies of working-class families in England, argues that the lower classes adopted middle-class family norms during the nineteenth century, resulting in a decline in family violence. See Nancy Tomes, "A 'Torrent of Abuse'" and Ellen Ross, "'Fierce Questions and Taunts.'"

CHAPTER 1. *La Vie Intime*

1. AVP, D2U8/198, Merle, 3 March 1886. That Béziade signed a statement before the trial indicating that he wanted to abandon the case against her may have facilitated her acquittal. In giving up the case, he was effectively condoning her right to retaliate against him for breaking his promises to her.
2. For work in the traditional, demographic vein of family history, see Wesley D. Camp, *Marriage and the Family in France Since the Revolution*. On the history of homosexuality in France, see Jeffrey Merrick and Bryant T. Ragan Jr., eds., *Homosexuality in Modern France*, and William A. Peniston, *Pederasts and Others*.
3. Guy Richard, *Histoire de l'amour en France du Moyen Age à la Belle Epoque*, 276.
4. The evolving complexity of analysis of these trends is represented by the following works: Philippe Ariès, *Histoire des populations françaises et de leurs attitudes devant la vie depuis le 18e siècle*, Jacques Dupâquier and Denis Kessler, eds., *La Société française au 19e siècle*; Noël Bonneuil, *Transformation of the French Demographic Landscape, 1806–1906*.
5. Elinor Accampo, *Industrialization, Family Life, and Class Relations*.
6. Patricia Hilden, *Working Women and Socialist Politics in France*.
7. Laure Adler, *Secrets d'alcôve*, 12.
8. Michel Foucault, *History of Sexuality*, 1:121, 122.
9. Anne-Marie Sohn, *Du Premier baiser à l'alcôve*, 284, 307, 308.
10. Edward Shorter, *The Making of the Modern Family*, esp. chap. 3.
11. While insisting on the great diversity of marriage strategies throughout Europe in the nineteenth century, a synthesis of more recent scholarship contends that "it was above all members of the lower classes who enjoyed a high degree of autonomy in the choice of a partner." See Josef Ehmer, "Marriage," in David I. Kertzer and Mario Barbagli, eds., *Family Life in the Long Nineteenth Century*, 313.
12. Martine Segalen, *Love and Power in the Peasant Family*, esp. 14–20.
13. Rachel G. Fuchs, *Poor and Pregnant in Paris*, 20, n. 26.
14. Lenard R. Berlanstein, *The Working People of Paris*, 33–34.
15. AVP, D2U8/268, Gadel, 17 January 1891.
16. AVP, D2U8/152, Hillairain de Saint-Priest, 29 September 1883.
17. AVP, D2U8/181, Millim, 23 April 1885.
18. AVP, D2U8/288, Rochat, 6 January 1892.
19. AVP, D2U8/200, Badran, 22 April 1886.
20. AVP, D2U8/271, Verhoost, 14 March 1891.
21. AVP, D2U8/219, Beulle, 21 April 1887.
22. AVP, D2U8/32, Helfrich, 26 October 1874.

23. AVP, D2U8/144, Chervey, 29 March 1883.
24. AVP, D2U8/295, Cousin, 28 December 1892.
25. AVP, D2U8/171, Deffendi, 13 October 1884.
26. AVP, D2U8/161, Féral, 9 May 1884. She was acquitted.
27. The authoritative history on paternity suits in France is Rachel Fuchs, *Contested Paternity*.
28. AVP, D2U8/285, Croissant, 26 October 1881.
29. AVP, D2U8/78, Dubien, 25 October 1878.
30. AVP, D2U8/21, Clément, 21 July 1880.
31. Ibid.
32. AVP, D2U8/35, Michaud, 25 January 1875. Guerval's former lover, a coworker, killed her when he discovered her plans for marriage. He was convicted of murder.
33. AVP, D2U8/61, Gendarme, 28 May 1877. Gendarme was convicted of murder.
34. AVP, D2U8/290, Bertal, 23 March 1892.
35. AVP, D2U8/291, Langlois, 30 June 1892.
36. AVP, D2U8/265, Henry, 13 November 1890.
37. AVP, D2U8/122, Guillet, 11 October 1881. The court fined her 5,000 francs—an unusually high sum—for blinding her victim with acid.
38. AVP, D2U8/80, Guillot, 25 November 1878. He was convicted of murder.
39. AVP, D2U8/272, Teste, 11 April 1891.
40. This is an entirely typical interaction with the police; see chap. 5.
41. *Gazette des Tribunaux*, 12 April 1891.
42. AVP, D2U8/32, Duc, 28 September 1874.
43. *Gazette des Tribunaux*, 18–19 September 1874.
44. AVP, D2U8/101, Richelet, 20 July 1880. Ironically, the investigating magistrate was named Mariage.
45. AVP, D2U8/114, Koenig, 8 March 1881.
46. AVP, D2U8/141, Ancelin, 28 November 1882.
47. AVP, D2U8/152, Hillairain de Saint-Priest, 29 September 1883.
48. AVP, D2U8/288, Méhu, 20 January 1892.
49. AVP, D2U8/96, Bière, 5 April 1880.
50. AVP, D2U8/285, Herbellot, 27 October 1891.
51. AVP, D2U8/264, Alquier, 25 September 1890.
52. AVP, D2U8/212, Lechevallier, 22 December 1886. The one circumstance Lechevallier and Méro could agree on was that she wanted to leave him. He was convicted on a lesser charge of assault. In another case, Victorine Lelong *was* fired from a longtime job as a domestic servant when her employer discovered she had a lover (AVP, D2U8/38, Lelong, 9 July 1875).
53. AVP, D2U8/139, Jean, 14 November 1882.
54. AVP, D2U8/75, Lerondeau, 29 June 1878. They lived in Châteaufort, Seine-et-Oise, where she was initially convicted of poisoning him. The assize court of the Seine later acquitted her, based on more extensive scientific evidence.
55. AVP, D2U8/32, Forestier, 27 October 1874. He was convicted and given a life sentence.
56. AVP, D2U8/271, Verhoost, 14 March 1891.
57. AVP, D2U8/200, Badran, 22 April 1886.

58. AVP, D2U8/241, Nodin, 11 August 1888. They lived just outside Paris, in St. Ouen.
59. AVP, D2U8/53, Marie, 7 October 1876. He shot at her, missed, and was acquitted of attempted murder.
60. *Gazette des Tribunaux*, 25–26 January 1892. "Un pantalon fermé," drawers with a closed inseam, would have been an unusual garment for a lower-class woman at this time. Most women just wore a *chemise*, or slip, as underwear, and even drawers for upper-class women (more sensitive to hygiene, perhaps, and with the extra cash to purchase and care for delicate textiles) were designed with the seam between the legs unsewn.
61. AVP, D2U8/153, Legrand, 22 October 1883.
62. AVP, D2U8/35, Michaud, 25 January 1875.
63. AVP, D2U8/271, Verhoost, 14 March 1891.
64. AVP, D2U8/280, Robert, 31 August 1891.
65. AVP, D2U8/202, De Verneuil, 28 May 1886. De Verneuil had to pay 3,000 francs in civil damages to his rival's family.
66. AVP, D2U8/288, Méhu, 20 January 1892. She was convicted of assault and causing the loss of an eye.
67. AVP, D2U8/83, Pourcher, 3 April 1879. Pourcher was acquitted.
68. AVP, D2U8/109, Pautard, 13 December 1880.
69. AVP, D2U8/135, Gy, 15 July 1882.
70. AVP, D2U8/241, Masset, 10 August 1888.
71. AVP, D2U8/53, Marie, 7 October 1876.
72. AVP, D2U8/114, Koenig, 8 March 1881.
73. AVP, D2U8/53, Marie, 7 October 1876.
74. AVP, D2U8/101, Clément, 21 July 1880.
75. AVP, D2U8/194, Catherine, 4 December 1885.
76. *Gazette des Tribunaux*, 1 March 1871.
77. AVP, D2U8/16, Perney, 28 December 1872.
78. *Gazette des Tribunaux*, 29 December 1872.
79. *Gazette des Tribunaux*, 15 February 1894.
80. AVP, D2U8/209, Schumacher, 30 October 1886. Sohn mentions this case to illustrate "the total rejection of group sexuality" (*Chrysalides*, 86). In contrast, this analysis highlights the importance of Duflot's alleged infidelity in the case.
81. AVP, D2U8/291, Langlois, 30 June 1892.
82. *Gazette des Tribunaux*, 29 March 1870.
83. AVP, D2U8/272, Teste, 11 April 1891. The ellipses are in the original, as the stenographers were reluctant to write down impolite expressions in their entirety. The complete phrase here might be "*chasseur d'affaires*," where *affaires* was slang for male genitalia.
84. The notorious case of Félix Lemaître, which filled the pages of popular dailies in the summer of 1881, also involved suspicions of homosexuality. Lemaître, who himself was only fifteen, took a six-year-old boy to his room and eviscerated him. In the investigation, the magistrate persisted in asking Lemaître if he hadn't lured the boy to his room "to satisfy [his] desires," or make a "shameful proposition." Lemaître denied it, and the famous Dr. Brouardel was unable to find any traces of sexual violence on the victim's body (AVP, D2U8/117, Lemaître, 15 July 1881).
85. AVP, D2U8/145, Perrette, 28 April 1883.
86. On the existence of a male homosexual subculture as early as the 1870s in Paris,

see Peniston, *Pederasts and Others*. According to evidence Peniston collected from the police archives, many men were arrested along the Champs-Elysées for soliciting homosexual acts.

87. AVP, D2U8/289, Vaubourg, 5 February 1892. Participants in the homosexual subculture commonly used feminine nicknames. See Peniston, *Pederasts and Others*, 104–5. For more evidence of men living together as couples in this era, see Régis Revenin, *Homosexualité et prostitution masculines à Paris*, 65–68.

88. AVP, D2U8/141, Grodet, 24 November 1882.

89. At midcentury, the great actress Rachel was rumored to have had female lovers. See Rachel M. Brownstein, *Tragic Muse*, 53.

90. AVP, D2U8/258, Daouze, 20 March 1890.

91. For thorough studies of the practice and regulation of prostitution, see Alain Corbin, *Les Filles de noce*, and Jill Harsin, *Policing Prostitution in Nineteenth-Century Paris*. The focus here on the social lives of prostitutes resonates more with the approach in Judith Walkowitz's classic, *Prostitution and Victorian Society*.

92. D2U8/16, Perney, 28 December 1872.

93. *Gazette des Tribunaux*, 29 December 1872.

94. *Gazette des Tribunaux*, 21 June 1893.

95. Jennifer Waelti-Walters and Steven C. Hause, eds., *Feminisms of the Belle Epoque*, 1. Specifically, the figure Waelti-Walters gives is forty *sous*. Twenty *sous* made one franc. In another case, Honorine Brossard, who was prosperous enough to have decent linens and gold jewelry, asked for five francs but received ten from one client (AVP, D2U8/61, Gendarme, 28 May 1877).

96. AVP, D2U8/202, Gérard, 5 June 1886. Gérard insisted that she was the one who had ended their relationship; he had not left her, and she had stabbed him not out of vengefulness but by mistake.

97. AVP, D2U8/289, Dogmatschoff, 2 February 1892.

98. D2U8/194, Amichot, 7 December 1885. During the investigation, Amichot requested that fifty francs seized from him at the time of his arrest be returned. Jorand insisted that the money be returned to her, since she was the one who had earned it.

99. D2U8/28, Zick, 30 May 1874.

100. *Gazette des Tribunaux*, 31 May 1874.

101. *Gazette des Tribunaux*, 8 February 1891. He was sentenced to forced labor for life.

102. AVP, D2U8/144, Perrin, 30 March 1883.

103. Ibid.

104. AVP, D2U8/109, Joulain, 27 December 1880.

105. *Gazette des Tribunaux*, 16 March 1870.

106. AVP, D2U8/12, Bernou, 29 September 1871.

107. AVP, D2U8/207, Léra, 17 September 1886.

108. AVP, D2U8/152, Hillairin de Saint-Priest, 29 September 1883.

109. AVP, D2U8/272, Boudet, 2 March 1891.

110. AVP, D2U8/285, Malmézac, 24 October 1891.

111. AVP, D2U8/16, Béal, 7 December 1872.

112. AVP, D2U8/141, Ancelin, 28 November 1882.

113. AVP, D2U8/156, Sanglé, 25 January 1884.

114. AVP, D2U8/218, Rault, 12 April 1887.

115. AVP, D2U8/198, Catelier, 22 March 1886.

116. AVP, D2U8/117, Schmittgall, 8 June 1881.
117. AVP, D2U8/200, Badran, 22 April 1886.
118. AVP, D2U8/139, Jean, 14 November 1882.
119. Georges Solhart, a lazy man who nearly beat his wife to death when she left him, claimed during his interrogation, "I love her more than she believes." He did not back up this statement with any evidence of his devotion, and it passed without further comment by anyone involved in the investigation (AVP, D2U8/23, Solhart, 26 November 1873). The same was true for Jean Deschutter, who declared, "I regret the act I committed. I loved la fille Bonjour, and if I struck her mortally, I acted out of anger and jealousy." His statement of love was not integrated into the story of the crime and appeared to be simply tacked on at the end of his first interrogation (AVP, D2U8/207, Deschutter, 25 September 1886).
120. AVP, D2U8/158, Froquières, 11 March 1884. He was convicted of murder.

CHAPTER 2. Material and Symbolic Household Management

1. *Le foyer*, which designates at once the people of the household and the architectural structure that contains them, was used quite rarely in this milieu.
2. Pierre Bourdieu, *La Domination masculine*, 108.
3. For a complete description of Khabyle society, see Pierre Bourdieu, *Outline of a Theory of Practice*.
4. Lenard Berlanstein, *The Working People of Paris*, 3.
5. For instance, about half a dozen people mentioned the Commune, but only as a way of situating an event chronologically. One man, a blacksmith, had been imprisoned for taking part in the insurrection in Paris (AVP, D2U8/31, Breffeil, 24 September 1874). Another man described his wife as being "like Louise Michel, since she was interested in politics" (AVP, D2U8/288, Rochat, 6 January 1892). In addition, calling someone a Prussian was an insult during this era; one man used to call his mother-in-law Bismarck (AVP, D2U8/80, Guillot, 25 November 1878). In a rather distant brush with greatness, one woman on trial for attacking her husband had formerly worked for five months as head housemaid for Madame Dosne, *belle-mère* of Adolphe Thiers (AVP, D2U8/154, Genuit, 12 November 1883). Finally, half a dozen people mentioned attending one of the Universal Expositions held in Paris; one man used a knife with a handle shaped like the Eiffel Tower to stab his wife (AVP, D2U8/260, Keiffer, 12 June 1890).
6. Berlanstein, *Working People of Paris*, 43, 40.
7. Ibid., 44–45.
8. Anne Martin-Fugier, *La Bourgeoise*, 10–11.
9. Bonnie G. Smith, *Ladies of the Leisure Class*.
10. In Berlanstein's study, 66% of "wage-earning" couples had wives who worked, while 48.8% of clerks' wives worked. He notes, "Employees did not shrink, from considerations of status, from having their wives bring home an income" (*The Working People of Paris*, 71).
11. Christophe Charle, *Histoire sociale de la France au 19e siècle*, 292.
12. AVP, D2U8/61, Kemps, 14 June 1877; AVP, D2U8/38, Lelong, 9 July 1875; AVP, D2U8/219, Beulle, 21 April 1887; AVP, D2U8/271, Verhoost, 14 March 1891.
13. AVP, D2U8/61, Kemps, 14 June 1877; AVP, D2U8/144, Perrin, 30 March 1883; AVP, D2U8/272, Boudet, 2 March 1891; AVP, D2U8/239, Dabon, 13 June 1888.

14. AVP, D2U8/188, François, 19 August 1885.
15. AVP, D2U8/127, Larue, 27 January 1882.
16. AVP, D2U8/80, Guillot, 25 November 1878.
17. AVP, D2U8/23, Solhart, 26 November 1873.
18. AVP, D2U8/251, Ecoiffier, 20 September 1889.
19. AVP, D2U8/12, Brossier, 20 September 1889.
20. AVP, D2U8/202, Gérard, 5 June 1886.
21. AVP, D2U8/173, Martinière, 10 December 1884.
22. AVP, D2U8/141, Grodet, 24 November 1882.
23. AVP, D2U8/158, Froquières, 11 March 1884.
24. AVP, D2U8/271, Verhoost, 14 March 1891.
25. AVP, D2U8/101, Clément, 21 July 1880.
26. AVP, D2U8/94, Guerrier, 6 February 1880.
27. AVP, D2U8/127, Larue, 27 January 1882.
28. Ibid.
29. AVP, D2U8/207, Deschutter, 25 September 1886.
30. AVP, D2U8/239, Dabon, 13 June 1888.
31. *Gazette des Tribunaux*, 11 May 1870.
32. This practice was well known to nineteenth-century social observers. See, e.g., Denis Poulot, *Le Sublime*, 265–66; and F. Le Play and A. Fogillon, "Charpentier de Paris de la Corporation des Compagnons du devoir," 27–43, 30.
33. *Gazette des Tribunaux*, 11 October 1894.
34. AVP, D2U8/272, Cholat, 26 March 1891.
35. AVP, D2U8/284, Durban, 13 October 1891.
36. AVP, D2U8/239, Derreux, 27 June 1888.
37. AVP, D2U8/75, Lerondeau, 29 June 1878.
38. AVP, D2U8/114, Jacob, 26 March 1881.
39. AVP, D2U8/144, Roulland, 7 April 1883.
40. AVP, D2U8/188, François, 19 August 1885.
41. Quotation marks appear in the original document.
42. *Gazette des Tribunaux*, 23 January 1873.
43. AVP, D2U8/207, Deschutter, 25 September 1886.
44. Only in one other case did a man seem to identify himself as a worker. After he stabbed his supposed lover la veuve Bochinger, Joseph Hahn was heard to cry, "That will teach her to mock workers!" but this statement has no clear link with the circumstances of the case (AVP, D2U8/264, Hahn, 18 September 1890).
45. AVP, D2U8/219, Duchène, 21 May 1887. Quotation marks appear in the original.
46. AVP, D2U8/288, Méhu, 20 January 1892.
47. AVP, D2U8/38, Lelong, 9 July 1875. The identical surname in this and the Méhu case is apparently only a coincidence.
48. AVP, D2U8/281, De Moor, 10 September 1891.
49. AVP, D2U8/284, Durban, 13 October 1891. Spelling of la fille Eizeinkreimer's name varies throughout the dossier.
50. For a richly detailed analysis of the roles of fathers in family life in this era, see Rachel Fuchs, *Contested Paternity*.
51. AVP, D2U8/161, Féral, 9 May 1884.

52. AVP, D2U8/38, Lelong, 9 July 1875. Although Langlois died from the acid burns, Lelong was convicted of *coups et blessures*, not homicide, and sentenced to five years of prison.
53. AVP, D2U8/135, Gy, 15 July 1882.
54. AVP, D2U8/284, Cotard, 14 October 1891. She was acquitted.
55. *Gazette des Tribunaux*, 10 July 1875.
56. Rachel Fuchs, *Poor and Pregnant in Paris*, 152–53.
57. AVP, D2U8/230, Legrand, 6 December 1887.
58. AVP, D2U8/260, Keiffer, 12 June 1890.
59. AVP, D2U8/53, Marie, 7 October 1876.
60. AVP, D2U8/272, Teste, 11 April 1891.
61. The classic statement of this position for France is Philippe Ariès, *Centuries of Childhood*. Shorter addressed the transfer of intensive mothering from the upper to lower classes in the late eighteenth to early nineteenth centuries in *The Making of the Modern Family*. Louise Tilly and Joan Scott place the transition in the second half of the nineteenth century (*Women, Work, and Family*).
62. Charles Rearick, *Pleasures of the Belle Epoque*; W. Scott Haine, *The World of the Paris Café*; Rosalind H. Williams, *Dream Worlds*.
63. AVP, D2U8/219, Duchène, 21 May 1887.
64. AVP, D2U8/268, Gadel, 17 January 1891.
65. AVP, D2U8/23, Solhart, 26 November 1873.
66. AVP, D2U8/264, Fétat, 10 September 1890.
67. AVP, D2U8/175, Berquet, 28 January 1885.
68. AVP, D2U8/139, Aubriot, 15 November 1882.
69. AVP, D2U8/156, Sanglé, 25 January 1884. I have added punctuation to this passage, which in the original French is one long, run-on sentence.
70. See, e.g., Jean-Paul Aron, *Le Mangeur du 19e siècle*.
71. Cited in Charle, *Histoire sociale*, 287.
72. Berlanstein, *Working People of Paris*, 46.
73. For more on the role of alcohol consumption in crimes of passion, see chap. 6.
74. AVP, D2U8/16, Perney, 28 December 1872.
75. AVP, D2U8/17, Jouault, 11 February 1873.
76. AVP, D2U8/239, Boullevaut, 15 June 1888.
77. AVP, D2U8/200, Badran, 22 April 1886.
78. AVP, D2U8/80, Guillot, 25 November 1878.
79. AVP, D2U8/239, Dabon, 13 June 1888.
80. AVP, D2U8/200, Badran, 22 April 1886.
81. AVP, D2U8/38, Lelong, 9 July 1875. The woman who gave Lelong charity had formerly employed her as a domestic servant.
82. AVP, D2U8/239, Derreux, 27 June 1888.
83. AVP, D2U8/94, Guerrier, 6 February 1880.
84. AVP, D2U8/156, Sanglé, 25 January 1884.
85. AVP, D2U8/260, Keiffer, 12 June 1890.
86. AVP, D2U8/40, Charrier, 19 October 1875.
87. Shapiro, *Breaking the Codes*, 73–74. On women as poisoners, see also Lisa Downing, "Murder in the Feminine."
88. Laure Adler, *L'Amour à l'arsenic*, 124–26.

89. These totals are based on statistics reported by Adler for 1825–85 (Adler, *L'Amour à l'arsenic*, 132–33) and my own research using the *Comte général de l'administration de la justice criminelle en France* for 1887–1900.

90. Adler, *L'Amour à l'arsenic*, 132–33.

91. AVP, D2U8/75, Lerondeau, 29 June 1878. Doctors Charles Adolphe Wurtz, Edmé Félix Alfred Vulpian, and Georges Bergeron, all at the Faculté de Medicine de Paris, performed experiments by poisoning dogs with oxalic acid in various doses and observing how they died. François Lerondeau's lingering agony, they concluded, was not consistent with the brief sufferings of the poisoned dogs. As in the infamous trial of Marie Lafarge, documented by Laure Adler, poisoning could be a difficult crime to prove.

92. Note that the Lerondeau couple did not live in Versailles, as Shapiro reported (*Breaking the Codes*, 83), but in the smaller town of Châteaufort. Versailles was the location of the court that had jurisdiction in the original trial.

93. See a further discussion of this point in chap. 1.

94. AVP, D2U8/139, Jean, 14 November 1882.

95. AVP, D2U8/154, Buire, 26 November 1883.

96. AVP, D2U8/239, Dabon, 13 June 1888.

97. AVP, D2U8/207, Fournet, 6 October 1886.

98. AVP, D2U8/188, Vigineix, 20 August 1885. The spelling of the accused's last name varies in the dossier.

99. AVP, D2U8/101, Richelet, 20 July 1880.

100. AVP, D2U8/194, Catherine, 4 December 1885.

101. AVP, D2U8/200, Badran, 22 April 1886.

102. AVP, D2U8/284, Durban, 13 October 1891.

103. AVP, D2U8/230, Legrand, 6 December 1887.

104. AVP, D2U8/17, Jouault, 11 February 1873.

105. AVP, D2U8/219, Beulle, 21 April 1887. The busk is the relatively wide, flat, center stay of a corset. It was likely to be made of steel in this era. See Valerie Steele, *The Corset*, 48.

106. AVP, D2U8/40, Charrier, 19 October 1875.

107. AVP, D2U8/75, Lerondeau, 29 June 1878.

108. AVP, D2U8/281, De Moor, 10 September 1891.

109. AVP, D2U8/202, Gérard, 5 June 1886.

110. AVP, D2U8/139, Jean, 14 November 1882.

111. AVP, D2U8/260, Levielle, 4 June 1890.

112. AVP, D2U8/289, Dogmatschoff, 2 February 1892.

113. AVP, D2U8/114, Jacob, 26 March 1881.

114. Ibid.

115. AVP, D2U8/83, Pourcher, 3 April 1879.

116. AVP, D2U8/295, Cousin, 28 December 1892.

117. AVP, D2U8/288, Rochat, 6 January 1892.

118. AVP, D2U8/135, Gy, 15 July 1882.

119. *Gazette des Tribunaux*, 6 December 1871.

120. In her autobiography, Jeanne Bouvier describes her careful efforts to purchase her own bed frame by scrimping and saving her meager wages as a novice seamstress. Jeanne Bouvier, *Mes Mémoires*, 83.

121. AVP, D2U8/239, Dabon, 13 June 1888.

122. Pierre Bourdieu, *La Domination masculine*, 107.

123. For an analysis of upper-class taste in interior decoration, see Deborah L. Silverman, *Art Nouveau in Fin-de-Siècle France*, and Leonore Auslander, *Taste and Power*. Anne Martin-Fugier described the decoration of the bourgeois abode as an activity that involved men and women: the husband usually chose and purchased the furniture before the marriage, while his wife decorated the home "in her image" (*La Bourgeoise*, 157–75).

124. AVP, D2U8/47, Trouvé, 12 May 1876.

125. AVP, D2U8/200, Badran, 22 April 1886.

126. AVP, D2U8/291, Langlois, 30 June 1892.

127. AVP, D2U8/207, Léra, 17 September 1886.

128. AVP, D2U8/114, Koenig, 8 March 1881.

129. AVP, D2U8/212, Barbier, 22 December 1886.

130. AVP, D2U8/158, Froquières, 11 March 1884. Quotation marks appear in the original French.

131. AVP, D2U8/154, Buire, 26 November 1883. Her lover, however, said she only attacked him for revenge because he was leaving her to marry another woman.

132. AVP, D2U8/23, Solhart, 26 November 1873.

133. AVP, D2U8/260, Levielle, 4 June 1890.

134. AVP, D2U8/230, Périchon, 7 December 1887.

135. AVP, D2U8/289, Dogmatschoff, 2 February 1892.

136. AVP, D2U8/16, Perney, 28 December 1872.

137. AVP, D2U8/17, Jouault, 11 February 1873.

138. AVP, D2U8/31, Breffeil, 24 September 1874.

139. On café sociability, see Haine, *World of the Paris Café*.

CHAPTER 3. Networks of Knowledge

1. This is certainly not always the case in crowded conditions, as William M. Reddy demonstrates in his study of divorce cases in the first half of the nineteenth century. Reddy found that people tried to close their eyes and ears to the conflicts they witnessed or even tried to deny the knowledge that they had inadvertently gathered ("Marriage, Honor, and the Public Sphere in Postrevolutionary France," 437–72).

2. David Garrioch, *Neighborhood and Community in Paris*, 6.

3. Roger V. Gould, *Insurgent Identities*, 121–22, 156.

4. The dangerous rootlessness of the urban worker was a ubiquitous theme, from Frédéric Le Play (*Les Ouvriers européens*) to Emile Durkheim (*The Division of Labor in Society*). These nineteenth-century themes are amplified in Louis Chevalier's classic work, *Laboring Classes and Dangerous Classes*. William H. Sewell Jr. has found that transient, unmarried migrants in Marseilles were slightly more likely to commit certain crimes than their fellow migrants who settled down in stable partnerships; see *Structure and Mobility*, esp. 232.

5. Joëlle Guillais, *La Chair de l'autre*, 54–55.

6. Philippe Ariès, *Histoire des populations françaises*, 170–72. Data from the judicial dossiers does not permit any conclusions about people from certain geographic regions being more prone to violence than others.

7. Leslie Page Moch, *Paths to the City*.

8. AVP, D2U8/61, Gendarme, 28 May 1877.

9. AVP, D2U8/81, Guignot, 24 December 1878.
10. AVP, D2U8/265, Henry, 13 November 1890.
11. AVP, D2U8/118, Thauvin, 12 August 1881.
12. AVP, D2U8/162, Genuyt, 30 May 1884.
13. AVP, D2U8/12, Bernou, 29 September 1871.
14. AVP, D2U8/17, Santin, 13 March 1873. The letter was actually dated 4 March, and the trial was held on 13 March, apparently enough time for the letter to reach Paris. In spite of this warm recommendation for leniency, Santin was condemned to forced labor for life for killing his wife.
15. AVP, D2U8/101, Clément, 21 July 1880. Although convicted of murdering his wife, Clément received a light sentence of five years in prison.
16. In another case, ten men signed a letter from Castelnaudary (Aude) in defense of Paul Alquier, a shoemaker, and they also listed their professions: barber, furniture maker, commercial employee, tailor, café owner, locksmith—working men with skilled trades but certainly no exalted social status. They wrote that Alquier "was of a frank and loyal character, but weak and limited by the fact [that he was] easy to anger. They declare nevertheless that his fits of anger, although sudden and frequent, did not last and that he immediately regretted the foolish acts he committed." Claiming the continuity of their own relationship with the accused, they also implicitly claim the continuity of the character of the accused (AVP, D2U8/264, Alquier, 25 September 1890).
17. AVP, D2U8/117, Schmittgall, 8 June 1881.
18. AVP, D2U8/109, Pautard, 13 December 1880.
19. *Gazette des Tribunaux*, 8 December 1872.
20. AVP, D2U8/114, Koenig, 8 March 1881. Koenig was actually born in Paris, although he clearly spent most of his youth in Besançon.
21. AVP, D2U8/171, Deffendi, 13 October 1884.
22. AVP, D2U8/135, Georges, 28 June 1882.
23. AVP, D2U8/84, Balade, 29 April 1879.
24. AVP, D2U8/139, Jean, 14 November 1882.
25. *Gazette des Tribunaux*, 13 December 1871.
26. AVP, D2U8/289, Dogmatschoff, 2 February 1892.
27. AVP, D2U8/84, Balade, 29 April 1879.
28. AVP, D2U8/207, Léra, 17 September 1886.
29. AVP, D2U8/53, Prévot, 12 October 1876.
30. AVP, D2U8/272, Boudet, 2 March 1891.
31. AVP, D2U8/198, Catelier, 22 March 1886.
32. AVP, D2U8/101, Clément, 21 July 1880.
33. AVP, D2U8/181, Fontaine, 12 May 1885.
34. AVP, D2U8/61, Kemps, 14 June 1877.
35. The cousin worked as a dyer, and the wife sewed pants for the Belle Jardinière department store, earning three or four francs a week, while the husband allegedly made forty to fifty francs a week hanging wallpaper. Other witnesses, however, claimed that he did not work regularly and often harassed his wife to give him money, indicating that the household was not as financially secure as these figures might suggest.
36. AVP, D2U8/75, Lerondeau, 29 June 1878.
37. AVP, D2U8/139, Jean, 14 November 1882.

38. AVP, D2U8/173, Maxant, 6 December 1884. In the end, he stayed and was acquitted for killing his wife.
39. AVP, D2U8/219, Duchène, 21 May 1887.
40. AVP, D2U8/272, Boudet, 2 March 1891.
41. AVP, D2U8/53, Marie, 7 October 1876. Marie was acquitted of attempted murder, but it is not clear how much of this verdict can be attributed to the doubt cast on his wife's character throughout his testimony or to the fact that when he shot her he did not actually wound her.
42. AVP, D2U8/109, Joulain, 27 December 1880.
43. AVP, D2U8/ 291, Langlois, 30 June 1892.
44. AVP, D2U8/162, Genuyt, 30 May 1884.
45. One historian has argued that among eighteenth-century English gentry, women's nervous illness was a strategy for calling attention to a husband's violent behavior. See Elizabeth Foyster, "Creating a Veil of Silence?"
46. *Gazette des Tribunaux*, 13 April 1870.
47. *Gazette des Tribunaux*, 25–26 January 1892.
48. AVP, D2U8/207, Fournet, 6 October 1886.
49. AVP, D2U8/144, Perrin, 30 March 1883.
50. AVP, D2U8/241, Masset, 10 August 1888.
51. AVP, D2U8/260, Kieffer, 12 June 1890.
52. AVP, D2U8/241, Masset, 10 August 1888.
53. AVP, D2U8/156, Sanglé, 25 January 1884.
54. AVP, D2U8/188, Vigineix-Roche, 20 August 1885. Spelling of the last name varies in the dossier.
55. AVP, D2U8/212, Barbier, 22 December 1886.
56. AVP, D2U8/109, Pautard, 13 December 1880.
57. AVP, D2U8/156, Sanglé, 25 January 1884.
58. AVP, D2U8/181, Fontaine, 12 May 1885.
59. AVP, D2U8/284, Durban, 13 October 1891.
60. AVP, D2U8/219, Duchène, 21 May 1887.
61. AVP, D2U8/181, Millim, 23 April 1885.
62. AVP, D2U8/61, Kemps, 14 June 1877.
63. AVP, D2U8/198, Catelier, 22 March 1886. The witness's name was Delphin Felicien Magneny.
64. AVP, D2U8/281, De Moor, 10 September 1891. In this case, although the victim was a seamstress who made shirts, her husband was a day laborer, and other women in their building were employed in similarly humble professions (*lingère, cartonnière*) throughout the file they are referred to, and refer to each other, as *madame*. This is certainly atypical for this milieu, and I suspect it is due to the initiative of the clerk who recorded their testimony.
65. AVP, D2U8/12, Bernou, 29 September 1871.
66. AVP, D2U8/135, Gy, 15 July 1882.
67. AVP, D2U8/17, Santin, 13 March 1873.
68. *Gazette des Tribunaux*, 28 October 1874.
69. AVP, D2U8/207, Deschutter, 25 September 1886.
70. AVP, D2U8/194, Catherine, 4 December 1885.

71. AVP, D2U8/135, Gy, 15 Juillet 1882.
72. AVP, D2U8/285, Croissant, 26 October 1891.
73. AVP, D2U8/17, Jouault, 11 February 1873.
74. AVP, D2U8/188, Vigineix, 20 August 1885.
75. AVP, D2U8/32, Duc, 28 September 1874.
76. Julie Hardwick, "Early Modern Perspectives on the Long History of Domestic Violence" and Mary Trouille, *Wife Abuse*, esp. chap. 1. (Hardwick's book *Family Business*, which analyzes domestic violence in the larger context of seventeenth-century political economy, was forthcoming as this book went to press.)
77. Leslie Page Moch and Rachel G. Fuchs, "Getting Along." Christine Stansell analyzes the importance of women's networks in early nineteenth-century New York in *City of Women*.
78. Roderick Phillips, "Women, Neighborhood, and Family in the Late Eighteenth Century."
79. AVP, D2U8/75, Lerondeau, 29 June 1878.
80. AVP, D2U8/218, Rault, 12 April 1887. Since her husband died shortly after she stabbed him, la veuve Rault was referred to as a widow throughout the investigation and trial.
81. AVP, D2U8/12, Bernou, 29 September 1871.
82. AVP, D2U8/288, Méhu, 20 January 1892. The concierge was the only nonprofessional witness interviewed besides the couple themselves in the case of Rose Méhu.
83. AVP, D2U8/295, Cousin, 28 December 1892.
84. AVP, D2U8/ 280, Robert, 31 August 1891. Robert was acquitted for the murder of his unfaithful wife.
85. AVP, D2U8/29, Vallaud, 28 July 1874.
86. AVP, D2U8/61, Kemps, 14 June 1877.
87. AVP, D2U8/101, Clément, 21 July 1880.
88. AVP, D2U8/16, Perney, 28 December 1872.
89. *Gazette des Tribunaux*, 8 November 1872.
90. AVP, D2U8/94, Guerrier, 6 February 1880.
91. AVP, D2U8/230, Legrand, 6 December 1887.
92. *Gazette des Tribunaux*, 8 November 1872.
93. AVP, D2U8/28, Zick, 30 May 1874.
94. AVP, D2U8/61, Kemps, 14 June 1877.
95. AVP, D2U8/29, Vallaud, 28 July 1874.
96. AVP, D2U8/258, Daouze, 20 March 1890.
97. AVP, D2U8/23, Solhart, 26 November 1873.
98. AVP, D2U8/36, Degrange, 13 March 1875.
99. AVP, D2U8/285, Herbellot, 27 October 1891.
100. AVP, D2U8/114, Jacob, 26 March 1881.
101. AVP, D2U8/53, Michel, 13 October 1876.
102. AVP, D2U8/272, Teste, 11 April 1891.
103. A woman and her daughter watched from their window as Adélaïde Marguerite Goix femme Ledoux beat her husband to death in an empty lot across the street (D2U8/82, Ledoux, 7 January 1879). An old, deaf man peacefully went to sleep after he watched through a hole in his floor as Pierre Schumacher strangled his mistress and then

had sex with the corpse—but that particular case surely belongs in the realm of pathology (D2U8/209, Schumacher, 30 October 1886).

104. AVP, D2U8/80, Guillot, 25 November 1878.
105. AVP, D2U8/127, Larue, 27 January 1882.
106. AVP, D2U8/207, Fournet, 6 October 1886.

CHAPTER 4. Reciprocity and Retribution

1. Alexandre Dumas fils, *L'Homme-femme*.
2. For a transcript of the trial proceedings, see *La Gazette des Tribunaux*, 15 June 1872. The trial dossier no longer exists in the archives of the Cour d'assises de la Seine.
3. Ann-Louise Shapiro, *Breaking the Codes*, 182. D'Ideville's article is reprinted in Henri d'Ideville, *L'Homme qui tue*.
4. See, e.g., *Le Petit Parisien*, 17 December 1876 and 11 October 1877.
5. See Shapiro, *Breaking the Codes*, 183–84; Odile Krakovitch, "Misogynes et féministes," and James F. McMillan, *France and Women*, 103.
6. Paulin Moniquet, *Autopsie de l'homme-femme*, 4. See also *Ni homme ni femme* for a pertinent Catholic defense of the indissolubility of marriage.
7. Jules Girard, *À Propos de l'homme-femme*.
8. See, e.g., Emile de Girardin, *L'Homme et la femme*.
9. Hermance Lesguillon, *L'Homme*, 36, 37.
10. Ibid., 43.
11. Maria Deraismes, *Ève contre M. Dumas fils*, 26.
12. Ibid., 41–42, 48, 49.
13. A few French feminists were known to be victims of violence themselves. Flora Tristan, most notably, was shot by her estranged husband on the rue du Bac in September 1838. She survived a serious wound, and her husband was convicted of attempted murder and sentenced to twenty years' hard labor (Susan Grogan, *Flora Tristan*, 26–33). Perhaps because of her personal experience, she cited the high proportion of murders among unhappily married spouses in her petition to abolish the death penalty in 1838. She wrote, "Two-thirds of the cases of poisoning and assassinations are caused by jealousy, the feelings which result from the indissolubility of marriage and woman's servitude," and she claimed that all countries without legal divorce have similarly high rates of spousal murder (Felicia Gordon and Máire Cross, eds., *Early French Feminisms*, 47, 55). Hubertine Auclert claimed that her feminism was inspired by the experience of male violence in her childhood: "Man's brutality against women, which terrified my childhood, prepared me early to claim independence and respect for my sex," she wrote in *Les Femmes au gouvernail* (Claire Goldberg Moses, *French Feminism in the Nineteenth Century*, 213). For Jeanne Schmahl, it was not her own experience of violence but the experience of one of her patients that helped motivate her activism. The patient's alcoholic husband beat her frequently, took her pay, and caused her to lose her job. This terrible story inspired Schmahl to begin her fight for married women's property rights, which was ultimately successful in 1907 (Steven C. Hause with Anne R. Kenney, *Women's Suffrage and Social Politics*, 56).
14. Marguerite Durand, *Congrès international*, 236–37, 197.
15. G.-M. Ragonod, *Autour du foyer domestique*, 127–29.

16. Ibid., 129.
17. AVP, D2U8/230, Périchon, 7 December 1887.
18. AVP, D2U8/291, Langlois, 30 June 1892.
19. AVP, D2U8/288, Rochat, 6 January 1892.
20. AVP, D2U8/239, Dabon, 13 June 1888.
21. AVP, D2U8/284, Durban, 13 October 1891; AVP, D2U8/288, Giacardo, 29 December 1891; AVP, D2U8/218, Rault, 12 April 1887.
22. AVP, D2U8/12, Bernou, 29 September 1871.
23. AVP, D2U8/268, Gadel, 17 January 1891.
24. AVP, D2U8/23, Solhart, 26 November 1873.
25. AVP, D2U8/284, Cotard, 14 October 1891.
26. Shapiro, *Breaking the Codes*, 76–79. I have chosen to translate *vitriol* as sulfuric acid, since the phrase is more precise than the English homologue "vitriol."
27. AVP, D2U8/152, Valadon, 21 September 1883.
28. AVP, D2U8/207, Fournet, 6 October 1886.
29. AVP, D2U8/127, Larue, 27 January 1882.
30. AVP, D2U8/173, Maxant, 6 December 1884, and AVP, D2U8/264, Fétat, 10 September 1890.
31. AVP, D2U8/17, Jouault, 11 February 1873.
32. AVP, D2U8/173, Martinière, 10 December 1884.
33. AVP, D2U8/114, Chalandre, 6 April 1881.
34. AVP, D2U8/114, Koenig, 8 March 1881.
35. AVP, D2U8/29, Vallaud, 28 July 1874.
36. AVP, D2U8/281, De Moor, 10 September 1891. Ellipses in original.
37. AVP, D2U8/80, Guillot, 25 November 1878.
38. AVP, D2U8/135, Gy, 15 July 1882.
39. AVP, D2U8/181, Millim, 23 April 1885.
40. AVP, D2U8/207, Deschutter, 25 September 1886.
41. AVP, D2U8/17, Santin, 13 March 1873.
42. AVP, D2U8/94, Guerrier, 6 February 1880. She dodged the shot.
43. AVP, D2U8/36, Degrange, 13 March 1875.
44. AVP, D2U8/53, Michel, 13 October 1876.
45. AVP, D2U8/218, Rault, 12 April 1887.
46. AVP, D2U8/139, Jean, 14 November 1882.
47. AVP, D2U8/194, Catherine, 4 December 1885.
48. AVP, D2U8/258, Daouze, 20 March 1890.
49. AVP, D2U8/12, Brossier, 7 October 1871.
50. AVP, D2U8/202, Gérard, 5 June 1886. It was alleged that she had stabbed him once before, but she said she had only struck him with an umbrella.
51. AVP, D2U8/268, Gadel, 17 January 1891.
52. AVP, D2U8/120, Velay, 15 September 1887.
53. AVP, D2U8/264, Denis, 20 September 1890.
54. AVP, D2U8/38, Lelong, 9 July 1875.
55. AVP, D2U8/251, Brudieux, 21 October 1889.
56. AVP, D2U8/198, Catelier, 22 March 1886.
57. AVP, D2U8/260, Levielle, 4 June 1890.
58. AVP, D2U8/84, Gaudot, 10 May 1879.

59. AVP, D2U8/260, Keiffer, 12 June 1890.
60. AVP, D2U8/284, Cotard, 14 October 1891. She was acquitted of throwing sulfuric acid on him after he consented to the abandonment of their child.
61. AVP, D2U8/114, Jacob, 26 March 1881.
62. AVP, D2U8/75, Lerondeau, 29 June 1878.
63. AVP, D2U8/200, Badran, 22 April 1886.
64. AVP, D2U8/32, Duc, 28 September 1874.
65. AVP, D2U8/162, Genuyt, 30 May 1884.
66. AVP, D2U8/291, Langlois, 30 June 1892. When la femme Lerondeau filed for divorce, she used public assistance (*assistance judiciare*) to cover the costs, an indication of her dire financial straits.
67. Robert Nye, *Masculinity and Male Codes of Honor in Modern France*, 280.
68. William M. Reddy, *The Invisible Code*, 104.
69. AVP, D2U8/32, Duc, 28 September 1874.
70. *Gazette des Tribunaux*, 6 June 1872.
71. *Gazette des Tribunaux*, 15 June 1872.
72. Pierre-Etienne Carraby, *Affaire de M. Arthur Leroy du Bourg*, 10, 55, 57.
73. *Gazette des Tribunaux*, 27 May 1894. Daly earned three hundred francs per month, and his wife earned two hundred francs a month sewing cravats.
74. In four cases men made a point of turning themselves in to the police after committing an attack; see AVP, D2U8/117, Schmittgall, 8 June 1881; AVP, D2U8/173, Liénard, 28 November 1884; AVP, D2U8/173, Maxant, 6 December 1884; and AVP, D2U8/207, Léra, 17 September 1886.
75. AVP, D2U8/202, de Verneuil, 28 May 1886.
76. AVP, D2U8/84, Balade, 29 April 1879.
77. AVP, D2U8/109, Joulain, 27 December 1880. In another case, a prostitute was rumored to have challenged her former pimp's new mistress to a duel (AVP, D2U8/202, Gérard, 5 June 1886).
78. AVP, D2U8/80, Guillot, 25 November 1878.
79. AVP, D2U8/152, Hillairin de Saint-Priest, 29 September 1883.
80. AVP, D2U8/60, Barbot, 11 October 1877.
81. AVP, D2U8/101, Richelet, 20 July 1880.
82. AVP, D2U8/154, Genuit, 12 November 1883.
83. AVP, D2U8/198, Merle, 3 March 1886.
84. AVP, D2U8/109, Pautard, 13 December 1880.
85. AVP, D2U8/219, Duchène, 21 May 1887.
86. AVP, D2U8/101, Richelet, 20 July 1880.
87. See, e.g., David D. Gilmore, ed., *Honor and Shame*. In the Richelet case, other witnesses said that the wife's failure was due in part to her husband's laxity in controlling her. The husband said that he bought a gun with the intention of shooting his wife and her lover "*en flagrant délit*," but he also tried to make his wife's lover sign a pact giving the lover his wife, right before he shot her.
88. AVP, D2U8/152, Valadon, 21 September 1883.
89. AVP, D2U8/161, Féral, 9 May 1884.
90. AVP, D2U8/285, Croissant, 26 October 1891.
91. AVP, D2U8/207, Fournet, 6 October 1886.
92. If women could use violence in defense of their sexual honor, this capacity did not

seem to extend to other areas of honorability. Robert Nye has argued that women's exclusion from the masculine honor code worked to exclude them from the professions in the nineteenth century; women could not be challenged to a duel to defend the veracity of their scientific claims ("Medicine and Science as Masculine 'fields of Honor'").
93. AVP, D2U8/188, Vigineix, 20 August 1885.
94. AVP, D2U8/291, Langlois, 30 June 1892.
95. AVP, D2U8/16, Perney, 28 December 1872.
96. AVP, D2U8/114, Koenig, 8 March 1881.
97. AVP, D2U8/285, Malmézac, 24 October 1891.
98. AVP, D2U8/109, Pautard, 13 December 1880.
99. AVP, D2U8/153, Legrand, 22 October 1883.
100. AVP, D2U8/291, Langlois, 30 June 1892. Rosine Langlois was a bourgeoise, so it may seem surprising that she believed it would be more shameful to stay married to a bad man than divorce him.
101. Thanks to William Reddy for this observation.
102. AVP, D2U8/42, Marambat, 20 December 1875. Vittore del Greco, an Italian immigrant, also avenged his daughter's dishonor by killing a faithless suitor (AVP, D2U8/268, del Greco, 3 January 1891.) Del Greco and three codefendants were convicted of murder, perhaps because they ambushed the man, perhaps because no child had been born following the engagement, or perhaps because the courts may have treated immigrants more harshly.
103. AVP, D2U8/264, Denis, 20 September 1890.
104. AVP, D2U8/153, Legrand, 22 October 1883. He was acquitted of murder.
105. Gordon Wright, *Between the Guillotine and Liberty*.
106. On the history of prison reform in France, see Patricia O'Brien, *The Promise of Punishment*, and Michel Foucault, *Discipline and Punish*.

CHAPTER 5. Local Knowledge and State Power

1. Emile Yvernès, *Le Crime et le criminel devant le jury*, 14, 21.
2. Raoul de la Grassière, *Des Origines, de l'évolution, et de l'avenir du jury*, 30.
3. Whether systems of law are better understood as rules or processes is not a new debate for anthropologists, but it remains a fruitful one for historians. See, e.g., John L. Comaroff and Simon Roberts, *Rules and Processes*, and Clifford Geertz, "Local Knowledge: Fact and Law in Comparative Perspective," in *Local Knowledge*.
4. Pierre Bourdieu, *Outline of a Theory of Practice*.
5. A classic text of this genre is Douglas Hay et al., *Albion's Fatal Tree*.
6. Norbert Elias, *The Civilizing Process*.
7. Michel Foucault, *Discipline and Punish*.
8. A notable exception is Natalie Zemon Davis, *Fiction in the Archives*. Using tools of literary analysis, Davis found that pardon tales had to conform to certain conventions of legal procedure to be intelligible to the court but that they nonetheless preserved the individual voice of the accused. Thus such tales could reveal evidence about how ordinary people understood their place in the world and proper behavior for men and women.
9. See, e.g., Martin Wiener, *Men of Blood*; Barbara Alpern Engel, "In the Name of the Tsar"; and Astrid Cubano-Iguina, "Legal Constructions of Gender and Violence against

Women in Puerto Rico." Kimberly Gauderman has found that the colonial Spanish judicial system in Quito worked to undermine the authority of male heads of households while local community members readily intervened to limit husbands' violence and infidelity. Here, wife abuse and the husband's adultery were legally defined crimes. See *Women's Lives in Colonial Quito*, esp. chap. 3.

10. Steve Stern, *The Secret History of Gender*, chap. 4.

11. On the creation of the modern criminal justice system in France, see Gordon Wright, *Between the Guillotine and Liberty*; Robert A. Nye, *Crime, Madness, and Politics in Modern France*; Patricia O'Brien, *The Promise of Punishment*.

12. Article 10 reads: "Les tribunaux ne pourront prendre directement ou indirectement aucune part à l'exercise du pouvoir législative, ni empêcher ou suspendre l'exécution des décrets du Corps législatif [sanctionnés par le Roi], à peine de forfaiture." (Courts are not, on pain of "forfeiture," permitted to take part, directly or indirectly, in the exercise of the legislative power, nor can they prevent or adjourn the execution of any decree issued by the legislature.) Cited in Eva Steiner, *French Legal Method*, 77. The principle is stated even more directly in Article 5 of the present civil code: "Il est défendu aux juges de prononcer par voie de disposition générale et réglementaire sur les causes qui leur sont soumises" (Judges are not permitted to adjudicate by means of general and statutory rulings in the cases brought before them.) (Steiner, 78).

13. Jurors had to affirm the following oath at the beginning of an assize court trial: "You swear and promise, before God and man, to examine with the most scrupulous attention the charges brought against [the accused]; to betray neither the interests of the accused, nor those of the society that accuses him; to communicate with nobody until after your verdict; to heed neither hate nor meanness, neither fear nor affection; following your conscience and your inner conviction, with the impartiality and the firmness that are appropriate to a free and honest man." Cited in Jean Cruppi, *La Cour d'assises*, 71. This oath emphasized the importance of the jurors' individual judgment, and their dual responsibility to the accused and to society as a whole—not adherence to the law.

14. Laura Ann Mason, "The 'Bosom of Proof,'" 35. This legacy accounts for the fact that the French judicial system still does not create its own transcripts of exactly what is done and said in jury trials. The *procès verbal* only records the laws and procedures that were followed during the course of the trial. Verbatim transcripts for fin-de-siècle trials are only to be found in the popular press or semiprofessional publications such as the *Gazette des Tribunaux*.

15. André Bougon, *De la Participation du jury à l'application de la peine*; M. Charmeil, *De l'Institution du juré en France*; Henri Coulon, *Une Réforme nécessaire*; de la Grassière, *Des Origines*; Félix Grélot, *Loi du 21 novembre sur le jury votée par l'Assemblée Nationale*; Adolphe Guillot, *Le Jury et les meours*; Corentin Guyho, *Les Jurés, "maîtres de la peine."* For a review of professional jurists' positions, see James F. Donovan, "Magistrates and Juries in France, 1791–1952."

16. On the depiction of crimes of passion in the popular press, see Dominique Kalifa, *L'Encre et le sang*; Kalifa, *Crime et culture au 19e siècle*, chap. 6; and Ann-Louise Shapiro, *Breaking the Codes*.

17. Benjamin F. Martin, *Crime and Criminal Justice under the Third Republic*, 4. Martin bases his analysis on the annual volumes of the *Comte général de l'administration de la justice criminelle*, which this author has verified.

18. Joëlle Guillais, *La Chair de l'autre*, 320.

19. Ann-Louise Shapiro, *Breaking the Codes*, 150–151.
20. AVP, D2U8/207, Fournet, 6 October 1886.
21. Shapiro, *Breaking the Codes*, 151.
22. Ruth Harris, *Murders and Madness*.
23. AVP, D2U8/94, Magerus, 10 February 1880.
24. Bernard Marchand, *Paris*, 162. In other departments the number of potential jurors ranged between four hundred and six hundred, depending on the size of the population.
25. Bougon, *De la Participation*, 5.
26. AVP, D2U8/35, Michaud, 25 January 1875.
27. AVP, D2U8/288, Rochat, 6 January 1892.
28. See chap. 2 for a detailed discussion of wages and material resources among trial participants.
29. This summary of the organization of the police force in Paris is drawn from the detailed account in Martin, *Crime*. For the creation of the nationwide police system in the first half of the nineteenth century, see John Merriman, *Police Stories*.
30. Martin, *Crime*, 42
31. Arlette Farge, *La Vie fragile*, 56. See also Alan Williams, *The Police of Paris*.
32. As one *gardien de la paix* reported, a man named Jean-Baptiste Denis complained during his arrest for stabbing his wife that "he did not understand our intervention in a household discussion" (AVP, D2U8/264, Denis, 20 September 1890). While that statement is unique among the dossiers, police occasionally declined to intervene unless a conflict appeared to have reached a dangerous level. Concierge Constant Chauvin once called the police during a noisy fight between a couple in his building, but when the officer refused to intervene, Chauvin had to put an end to the conflict himself (AVP, D2U8/258, Daouze, 20 March 1890). In another case, hearing the sounds of a violent argument but not daring to intervene, a neighbor of Alphonse Catelier summoned the police. When they arrived, all was quiet, so they refused to break in the apartment door; if they had, they might have found Catelier's mistress before she died of his beatings (AVP, D2U8/198, Catelier, 22 March 1886). It is not clear in these cases why the police decided not to intervene when they were appealed to for help. Maybe the individual officers involved would have agreed with Denis that police should not get involved in household arguments. Or maybe they did not feel that the situation was dangerous enough to require intervention. While the attitudes of individual officers may have varied, police seem generally to have responded with alacrity to requests for help.
33. AVP, D2U8/17, Jouault, 11 February 1873.
34. AVP, D2U8/188, Vigineix, 20 August 1885.
35. AVP, D2U8/152, Valadon, 21 September 1883.
36. AVP, D2U8/285, Herbellot, 27 October 1891.
37. AVP, D2U8/219, Duchène, 21 May 1887.
38. In a few cases, police were the attackers. Four separate cases involved men who were employed (or recently employed) as *gardiens de la paix*. Each was tried for committing murder or attempted murder, and two of them made use of their service revolvers in their crimes (AVP, D2U8/173, Maxant, 6 December 1884, and AVP, D2U8/264, Fétat, 10 September 1890). Other cases are Koenig (AVP, D2U8/114, 8 March 1881) and Michel, who had previously been fired from his job (AVP, D2U8/53, 13 October 1876). Another attacker worked as a clerk at the *commissaire de police* of the St. Victor quarter

(AVP, D2U8/175, Berquet, 28 January 1885). It may be tempting to speculate that police officers were more likely to be violent, given their frequent contact with criminals and familiarity with firearms, but they did not distinguish themselves from the rest of the defendants through a greater regard for the law or a commitment to curbing private violence, both of which might also be expected as a result of their profession.

39. AVP, D2U8/47, Trouvé, 12 May 1876.
40. AVP, D2U8/53, Michel, 13 October 1876.
41. AVP, D2U8/251, Brudieux, 21 October 1889.
42. AVP, D2U8/31, Breffeil, 24 September 1874.
43. AVP, D2U8/17, Jouault, 11 February 1873.
44. AVP, D2U8/284, Cotard, 14 October 1891.
45. AVP, D2U8/181, Fontaine, 12 May 1885.
46. According to the Naquet law, divorce could be obtained only on the following grounds: the wife's adultery, the husband's adultery in the conjugal abode, either spouse's "outrageous conduct, abuse, or grievous insult," or either spouse's condemnation to a defamatory criminal punishment. Alfred Naquet, *Le Divorce*, 221. For an innovative analysis of the debates around the divorce law, see Jean Pedersen, *Legislating the French Family*.
47. AVP, D2U8/17, Jouault, 11 February 1873.
48. AVP, D2U8/114, Koenig, 8 March 1881.
49. Arlette Farge and Michel Foucault, *Le Désordre des familles*, 26 and 29.
50. AVP, D2U8/230, Legrand, 6 December 1887.
51. However, if the investigating magistrate wanted to try a case as a misdemeanor in correctional court instead of as a felony in the assize court, the consent of the victim was required.
52. The vast majority of the witnesses and defendants in this study were able to read and sign legibly, attesting to the effectiveness of the French national education system. See chap. 6 for a further discussion of literacy among participants in assize court trials.
53. One example appears in the *acte d'accusation* for the trial of Marie Gadel, who was acquitted of assault in the stabbing death of her husband (AVP, D2U8/268, Gadel, 17 January 1891). Part of the indictment reads, "L'accusée, toujours ivre, ne manifesta alors qu'une seule préoccupation, celle de se débarasser le plus rapidement possible du cadavre de sa victime, ajoutant, 'je ne veux pas le faire enterer; il m'a mangé trop d'argent. Il m'a mise sur la paille!'" (The accused, still drunk, evinced only one preoccupation, to get rid of her victim's cadaver as quickly as possible, adding, "I don't want to have him buried; he squandered too much of my money. He made me broke!") Although unattributed in the indictment, the quotation is from a deposition given six days after the crime by the couple's neighbor, a wine seller, recounting what she had said to him when the victim died.
54. For example, *Le Petit Parisien* of 12 October 1877 reproduced much of the *acte d'accusation* from the case of Louis Barbot (AVP, D2U8/60, Barbot, 11 October 1877) who was convicted of murdering his wife: "L'accusé ne pouvait entrer dans une famille plus honorable, de l'aveu de tous ceux qui la connaissait. Au dire des témoins, la jeune femme était d'une reputation intacte. Déporvue d'instruction et d'une intelligence médiocre, elle avait un caractère doux jusqu'à la timidité, et elle était incapable de résister à la ménace." (The accused could not have joined a more honorable family, as all those who knew [his wife's family] swore. According to the witnesses, the young woman had a

spotless reputation. Completely lacking education, and of mediocre intelligence, she had a character that was docile to the point of timidity, and she was incapable of resisting threats.)

55. The process of diverting cases to the lower court was known as *correctionalisation*. It could only be done with the crime victim's consent. In correctional court, a panel of judges tried cases, and the acquittal rate was consequently much lower: less than 10% in this era, according to Benjamin Martin (*Crime*, 4). James Donovan has explained that the practice of *correctionalisation* was an explicit strategy magistrates employed to reduce the power of juries and increase their own professional authority, an analysis is in line with recent French legal scholarship. See James M. Donovan, "Magistrates and Juries in France." See also Françoise Lombard, "'Les Citoyens-juges.'" She writes, "L'histoire du jury est, en effet, pour large partie l'histoire de la lente reconquête par les magistrats de la maîtrise de leur espace professionnel en matière de justice criminelle, espace confisqué en 1791 par l'Assemblé constituante" (775).

56. Even more detailed summaries of court procedures can be found in Cruppi, *La Cour d'assises*, and A. Surraud, *Code de la Cour d'assises*.

57. An earlier law (25 June 1824) provided that the court should decide on extenuating circumstances before deciding the punishment. Permitting the jury to find extenuating circumstances was widely perceived as an incentive for the jurors to find more defendants guilty. Jurors could not choose to find the defendant guilty of a lesser offense on their own initiative. Only the presiding magistrate could raise new charges against the defendant.

58. Excusable murder of an adulterous wife and her accomplice was instituted in Roman law, and confirmed with the laws of the ancien régime. According to Natalie Zemon Davis, the principle was established in French jurisprudence by the time of the sixteenth century (*Pardon Tales*, 95).

59. Paul Peyssonnié, *Le Meurtre excusable*, 3.

60. *Carnet du juré d'assises*, 40.

61. M. Charmeil, *De l'Institution du juré en France*, 23. Emphasis in the original.

62. Adolphe Guillot, *Le Jury et les mœurs*, 15.

63. Raoul de la Grassière, *Des Origines, de l'évolution et de l'avenir du jury*, 26. Emphasis in original.

64. Adolphe Guillot, *Le Jury et les meours*, 22–23. This essay was first published in the *Gazette des Tribunaux* on 2 and 4 January 1885 before being published as a book.

65. *Carnet du juré d'assises*.

66. Charles Berriat de Saint-Prix, *Le Jury en matière criminelle*.

67. Constant Fenet. *Code-Manuel du juré d'assises*.

68. Jules Lévy, *Le Jury en matière criminelle*, 19–20.

69. John M. Conley and William M. O'Barr, *Rules versus Relationships*.

70. It was during the late eighteenth century that the process of "lawyerization" and the silencing of the accused came about in British courts. See John H. Langbien, *The Origins of the Adversary Criminal Trial*, and Martin J. Weiner, "Judges v. Jurors." French jury trials, though largely based on an eighteenth-century British model, did not follow this evolution.

71. AVP, D2U8/114, Koenig, 8 March 1881.

72. For details on the evolution of the assize court, see Jean Pradel, "Les Méandres de la Cour d'assises françaises."

73. Françoise Lombard, "Les Citoyens-juges."

74. Pradel, "Les Méandres," 135.

CHAPTER 6. Reading and Writing Stories of Intimate Violence

1. Pierre Decourcelle, *Crime de femme*, 8–9. The investigating magistrate turns out to be the father of Lydia's sister's illegitimate child. He dies after accidentally ingesting poison from the case of a pharmacist accused of poisoning his wife.
2. On popular literacy and serial novels, see Anne-Marie Thiesse, *Le Roman du quotidien*.
3. Dominique Kalifa, *L'Encre et le sang*; Ann-Louise Shapiro, *Breaking the Codes*.
4. Michel de Certeau, *The Practice of Everyday Life*, 169.
5. Vanessa Schwartz recounts the case to illustrate "how the public, the morgue administrators and the popular press transformed this real-life crime into a spectacle" (*Spectacular Realities*, 72). Schwartz's account draws on police archives and the popular press, while my account draws on police and court archives together in order to shed light on the circumstances leading up to the crime.
6. Archives de la Préfecture de Police, Series Ba, carton 81. All translations are by the author.
7. AVP, D2U8/59, Billoir, 14–15 March 1877.
8. *Le Petit journal supplément littéraire*, 12 November 1892.
9. Séverin Icard, *De la Contagion du crime et du suicide par la presse*.
10. Deborah Silverman, *Art Nouveau in Fin-de-Siècle France*, 83–84.
11. Icard, *De la Contagion*, 9. Emphasis in the original.
12. See Ruth Harris, *Murders and Madness*; Robert A. Nye, *Crime, Madness, and Politics in Modern France*; and Gordon B. Wright, *Between the Guillotine and Liberty*.
13. Paul Aubry, *La Contagion du meurtre*, 95.
14. Ibid., 98–99.
15. Armand Corre, *Crime et suicide*, 217–23.
16. Gabriel Tarde, *Les Lois de l'imitation*, 73.
17. Ibid., 209.
18. Ibid., 83.
19. Shapiro, *Breaking the Codes*, 47.
20. Aubry, *La Contagion du meurtre*, xxi.
21. Louis Proal, *Le Crime et le suicide passionnels*, 613.
22. Hélie Courtois, *Etude médico-légale des crimes passionnels*, 12.
23. See, e.g., Cesare Beccaria, *On Crimes and Punishments*. Beccaria's work was first published in 1764 and immediately went through many editions throughout Europe, influencing all major legal reforms of the era.
24. Anatole Bérard des Glajeux, *Accusés et juges, Accusateurs et avocats*, 43.
25. Anatole Bérard des Glajeux, *Les Passions criminelles*, 40–41.
26. Louis Holtz, *Les Crimes passionnels*, 3.
27. H. Maudsley, *Le Crime et la folie*, 263.
28. Proal, *Le Crime et le suicide passionnels*, 428.
29. Didier Nourrisson, *Le Buveur du 19e siècle*, 66. Just after the turn of the century, average annual consumption was estimated at 22.93 liters of pure alcohol per person, followed rather distantly by Italy, with 17.29 liters per capita, and Spain with 14.2.
30. M. Marambat, *L'Alcoolisme et la criminalité*, 5.
31. Ibid., 8–11.

32. Ibid., 34.
33. Holtz, *Les Crimes passionnels*, 68.
34. AVP, D2U8/101, Richelet, 20 July 1880.
35. AVP, D2U8/153, Legrand, 22 October 1883.
36. AVP, D2U8/212, Barbier, 22 December 1886.
37. AVP, D2U8/16, Perney, 28 December 1872.
38. AVP, D2U8/160, Gobert, 19 March 1884.
39. AVP, D2U8/31, Breffeil, 24 September 1874; AVP, D2U8/67, Gassion, 8 November 1877; AVP, D2U8/264, Fétat, 10 September 1890; AVP, D2U8/285, Herbellot, 27 October 1891.
40. AVP, D2U8/173, Martinière, 10 December 1884.
41. Late twentieth-century cross-cultural studies of drunken behavior have demonstrated convincingly that when people "lose control" after drinking, they do so in culturally determined ways. Violence is not universally associated with drunkenness. See Craig MacAndrew, *Drunken Comportment*.
42. Although he did not address the issue of crimes of passion specifically, Durkheim too would have agreed that social control and self-control were proving to be inadequate bulwarks against antisocial behavior in his era. See Emile Durkheim, *The Division of Labor in Society*.
43. AVP, D2U8/138, Lachaize, 19 October 1882.
44. AVP, D2U8/144, Roulland, 7 April 1883.
45. AVP, D2U8/285, Malmézac, 24 October 1891.
46. AVP, D2U8/198, Merle, 3 March 1886.
47. AVP, D2U8/17, Jouault, 11 February 1873.
48. AVP, D2U8/84, Balade, 29 April 1879.
49. AVP, D2U8/289, Dogmatschoff, 2 February 1892.
50. Likewise, in what was arguably the most famous murder of the fin de siècle, that of the bailiff Gouffé by Gabrielle Bompard and Michel Eyraud, illustrations in the popular press led to Eyraud's arrest in Cuba (AVP, D2U8/267, Eyraud/Bompard, 20 December 1890).
51. AVP, D2U8/230, Périchon, 7 December 1887.
52. AVP, D2U8/265, Henry, 13 November 1890.
53. AVP, D2U8/15, Schenk, 21 November 1872.
54. AVP, D2U8/239, Delthil, 5 June 1888. The dossier on Georges Bonfils still contains an issue of *Le Petit Populaire Illustré*, splattered with blood from the young woman he attacked with a hammer—surely a unique blending of crime and the printed page (AVP, D2U8/134, Bonfils, 27 May 1882).
55. AVP, D2U8/12, Brossier, 7 October 1871.
56. AVP, D2U8/15, Schenk, 21 November 1872.
57. AVP, D2U8/295, Cousin, 28 December 1892.
58. AVP, D2U8/94, Guerrier, 6 February 1880.
59. For more on this point, see chap. 5.
60. Michelle Perrot, "Le Secret de la correspondance au 19e siècle," 184–88.
61. Most of these dossiers contain just a few letters, written by one person, but some contain extensive collections of love letters transcribed into booklets during the investigation. AVP, D2U8/271, Bleszinsky, 21 March 1891 (370 transcribed letters); AVP, D2U8/96, Bière, 7 April 1880 (82 transcribed letters and related documents).

62. See, e.g., Barry Reay, "The Context and Meaning of Popular Literacy."
63. AVP, D2U8/84, Gaudot, 10 May 1879.
64. AVP, D2U8/118, Thauvin, 12 August 1881.
65. AVP, D2U8/38, Lelong, 9 July 1875.
66. AVP, D2U8/153, Legrand, 22 October 1883.
67. Cécile Dauphin, Pierette Lebrun-Pézerat, and Danièle Poublan, *Ces Bonnes lettres*, 194.
68. Ibid., 131.
69. Cécile Dauphin, *Prête-moi ta plume*. To be sure, the well-to-do family featured in *Ces Bonnes lettres* did not slavishly follow the dictates of epistolary handbooks either, but their practices followed other codes established through the course of their correspondence.
70. AVP D2U8/84, Gaudot, 10 May 1879. After arguing with her lover Charles Gaudot, Léontine drank a glass of water and *vert de Mittis* that he gave her; she died five days later. Used as a green tint in painting, vert de Mittis (also known as vert de Vienne or vert métis) contains copper and arsenic. The chemical analysis of the poisoning is described in Bergeron, Delens, and L'Hôte, "Empoisonnement par le vert de Mittis."
71. For instance, Victor Gasson, a bronzer, in the midst of his army service, noted that his lover Berthe Delmas wrote him regularly twice a week, while he ordinarily only wrote her once weekly (AVP, D2U8/249, Gasson, 10 April 1889). See also AVP, D2U8/127, Guyard, 31 January 1882; D2U8/284, Bellon, 30 September 1891.
72. AVP, D2U8/144, Perrin, 30 March 1883; D2U8/207, Fournet, 6 October 1886; D2U8/244, Parrain, 2 November 1888.
73. AVP, D2U8/260, Levielle, 4 June 1890.
74. AVP, D2U8/188, Vigineix, 20 August 1885.
75. AVP, D2U8/139, Jean, 14 November 1882. The newspaper clipping gives the correct address (1, rue Lourmel) and correctly reports that she fired three shots without hitting him, but it names her as Henry (Jeanne) Laveau. In fact, her husband was named Henri Jean but was called Delaveau, and her name was Eulalie.
76. AVP, D2U8/264, Denis, 20 September 1890. He stabbed her in the thigh, severing her femoral vein, according to the autopsy report.
77. "I recommend that you not speak to me about anything in my letter... It is not worth it to write me back before I write you again... Above all do not write me back about anything that I write you."
78. The closing reads, "Je finie ma letter en vous embrassan de tous Coeur toute la famille sent oublier ma fille, votre fille devouer."
79. AVP, D2U8/158, Foquières, 11 March 1884.
80. AVP, D2U8/207, Fournet, 6 October 1886.
81. AVP, D2U8/156, Sanglé, 25 January 1884.
82. AVP, D2U8/144, Perrin, 30 March 1883.
83. See chap. 1 for a further discussion of the content of Perrin's letter.
84. In Rimbaud's 1871 poem, the poet associates the sounds of the vowels with colors and images. Here is Rimbaud's verse on the letter O: "O, suprême Clairon plein des strideurs étranges,/Silences traversés des Mondes et des Anges:/O l'Oméga, rayon violet de Ses Yeux !" And here is part of Perrin's composition: "Ta beauté?... Oh! Oh! Oh!..../C'était vingt printemps à peine, fleur déjà sans parfum et mi-close!.../Tes yeux purs?.... Ah! Ah! Ah!.../C'était la couleur de vipérine!!!/Ta voix douce ?.... Eh! Eh!

Eh!.../C'était celle de la perfide sirène!.../Ange? mais déchu!... un démon!" It seems quite possible that Perrin's alphabet of a broken heart was inspired on some level by Rimbaud's example, with its repetition of vowel sounds and references to angels and eyes.

85. AVP, D2U8/144, Perrin, 30 March 1883.

86. *Le Gaulois*, 3 July 1887; *La Patrie*, 3 July 1887 (in Ba82, Archives de la Préfecture de Police).

CONCLUSION. "Men Who Kill and Women Who Vote"

1. Alexandre Dumas, *Les Femmes qui tuent et les femmes qui votent*.
2. Dumas reported that a jurist seated next to him at the trial said, "That is where your *Tue-la* leads!" (55). The dossier for Bière's trial is AVP, D2U8/96, Bière, 7 April 1880.
3. *Les Femmes qui tuent*, 6.
4. Dumas's change of heart was reportedly due to the influence of Hubertine Auclert. See Patrick Kay Bidelman, *Pariahs, Stand Up!* 126–27.
5. Emile de Girardin, *L'Égale de l' homme*, 8, 25, 43, 46. De Girardin further proposed that since women's "highest law" is motherhood (56), mothers should have exclusive parental rights over their children (60).
6. Gill Allwood, *French Feminisms*, 101. Allwood decries Anglo-American scholars' overemphasis on highly theoretical French feminists like Hélène Cixous and Luce Irigaray, whose ideas are quite peripheral to the activism of many French feminists engaged in social reform. Although Allwood documents feminist activists' consistent engagement against domestic violence through the 1970s and 1980s, this issue is mentioned only in passing if at all in most historical accounts of the twentieth-century French feminist movement. One scholar has noted that the Flora Tristan shelter was immediately involved in protecting North African women from excision and infibulation (Françoise Picq, *Libération des femmes*, 272.) Erin Pizzey founded the first shelter for battered women in Europe in the London suburb of Chiswick in 1973. Pizzey purposefully publicized the shelter and the problem of wife abuse in general, and the facility was soon widely imitated (Elizabeth Pleck, *Domestic Tyranny*, 190).
7. Monique Rémy, *Histoire des Mouvements de femmes*, 76.
8. Ibid., 75.
9. Dominique Viriot-Barrial, "Commentaire de la loi no. 2006–399 du 4 avril 2006."
10. Civil Code, Article 515–18.
11. The complete text of the law can be found on www.legifrance.gouv.fr (accessed 7 January 2009).
12. Specifically, the law addresses torture, assault, murder, rape, and sexual violence. For rape and sexual violence, the fact of being partnered with the victim had previously been defined as an aggravating circumstance.
13. Nouveau Code Pénal, Article 132–80 (Loi numéro 2006–399 du 4 avril 2006, article 7):

> Dans les cas prévus par la loi, les peines encourues pour un crime ou un délit sont aggravées lorsque l' infraction est commise par le conjoint, le concubin ou le partenaire lié à la victime par un pacte civil de solidarité. La circonstance aggravante prévue au premier alinéa est également constituée lorsque les faits sont commis par l' ancien conjoint, l' ancien concubin ou l' ancien partenaire lié à la victime par un pacte civil de

solidarité. Les dispositions du présent alinéa sont applicables dès lors que l' infraction est commise en raison des relations ayant existé entre l' auteur des faits et la victime.

14. Viriot-Barrial, "Commentaire," note 5.
15. See http://ec.europa.eu/justice_home/daphnetoolkit/html (accessed 26 February 2009).
16. Historians of crime in England have hotly debated this topic. See J. A. Sharpe, "The History of Violence in England"; Lawrence Stone, "The History of Violence in England," and "Interpersonal Violence in English Society," 22–23. One regional study offers evidence of a striking increase of family murders as a proportion of all murders in nineteenth-century France. See Anne Parrella, "Industrialization and Murder."
17. Norbert Elias, *The Civilizing Process*.
18. In Great Britain, early feminists such as Mary Wollstonecraft, Harriet Taylor Mill, and John Stuart Mill explicitly linked the problem of intimate violence to women's rights. Francis Power Cobbe amplified this connection; she, in turn, influenced American reformers such as Lucy Stone. See Elizabeth Pleck, *Domestic Tyranny*; Russel P. Dobash and R. Emerson Dobash, *Violence Against Wives*; Carol Bauer and Lawrence Ritt, "Wife-Abuse, Late-Victorian Feminists, and the Legacy of Frances Power Cobbe." Whatever influence these Anglo-American feminists may have had on their French counterparts regarding this issue remains elusive. By contrast, historians are well aware of the movement against corporal punishment of children in France. See Jean-Claude Caron, *À l'École de la violence*.
19. *Gazette des Tribunaux*, 15 June 1872.
20. Annelise Maugue, *L'Identité masculine en crise*, 66, 88–94. On the fin-de-siècle crisis of masculinity, see also Christopher Forth, *The Dreyfus Affair*, and Judith Surkis, *Sexing the Citizen*.
21. Ibid., 114–24.
22. This is in sharp contrast to the history of violence and masculinity in Britain in the same era. Surveying virtually all cases of spousal murder and numerous cases of spousal manslaughter tried in England during the Victorian era, Martin Wiener finds that court verdicts as well as public opinion treated men's violence against wives with increasing harshness. While it was increasingly likely for a woman be acquitted for killing her abusive husband toward the end of the century, no man was acquitted of killing his wife after 1872 (*Men of Blood*, 214). The contrast with the verdicts of French courts in similar cases is astonishing, and it did not escape the notice of contemporaries, who pointedly compared the leniency of French courts in "crimes of passion" with the rigor of English justice (235–38). Wiener concludes, "'Englishness' involved both self-control and care for the weaker sex, restraints upon violence, and protection of women" (239). Nonetheless, social historians of the working people in late nineteenth-century London are unanimous in describing violence against women as endemic. See Ellen Ross, *Love and Toil*.
23. In *The Struggle for the Breeches*, Anna Clark argues that English artisans increasingly used violence against their wives as they lost professional status during the Industrial Revolution.
24. Jean-Yves Le Naour, *Misères et tourments de la chair durant la grande guerre*, 237–44.
25. A similar point is developed in Tove Stang Dahl and Annika Snare, "The Coercion of Privacy."
26. Mina Kruseman, *Lettre à M. Alexandre Dumas fils*, 1872.

Bibliography

ARCHIVAL SOURCES

Archives de la Ville de Paris et du Département de la Seine (AVP)
Archives de la Préfecture de Police de Paris

NEWSPAPERS AND PERIODICALS

Annales d'Hygiène Publique et de Médecine Légale
Archives d'Anthropologie Criminelle et des Sciences Pénales
La Gazette des Tribunaux, Journal de Jurisprudence et des Débats Judiciares
L'Illustration
Le Journal Illustré
Les Ouvriers des Deux Mondes
Le Petit Journal
Le Petit Parisien
Le Petit Parisien Supplément Littéraire
Le Receuil de la Gazette des Tribunaux

PRINTED PRIMARY SOURCES

Albanel, Louis. *Le Crime dans la famille*. Paris: J. Reuff, 1900.
Andrieux, L. *Souvenirs d'un préfet de police*. Paris: Jules Rouff, 1885.
Aubry, Paul. *La Contagion du meurtre: Étude d'anthropologie criminelle*. 2nd ed. Paris: Alcan, 1894.
Baggio, C. *Catéchisme de l'ouvrier: Les maux de la vie ouvrière, leurs causes et leurs rémèdes ou le socialisme pratique*. Carvin: Plouvier et Chartreux, 1899.
Bataille, Albert. *Causes criminelles et mondaines de 1891*. Paris: Librairie Dentu, 1892.
———. *Causes criminelles et mondaines de 1892*. Paris: Librairie Dentu, 1893.
———. *Causes criminelles et mondaines de 1896*. Paris: Librairie Dentu, 1897.
Bauchéry, Roland. *La Femme de l'ouvrier, précédé d'un essai sur l'influence des romans moraux dans les classes ouvrières*. Paris: A. de Vresse, 1859.
Bayeux, Marc. *Histoire d'une ouvrière*. Paris: Calman Lévy, 1866.
Bérard des Glajeux, Anatole. *Accusés et juges, Accusateurs et avocats*. Vol. 1 of *Souvenirs d'un président d'assises*. Paris: Plon, Nourrit, 1892.
———. *Les Passions criminelles: Leurs causes et leurs remèdes*. Vol. 2 of *Souvenirs d'un président d'assises*. Paris: Plon, Nourrit, 1893.

Bergeron, Delens, and l'Hôte. "Empoisonnement par le vert de Mittis (arséniac de cuivre). Relation médico-légale de l'affaire Gaudot." *Annales d'hygiène publique et de médecine légale*, ser. 3, no. 3 (1880): 23–32.
Berriat de Saint-Prix, Charles. *Le Jury en matière criminelle: Manuel des jurés à la cour d'assises*. 5th ed. Paris: Imprimerie et librairie générale de jurisprudence, 1875.
Bertrand, Ernest. *Moralité comparée des classes ouvrières*. Paris: Berger-Levraut, n.d.
Bogdan, Georges. *Suicide ou assassinat? Deux rapports médico-légaux*. Clermont: Imprimerie Daix Frères, 1897.
Bougon, André. *De la Participation du jury à l'application de la peine*. Paris: Librairie de droit et de jurisprudence, 1900.
Bouvier, Jeanne. *Mes Mémoires, ou 59 années d'activité industrielle, sociale et intellectuelle d'une ouvrière, 1876–1935*. Edited by Daniel Argomath. Paris: La Découverte/Maspero, 1983.
Carnet du juré d'assises, contenant tout ce qui a rapport à ses fonctions, à ses droits, à ses devoirs et obligations. Par un avocat. Douai: L. Crépin, 1883.
Carraby, Pierre-Etienne. *Affaire de M. Arthur Leroy Du Bourg, Plaidorie*. Paris: Renou et Maulde, 1872.
Caron, Maurice. *Le Mariage de l'ouvrier*. Caen: C. Valin, 1901.
Cetty, H. *Le Mariage dans les classes ouvrières*. Paris: Lecoffre, 1905.
Charmeil, M. *De l'Institution du juré en France; de ses origines, de son fonctionnement en matière criminelle et de son extension en divers matières*. Grenoble: Bartier et Dardalet, imprimeurs de la Cour d'appel, 1885.
Cobbe, Frances Power. "Wife Torture in England." In *Criminals, Idiots, Women, and Minors: Nineteenth-Century Writing by Women on Women*, edited by Susan Hamilton, 132–70. Ontario: Broadview, 1995.
Corre, A. *Crime et suicide, étiologie générale, facteurs individuels, sociologiques, et cosmiques*. Paris: Octave Doin, 1891.
Coulon, Henri. *Une Réforme nécessaire: Le jury correctionnel, projet de loi*. 2nd ed. Paris: Marchal et Billard, 1900.
Courtois, Hélie. *Étude médico-légal des crimes passionels*. Toulouse: Ch. Diron, 1900.
Cruppi, Jean. *La Cour d'assises*. Paris: Calmann Lévy, 1898.
Dallemagne, Jules. *Stigmates anatomiques de la criminalité*. Paris: G. Masson, [1896].
Decourcelle, Pierre. *Crime de femme*. 4th ed. Paris: E. Dentu, n.d.
Deraismes, Maria. *Ève contre Monsieur Dumas fils*. Paris: E. Dentu, 1872.
Desmaisons, L.Ch. *"Tu seras ouvrière": Simple histoire*. Paris: Armand Colin, n.d.
D'Ideville, Henry. *L'Homme qui tue et l'homme qui pardonne. Précédé d'une lettre à M. Alexandre Dumas fils*. Paris: Dentu, 1872.
Dumas, Alexandre, fils. *Les Femmes qui tuent et les femmes qui votent*. Paris: Calman Lévy, 1880.
———. *L'Homme-femme: Réponse à M. Henry D'Ideville*. 4th ed. Paris: Michel Lévy, 1872.
Durand, Marguerite. *Congrès international de la condition et des droits des femmes, Tenu les 5, 6, 7, et 8 Septembre 1900*... Paris: Imprimerie des arts et manufactures, 1901.
Durkheim, Emile. *The Division of Labor in Society*. Translated by W. D. Hall. New York: Free Press, 1984.
Espanet, A. *Une Famille d'ouvriers, études*. Fontainebleau: Pouyé, 1877.

Favier, J. *Des Fonctions du président de la cour d'assises.* Paris: A. Pedone, 1895.
Fenet, Constant. *Code-manuel du juré d'assises avec un résumé synoptique de ce que doivent savoir des jurés.* 3rd ed. Paris: A. Cotillon, 1879.
Ferri, Enrico. *Les Criminels dans l'art et la littérature.* Translated by Eugène Laurent. Paris: Félix Alcan, 1897.
———. *La Sociologie criminelle.* Translated by Léon Terrier. Paris: Félix Alcan, 1905.
Fouillée, Alfred. *La France au point de vue morale.* Paris: Félix Alcan, 1900.
Garçon, Emile. *Du Crime dans ses rapports avec l'art dramatique et la littérature.* Paris: Université de Paris Faculté de Droit, 1922.
Gascogne, Jean. *Assassin!* Paris: Paul Ollendorff, 1887.
Girard, Jules. *À Propos de l'homme-femme, réponse d'un libre penseur, précédé d'une lettre de Louis Blanc.* Bordeaux: Féret, 1872.
de Girardin, Émile. *L'Égale de l' homme: Letter à M. Alexandre Dumas fils.* Paris: Calman Lévy, 1881.
———. *L'Homme suzerain et la femme vassale.* Paris: Calman Lévy, 1872.
Goron, Marie-François. *L'Amour criminel.* Paris: flammarion, 1899.
Grélot, Félix. *Loi du 21 novembre 1872 sur le jury votée par l'Assemblé Nationale commentée et annotée.* Paris: Maresco Aîné, 1872.
Grün, Alph. *De la Moralisation des classes laborieuses.* Paris: Guillaumin, 1851.
Guillot, Adolphe. *Le Jury et les moeurs.* Paris: Chaix, 1885.
Guyho, Corentin. *Les Jurés, "Maîtres de la peine."* Paris: A. Pedone, 1908.
Hamon, A. *Déterminisme et responsabilité.* Paris: Schleicher frères, 1898.
Haussonville, le compte de. *Salaire et misère des femmes.* Paris: Calman Lévy, 1900.
Holtz, Louis. *Les Crimes passionnels, thèse pour le doctorat.* Châteauroux and Paris: A. Mellotte, 1904.
Hude, Albert. *Le Roman, son influence sur la criminalité. Discours prononcé le 4 décembre 1909 à la séance solonelle de rentrée de la conférence des avocats stagiaires.* Poitiers: Blais et Roy, 1910.
Hugues, Henry. *La Cour d'assises et le nouveau code d'instruction criminelle: Simple notes.* Paris: A. Duran et Pedone-Lauriel, 1887.
Icard, Séverin. *De la Contagion du crime et du suicide par la presse.* Paris: Editions de la Nouvelle Revue, 1902.
Institut Général de Psychologie (Section de Psychologie morale et criminelle). *L'Action de presse en matière de criminalité.* Paris: Au Siège de la Société, 1910.
Jean. *Les Bas-fonds du crime et de la prostitution, par M. Jean, ancien inspecteur général de la sûreté.* Paris: Bibliothèque du journal fin-de-Siècle, 1899.
Joly, Henri. *Le Crime: étude sociale.* Paris: Léopold Cerf, 1888.
———. *La France criminelle.* Paris: Cerf, 1889.
Kruseman, Mina [Mlle. S. Oristorio di Frama, pseud.]. *Lettre à M. Alexandre Dumas fils au sujet de son livre l'Homme-Femme, par Mlle. Oristorio di Frama, cantatrice.* Paris: Lachaud, 1872.
Laboulet, Lucie (née Chenot). *Considérations sur l'amélioration du sort moral et materiel de l'ouvier.* Paris: Laporte, 1873.
Lemer, Julien. *L'Homme qui tue sa femme, roman parisien.* Paris: Guérin, 1884.
La Grassière, Raoul de. *De la Criminologie des collectivités.* Paris: Giard et Brière, 1903.

———. *Des Origines, de l'évolution et de l'avenir du jury*. Paris: Giard et Brière, 1897.
Le Play, F., and A. Fogillon. "Charpentier de Paris de la Corporation des Compagnons du Devoir." In vol. 1 of *Les Ouvriers des deux mondes: Études sur les travaux, la vie domestique, et la condition morale des populations ouvrières des divers contrées et sur les rapports qui les unissent aux autres classes, publiées sous forme de monographies par la Societé Internationale des études pratiques d'économie sociale*. Paris: J. Claye, 1857.
Le Play, Frédéric. *Les Ouvriers européens: Étude sur les travaux, la vie domestique et la condition morale des populations ouvrières de l'Europe*. 2nd ed. Tours: A. Mame et fils, 1877–79.
Le Roux, Hugues. *Le Chemin du crime*. 3rd ed. Paris: Victor-Havard, 1889.
Leroy-Beaulieu, Paul. *Le Travail des femmes au 19e siècle*. Paris: Charpentier, 1873.
Lesguillon, Hermance. *L'Homme, réponse à M. Alexandre Dumas fils, par Mme Hermance Lesguillon, auteur de Les Femmes dans cent ans*. Paris: Tresse, 1872.
Le Tellier, L'abbé. *Le Guide des jeunes ouvrières, ouvrage particulièrement destiné aux patronages de jeunes filles appelées à vivre au milieu du monde*. Paris: Lucien Roy, 1862.
Lévy, Jules. *Le Jury en matière criminelle: Origine de son institution, son histoire et son organisation ancienne et actuelle*. Paris: A. Amresque Aîné, 1875.
Macé, G. *Le Service de la sûreté, par son ancien chef*. Paris: Charpentier, 1884.
Marambat, M. *L'Alcoolisme et la criminalité*. Paris: Imprimerie de Typographe, 1887.
Marie, Jean. *La Famille de l'ouvrier, ses joies et ses devoirs*. Caen: E. Brunet, 1894.
Mathé, Lucien. *La Responsabilité atténuée: Lois faites dans les divers pays, lois à faire concernant les criminels à responsabilité atténuée*. Paris: Vigot Frères, 1911.
Maudsley, H. *Le Crime et la folie*. Paris: Librairie Germer Ballière, 1880.
Meunier, Georges. *Le Crime: Réquisitoire social*. Paris: Cercle Germinal, 1890.
Mill, Harriet Taylor. "Enfranchisement of Women." 1851. In *Essays on Sex Equality: John Stuart Mill and Harriet Taylor Mill*, edited by Alice Rossi, 89–121. Chicago: University of Chicago Press, 1970.
Mill, John Stuart. "The Subjection of Women." 1869. In *Essays on Sex Equality: John Stuart Mill and Harriet Taylor Mill*, edited by Alice Rossi, 125–242. Chicago: University of Chicago Press, 1970.
Ministère de la Justice. *Compte Général de l'administration de la justice criminelle en France*. Paris: Imprimerie Nationale, 1873–1902.
Moniquet, Paulin. *Autopsie de l'homme-femme, par l'Abbé P. Moniquet du clergé de Paris*. Paris: Haton, 1872.
de Montépin, Xavier. *Le Crime d'Asnières: L'entremetteuse*. Paris: E. Dentu, 1885.
Moreau de Tours, A. *Suicides et crimes étranges*. Paris: Société d'éditions scientifiques, 1899.
Morin, M. L.-J. *Manuel du juré en matière criminelle. Précédé d'un commentaire de la loi du 21 novembre 1872*. Angers: Barassé, and Paris: Cosse, Marchal, 1875.
Naquet, Alfred. *La Loi du divorce*. Paris: Calmann Lévy, 1880.
Ni homme ni femme par un auvergnat, réponse à MM. Alexandre Dumas fils et Emile de Girardin. Paris: Dentu, 1872.
Nourrisson, Paul. *L'Association contre le crime*. Paris: Librairie de la Société du receuil générale des lois et arrêts et du journal du palais, 1901.
Petit livre de l'ouvrière. Nancy: Wagner, 1885.
Peyssonnié, Paul. *Le Meurtre excusable*. Orléans: Imprimerie Gaston Morand, 1897.
Poulot, Denis. *Le Sublime, ou le travailleur comme il est en 1870 et ce qu'il peut être*. Introduction by Alain Cottereau. Paris: Maspero, 1980.

Proal, Louis. *Le Crime et le suicide passionnels.* Paris: Ancienne Librairie Germier, Félix Alcan, 1900.
Prudhon, P.-J. *La Pornocratie, ou Les Femmes dans les temps modernes.* Paris: A. Lacroix, 1875.
Ragonod, G.-M. *Autour du foyer domestique: Discours populaire.* Neuchâtel: Delachaux et Niestlé, 1894.
de Schlumberger, Mme. Paul. *Aux Jeunes ouvrières, conseils d'une mère.* Paris: Fischbacher, 1911.
Sighele, Scipio. *Littérature et criminalité.* Translated by Erick Adler. Paris: Giard et Brière, 1908.
Simon, Jules. *L'Ouvrière.* Paris: Hachette, 1861.
Smyers, L. *Souvenirs d'un vieux chroniqueur judiciaire: Le Jury en matière criminelle.* Nice: Imprimerie Adroin Frères, 1885.
Sumien, Paul. *Essai sur la théorie de la responsabilité atténuée de certains criminels.* Paris: F. Pichon, 1897.
Surraud, A. *Code de la Cour d'assises, avec jurisprudence et formules.* Poitiers and Paris: Lecène Oudin, 1891.
Tallon, Eugène. *La Vie morale et intellectuelle des ouvriers.* 2nd ed. Paris: Plon, 1877.
Tarde, Gabriel. *Les Lois de l'imitation.* 1886. Edited by Bruno Karsenti. Paris: Kimé, 1993.
Tardieu, Ambroise. *Les Attentats aux moeurs.* Edited by Georges Vigarello. Paris: Jérôme Millon, 1995.
Vibert, Georges. *Du Plus grand crime au plus petit délit.* Paris: Jouvet, 1888.
de Vitis, Charles. *Le Roman de l'ouvrière.* Tours: A. Mame et fils, n.d.
Wollstonecraft, Mary. *A Vindication of the Rights of Women.* 1792. 2nd ed. Edited by Carol H. Poston. New York: W. W. Norton, 1988.
Yvernès, Émile. *Le Crime et le criminel devant le jury.* Paris: Berger-Levrault, 1894.

SECONDARY SOURCES

Accampo, Elinor. *Industrialization, Family Life, and Class Relations: Saint Chamond, 1815–1941.* Berkeley and Los Angeles: University of California Press, 1989.
Accampo, Elinor, Rachel G. Fuchs, and Mary Lynn Stewart, eds. *Gender and the Politics of Social Reform in France, 1870–1914.* Baltimore: Johns Hopkins University Press, 1995.
Adler, Laure. *L'Amour à l'arsenic: Histoire de Marie Lafarge.* Paris: Denoël, 1985.
———. *Secrets d'alcôve: Histoire du couple, 1830–1930.* Paris: Hachette, 1983.
Allwood, Gill. *French Feminisms: Gender and Violence in Contemporary Theory.* London: University College London Press, 1998.
Amussen, Susan Dwyer. "'Being Stirred to Much Unquietness': Violence and Domestic Violence in Early Modern England." *Journal of Women's History* 6 (Summer 1994): 70–89.
Ariès, Philippe. *Centuries of Childhood: A Social History of Family Life.* Translated by Robert Baldick. New York: Alfred A. Knopf, 1962.
———. *Histoire des populations françaises et de leurs attitudes devant la vie depuis le XVIIIe siècle.* Paris: Seuil, 1971.

Ariès, Philippe, and Georges Duby, eds. *From the Fires of Revolution to the Great War*. Vol. 4 of *A History of Private Life*. Cambridge, MA: Belknap, 1987.

Aron, Jean-Paul. *Le Mangeur du 19e siècle*. Paris: Payot, 1989.

Auslander, Leora. *Taste and Power: Furnishing Modern France*. Berkeley and Los Angeles: University of California Press, 1996.

Bauer, Carol, and Lawrence Ritt. "'A Husband Is a Beating Animal': Frances Power Cobbe Confronts the Wife-Abuse Problem in Victorian England." *International Journal of Women's Studies* 6 (March–April 1983): 99–118.

———. "Wife-Abuse, Late-Victorian Feminists, and the Legacy of Frances Power Cobbe." *International Journal of Women's Studies* 6 (May–June 1983): 195–207.

Beik, Doris, and Paul Beik. *Flora Tristan, Utopian Feminist: Her Travel Diaries and Personal Crusade*. Bloomington: Indiana University Press, 1993.

Berenson, Edward. *The Trial of Madame Caillaux*. Berkeley and Los Angeles: University of California Press, 1992.

Berlanstein, Lenard R. *The Working People of Paris, 1871–1914*. Baltimore: Johns Hopkins University Press, 1984.

Bidelman, Patrick Kay. *Pariahs, Stand Up! The Founding of the Liberal Feminist Movement in France, 1858–1889*. Westport, CT: Greenwood, 1982.

Bonneuil, Noël. *Transformation of the French Demographic Landscape, 1806–1906*. Oxford: Clarendon, 1997.

Bourdieu, Pierre. *Distinction: A Social Critique of the Judgment of Taste*. Translated by Richard Nice. Cambridge, MA: Harvard University Press, 1984.

———. *La Domination masculine*. Paris: Seuil, 1999.

———. *The Field of Cultural Production: Essays on Art and Literature*. Edited by Randal Johnson. New York: Columbia University Press, 1993.

———. *Outline of a Theory of Practice*. Translated by Richard Nice. Cambridge: Cambridge University Press, 1977.

Bourdieu, Pierre, and Loïc J.D. Wacquant. *An Invitation to Reflexive Sociology*. Chicago: University of Chicago Press, 1992.

Brownstein, Rachel M. *Tragic Muse: Rachel of the Comédie Française*. Durham, NC: Duke University Press, 1995.

Breines, Wini, and Linda Gordon. "The New Scholarship on Family Violence." *Signs* 8 (Spring 1983): 490–531.

Calhoun, Craig, Edward LiPuma, and Moishe Postone. *Bourdieu: Critical Perspectives*. Chicago: University of Chicago Press, 1993.

Camp, Wesley D. *Marriage and the Family in France Since the Revolution*. New York: Bookman, 1961.

Caron, Jean-Claude. *À l'École de la violence: Châtiments et sévices dans l'institution scolaire au 19e siècle*. Paris: Aubier, 1999.

de Certeau, Michel. *The Practice of Everyday Life*. Translated by Steven Rendell. Berkeley and Los Angeles: University of California Press, 1984.

Charle, Christophe. *Histoire sociale de la France au 19e siècle*. Paris: Seuil, 1991.

Chauvaud, Frédéric. *Les Passions villageoises au 19e siècle: Les émotions rurales dans les pays de Beauce, de Hurepoix et du Mantois*. Paris: Publisud, 1995.

———. *De Pierre Rivière à Landru: La violence apprivoisée au 19e siècle*. n.p.: Brepols, 1991.

Chesnais, Jean Claude. *Histoire de la violence en occident de 1800 à nos jours.* Paris: Éditions Robert Lafont, 1981.
Chevalier, Louis. *Laboring Classes and Dangerous Classes in Paris During the first Half of the Nineteenth Century.* Translated by Frank Jellinek. New York: Howard Fertig, 1973.
Clark, Anna. "Humanity or Justice: Wifebeating and the Law in the Eighteenth and Nineteenth Centuries." In *Regulating Womanhood,* edited by Carol Smart, 187–206. New York: Routledge, 1992.
———. *The Struggle for the Breeches: Gender and the Making of the British Working Class.* Berkeley and Los Angeles: University of California Press, 1995.
Claverie, Elisabeth, and Pierre Lamaison. *L'Impossible mariage: Violence et parenté en Gévaudan, 17e, 18e, et 19e siècles.* Paris: Hachette, 1982.
Cockburn, J. S. "Patterns of Violence in English Society: Homicide in Kent, 1560–1985." *Past and Present* 130 (February 1991): 70–106.
Comaroff, John L., and Simon Roberts. *Rules and Processes: The Cultural Logic of Dispute in an African Context.* Chicago: University of Chicago Press, 1981.
Conley, John. M, and William M. O'Barr. *Rules versus Relationships: The Ethnography of Legal Discourse.* Chicago: University of Chicago Press, 1990.
Corbin, Alain. *Les Filles de noce: Misère sexuelle et prostitution au 19e et 20 siècles.* Paris: Aubier Montaigne, 1978.
Cubano-Iguina, Astrid. "Legal Constructions of Gender and Violence against Women in Puerto Rico under Spanish Rule, 1860–1895." *American Society for Legal History* 22 (Autumn 2004): 531–64.
Dauphin, Cécile. *Prête-moi ta plume... Les Manuels épistolaires au 19e siècle.* Paris: Éditions Kimé, 2000.
Dauphin, Cécile, and Arlette Farge, eds. *De la Violence et des femmes.* Paris: Albin Michel, 1997.
Dauphin, Cécile, Pierette Lebrun-Pézerat, and Danièle Poublan. *Ces Bonnes lettres: Une Correspondance familiale au 19e siècle.* Paris: Albin Michel, 1995.
Davis, Natalie Zemon. *Fiction in the Archives: Pardon Tales and Their Tellers in Sixteenth-Century France.* Stanford: Stanford University Press, 1996.
———. *Society and Culture in Early Modern France: Eight Essays.* Stanford: Stanford University Press, 1975.
Dobash, Russel P., and R. Emerson Dobash. "Community Response to Violence Against Wives: Charivari, Abstract Justice, and Patriarchy." *Social Problems* 28 (June 1981): 563–81.
———. *Violence Against Wives: A Case Against the Patriarchy.* New York: Free Press, 1979.
Donovan, James F. "Magistrates and Juries in France, 1791–1952." *Journal of French Historical Studies* 22 (Summer 1999): 379–420.
Downing, Lisa. "Murder in the Feminine: Marie Lafarge and the Sexualization of the Nineteenth-Century Criminal Woman." *Journal of the History of Sexuality* 18 (January 2009): 121–38.
Dupâquier, Jacques, and Denis Kessler, eds. *La Société française au 19e siècle.* Paris: Fayard, 1992.
Dupeux, Georges. *French Society, 1789–1970.* Translated by Peter Wait. London: Methuen, 1976.

Edwards, Laura F. "Law, Domestic Violence, and the Limits of Patriarchal Authority in the Antebellum South." *Journal of Southern History* 65 (November 1999): 733–70.

Elias, Norbert. *The Civilizing Process*. Translated by Edmund Jephcott. Vol. 1 of *The History of Manners*. New York: Pantheon Books, 1978.

———. *Power and Civility*. Translated by Edmund Jephcott. Vol. 2 of *The History of Manners*. New York: Pantheon Books, 1982.

Engel, Barbara Alpern. "In the Name of the Czar: Competing Legalities and Marital Conflict in Late Imperial Russia." *Journal of Modern History* 77 (March 2005): 70–96.

Farge, Arlette. *La Vie fragile: Violence, pouvoirs, et solidarités à Paris au 18e siècle*. Paris: Hachette, 1986.

Farge, Arlette, and Michel Foucault, eds. *Le Désordre des familles: Lettres de cachet des Archives de la Bastille au 18e siècle*. Paris: Gallimard, 1982.

Flandrin, Jean-Louis. *Les Amours paysannes (16e–19e siècle)*. Paris: Gallimard, 1975.

Forth, Christopher E. *The Dreyfus Affair and the Crisis of French Manhood*. Baltimore: Johns Hopkins University Press, 2004.

Foucault, Michel. *Discipline and Punish: The Birth of the Prison*. Translated by Alan Sheridan. New York: Vintage, 1995.

———. *History of Sexuality*. Vol. 1, *An Introduction*. Translated by Robert Hurley. New York: Vintage, 1990.

———, ed. *I, Pierre Rivière, Having Slaughtered My Mother, My Sister, and My Brother: A Case of Parricide in the Nineteenth Century*. Translated by Frank Jellinek. Lincoln: University of Nebraska Press, 1982.

Foyster, Elizabeth. "Creating a Veil of Silence? Politeness and Marital Violence in the English Household." *Transactions of the Royal Historical Society* 12 (2002): 395–415.

Fuchs, Rachel. *Contested Paternity: Constructing Families in Modern France*. Baltimore: Johns Hopkins University Press, 2008.

———. *Poor and Pregnant in Paris: Strategies for Survival in the Nineteenth Century*. New Brunswick, NJ: Rutgers University Press, 1992.

Garrioch, David. *Neighborhood and Community in Paris, 1740–1790*. Cambridge: Cambridge University Press, 1986.

Gauderman, Kimberly. *Women's Lives in Colonial Quito: Gender, Law, and Economy in Spanish America*. Austin: University of Texas Press, 2003.

Geertz, Clifford. *Local Knowledge: Further Essays in Interpretive Anthropology*. New York: Basic Books, 1983.

Giddens, Anthony. *Central Problems in Social Theory: Action, Structure, and Contradiction in Social Analysis*. Berkeley and Los Angeles: University of California Press, 1994.

Gilmore, David D. *Honor and Shame and the Unity of the Mediterranean*. Washington, DC: American Anthropological Association, 1987.

Ginzburg, Carlo. *The Cheese and the Worms: The Cosmos of a Sixteenth-Century Miller*. Translated by John and Anne Tedeschi. Baltimore: Johns Hopkins University Press, 1980.

Gordon, Felicia, and Máire Cross, eds. *Early French Feminisms, 1830–1840: A Passion for Liberty*. Cheltenham, UK: Edward Elgar, 1996.

Gordon, Linda. *Heroes of Their Own Lives: The Politics and History of Family Violence, Boston, 1880–1960*. New York: Viking, 1988.

Gould, Roger V. *Insurgent Identities: Class, Community, and Protest in Paris from 1848 to the Commune*. Chicago: University of Chicago Press, 1995.

Grogan, Susan. *Flora Tristan: Life Stories*. New York: Routledge, 1998.
Guillais, Joëlle. *La Chair de l'autre: Le Crime passionnel au 19e siècle*. Paris: Olivier Orban, 1986.
Haine, W. Scott. *The World of the Paris Café: Sociability Among the French Working Class, 1789–1914*. Baltimore, MD: Johns Hopkins University Press, 1996.
Hammerton, A. James. *Cruelty and Companionship: Conflict in Nineteenth-Century Married Life*. London: Routledge, 1992.
———. "The Targets of 'Rough Music': Respectability and Domestic Violence in Victorian England." *Gender and History* 3 (Spring 1991): 23–44.
Hardwick, Julie. "Early Modern Perspectives on the Long History of Domestic Violence: The Case of Seventeenth-Century France." *Journal of Modern History* 78 (March 2006): 1–36.
———. *Family Business: Litigation and the Political Economics of Daily Life in Early Modern France*. Oxford: Oxford University Press, 2009.
———. "Seeking Separations: Gender, Marriages, and the Household Economies in Early Modern France." *French Historical Studies* 21.1 (1998): 157–80.
Harris, Ruth. *Murders and Madness: Medicine, Law, and Society in the Fin-de-Siècle*. Oxford: Clarendon, 1989.
Harsin, Jill. *Policing Prostitution in Nineteenth-Century Paris*. Princeton, NJ: Princeton University Press, 1985.
Hause, Steven C., with Anne R. Kenney. *Women's Suffrage and Social Politics in the French Third Republic*. Princeton: Princeton University Press, 1984.
Hay, Douglas, Peter Linebaugh, John G. Rule, E. P. Thompson, and Cal Winslow. *Albion's Fatal Tree: Crime and Society in Eighteenth-Century England*. New York: Pantheon, 1975.
Hilden, Patricia. *Working Women and Socialist Politics in France, 1880–1914: A Regional Study*. Oxford: Clarendon, 1986.
Hunt, Margaret. "Wife Beating, Domesticity, and Women's Independence in Eighteenth-Century London." *Gender and History* 4 (Spring 1992): 10–33.
Kalifa, Dominique. *Crime et culture au 19e siècle*. Paris: Perrin, 2005.
———. *L'Encre et le sang: Récits de crimes et société à la Belle Époque*. Paris: Librairie Arthème Fayard, 1995.
Kertzer, David I., and Mario Babagli, eds. *Family Life in the Long Nineteenth Century, 1789–1913*. Vol. 2 of *The History of the European Family*. New Haven, CT: Yale University Press, 2002.
Krakovitch, Odile. "Misogynes et féministes, il y a cent ans (I)." *Questions féministes* 8 (May 1980): 85–113.
Langbien, John H. *The Origins of the Adversary Criminal Trial*. Oxford: Oxford University Press, 2003.
Le Naour, Jean-Yves. *Misères et tourments de la chair durant la grande guerre: Les moeurs sexuelles des Français, 1914–1918*. Paris: Aubier, 2002.
Le Roy Ladurie, Emmanuel. *Montaillou: The Promised Land of Error*. Translated by Barbara Bray. New York: George Braziller, 1978.
Lombard, Françoise. "Les Citoyens-Juges: La Réforme de la cour d'assises ou les limites de la souveraineté populaire. " *Revue de science criminelle et de droit pénal comparé* 4 (1996): 773–97.

MacAndrew, Craig. *Drunken Comportment: A Social Explanation*. Chicago: Aldine, 1969.
Marchand, Bernard. *Paris: Histoire d'une ville, 19e–20e siècles*. Paris: Seuil, 1993.
Martin, Benjamin F. *Crime and Criminal Justice under the Third Republic: The Shame of Marianne*. Baton Rouge: Louisiana State University Press, 1990.
Martin-Fugier, Anne. *La Bourgeoise: Femme au temps de Paul Bourget*. Paris: Bernard Grasset, 1983.
———. *La Place des Bonnes: La domesticité féminine à Paris en 1900*. Paris: Grasset, 1979.
Mason, Laura Ann. "The 'Bosom of Proof': Criminal Justice and the Renewal of Oral Culture during the French Revolution." *Journal of Modern History* 76 (March 2004): 29–61.
McMillan, James F. *France and Women, 1789–1914: Gender, Politics, and Society*. London: Routledge, 2000.
Merrick, Jeffrey, and Bryant T. Ragan, eds. *Homosexuality in Modern France*. New York: Oxford, 1996.
Merriman, John. *Police Stories: Building the French State, 1815–1851*. Oxford: Oxford University Press, 2006.
Moch, Leslie Page. *Paths to the City: Regional Migration in Nineteenth-Century France*. Beverly Hills: Sage, 1983.
Moch, Leslie Page, and Rachel G. Fuchs. "Getting Along: Poor Women's Networks in Nineteenth-Century Paris." *French Historical Studies* 18 (Spring 1993): 34–49.
Moi, Toril. "Appropriating Bourdieu: Feminist Theory and Pierre Bourdieu's Sociology of Culture." *New Literary History* 22 (1991): 1017–49.
Moses, Claire Goldberg. *French Feminism in the Nineteenth Century*. Albany: State University of New York Press, 1984.
Muchambled, Robert. "Anthropologie de la violence dans la France moderne (15e–18e siècle)." *Revue de Synthèse* 4 (January–March 1987): 31–55.
Murphy, Jeffrie. *Retribution, Justice, and Therapy: Essays in the Philosophy of Law*. Dordecht, Holland, and Boston: D. Reidel, 1979.
———. *Retribution Reconsidered: More Essays in the Philosophy of Law*. Dordecht, Holland, and London: Kluwer, 1992.
Noiriel, Gérard. *Workers in French Society in the 19th and 20th Centuries*. New York and Oxford: Berg, 1990.
Nourrisson, Didier. *Le Buveur du 19e siècle*. Paris: Albin Michel, 1990.
Nye, Robert A. *Crime, Madness, and Politics in Modern France: The Medical Concept of National Decline*. Princeton: Princeton University Press, 1984.
———. *Masculinity and Male Codes of Honor in Modern France*. New York: Oxford University Press, 1993.
———. "Medicine and Science as Masculine 'Fields of Honor.'" *Osiris* 12 (1997): 60–79.
O'Brien, Patricia. *The Promise of Punishment: Prisons in Nineteenth-Century France*. Princeton: Princeton University Press, 1982.
Ortner, Sherry B. *Making Gender: The Politics and Erotics of Culture*. Boston: Beacon Press, 1996.
Parella, Anne. "Industrialization and Murder: Northern France, 1815–1904." *Journal of Interdisciplinary History* 22 (Spring 1992): 627–54.
Pedersen, Jean Elisabeth. *Legislating the French Family: Feminism, Theater, and Republican Politics, 1870–1920*. New Brunswick, NJ: Rutgers University Press, 2003.

Peniston, William A. *Pederasts and Others: Urban Culture and Sexual Identity in Nineteenth-Century Paris*. New York: Harrington Park, 2004.
Perrot, Michèle. *Les Femmes ou les silences de l'histoire*. Paris: Flammarion, 1998.
———. "Le Secret de la correspondance au 19e siècle." In *L'Epistolarité à travers les siècles*, edited by Mireille Bossis and Charles A. Poper, 184–88. Stuttgart: Franz Steiner, 1990.
Phillips, Roderick. "Gender Solidarities in Late Eighteenth-Century Urban France: The Example of Rouen." *Histoire Sociale-Social History* 13 (November 1980): 235–337.
———. *Putting Asunder: A History of Divorce in Western Society*. Cambridge: Cambridge University Press, 1988.
———. "Women, Neighborhood, and Family in the Late Eighteenth Century." *French Historical Studies* 18 (Spring 1993): 1–12.
Picq, Françoise. *Libération des femmes: Les Années mouvement*. Paris: Seuil, 1993.
Pleck, Elizabeth. *Domestic Tyranny: The Making of American Social Policy Against Family Violence from Colonial Times to the Present*. New York: Oxford University Press, 1987.
Pradel, Jean. "Les Méandres de la cour d'assises française de 1791 à nos jours." *Revue juridique Thémis* 32 (1997): 135–53.
Rearick, Charles. *Pleasures of the Belle Epoque: Entertainment and Festivity in Turn-of-the-Century France*. New Haven: Yale, 1985.
Reay, Barry. "The Context and Meaning of Popular Literacy: Some Evidence from Nineteenth-Century Rural England." *Past and Present* 131 (May 1991): 89–129.
Reddy, William M. *The Invisible Code: Honor and Sentiment in Postrevolutionary France, 1814–1848*. Berkeley and Los Angeles: University of California Press, 1997.
———. "Marriage, Honor, and the Public Sphere in Postrevolutionary France: *Séparations de Corps*, 1815–1848." *Journal of Modern History* 65 (September 1993): 437–72.
———. *The Navigation of Feeling: A Framework for the History of Emotions*. Cambridge: Cambridge University Press, 2001.
Rémy, Monique. *Histoire des mouvements de femmes: De l'Utopie à l'intégration*. Paris: L'Harmattan, 1990.
Revenin, Régis. *Homosexualité et prostitution masculines à Paris: 1870–1918*. Paris: Harmattan, 2005.
Richard, Guy. *Histoire de l'amour en France du Moyen Age à la Belle Epoque*. N.p.: Editions Jean-Claude Lattès, 1985.
Ross, Ellen. "'Fierce Questions and Taunts': Married Life in Working-Class London, 1870–1914." *Feminist Studies* 8 (Fall 1982): 575–602.
———. *Love and Toil: Motherhood in Outcast London, 1870–1918*. Oxford: Oxford University Press, 1993.
Ruff, Julius Ralph. *Violence in Early Modern Europe, 1500–1800*. Cambridge: Cambridge University Press, 2001.
Schaefer, Sylvia. *Children in Moral Danger and the Problem of Government in Third Republic France*. Princeton, NJ: Princeton University Press, 1997.
Schwartz, Vanessa. *Spectacular Realities: Early Mass Culture in Fin-de-Siècle Paris*. Berkeley and Los Angeles: University of California Press, 1998.
Segalen, Martine. *Love and Power in the Peasant Family: Rural France in the Nineteenth Century*. Translated by Sarah Matthews. Chicago: University of Chicago Press, 1983.
Sewell, William H. *Structure and Mobility: The Men and Women of Marseille, 1820–1870*. Cambridge: Cambridge University Press, 1985.

Shapiro, Ann-Louise. *Breaking the Codes: Female Criminality in Fin-de-Siècle Paris*. Stanford: Stanford University Press, 1996.
Sharpe, J. A. "Domestic Homicide in Early Modern England." *Historical Journal* 24 (1981): 29–48.
———. "The History of Violence in England: Some Observations." *Past and Present* 108 (August 1985): 216–24.
Shorter, Edward. *The Making of the Modern Family*. New York: Basic Books, 1975.
Silverman, Deborah L. *Art Nouveau in Fin-de-Siècle France: Politics, Psychology, and Style*. Berkeley and Los Angeles: University of California Press, 1989.
Smith, Bonnie. *Ladies of the Leisure Class: The Bourgeoises of Northern France in the Nineteenth Century*. Princeton, NJ: Princeton University Press, 1981.
Smith, Paul. *Feminism and the Third Republic: Women's Political and Civil Rights in France, 1918–1945*. Oxford: Clarendon, 1996.
Sohn, Anne-Marie. *Chrysalides: Femmes dans la vie privée (19e–20e siècles)*. 2 vols. Paris: Publications de la Sorbonne, 1996.
———. *La Correspondance, un document pour l'histoire*. Rouen: Publications de l'Université de Rouen, 2002.
———. *Du Premier baiser à l'alcôve: La sexualité des Français au quotidien (1850–1950)*. Paris: Aubier, 1996.
Stang Dahl, Tove, and Annika Snare. "The Coercion of Privacy: A Feminist Perspective." In *Women, Sexuality and Social Control*, edited by Carol and Barry Smart, 8–26. London: Routledge and Kegan Paul, 1978.
Stansell, Christine. *City of Women: Sex and Class in New York, 1789–1860*. New York: Knopf, 1986.
Steele, Valerie. *The Corset: A Cultural History*. New Haven: Yale University Press, 2003.
Steiner, Eva. *French Legal Method*. Oxford: Oxford University Press, 2002.
Stone, Judith. *The Search for Social Peace: Reform Legislation in France, 1890–1914*. New York: State University of New York Press, 1985.
Stone, Lawrence. *Broken Lives: Separation and Divorce in England, 1660–1857*. Oxford: Oxford University Press, 1993.
———. *The Family, Sex, and Marriage in England, 1500–1800*. New York: Harper Colophon, 1979.
———. "The History of Violence in England: Some Observations: A Rejoinder." *Past and Present* 108 (August 1985): 216–24.
———. "Interpersonal Violence in English Society, 1300–1980." *Past and Present* 101 (November 1983): 22–23.
———. *Road to Divorce: England, 1530–1987*. Oxford: Oxford University Press, 1990.
Surkis, Judith. *Sexing the Citizen: Morality and Masculinity in France, 1870–1920*. Ithaca: Cornell University Press, 2006.
Thiesse, Anne-Marie. *Le Roman du quotidian: Lecteurs et lectures populaires à la Belle Époque*. Paris: Seuil, 2000.
Thompson, E.P. "'Rough Music': Le Charivari Anglais." *Annales* (March–April 1972): 285–312.
Tilly, Louise A., and Joan W. Scott. *Women, Work, and Family*. New York: Holt, Reinhart, and Winston, 1978.

Tomes, Nancy. "A 'Torrent of Abuse': Crimes of Violence Between Working-Class Men and Women in London, 1840–1875." *Journal of Social History* 11 (1978): 329–45.
Trouille, Mary. *Wife-Abuse in Eighteenth-Century France*. Oxford: Voltaire Foundation, 2009.
Viriot-Barrial, Dominique. "Commentaire de la loi no. 2006–399 du 4 avril 2006 renforçant la prévention et la répression des violences au sein du couple ou commises contre les mineurs" *Recueil Dalloz* 182 (2006): 2350. *http://decouvrirdalloz.fr*. Accessed 7 January 2009.
Waelti-Walters, Jennifer, and Steven C. Hause, eds. *Feminisms of the Belle Époque: A Historical and Literary Anthology*. Lincoln: University of Nebraska Press, 1994.
Walkowitz, Judith R. *Prostitution and Victorian Society: Women, Class, and the State*. Cambridge: Cambridge University Press, 1980.
Weber, Eugen. *France, Fin-de-Siècle*. Cambridge, MA: Belknap, 1986.
———. *Peasants into Frenchmen: The Modernization of Rural France, 1870–1914*. Stanford: Stanford University Press, 1976.
Weber, Max. *Economy and Society: An Outline of Interpretive Sociology*. Edited by Guenther Roth and Claus Wittich. Translated by Ephraim Fischoff. Berkeley and Los Angeles: University of California Press, 1978.
Weiner, Martin J. "Judges v. Jurors: Courtroom Tensions in Murder Trials and the Law of Criminal Responsibility in Nineteenth-Century England." *Law and History Review* 17 (Autumn 1999): 467–506.
———. *Men of Blood: Violence, Manliness, and Criminal Justice in Victorian England*. Cambridge: Cambridge University Press, 2004.
Williams, Alan. *The Police of Paris, 1718–1789*. Baton Rouge: Louisiana State University Press, 1979.
Williams, Rosalind. *Dream Worlds: Mass Consumption in Late Nineteenth-Century France*. Berkeley and Los Angeles: University of California Press, 1982.
Wright, Gordon. *Between the Guillotine and Liberty: Two Centuries of the Crime Problem in France*. New York: Oxford University Press, 1983.

Index

Accampo, Elinor, 21
acquittals: controversy over, 178; controversy over rates of, 183–85; for crimes of passion, 1–2, 10–11, 156, 161–62; gender and, 184–85; increase in rates of, 156–58; for infidelity, 38–39; jurors and, 175–79; of Koenig, 171, 180, 182; of Maxant, 5, 17; of Merle, 19; of Perrin, 48; as protests against legal structure, 176–77
actes d'accusation (official indictments), 8, 173–74
Adler, Laure, 21, 79–80
admissions of guilt, 5, 7
alcohol: drinking of, 90–91; food resources traded for, 76–77, 131; role of, in crimes, 164–65, 194–95
Allwood, Gill, 210
Ancel, Alphonsine, 62, 136
appearances, concern for, 84, 147
archives, judicial, 6, 9–10
assize court (*cour d'assises*): archives of, 6–7; cases, 9; described, 172–74; presentation of evidence in, 178–79; retributive justice and, 182–83. *See also* defendants; jurors; witnesses
attitudes toward violence, 182–83, 184–85. *See also* retributive justice
Aubry, Paul, 191, 192
awls, as weapons, 135

Badault, François, 62, 204
Badran, Louis, 25, 37, 53, 77, 87, 144
Balade, Charles, 99, 149
Barbier, Louis, 195
Barbier, Zoé, 88, 107
Barbot, Louis, 149, 239–40n54
Barthélemy, Annette, 97, 101
Béal, Célestine, 52, 98
Bérard des Glajeax, Anatole, 193
Berlanstein, Lenard, 24, 58, 59
Bernheim, Hippolyte, 190
Bernou, Jean-Baptiste, 50, 96–97, 118–19, 135
Berriat de Saint-Prix, Charles, 177
Béziade, Henri, 18–20, 150
Bière, Marie, 34, 209
Billoir, Sébastien-Joseph, 188–90
Biver, Marie, 106
Biver, Pierre, 82, 125, 151
blades, as weapons, 135
Blanc, Louis, 129
Bonjour, Esther, 64, 68, 112
Bonnefoy, Jeanne, 200, 205–6
Bougon, André, 166
Bourdeaux, Mathilde, 60, 63–64, 125
Bourdieu, Pierre: on discursive strategies, 14; and "feel for the game," 158, 214; on practice theory, 11–13; on social capital, 94; on symbolic capital, 56
bourgeois class: code of honor of, 146–48; family involvement and, 104–6; jurors from, 165–67; toleration of violence and, 144–46; wage labor and, 59
bourgeois habits: notion of couple and, 21; sexuality, 21–22; trickle-down theory of, 16, 213
Brossier, Philiberte, 61–62, 142
Brunette, Cécile, 47
business interests: domestic disputes and, 61–62; honor and, 152; marriage and, 29–32

Index

cafés and cabarets, 40, 75, 90–91, 189
Catelier, Alphonse, 53, 101, 110, 143, 238n32
Catherine, Augustine, 40, 82, 112, 141
Catherine, Pierre, 40, 82, 112
Ces Bonnes lettres, 201–2
Chalandre, Alexine, 136
Charcot, Jean-Martin, 190
Charle, Christophe, 60
Charmeil, M., 176–77
Charrier, Antoine and Marie, 79, 83
Chauvalin, Frédéric, 15
children: dissolution of unions and, 102–3; illegitimate, 30, 70; parenting of, 70–74
civil code: article 213, 32–33; article 1536, 29; reforms to, 210–11. *See also* penal code
civil court processes, 171
Clément, François, 40, 62–63, 97
clothing, 38, 82–85
Code Pénal. See penal code
commissaires de police (police captains), 159, 167, 168–70
community-based justice. *See* retributive justice
concierges: intervention in disputes by, 31; testimony of, 3, 4, 40, 119–21, 180, 189
concubinage: definition of, 8, 24; reform to law regarding, 210–11; as trial period before marriage, 25
consumption of household goods, 74–76
control, loss of, 195–96
Corre, Armand, 192
correctional courts, 239n51, 240n55
corsets, 83
Cotard, Ernest, 71–72, 143, 171
Cotard, Marie, 71–72, 135
couple: bourgeois notion of, 21; eroticization of, 22–23, 55, 216; formation of, 24–32. *See also* domestic partners
Courtois, Hélie, 192–93
Courtois, Jules, 26–27, 70–71
courtship: family involvement in, 28–29, 180; sexual relations and, 19–20
coworkers, as witnesses, 64–65
crime: definition of, 159–60; magnitude of, and punishment for, 176–77; medicalization of, 10–11, 164–65; against property, 156. *See also* acquittals; crimes of passion

Crime de Femme (Decourcelle), 186–87
crimes of passion: acquittals for, 1–2, 10–11, 156, 161–62; alcohol and, 164–65, 194–95; definition of, 1; discourses on, 13–14, 213; honor defense in, 146–47; love and, 49–50, 54–55; madness and, 164–65, 198–99; popular press and, 161–62, 186–88, 198–99; retributive justice and, 183; stories of, 162–63
Croissant, Marie, 27, 113, 151, 152

Dabon, Charles, 64, 77, 81–82, 86, 135
Damotte, Henriette, 46, 84, 89, 100, 197
Daouze, Marie, 45, 122, 141
Daphne Initiative, 211
death sentence, and murder, 175–76
de Certeau, Michel, 187
Decourcelle, Pierre (*Crime de Femme*), 186–87
defendants: claims of emotion and madness by, 198–99; jurors and, 178; as objects of normalizing discourses, 164; presiding magistrates and, 174; as working people, 165, 167
de Girardin, Emile, 209–10
de La Grassière, Raoul, 157, 177
Delinon, Auguste, 75–76, 206
De Moor, Catherine, 69–70, 84, 110–11
De Moor, Jean-Jacques, 110, 137
Denis, Clarisse, 153, 203–4
Deraismes, Maria, 130
Deschutter, Jean, 64, 68, 225n119
de Verneuil, Eudoxe, 38, 126, 148–49
disguises, 84–85, 187
divorce, 171–72
Dogmatschoff, Eugène, 46, 89, 100
domestic partners: choice of, 14, 54–55; definition of, 8; obligations of, 24–25, 33, 132–33, 216. *See also* couple
domestic partnerships: boundaries of acceptable behavior in, 212–13; business interests and, 29–32, 61–62; formation of, 24–32; leaving, 154; love and, 49–55; negotiations in, 16–17. *See also* gendered division of labor; household; marriage
domestic servants, 113–14
Douët, Jeanne, 54, 88, 204
dowry, 19, 33
Dreyfuss, Constance, 52–53

drinking. *See* alcohol
du Bourg, Charles-Arthur Leroy, 128, 148, 214
Duc, François and Alexandrine, 33, 113–14, 144, 147
Duchène, Charles, 68–69, 150
Duchène, Eugénie, 68–69, 103, 107–8, 169
Ducret, Georges, 207
duels, 147, 149, 214
Dufaure law, 161, 165–66
Dumas, Alexandre (fils), 128–29, 132, 209–10
du Mesnil, Octave, 59

échivenage, 184
economic capital, 13, 56
Eizenkreimer, Marguerite, 70, 83, 107
Elias, Norbert, 15, 158, 213–14
emotion: crimes of passion and, 49–50, 195–96, 198–99; in domestic relationships, 212; expression of, through violent behavior, 165, 182; love, 49–55, 216–17
employers, as witnesses, 62–65, 117
employment, 59–61, 62–65
epistolary pact, 201–2
ethnography, 11, 15
European Union, 211
excusable murder (article 324), 5, 131, 175–76, 210, 211
extenuating circumstances, 9, 175

family involvement: honor and, 147, 149–50, 152–53; letters and, 203–4; in marriages, 28–29; in networks of knowledge, 99–108; from *pays*, 98–99
Farge, Arlette, 6, 168, 172
fathers, 70–71, 106–7
feminism: Dumas and, 128–29, 209, 217; in France, 129–31; in Great Britain, 245n18; intimate violence and, 210–11, 217; methodology and, 11
feminists, as victims of violence, 233n13
Fenet, Constant, 177
Féral, Marie, 26–27, 71, 151, 152
fighting back, 139–42
Fischer, Alain, 210
Folies Bergères, 48, 206
food, disagreements related to, 76–82

Forestier, Louis-François, 36–37, 112
Foucault, Michel, 10, 21–22, 158, 172
Fournet, Marie, 82, 125, 135, 151, 152, 163–64, 204–5
Fragonard, Marie, 63–64
Froquières, Augustin, 54, 88, 204
Fuchs, Rachel, 24, 73, 114
furniture, 86, 87–88

Gadel, Marie, 24, 74, 135, 142, 239n53
Gallier, Blanche, 25, 37, 53, 77, 78, 83, 87
Garrioch, David, 94
Gaudot, Charles, 143, 200–201
gender: acquittals and, 2, 9, 184–85; assistance in crisis and, 114; construction of, in everyday life, 126–27; infidelity and, 38–39, 133; power of suggestion and, 192–93; violence and, 15–17, 133–34, 213–17. *See also* men; women
gendered division of labor: agricultural, 14; conflicts over household goods and, 91–92; drinking alcohol and, 90–91; household and, 58, 76; urban, 14
Genuyt de Beaulieu, Edouard, 96, 144–45
Genuyt de Beaulieu, Emilie, 105–6, 144–45
Gérard, Charlotte, 46, 84, 142
gifts, 51–52
Ginzburg, Carlo, 10
Gould, Roger, 94
Great Britain: feminism in, 245n18; history of violence and masculinity in, 245n22
Guerrier, Georges, 78, 139
Guerrier, Jeanne, 63, 121
Guillais, Joëlle, 94, 162, 219n3
Guillot, Adolphe, 177
Guillot, Joséphine, 2–3
Guillot, Modeste and Zélie: business interests and, 29–30, 61; food resources and, 77; testimony of witnesses about, 124–25, 137–38, 149
guilt, admissions of, 5, 7
guns, as weapons, 83, 135–36
Gy, Marie, 39, 71, 85, 111, 113, 138

habitus, 12
Hardwick, Julie, 114
Harris, Ruth, 146, 164, 219n3

hearsay, 112–14, 179
Henry, Eugène, 29, 96, 197
Herbellot, Emile, 169
Herbellot, Marguerite, 35, 123
Hilden, Patricia, 21
Hillairain de Saint-Priest, M., 34, 51, 149
Holtz, Louis, 193–94
homicide, acquittals for, 9, 156
homosexuality, 42–45
honor, and reputation, 146–55
household: definition of, 56; distribution of power in, 57; finances of, 58–59, 61–62, 67–70; management of, 66; material resources of, 59–70; mutual assistance in, 62, 69; provision for, 65–67. *See also* domestic partnerships; gendered division of labor
household goods: clothing, 82–85; consumption of, 74–76; disputes over, 85–92; food, disputes related to, 76–82; furniture, 86, 87–88; marriage and, 87; pawning of, 89–90
housing conditions, 3, 93, 108–9, 145–46
husbands, responsibility of, for wives, 129, 130, 132, 181

Icard, Séverin, 190, 191
Iltis, Marie, 47–49, 106, 206
images, suggestive, 190–91
indictments (*actes d'accusation*), 8, 173–74
infidelity: evidence of, 39–40; female reactions to, 39; gender and, 133; honor and, 153–54; male reactions to, 38–39; of wives, 33–34, 180–81
International Congress on the Condition and Rights of Women, 131
intervention in violent conflicts: by family members, 122–24; by neighbors, 122–24; networks of knowledge and, 121–26; versus nonintervention, 124–26; by police, 168–71
intimacy, 212–13, 216
intimate violence, efforts to end, 210–11, 216–17
investigating magistrates (*juges d'instruction*), 172–73
irrationality, theories of, 190–96

Jacob, la femme, 84–85, 123
Jacob, Nicolas, 66, 123, 143

Jacques, Joséphine, 27
jealousy, sexual, 38–39, 47
Jean, Eulalie: clothing of, 84; cooking and, 81; family of, 99, 103; letters of, 203; on love, 53–54; on self-defense, 141; on sexual relationship with husband, 35
Jean, Henri, 53–54
Jouault, Louis, 113, 136, 171, 196–97
Jouault, Virginie, 77, 83, 90, 168
Joulain, Charles, 50, 99, 104, 149
judicial archives, 6, 9–10
judicial system: growth of, 159–61; social control and, 158–59. *See also* retributive justice; utilitarian justice
juges d'instruction (investigating magistrates), 172–73
jurors: acquittals and, 175–79; criticism of, 156–57, 161, 177–78; defendants and, 178; handbooks for, 177; motivations of, 165; oath affirmed by, 237n13; socioeconomic status of, 165–67
jury trials: acquittal rates and, 1–2, 9, 156–58; decisions made in, 174; establishment of, 160; public opinion and, 160, 185; purpose of, 161
justice: jury trials and, 161; systems of, 154–55, 157–58, 182, 193–94; utilitarian, 154–55, 160, 182–83. *See also* retributive justice

Kalifa, Dominique, 187
Keiffer, Gaspard, 79, 107, 143
Kemps couple, 109, 120, 122
knives, as weapons, 135
Koenig, Georges: acquittal of, 171, 180, 182; case of, 180–82; family of, 98, 152; furniture of, 87–88; relationship with wife, 34, 136; venereal disease of, 40

Langlois, Georges, 29, 42–43, 71, 104–5, 145, 152
Langlois, Rosine, 152–53
Larue, Alexandre, 60, 63–64, 125, 135
leaving partnerships, 154, 212
Lechevallier, Edmé, 35
legitimate violence: jury trials and, 158; need for punishment and, 137–38, 142–43; as retribution, 214

Legrand, Jean, 38, 152, 154, 195, 201
Legrand, Juliette, 73, 83, 121
Lelong, Paul, 34, 69
Lelong, Victorine, 69, 71, 72, 78, 142, 201, 222n52
Lemaître, Félix, 223n84
Le Manach, Jeanne Marie, 188–90
Le Naour, Jean-Yves, 215
Léra, Louis, 50–51
Lerondeau, François, 36, 66, 80–81, 102–3, 143–44
Lerondeau, Mélanie, 36, 80–81, 83–84, 114–15
lesbianism, 44–45
Lesguillon, Hermance, 129
letters/letter-writing: epistolary pact in, 201–2; between family members, 180, 203–4; to investigating magistrates, 197, 201; between lovers or spouses, 200–201, 204–6; by notables, 95–97; self-representation of authors in, 206–7; separation and, 202–3
Levielle, Eugéne, 143
Levielle, Octavie, 84, 88–89, 202
Lévy, Jules, 177–78
L'Homme-femme (Dumas), 128–29
libre de ma personne, 26
Ligue du droit des femmes, 210
Ligue française pour le droit des femmes, 209
literacy: letter writing and, 199–206; spread of, 208; of working people, 206–7
loss of control, 195–96
love/romantic love: in domestic partnerships, 33, 49–55; intimate violence and, 1, 52–55, 216–17; marriage and, 129; prostitutes and, 47–48

madness/insanity, 164–65, 198–99
magistracy: of assize courts, 172–73; of correctional courts, 240n55; échivenage and, 184; as neutral, 160; as professional, 161
male privilege, violence as tool for enforcement of, 136–37, 148, 181–82, 214–15
Malmézac, Guillaume, 152, 196
Mangenot, Charles, 59
Marie, Jean-Marie, 73, 103–4

Marie, Julie, 37–38, 40, 103–4
marriage: antipathy toward, 25–26; business interests and, 29–32, 61–62; family involvement in, 28–29; household goods and, 87; in nineteenth century, 22; promises of, 18–19, 26–27; property of wives and, 29–30; requirements for, 24; rights of women in, 129, 130, 133; sex before, 27–28; sexuality in, 32–41; sexual relationships in, 32–41; statistics related to, 20–21. *See also* domestic partnerships; spouse
Martinage, Sophronie, 25, 37, 62
Martin-Fugier, Anne, 59, 229n123
Martinière, Louis, 62, 195
Mason, Laura, 160
Masset, Georges, 40, 107
Maudsley, Henry, 194
Maugue, Annelise, 214–15
Maxant, Joseph, 1, 2–5, 17, 103
Maxant, Margot, 1, 2–5, 17
medicalization of crime, 10–11, 164–65
Méhu, Rose, 34, 39, 69
melodramatic narrative, 10–11
men: as controlling women's behavior, 128–29, 131–32, 133–34; as fathers, 70–72; homosexuality of, 42–44; monopolization of violence by, 15; presentation of selves in letters, 206–7; as providers, 58, 66–67, 70, 79; role of, 57; single, eating with families, 82; supported by women, 67–69; as workers, 65–66
Merle, Angélina, 18–20, 23, 196
Méro, Louise, 35
methodology, 9–14
Michaud, Emile, 38, 166–67
Michel, Jules Alphonse, 139, 170
migration to Paris, 14, 23, 94–95
Millim, Dominique, 24, 109, 138
mobility of population, 14, 212. *See also* migration to Paris
Moch, Leslie Page, 95, 114
mothers, 72–74
Mouvement de Libération de Femmes, 210
murder: acquittals for, 156; excusable (article 324), 5, 131, 175–76, 210, 211; woman cut in two, case of, 188–90, 197

266 Index

neighbors: assistance from, 114–19; concierges, 119–21; hearsay and, 112–14, 179; intervention by, 121–26; knowledge of, 93–94; from *pays*, links to, 94–99; privacy, living conditions, and, 108–12, 125–26, 216; testimony of, 3–5, 7–8; well-to-do couples and, 145–46; as witnesses, 111–12
networks of knowledge: family and, 99–108; overview of, 93–94; in *pays*, 94–99; well-to-do-couples and, 145–46; witnesses and, 179. See also neighbors
Neu, Marie, 73, 79, 107
newspapers, as historical sources, 8. See also popular press
notables, letters and reports from, 95–97
Nourrisson, Didier, 194
novels, murder cases in, 186–87
Nye, Robert, 146–47, 149, 236n92

oral testimony, value placed on, 160, 207–8
Ortner, Sherri, 11, 12, 13

parenting, 70–74
parents: relationships with, 100–101; responses of, 101–2; sides taken by, 103–6, 106–8. See also fathers; mothers
Parrain, Louis, 200, 205–6
Pautard, Adèle, 39, 97–98, 107, 150, 152
pawning of household goods, 89–90
pays (native region), links to, 94–99, 126
Pellentz, Félix, 50
penal code: article 324, 131, 175–76, 210, 211; article 326, 175; article 463, 175; articles 321–326, 219n6. See also civil code
Périchon, Louis, 134, 197
Perney, Ernestine, 41–42, 45, 90, 120–21
Perney, Pierre-Auguste, 120–21, 195
Perrin, Emile, 47–49, 106, 206–7
Perrot, Michèle, 15
Peyssonnié, Paul, 176
Phillips, Roderick, 114
players in game, social actors likened to, 12–13, 158
Pluchet, Estelle, 26, 85, 119
poisoning, 79–81
police, 2, 159, 167–71
Police Municipale, 167

popular press: active role of, 197–98; as agent of criminal inspiration, 190–92, 196; crimes of passion and, 161–62, 187–88, 198–99; exploits appearing in, 196–97, 203; indictments reproduced in, 173; novels, 186–87; transcriptions in, 8, 237n14; woman cut in two, case of, in, 188–90, 197
Pourcher, Marie, 39, 85
practice theory, 11–13, 23
precedent, in French law, 160
pregnancy: abandonment and, 27; financial support and, 69, 70
presiding magistrates (*présidents*), 173–74
Prévost, Elisabeth, 100
privacy: intervention in conflicts and, 125–26; living conditions and, 108–12; move toward, 216
Proal, Louis, 192, 194
property: acquittals for crimes against, 156; definition of, 58; of women in marriage, 29–30
prostitution, 45–49, 136–37
provocation of violence, 138–39
public displays of affection, 51–52
public opinion, and jury trials, 160, 185
punishment: legitimate violence and, 137–38, 142–43; retributive justice and, 182–83
Puthomme, Léontine, 202

Ragonod, G.-M., 131–32
Rault, Marie, 53, 115–18, 135, 139–41
reading, attitudes toward, 197–98
reciprocity, 132, 146
Reddy, William, 147
reputation: honor and, 146–55; of men, 57; networks of knowledge and, 94; in *pays*, 96; as symbolic capital, 13; of women, 40–41, 57
retributive justice: assize court trials and, 182–83; domestic partnerships and, 132–34; infidelity and, 153–54; irrationality and, 193–94; utilitarian models of justice and, 154–55; verdicts of courts and, 157–58, 184–85; violence and, 214
Richard, Guy, 20
Richard, Hippolyte, 45, 122, 141

Richelet, Rose, 150–51
Richelet, Simon, 33–34, 82, 149–50, 150–51, 195
rights of married women, 131
Rivière, Pierre, 10
Robert, Barthélemy and Louise, 119–20
Rochat, Marie, 85, 134, 167
Roché, Charles, 46–47, 122
Roulland, Denis, 66, 196
rumor, 113, 179

safety lines: family as, 100, 106–8; neighbors as, 114–19; *pays* as, 99
Sanglé, Marie, 53, 75–76, 78–79, 107, 206
Santin, Jean-Baptiste, 97, 111–12, 138–39
Sauvan, Anaïs, 111, 118–19
Schlesser, Eugénie, 45–46
Schmittgall, Henri, 53, 97
self-defense, 139–42
sentencing, 175–77
separation, legal, 32, 171–72, 181
servants, domestic, 113–14
sexual relationships: of bourgeois, 21–22; courtship and, 19–20; desire for, 34–35; deviant practices in, 41–42; differences in understandings of, 26–27; fidelity in, 133, 153–54; honor and, 151–52; jealousy in, 38–39, 47; in marriage, 32–41; of ordinary people, 22–23; as personal decision, 27–28; propriety, standards of, 23–24; refusal of, and violence, 36–38; venereal disease and, 37–38, 40. *See also* infidelity
Shapiro, Ann-Louise, 79, 135, 163, 187, 192, 219n3
Shorter, Edward, 22–23
Silverman, Deborah, 190
Smith, Bonnie, 59
social capital, 13, 94
social control, systems of, 158–59, 213
social interactions, complexity of, 13–14
Sohn, Anne-Marie, 22–23
Solhart, Désirée, 61, 75, 122–23
Solhart, Georges, 88, 135, 225n119
S.O.S. Femmes Battues, 210
spouse: choice of, 14, 54–55; murder of (article 324), 5, 131, 175–76, 210, 211
state: monopolization of violence by, 15, 213–14; system of justice of, 154–55, 157–58, 182, 193–94
Stern, Steve, 159
suggestion, power of, 190–93
suicide, 187, 197; murder-suicide, 29, 34, 52, 96, 98, 105, 192, 206
sulfuric acid, as weapon, 19, 39, 75, 85, 135, 196
Sûreté (*Police Judiciare*), 167
symbolic capital: economic capital and, 56; reputation as, 13; women and, 86–87

Tarde, Gabriel, 192
Teste, Blanche Lecoeur, 30–32, 43, 73, 124
Teste, Ernest, 30–32, 43, 73, 124
testimony: of concierges, 4, 119–21; of neighbors, 3–5, 7–8; oral, value placed on, 160, 207–8; of witnesses, 162, 163–64, 178–79, 183, 207–8
Thiéron, Marie, 99, 100, 197
Third Republic, 158, 161
Traber, Marie, 26, 98
trickle-down theory of bourgeois habits, 16, 213
Troppmann case, 188, 196
Trouille, Mary, 114
Trudersheim, Célestine, 107, 171
Trudersheim, Ignace, 102

urban population growth, 94
utilitarian justice, 154–55, 160, 182–83

Valadon, Désirée, 135, 151, 152
venereal disease, 37–38, 40
vengeance. *See* retributive justice
Verhoost, Jean-Baptiste, 25, 38
Vigineix-Roche, Jeanne, 107, 113, 152, 168
violence: bourgeois attitudes toward, 144–45; community monitoring of, 126–27; as condoned, 184–85; debate over, 129–30; desensitization to, 124; Dumas and, 128–29; gender and, 15–17, 133–34, 213–17; as masculine entitlement, 136–37, 148, 181–82, 214–15; monopolization of, 15, 213–14; practices of, 134–46, 212–13; provocation of, 138–39; as punishment, 142–43, 182–83; Ragonod on, 131–32;

violence (*continued*)
  retributive justice and, 183, 184–85; social context of, 180–82; by women, 138, 139, 141, 215. *See also* legitimate violence
vitriol (sulfuric acid), as weapon, 19, 39, 75, 85, 135, 196
Voisin, Auguste, 164–65
voting rights for women, 210

wages: men handing over to partners, 65–66; women and, 58, 133; work for, 59–61
weapons, 134–36. *See also* sulfuric acid
Weber, Eugen, 16
Weber, Max, 15
wetnurses, 73, 75
witnesses: child caretakers as, 73; comments on appearance by, 84; coworkers as, 64–65; definition of, 8; depositions of, 158, 173, 179; employers as, 62–65, 117; investigating magistrates and, 173; neighbors as, 111–12; oral testimony and, 160, 207–8; from *pays*, 95–98; privileging of testimony of, 183; in Rault case, 115–17; testimony of, 3–5, 7–8, 162, 163–64, 178–79, 207–8; as working people, 7
woman cut in two, case of, 188–90, 197
women: clothing of, 83, 84; as criminals, 163; domestic contract and, 215–16; double burden of, 133; homosexuality of, 44–45; honor of, 151–52; household goods and, 86–87; legitimate violence by, 215; as mothers, 72–74; police and, 169–70; presentation of selves in letters, 205, 206; and prostitution, 45–46; reputation of, 40–41, 57; rights of, 129, 130, 131, 210; role of, 56–57; symbolic capital and, 56, 86; as workers, 58, 59–61, 133
working people: accounts of lives of, 20–21; defendants as, 165, 167; definition of, 58; literary efforts of, 207; as population in flux, 14; violence and, 16; witnesses as, 7
written evidence of literacy, 199–208

Yvernès, Emile, 156–57